CHURCHES, CITIES, AND
HUMAN COMMUNITY

Churches, Cities, and Human Community

URBAN MINISTRY IN
THE UNITED STATES, 1945-1985

Edited by

Clifford J. Green

WILLIAM B. EERDMANS PUBLISHING COMPANY
GRAND RAPIDS, MICHIGAN / CAMBRIDGE, U.K.

© 1996 Wm. B. Eerdmans Publishing Co.
255 Jefferson Ave. S.E., Grand Rapids, Michigan 49503
P.O. Box 163, Cambridge CB3 9PU U.K.

Printed in the United States of America

01 00 99 98 97 96   7 6 5 4 3 2 1

Library of Congress Cataloging-in-Publication Data

Churches, cities and human community : urban ministry
in the United States, 1945-1985 / edited by Clifford J. Green.
        p.   cm.
Includes index.
ISBN 0-8028-4208-9 (pbk. : alk. paper)
1. City churches — United States — History — 20th century.
2. City missions — United States — History — 20th century.
3. United States — Church history — 20th century.
I. Green, Clifford J.
BV637.C48 1996
253′.0973′091732—dc20   95-52403
                                                        CIP

Contents

Preface   vii

Acronyms   xi

1. History in the Service of the Future:
   Studying Urban Ministry
   Clifford Green   1

2. "Not by Might, nor by Power":
   Urban Ministry in American Baptist Churches
   George D. Younger   23

3. To Be Untrammeled and Free:
   The Urban Ministry Work of the CME Church, 1944-90
   Luther E. Smith Jr.   52

4. "My Soul Says Yes":
   The Urban Ministry of the Church of God in Christ
   Robert Michael Franklin   77

5. Seeking to Hear and to Heed in the Cities:
   Urban Ministry in the Postwar Episcopal Church
   *Norman Faramelli, Edward Rodman, and
   Anne Scheibner*   97

CONTENTS

6. Themes of Lutheran Urban Ministry, 1945-85
   Richard Luecke   123

7. Presbyterian Ministry in Urban America, 1945-80
   George Todd   151

8. Roman Catholic Approaches to Urban Ministry, 1945-85
   Frederick J. Perella Jr.   179

9. Retreat, Reentry, and Retrenchment:
   Urban Ministry in the United Church of Christ, 1945-80
   Donald R. Steinle   212

10. Urban United Methodism:
    Structures and Strategies, 1945-90
    *Loyde H. Hartley, William E. Ramsden, and
    Kinmoth Jefferson*   235

11. Urban Economic Development Strategies of
    African-American Baptist Clergy during
    the Cold War Era
    James Melvin Washington   258

12. Seeking Community in the Metropolis: Reflections
    for the Future
    Clifford Green   280

13. Urban Church Literature: A Retrospection
    Loyde H. Hartley   308

Contributors   364

Index   369

Preface

IN THE SUMMER OF 1991, the Reverend Jesse Jackson led a march through Connecticut to dramatize the plight of America's cities. Conjuring memories of the civil rights marches of the sixties, this one began in the state's largest city, Bridgeport, which had just declared bankruptcy. It continued through New Haven — home of Yale University and one of the poorest cities in the country — until it reached the state capital. Once home to famous manufacturing companies like Royal Typewriter and Colt, and still the home of great insurance companies and United Technologies, Hartford was also at the top of the poverty list — fourth poorest in the 1980 census, eighth poorest in 1990. The dramatic point of the march derived not only from the plight of these cities, but equally from their location in this particular state: in terms of per capita income, Connecticut was the richest state in the nation.

This march had parabolic power. It contrasted poverty and wealth. It highlighted the contrast between the predominantly white suburbs and towns of this affluent state and the predominantly black and Hispanic citizens of the poor cities. Linked in this contrast, as shadow is inseparably linked to light, the cities could not possibly be objectified and isolated as though they were cancers in an otherwise wholesome body politic. Rather, the parable showed that the whole body was ill, not just the cities.

The parable also had microcosmic power. For it pointed beyond the cities, towns, and suburbs of one state to remind us that the contrasts and disparities of suburb and city, affluence and poverty, whites and people of color, is the condition of the whole nation. More than that, it is the condition of the whole world, as the problematic terms *First World* and *Third*

vii

World clumsily describe it. So what begins as a concern with cities and urban life quickly becomes part of a national and global picture, a picture largely drawn by lines of class and colored by race.

In this context the authors in this book have come together to examine how churches have sought human community in the urban world. Specifically we wish to examine how churches have thought about cities and ministered in cities in the United States during the years since World War II. The word *community* in our title is rooted in a shared biblical understanding that human life before God is not the life of isolated, utilitarian individualists but life in community. In the chapters that follow, this effort of churches to reflect the divine commonwealth by building human community in the midst of urban life takes many forms. Common to them is the vision and hope that the prophet Jeremiah expressed so well. Writing to the exiles from Jerusalem in Babylon, exiles who longed to be somewhere else, he urged them to "Build houses and live in them; plant gardens and eat their produce. . . . Seek the peace of the city. . . . for in its peace you will find your peace. . . . For I know the plans I have for you, says the Lord, plans for peace and not for evil, to give you a future and a hope" (Jeremiah 29:5ff. RSV rev.). The word *peace* here is of course the famous biblical word *shalom.* More than the absence of conflict and death, this rich term fills out the word *community* by embracing well-being, contentment, wholeness, health, prosperity, safety, and rest. Knowing full well that these are not the terms used in the daily news to describe life in America's cities, we hope that this book will give inspiration, challenge critical reflection, and stimulate creative action.

This is not a book reserved for urban ministry specialists. The urban, national, and global picture sketched above confronts the whole church — urban and suburban; laity and clergy; congregations, synods, denominations, councils of churches, and ecumenical agencies. Indeed, I would argue that this picture of social contradiction, division, suffering, and injustice essentially defines the mission *context* of the church in North America today — locally, nationally, and globally. We must preach the gospel and live as the church community in ways that address this context. We dare not speak of evangelism, salvation, new life, repentance and reconciliation, community with God and with one another, the love of Christ, or the Christian life of faith, hope, and love apart from this context. The work of the Holy Spirit must be related to this public, social world, not confined to individualistic and subjective (spiritual!) interpretations.

The book covers the period of roughly four decades after World War II. Some authors stop at 1980, some at 1985, and some even reach to 1990. But the emphasis in most chapters is on the earlier part of the period.

In the eighties and nineties, as many of the activities documented here were cut back, other initiatives began to appear, especially among evangelicals. That is a new stage that needs to be documented and analyzed.

Any group of urban ministry leaders and researchers planning a work like this in the late 1980s would be keenly aware, as we were, of how many white males were in the room! Two important decisions were made to mitigate this situation. First, it was decided to increase the African American participation by inviting a contribution on the Church of God in Christ, a relatively new denomination born in this century, predominantly black and urban, and fast growing; Robert Franklin graciously agreed to write this chapter, and did so with exemplary dispatch. Second, authors agreed to seek the contributions and critique of people of color to their chapters, either by developing a team authorship (as in the Episcopal chapter) or by circulating their drafts to such colleagues for their comments.

When the chapters were completed, the editor was confronted with the order in which to print them. Aside from the fact that bibliographies come at the end of books, how were the other chapters to be ordered? Was there any logic in the practice of urban ministry that the chapters report, or in the history of the denominations, that would recommend an order? After discussion among several colleagues yielded no intrinsic logic, we resorted to a conventional solution that the perceptive reader will quickly discover. Chapters may therefore be read in any order, but we do urge readers to read all the chapters, and not only those of their own denominations.

Obviously the case could easily be made to include more chapters in the book. The CME chapter, for example, is a sample of work done by African American Methodists and cannot tell the whole story that would emerge if AME and AME Zion chapters could have been added. The chapter on black Baptists has a distinctive focus on clergy efforts for urban economic development, thereby making an important contribution, but at the cost of not being able to cover other aspects of urban ministry among black Baptists. It would be easy to list other chapters that might have been added, but a limit had to be made, and the picture that emerges from ten denominations covers a broad spectrum.

In addition to the contributors who are authors of chapters, several other people — all pioneers and leaders in urban ministry — made important contributions to this project by giving interviews, attending conferences, or consulting on manuscripts. They are Don Benedict, John De Boers, Ted Erickson, David Frenchak, John Heinemeier, Donna Schaper, Philip Newell, Dick Simpson, Sonny Stockwell, Bill and Helen Webber, and Gibson Winter: we offer them our thanks.

PREFACE

As editor I am happy to express my personal thanks and those of my colleagues to the following people and organizations: to the Lilly Endowment for the grant that supported our work, as part of a wider commitment to urban ministry; to Hartford Seminary for its generous promotion of faculty research and for sabbatical leave to work on this project; to Colleen Kruger and Patricia Onyia of Hartford Seminary for their word processing of chapters and their administrative assistance with the project; to Carolyn Sperl and Marie Rovero of Hartford Seminary Library for their friendly and unfailing assistance; and to Amy Bruch, who served in the summer of 1991 while a student at Union Theological Seminary as editorial and research assistant.

This project has given birth to another one. Readers will note many references to significant but fugitive documents, to organizations that assembled voluminous documentation and resources, and to people whose collections of papers are the raw material of future research. Loyde Hartley, contributor of two chapters in this book and author of the definitive bibliography *Cities and Churches: An International Bibliography* (three volumes, 1992), is recording interviews with urban church leaders, locating collections of material, and hoping to secure them for future research. The Lilly Endowment also supported his research, and its fruits will be a valuable companion to this book.

CLIFFORD GREEN
ADVENT 1994

Acronyms

ABCOTS	American Baptist Churches of the South
ABC/USA	American Baptist Churches in the U.S.A. (also ABC)
ABHMS	American Baptist Home Mission Societies
ABMAC	American Baptist Management Corporation
ACT	"Act in Crisis Today"
AELC	Association of Evangelical Lutheran Churches
AFDC	Aid to Families with Dependent Children
AHOP	Asylum Hill Organizing Project
AIDS	acquired immunodeficiency syndrome
ALC	American Lutheran Church
AME	African Methodist Episcopal Church
AMEZ	African Methodist Episcopal Zion Church
AME Zion	African Methodist Episcopal Zion Church
APSO	Appalachian People's Service Organization
ARTOS	Alternate Route to Ordained Service
BAM	Board for American Missions
BHM	Board for Homeland Ministries
BUILD	Baltimore United in Leadership Development
CAC	Christian Activities Council
CAP	Community Action Programs
CCUM	Catholic Committee on Urban Ministry
CHD	Campaign for Human Development
CHN	Coalition for Human Needs

xi

CICM	Conference on Inner City Ministries
CME	Christian Methodist Episcopal Church (also CME Church)
CNLC	Committee for the New Lutheran Church
COCU	Commission on Church Union
COGIC	Church of God in Christ
COPS	Communities Organized for Public Service
CORA	Commission on Religion in Appalachia
CORE	Congress of Racial Equality
CPE	clinical pastoral education
CSS/CFS	Catholic Social Services/Catholic Family Services
CWU	Church Women United
DAP	Development Assistance Program
ECCO	East Columbus Community Organization
ECW	Episcopal Church Women
EEOC	Equal Employment Opportunity Commission
EHPP	East Harlem Protestant Parish
ELCA	Evangelical Lutheran Church in America
ESCRU	Episcopal Society for Racial and Cultural Unity
EUB	Evangelical United Brethren Church
EUC	Episcopal Urban Caucus
FACT	Feminism and the Church Today
FBI	Federal Bureau of Investigation
FHA	Federal Housing Administration
FIGHT	For Integrity, God, Housing Today
GCSP	General Convention Special Program
HART	Hartford Areas Rally Together
HIV	human immunodeficiency virus
HUD	[Department of] Housing and Urban Development
IAF	Industrial Areas Foundation
ICCR	Interfaith Center on Corporate Responsibility
ICUIS	Institute on the Church in Urban Industrial Society
IFCO	Interreligious Foundation for Community Organizing
JNLC	Justice in the New Lutheran Church

JSAC	Joint Strategy and Action Committee
LCA	Lutheran Church in America
LCMS	Lutheran Church–Missouri Synod
LCUSA	Lutheran Council in the United States of America
LHRAA	Lutheran Human Relations Association of America
LMMA	Lutheran Metropolitan Ministry Association
MACC	Mexican American Cultural Center
MAP	Metropolitan Associates of Philadelphia
MFSA	Methodist Federation for Social Action
MFSS	Methodist Federation for Social Service
MLM	Metropolitan Lutheran Ministry
MRTI	Mission Responsibility through Investment
MUST	Metropolitan Urban Service Training
MUST-II	Methodists United for Service and Training
NAACP	National Association for the Advancement of Colored People
NCC	National Council of Churches
NCCC	National Council of the Churches of Christ
NCCIJ	National Catholic Conference for Interracial Justice
NICD	New Initiatives in Church Development
NLC	National Lutheran Council
NOBC	National Office of Black Catholics
OEO	Office of Economic Opportunity
OIC	Opportunities Industrialization Centers
OSC	Organization of the Southwest Community
PIIR	Presbyterian Institute of Industrial Relations
PNBC	Progressive National Baptist Convention
PUSH	People United to Save Humanity
SAAR	Study of Administrative Areas and Relationships
SBC	Southern Baptist Convention
SCLC	Southern Christian Leadership Conference
SCODS	Study Commission on Denominational Structure
SCOR	Study Commission on Regions
SCUPE	Seminary Consortium for Urban Pastoral Education

ACRONYMS

SECO	Southeast Community Organization
SNCC	Student Nonviolent Coordinating Committee
TCO	Twin Cities Organization
UBC	Urban Bishops Coalition
UBCL	Union of Black Clergy and Laity
UBE	Union of Black Episcopalians
UCC	United Church of Christ
UHC	United Holy Church of America
UMC	United Methodist Church
UMPE	United Ministries in Public Education
UNO	United Neighborhood Organization
URM	Urban Rural Mission
USCC	U.S. Catholic Conference
USSR	Union of Soviet Socialist Republics
UTC	Urban Training Center for Christian Mission
VIM	Venture in Mission
VIP	very important person
VISTA	Volunteers in Service to America
WABHMS	Women's American Baptist Home Mission Society
YMCA	Young Men's Christian Association
YWCA	Young Women's Christian Association

History in the Service of the Future: Studying Urban Ministry

CLIFFORD GREEN

How have churches in the United States understood and practiced their ministry in cities in the period following World War II? That is the question this book addresses. Since ministry in cities during this time has usually been summarized with the phrase "urban ministry," another way to state the main question is to ask: What has this central concept of urban ministry meant, and what are the main forms it has taken?

This study was done in the conviction that the issues of urban life present critical challenges to the churches — not optional questions of whether they will take on this or the other project, or engage in this or that service, but questions that challenge the very integrity of Christian existence in the contemporary and future urban world. Consequently this historical analysis is not done for the sake of merely chronicling urban ministry efforts since World War II, and certainly not out of nostalgia. Rather, it is "history in the service of the future." The contributors aim to present the history in an analytical and reflective way, so that we may learn from the past and offer insights for future practice.

This chapter will introduce the project in three sections. First, the goals of the project will be presented, delineating the basic issues to be addressed. Second, an overview of U.S. social history after 1945, especially as it relates to cities, will provide the context for the following chapters. Third, highlights of American church history during the period will be sketched, including reference to several activities directly related to the practice of urban ministry and frequently mentioned in the following chapters.

I

The aim of the study was to evaluate the guiding paradigm or paradigms shaping urban ministry since World War II, in order to help shape new paradigms and mission strategies for the future. At a planning conference at Union Theological Seminary, New York, in December 1989, a set of questions I had prepared as project director were discussed and accepted as the broad guidelines for our inquiries. These are the questions, with annotations.

(1) What has the central concept of "urban ministry" meant? What are the main forms it has taken? Closely related to this is another question: (2) What image, model, or paradigm of the city, inner city, or metropolitan area has informed the churches' policy and strategy in cities? Has this been intentional, or unconscious? Much lies behind the two key terms "urban" and "ministry." Does "urban" in fact mean "inner city," especially its residential neighborhoods, often poor and heavily populated by African Americans, Hispanics, other ethnic minorities, and poor whites? Does it mean the city as a whole, including its affluent neighborhoods; its business and commercial activities; its institutions of government, education, and culture; its professions like law and medicine? Or does "urban" mean a whole metropolitan area, both city and suburbs, poor and affluent, whites and people of color, with all their multitude of activities? How much did churches draw upon urban sociologists to help them understand the urban reality where they were ministering? How much were the approaches to urban ministry informed by an explicit understanding of how "urban" was being defined?

The term "ministry" likewise contains many assumptions about the church and about varying forms of ministry. Here the conference expressly articulated a question that was originally presupposed rather than listed. (3) What image, model, or paradigm of the church has informed the churches' policy and strategy in cities? This can be approached in terms of the *form* of the church. Does "church" mean local congregation, or a larger denominational form such as a diocese or synod, or a specialized agency like a city mission society, or an ecumenical structure such as a council of churches or a ministerial alliance, or an ad hoc coalition to accomplish a special purpose? Different forms of the church are clearly better suited to certain types of ministry. For example, a congregation or group of congregations may be better placed to address the concerns of a local neighborhood, while a diocese or council of churches may be more effective in lobbying a city council or mobilizing a network of laypeople.

The question of how the church is understood equally refers to its mission.[1] Is the gospel understood as intrinsically connected to the problems of urban life? Do churches regard questions of economics and politics as properly within their purview? If so, should a church encourage a service mentality, engage in legislative advocacy, or opt for political empowerment through community organizing? Or do churches seek to be primarily sanctuaries for individual souls?

Different understandings of the church have led to "ministry" being defined by different modes of Christian activity. For well over one hundred years the Salvation Army has engaged in a ministry of urban evangelism and service. More recently, many churches have pursued various forms of advocacy for peace and justice, particularly for civil rights. Community organizing, growing out of Saul Alinsky's movement, and shareholder movements for corporate responsibility, have also been important for many churches and religious orders in the last fifty years. Ministry, then, can have many meanings. And, presumably, one's paradigm or model of the city — whether conscious or unexamined — will affect the modes of ministry one engages in.

(4) What have been the main motives, interests, or concerns (theological or other) shaping a denomination's urban-metropolitan policy? This relates closely to the previous question about how ministry is understood. It also calls for comment on the ordering of this book by chapters on denominations. This was done not only for practical reasons but chiefly because that is how the churches organized themselves and operated during the period in question. The study did not assume a "preferential option for the denomination," as if resolutions by synods or national agencies were somehow more important than the actual practice of ministry in the cities.[2] Nor does this approach presume that denominations were the most appropriate form of ministry in the city, or that denominational structures were more appropriate to engage urban life than ecumenical forms. Indeed, as I shall argue in the concluding chapter, denominations as a *form* of the church are *incongruent* with urban life and institutions that are "ecumenical" by definition. Hence another of our guideline questions was, (5) To what extent have denominations worked ecumenically in given cities to pursue a common urban ministry with

---

1. For one investigation of how congregations relate to public life, which builds on the typologies of Troeltsch and H. Richard Niebuhr, see David A. Roozen, William McKinney, and Jackson W. Carroll, *Varieties of Religious Presence* (New York: Pilgrim Press, 1984).

2. Notes for authors from the December 1989 conference include this statement: "The framework of the study is denominational, without begging the question of what the actual relation of urban ministers and congregations was to the staff and policies of denominations."

other churches? A specific corollary of that question asks, (6) What, if any, has been the role of local citywide councils of churches in the denominations' urban-metropolitan strategies? In fact, as chapter after chapter will show, the encompassing character of urban life, and the fact that its problems were no respecters of denominations, repeatedly called forth ecumenical cooperation and organizations.

Another interesting question is whether different polities, and the theologies that support them, lead to different strategies in engaging urban life. For example, are congregationalists (e.g., United Church of Christ [UCC], Baptists) more disposed to see the local congregation as the chief agent of urban mission, while episcopal polities like Roman Catholics and Episcopalians are more inclined to look to larger entities such as a diocesan agency covering a metropolitan area?

A central question for the period under review is, (7) How have factors like urban poverty and racism been addressed in urban ministry? One of the major social events of our period has been the civil rights struggle, which had deep roots in the black churches and their leadership, and which attracted the support of thousands of active clergy and laity from white churches who marched, demonstrated, sang, prayed, and advocated together to overcome the blight of racism. Poverty, likewise, has been an enduring and increasing tragedy of urban life since World War II. The postwar suburban expansion, coupled with the northern migration of southern blacks, has led in city after city to what some have called the doughnut phenomenon and what Martin Luther King Jr. called "islands of poverty in a sea of affluence." All the contributors to this book consider racism and poverty — which so often victimize the same people — scandals in the eyes of God and issues that must be addressed in assessing the history of churches' ministry in cities.

Given the bifurcation of city and suburbs resulting from suburban expansion, black migration, and "white flight," it is crucial to ask, (8) What has been the relation between urban and suburban churches in urban-metropolitan strategies? At stake here are two factors, theological and contextual. It is a theological imperative of the gospel that breaking down the "dividing wall of hostility" (Ephesians 2:14, RSV) belongs to the essence of the church. The contextual factor is that a metropolis is an organic whole, even if suburbanites split it into workplace and dormitory. The coincidence of these two factors requires that we examine how urban ministry efforts have cultivated this relationship.

Another crucial question is, (9) What has been the role of the laity in urban ministry, seen from the perspective of their vocational institutions and public roles? The question here is not whether lay members of congregations have participated in efforts of their churches, such as housing a Head Start program or supporting a soup kitchen or shelter. Nor is it whether laypeople have served as volunteers in church urban mission organizations, or worked on special projects such as building low-income housing. Nor is it whether laypeople performed important roles as full-time employees of, say, a community organizing project. The focus, rather, is on lay church members *in their vocational institutions and public roles*. That is, how much have urban ministry strategies tried to learn from and mobilize those church members who, day by day, work in education, government, business and industry, the media — people who are often in positions of leadership, who are engaged in decision-making that affects the peace of the city, and who have access to power?

Two other questions complete our initial list, and are self-explanatory. (10) Which cities offer the best examples of a denomination's urban policy? (11) Have there been significant changes in policies or strategies during the period? If so, why, and with what results? This last question invites further reflection on the degree of self-consciousness and deliberateness with which urban ministry was pursued, on the extent to which assumptions were questioned, and whether such evaluation led to improved modes of ministry and engagement with the city.

Informing the initial set of questions were two basic assumptions, one sociological and the other theological. The sociological assumption was that it was not enough to define urban ministry simply as any ministry performed in a city. On the face of it, there are obviously dozens of different ministries congregations and individuals are pursuing in cities: Head Start programs, day care centers, tutoring programs, meal and visitation programs for the elderly, visitation of shut-ins, low-income housing projects, shelters for battered women, soup kitchens, homeless shelters, legislative advocacy, alcohol and drug abuse programs, employment programs, health programs, street evangelism, radio and television ministries — the list could easily expand to fill up the page. But mere geography, I contend, is not enough to qualify a ministry as "urban ministry." The fundamental sociological question is: What are the distinctive characteristics of urban life that Christian ministry needs to engage? What makes an "urbs"? What does it mean to live and minister in the urbs, rather than in a rural community? How does ministry in a city or metropolis present distinctive challenges to the Christian community?

This leads directly to the second and theological assumption, namely, the *contextual nature of ministry*. I regard "urban ministry" not as something

5

sui generis but as a contextual form of ministry per se. The whole ministry of the church involves worship, proclamation and witness, community life and pastoral care, Christian education, and doing justice in the world. A "contextual form of ministry" means that this ministry must assume forms appropriate to its context. This is obvious enough when one thinks of other contexts. A church in India, for example, faces the linguistic challenge of interpreting Hebrew and Greek Scriptures in the indigenous languages of that land, of embodying and articulating the gospel in a predominantly Hindu culture, and of dealing with characteristic problems in Indian society such as caste. In short, the Indian social and cultural system is the inescapable context in which a church lives its life and shapes its ministry. While an Indian church will have much in common with churches in Africa, Europe, or America, it will also have distinctive forms appropriate to its special context. The analogous question, therefore, is how the urban context presents distinctive challenges to church ministry in the United States in the past half century. Specifically, how did churches identify and engage those characteristic aspects of urban life?[3]

In the two historical sections that follow it is clearly impossible to chronicle every important social and cultural development of the period. In highlighting the following aspects of social and church history I sketch those events and developments that were most influential and appeared most important to the authors of the following chapters and the colleagues with whom they worked.

II. Social History

Key events in national life, major domestic and foreign policies of government, and decisive social movements inevitably shape life in American cities. Understanding the context of urban ministry therefore requires a brief sketch of social history in the postwar period.

One social movement that had a direct bearing on urban life and ministry after World War II was the *"Great Migration"* of southern blacks that began in the 1890s.[4] Provoked by racial attacks and lynchings, and

3. An obvious presupposition here, in terms of Troeltsch's church-sect typology, is that church life *ought* to be engaged with its social context, rather than isolating itself from its world.

4. See David M. Katzman in Eric Foner and John A. Garraty, eds., *The Reader's Companion to American History* (Boston: Houghton Mifflin, 1991), pp. 114f.

attracted by job opportunities in industrial cities, thousands and thousands of people moved from the countryside and small towns of the rural South to the cities of the North and Midwest. During World War I about half a million people migrated, and from 1916 through the 1960s more than six million people relocated in the North. In the decade from 1910 to 1920, Chicago's black population grew from 44,000 to 110,000. Migrating blacks often met in the North a hostility comparable to what they had left in the South: in 1919 alone there were over twenty major race riots. The migration tapered off during the 1960s. In fact, the tide turned during the 1970s and 1980s as more blacks moved into the South than out of it. This "reverse migration" was not only part of a move by the population at large into the Sunbelt; more specifically, this recent move has been motivated, as before, by the search for a better life in place of the problems in the northern urban ghettos: crime, drugs, unemployment, and poor, segregated schools.

The "Great Migration" changed the face of northern cities. It greatly increased the membership of older African American Methodist and Baptist churches in the North. It brought black and white urban church members together during the civil rights movement. But many whites turned their backs on the cities and made their own "great migration" in the phenomenon known at the time as white flight.

At the end of the Second World War, veterans returned home from Europe, Asia, and the Pacific keen to live normal lives, to resume their education and careers, and to marry and have families. The "baby boom" of the forties and fifties is linked to one of the decisive postwar developments mentioned in virtually every chapter of the book, namely, the phenomenal *growth of suburbs* around urban cores. Here are the roots of the bifurcation of suburb and core city, of affluence and poverty, of whites and people of color, so typical of metropolitan areas in the United States in the latter decades of the century.

In part the growth of suburbs reflected the expanding population, as parents of the baby boom generation sought new housing for their families. Many interpreters see in this movement toward a more "rural" type of environment and away from the density, ethnicity, and richness of the city a deep anti-urban prejudice in American culture. Sydney Ahlstrom, for example, noted "the strongly agrarian terms in which the American idea of the good life has been couched."[5] Others point out that the dominance of the automobile over more traditional types of urban transportation was

5. Sydney E. Ahlstrom, *A Religious History of the American People* (New Haven: Yale University Press, 1972), p. 1089.

an essential contributing factor, supported by massive postwar federal spending on interstate highways. Multilane, limited-access highways, which embraced cities in ring roads and often reached into the heart of downtown, made possible a relatively easy commute from semirural suburbs to central business districts.[6] One commentator observes that the American bias toward the automobile, which antedates the interstate highways, led to "the inevitable result . . . that by 1991 the United States had the world's best road system and very nearly its worst public transit offerings."[7] Another analyst argues that federal highway funding, along with government housing policies and "urban renewal," in spite of all good intentions, "sealed the fate of urban America."[8]

As a major development of the postwar period, suburbanization inescapably shapes the issue of how cities are to be understood and how churches can best minister in them.[9] By the year 1990, according to Kenneth Jackson, "more than 45 percent of the population, or more than 120 million people, lived in suburban areas, a far higher proportion than resided either in rural regions or central cities. Quite simply, the United States had become the world's first suburban nation."[10] Between 1950 and 1980, eighteen of the twenty-five largest cities recorded a net loss of population to the suburbs, while the independent suburbs gained over 60 million during the same period. The suburban population doubled from 34 million to 74 million between 1950 and 1970. Reviewing the fifteen largest metropolitan areas in 1980, Jackson points out that "only in Houston did a majority of residents live in the central city"; in the others (such as Baltimore, Atlanta, and Boston), the percentage of suburban residents was more than 60, 70,

---

6. The highway system is a link between urban policy and Cold War strategy. Among several reasons he gave for the system, Eisenhower wanted trucks and tanks to be able to travel speedily in the United States on a system of limited-access dual highways like the German autobahns. First funded in 1944, the name of the interstate system was changed in 1956 to the National System of Interstate and Defense Highways because of its "primary importance to the national defense"; cf. "Federal-Aid Highway Act of 1956" (PL 627, 29 June 1956), *United States Statutes at Large* 70, p. 378. More fundamental than the military aspect in the view of some analysts was the success of forces supporting road over rail; see Stephen B. Goddard, *Getting There: The Epic Struggle between Road and Rail in the American Century* (New York: Basic Books, 1994).

7. Kenneth T. Jackson, in Foner and Garraty, p. 885.

8. Stanley K. Schultz, in Foner and Garraty, p. 177.

9. For the following, see Kenneth T. Jackson, *Crabgrass Frontier: The Suburbanization of the United States* (New York: Oxford University Press, 1985), and his article on "Suburbanization" in Foner and Garraty, pp. 1040ff.

10. Jackson, in Foner and Garraty, p. 1040.

and 80 percent, respectively.[11] As the following chapters will show, building new churches and organizing new congregations in the burgeoning suburbs was a leading priority of denominations in these decades. Winthrop Hudson reports annual spending on new church building ranging from $26 million in 1945, to $775 million in 1956, to over $1 billion in 1960.[12]

Factors influencing the phenomenal growth of suburbs are complex. But, according to one expert, two factors are paramount: "racial prejudice and cheap housing."[13] One indication of the former is the way suburban migration accelerated after the 1954 Supreme Court decision declared school segregation unconstitutional. The result of the suburban explosion is patent:

> The . . . most important characteristic of the housing pattern is the socioeconomic distinction between the center and the periphery. In the United States, status and income correlate with suburbs, the area that provides the homes for an overwhelming proportion of those with college educations, those engaged in professional pursuits, and those in the upper-income brackets. Despite hopes and claims of a recent revival in American cities, the 1990 census revealed a widening disparity between residents of central cities and those of their surrounding suburbs not only in income but also in housing and family structure.[14]

This disparity, we must note, is in each city not only a microcosm of the whole nation, but also of the world. The bifurcation of poor city, largely populated by people of color, and affluent suburb, largely white, parallels the affluence and power of the so-called First World in relation to the so-called Third World. For churches with a theological mandate to seek the peace of the city, to break down the dividing walls of hostility, to create communities of love, justice, and hope that anticipate — even in fragmentary parables — the eschatological divine commonwealth, this local and

---

11. Jackson, *Crabgrass Frontier,* pp. 283ff.

12. See Winthrop S. Hudson, *Religion in America,* 2d ed. (New York: Charles Scribner's Sons, 1973), p. 382 n. 45. Extrapolating from Hudson's figures, we can estimate spending over $8 billion on new churches between 1945 and 1960.

13. Jackson, in Foner and Garraty, p. 1042. He regards the economic factor as the more powerful, pointing out that — compared to other nations — the cost of American housing is relatively low, that land and transportation are inexpensive, that the balloon frame technique of house building keeps costs down, and that government subsidizes home ownership through tax deductions of mortgage interest and property tax. While subsidizing suburban housing development, government is also concentrating public low-income housing in inner-city neighborhoods.

14. Jackson, in Foner and Garraty, p. 1041.

global paradigm of disparity, suffering, and injustice is an unavoidable context of all ministry, not only urban ministry.

The result of the spectacular development of suburbs around the urban core is a novel artifact compared to cities elsewhere in the world. Whether one thinks of Cairo, Rome, Barcelona, Vienna, Istanbul, Calcutta, Cape Town, Mexico City, Rio de Janeiro, or Caracas, the basic picture is the same: the prime living areas are near the center city; in the outer rings, at the margins, are to be found the slums, "townships," *favelas,* and shanty towns. Observing this novelty, Kenneth Jackson comments:

> Suburbia has become the quintessential physical achievement of the United States; it is perhaps more representative of its culture than big cars, tall buildings, or professional football. Suburbia symbolizes the fullest, most unadulterated embodiment of contemporary culture; it is a manifestation of such fundamental characteristics of American society as conspicuous consumption, a reliance upon the private automobile, upward mobility, the separation of the family into nuclear units, the widening division between work and leisure, and a tendency toward racial and economic exclusiveness.[15]

At the other end of the spectrum, reversing the pattern found elsewhere in the world, is abandonment in the inner core. Conjuring the images of "stripped automobiles, burned-out buildings, boarded-up houses, rotting sewers, and glass-littered streets," Jackson points out that "until the 1950s, there was no American precedent for the complete and absolute abandonment that has become so pervasive in the 1980s. Some streets are now so devoid of life that even the rats and roaming dogs are gone."[16] After reviewing the history of American cities, Stanley K. Schultz advances a comprehensive thesis to interpret the polarity Jackson describes.

> From the seventeenth century to the present, the cycle has come full circle. Despite generations of efforts by planning reformers enthusiastic about solving the physical, social and moral problems of urban America, cities remain as they began. They are containers for business, boasting vastly improved physical environments, to be sure, but they function as centers for the conduct of economic activities, not as humane habitats meant to enrich the lives of most of their citizens.[17]

15. Jackson, *Crabgrass Frontier,* p. 4.
16. Jackson, *Crabgrass Frontier,* pp. 285f.
17. Schultz, "City Planning," in Foner and Garraty, p. 177; see also his *Constructing*

Another characteristic of the earlier decades of the period was *urban renewal.* Already before the war, the federal government had come to the rescue of home owners threatened by foreclosure during the Depression. It also encouraged and supported local housing authorities to construct low-income public housing, and one hundred thousand units were built by 1939. After the war, the Housing Acts of 1949 and 1954 aimed to build new urban housing and wipe out city slums. But urban renewal proved to be at best a very problematic phenomenon. While some cities responded to dilapidated housing and run-down commercial properties ("urban blight," as it was usually called) with selective rebuilding and conservation, the most common method was to tear down whole blocks in the name of redevelopment. Every city can tell stories of former inner-city neighborhoods, often populated by ethnic and minority communities, which were torn down to be replaced by office towers, civic centers, and apartment housing for the well-to-do. In low-income residential areas, public housing often replaced poor two- and three-family homes but rarely accommodated most of the former residents. Over the years these "solutions" became part of the problem, the site of gangs, violence, and drugs — "factories of demoralization," as one black urban pastor called them. The displaced poor moved to other marginal neighborhoods.[18]

Foreign policy, as well as domestic developments, also affected urban life and church activities. The *Cold War* coincided almost exactly with the period of our study. From Winston Churchill's 1946 "iron curtain" speech in Fulton, Missouri, to the breakup of the Soviet Union after Gorbachev's reforms in the late eighties, ideological and military conflict with the USSR dominated Washington's foreign policy and the popular imagination, and controlled a large part of the federal budget. Crisis followed crisis, with the Korean War (1950-53) succeeded by the Bay of Pigs invasion (1961), the Cuban missile crisis (1962), and, above all, the Vietnam War (1961-74). Senator Joseph McCarthy led a witch-hunt in the 1950s to expose and punish alleged communists in all spheres of national life, including the churches. While the arms race consumed precious resources and the Cold War diverted attention from urgent urban needs, they did not prevent the formation of a new federal Department of Housing and Urban Develop-

---

Urban Culture: American Cities and City Planning, 1800-1920 (Philadelphia: Temple University Press, 1989).

18. See Schultz, "City Planning," in Foner and Garraty, p. 176, and George Younger, *The Church and Urban Renewal* (Philadelphia: Lippincott, 1965).

11

ment (HUD) in 1965,[19] nor Lyndon Johnson's War on Poverty. However, the Reagan administration policy of deep cuts in federal social funding had a crippling effect on urban programs such as low-income housing and other supports for the poor.

The *Vietnam War* brought the Cold War to the streets of America. If European theologians saw World War I as "shaking the foundations" (Tillich) of their civilization, the Vietnam War arguably had the same significance for the United States. The nation was more deeply divided over the morality of the war than over any issue since the Civil War a century before. More people expressed lack of confidence in government and "the system" than in the earlier or later decades of this century. Antiwar protests were a regular part of life. Young men burned draft cards in church services. On campuses the rhetoric of revolution came readily to students' lips. Clergy and other leading citizens were put on trial by the government for their antiwar activities, and a government official leaked the secret "Pentagon Papers" to the press and public.

By far the greatest number of urban ministry practitioners were opponents of the war. They took an active part in protest vigils, marches in Washington, demonstrations, and other antiwar activities. After a time, people like Martin Luther King Jr. began to make direct connections between the immorality of the war and the injustices of racism and poverty in the cities at home. At the height of the war and the antiwar protests in the late sixties and early seventies, Vietnam dominated all other issues. The end of the war in 1974 found the nation bitterly divided and exhausted; returning veterans received no heroes' welcome. What effect did the Vietnam War have on the urban ministry movement? Is it only a coincidence that the last several years of the war saw the closing of one urban training program after another?[20] Whatever future research may discover, we can safely say that the Vietnam War was a grave diversion from the critical issues of America's cities and the unfinished agenda of the civil rights movement for racial justice.

More directly related to urban ministry than the Cold War and the antiwar movement was the great moral mobilization that grew from a single act of courage (as small as a mustard seed), when Rosa Parks on December

19. Robert Weaver, its first head, was the first black cabinet member in U.S. history. In the Carter administration, a Catholic priest, Fr. Geno Baroni, joined HUD with special responsibility for neighborhood housing and economic development; see chapter 8.

20. See George Younger, *From New Creation to Urban Crisis: A History of Action Training Ministries, 1962-1975* (Chicago: Center for the Scientific Study of Religion, 1987), Appendix 7, pp. 235ff.

1, 1955, asserted her God-given human dignity and refused to give up her bus seat to a white passenger. Thus was born the *civil rights movement* led by Martin Luther King Jr. So deeply rooted was this movement in the black church that one could easily argue that it belongs in the next section of the chapter on church history. But the campaign led by the black preachers of the Southern Christian Leadership Conference (SCLC) soon expanded beyond the church to become a national movement, embracing people of all races, faiths, and party affiliation.

A monumental account of the civil rights movement is provided by the work of Taylor Branch.[21] Here only a few highlights of the movement must suffice. Near the end of World War II the classic study *An American Dilemma* by Gunnar Myrdal and a distinguished team of sociologists focused attention on the nation's most crucial issue.[22] The beginning of the civil rights movement a decade later is usually marked by the 1954 Supreme Court decision in *Brown v. Board of Education of Topeka,* which outlawed segregated education. This decision emboldened black citizens to boycott segregated buses in Montgomery, Alabama, for a year in 1955-56, a move that gained national and international attention. From this boycott was born in 1957 the SCLC, headed by Dr. King. His strategy was based on a marriage of the Christian doctrine of love and Gandhi's methods of nonviolent resistance.

In 1960, students in North Carolina adopted the desegregating strategy of lunch counter "sit-ins," a tactic that spread rapidly and quickly gave birth to the Student Non-Violent Coordinating Committee (SNCC).

In 1961, "freedom rides" became a highly visible part of the movement. Black and white bus riders protesting segregation at southern bus terminals rode buses together from Atlanta to Alabama in the spring, and from Atlanta to Mississippi in November. The Congress of Racial Equality (CORE) was a leader in these efforts, having organized the first such bus ride in 1947 to oppose segregation in interstate travel. Violence against the freedom riders was a catalyst for the federal Interstate Commerce Commission and the Justice Department to prohibit segregation in interstate transport and in terminals. These rulings and court judgments were reinforced by the Civil Rights Acts of 1964 and 1968.

21. Taylor Branch, *Parting the Waters: America in the King Years, 1954-1964* (New York: Simon and Schuster, 1988). Branch's second volume, entitled *Pillar of Fire,* will continue through the sixties and the Vietnam War. For a briefer summary of the movement, see Clayborne Carson's "Civil Rights Movement," in Foner and Garraty, pp. 177f.

22. Gunnar Myrdal (with Richard Sterner and Arnold Rose), *An American Dilemma: The Negro Problem and Modern Democracy* (New York: Harper and Brothers, 1944). See also James Washington's chapter below.

One decisive event in the history of the civil rights movement was the entry of James Meredith into the University of Mississippi in the fall of 1962. To accomplish this the full force of the federal government was necessary in the form of troops sent by the Kennedy administration.

A definite culmination of the early years was the March on Washington in August 1963, when over 250,000 people marched to the Lincoln Memorial and heard King give his "I Have a Dream" speech; King was awarded the Nobel Peace Prize the following year. Earlier in 1963, prompted by the National Catholic Conference for Interracial Justice, an interfaith civil rights effort arose. The National Conference on Religion and Race was held in Chicago in January 1963, and involved Catholic, Jewish, Protestant, and Orthodox representatives. The continuing organization they formed led to interfaith chapters in local areas, and this interfaith coalition helped to pass the civil rights legislation the following year.[23]

John F. Kennedy had begun to promote new civil rights legislation. Just months after his assassination on November 22, 1963, Lyndon Johnson pushed through Congress the landmark Civil Rights Act. It prohibited discrimination on grounds of race, color, religion, or national origin in restaurants, hotels, theaters, and so on; it also prohibited discrimination in employment and required desegregation of public schools. Additional legislation followed with the Voting Rights Act of 1965 to guarantee equal voting rights, and the Civil Rights Act of 1968, which sought to prevent discrimination in housing and real estate transactions.

Building on ideas of the Kennedy administration, Johnson launched his Great Society legislation, an extension of New Deal aims. This included a short-lived *War on Poverty* — efforts between 1964 and 1967 to eliminate poverty and expand social welfare. An act in 1964 created the Office of Economic Opportunity to promote antipoverty efforts, emphasizing education, job training, and community economic development, and stressing the participation of poor people themselves in shaping and running the programs. Three billion dollars were spent in those three years on programs such as Head Start, food stamps, neighborhood legal services, Upward Bound (to help poor high school students attend college), the Job Corps (to help poor young people learn job skills), and VISTA (Volunteers in Service to America), a sort of domestic Peace Corps. While escalating spending on the Vietnam War and resistance to community action programs brought the War on Poverty to an early end after 1967, programs like Head

23. Robert Handy, *A History of the Churches in the United States and Canada* (New York: Oxford University Press, 1977), p. 414.

Start and food stamps endured. Though poverty in general declined in the 1960s for a time, this "war" did not defeat poverty either in the inner city or in rural areas.

Many summers in the 1960s saw serious urban violence connected with the struggle for human rights and racial justice. Called riots by authorities and uprisings or rebellions by supporters, they occurred every year between 1963 and 1969. After the assassination of Martin Luther King Jr. in April 1968, violence broke out in 125 cities. Among the more serious outbreaks of violence were those in Birmingham, Alabama (1963), New York City (1964), the Watts district of Los Angeles (1965), and Chicago (1966). In 1967 urban violence occurred in Tampa, Cincinnati, Atlanta, Detroit, and three New Jersey cities — Newark, Plainfield, and New Brunswick.[24] Johnson appointed in the summer of 1967 the Commission on Civil Disorders, which produced the "Kerner Report" the following year, identifying white racism as the chief cause of the violence.[25]

If the civil rights movement and Martin Luther King were informed by the principle of *integration,* a principle that shaped government policy and organizations like the National Association for the Advancement of Colored People (NAACP) and CORE alike, another stream was gathering force in the sixties. When, as Taylor Branch writes, "the entire society shifted from 'Negro' to 'black' almost overnight,"[26] the *Black Power movement* was born. Although the slogan itself was popularized by Stokely Carmichael in 1966,[27] Malcolm X had been expressing similar sentiments for a decade. Black Power was essentially a political movement, though many whites paid more attention to the expressions of cultural self-affirmation, such as the Afro hairdo, the dashiki, and the slogan "Black is Beautiful." Reading the Black Power manifesto[28] more than two decades later, I find its actual social

24. See Henry Drewry, *Dictionary of American History* (New York: Scribner's, 1976), vol. 6, pp. 8-9.

25. See *Report of the National Advisory Commission on Civil Disorders* (New York: Dutton, 1968).

26. Branch, p. xii.

27. See James Cone, *For My People: Black Theology and the Black Church* (Maryknoll, N.Y.: Orbis, 1984), p. 10. Cone regarded his *Black Theology and Black Power* (New York: Seabury, 1969) as the theological arm of the Black Power movement. See also his more recent study, in which he brings together the two streams of the Afro-American movement of the 1960s, *Martin and Malcolm and America: A Dream or a Nightmare* (Maryknoll, N.Y.: Orbis, 1991). (Adam Clayton Powell had used the term "Black Power" in speeches in 1966, and in 1965 a conference had been held in Chicago to establish a Black Power organization; see John H. Bracey Jr., "Black Power," *Dictionary of American History* [New York: Scribner's, 1976], vol. 1, p. 316.)

28. Stokely Carmichael and Charles V. Hamilton, *Black Power: The Politics of Liberation*

goals do not appear to differ very much from those of Martin Luther King and the integration strategy. But Black Power was a watershed in differing from King's civil rights movement on two key points: it rejected integration, and it sanctioned violence in self-defense. The militant, angry rhetoric of Black Power, which so dismayed even liberal whites, communicated a paradigm shift. A conflictual social model was pitted against the traditional American homogeneous one. The goal was not desegregation, but self-determination, and this linked it philosophically with liberation movements in other parts of the world.

By the late sixties it was quite evident that rights declared by courts and enacted in law required an economic base to be actualized. By making such connections, Martin Luther King not only attacked the Vietnam War but also began a Poor People's Campaign, one of his last moves before he was assassinated in April 1968. An expanding black middle class became more evident in the seventies and eighties, partly aided by affirmative action policies. Nevertheless, "the distribution of the nation's wealth and income moved toward greater inequality during the 1970s and 1980s. Civil rights advocates acknowledged that desegregation had not brought significant improvements in the lives of poor blacks, but they were divided over the future direction of black advancement efforts."[29]

The civil rights movement was not a "background" to urban ministry in the sixties, but an integral part of it. Not only did urban pastors and church members participate in marches, demonstrations, and freedom rides in Washington and the South. They pursued racial justice in their own communities and cities for an obvious reason: cities, especially in the North, were increasingly populated by blacks as more and more whites moved to the suburbs. Hence, the peace of the city and justice for its black citizens were inseparable.

III. Aspects of U.S. Church History

The *life of churches overall* disclosed marked changes during the forty years under review. It begins with what historian Robert Handy calls a "many-faceted revival of religion." Church membership rose from about 50 percent

---

in America (New York: Random House, 1967). They advocated "an effective share in the total power of the society" (p. 41) and argued that new structures such as the Mississippi Freedom Democratic Party and "parallel community organizations" (p. 86) were vehicles by which blacks could run schools, police departments, city housing, etc.

29. Clayborne Carson, writing about 1990, in Foner and Garraty, p. 180.

of the population in 1940 to nearly 70 percent in 1960, and in 1955 nearly half the population attended religious services in a typical week. Denominations grew in size, parish renewal programs flourished, religious education and youth programs were updated, seminary enrollments grew, and campus ministry prospered.[30] But the tide quickly turned. Handy points out that while

> the religious, biblical, theological, liturgical, and ecumenical revivals had brought church membership and attendance to impressive heights . . . there was much that passed for revival that lacked spiritual depth; churches identified too easily with the cults of achievement and success then so strong in a prosperous nation without subjecting them to intense scrutiny in the light of their own historic traditions. Some were aware of the superficialities of the renewal; others were to see them only after the tide turned.[31]

The signs of decline began to appear about halfway through our period. The growth of church membership in Protestant denominations slowed in the 1950s, and by 1965 a noticeable drop was quite evident; this would eventually reduce funding for urban ministry and redirect attention to church growth. In 1968 the ten largest Protestant denominations reported fewer members than in the previous year. Church membership was not keeping up with the growth rate of the population. The United Methodist Church, which was the largest Protestant denomination in the country in the 1960s, lost over half a million members between 1968 and 1971.[32] Roman Catholic statistics, too, revealed some ominous drops. Catholic seminarians dropped from 48,046 in 1966 to 22,963 in 1972. Not as dramatic but still substantial were drops in the numbers of sisters and brothers in religious orders. The number of priests leaving the priesthood, many to marry, also increased markedly.[33]

One of the more promising characteristics of the immediate postwar period was its *ecumenical spirit* that led to many forms of cooperation between churches, and initially to enthusiastic hopes for Christian unity in the foreseeable future — at least among Protestants. No sooner had the

30. Handy, p. 396.

31. Handy, p. 407.

32. David A. Roozen and C. Kirk Hadaway, eds., *Church and Denominational Growth* (Nashville: Abingdon Press, 1993); Hudson, p. 413, citing Dean M. Kelley, *Why Conservative Churches Are Growing* (New York: Harper and Row, 1972).

33. Cf. Hudson, p. 416, citing the *Official Catholic Directory* for the relevant years.

rubble of war been cleared away in Europe than the first and founding assembly of the World Council of Churches, long in preparation, was held in Amsterdam in 1948. Two years later the National Council of the Churches of Christ in the U.S.A., comprising Protestant and Orthodox churches, was founded;[34] it included a Department of the Urban Church that held a convention on the city church in Columbus, Ohio, in January 1950. The world ecumenical movement came to the United States when the World Council held its Second Assembly in Evanston, Illinois, in 1954.

The optimistic hope that the ecumenical spirit might lead in the near future to organic union of several major churches gave birth to the Commission on Church Union (COCU) in 1960. It was made up of ten major denominations,[35] and actively put forward proposals for a number of years. Even Protestant–Roman Catholic dialogue flourished, so much so that "the president of Notre Dame predicted in 1970 that church reunion would come before the century's end."[36] By the eighties, however, COCU was moribund, and energy was being invested into bilateral discussions such as those between Lutherans and Episcopalians, Roman Catholics and Episcopalians, and Lutherans and Roman Catholics.

Also characteristic of the postwar years were unions between pairs of denominations, as well as between branches of divided denominations. The year 1957 saw the formation of the United Church of Christ (UCC) by union of the Congregational Church and the Evangelical and Reformed Church. The Presbyterian Church U.S.A., after merging in 1958 with another northern Presbyterian body, united in 1982 with its southern counterpart to form the Presbyterian Church (U.S.A.). The United Methodist Church was born of the union in 1968 of the Methodist Church and the Evangelical and United Brethren (EUB). In 1960 the American Lutheran Church (ALC) was formed from four Lutheran bodies; in 1962 four other Lutheran bodies joined together to form the Lutheran Church in America (LCA). These two churches, along with the Association of Evangelical Lutheran Churches (AELC), united as the Evangelical Lutheran Church in America (ELCA) in 1988.

Though the ecumenical enthusiasm of the first decades after the war has either waned or been channeled in other directions, it was an essential

---

34. The NCCC superseded the Federal Council of the Churches of Christ, founded in 1908, and included thirty-three denominations.

35. African Methodist Episcopal, American Baptist, African Methodist Episcopal Zion, Christian Methodist Episcopal, Disciples of Christ, Episcopal, Evangelical and United Brethren, Methodist, United Church of Christ, United Presbyterian.

36. Ahlstrom, p. 1083.

ingredient of many aspects of urban ministry. Whether one thinks of an experimental parish community such as the East Harlem Protestant Parish, or of urban training programs, or of organizations on the national level of denominational urban ministry leaders such as the Joint Strategy and Action Committee, or of a venture in a particular urban area such as Metropolitan Associates of Philadelphia, ecumenical cooperation was repeatedly found to be essential.

The *Second Vatican Council* (1962-65) was an historic and transforming event in the modern history of the Roman Catholic Church. Initiated by the charismatic Pope John XXIII, it was designed to "open the windows" of the church and to effect an *aggiornamento* to the modern world. Each autumn bishops and their advisers from all over the world assembled in Rome. The documents they produced inspired change and renewal that swept through the church. They approved vernacular masses, increased the role and standing of the laity, emphasized the church as "the whole people of God," and expressed a cooperative ecumenical attitude to other Christian communions and openness to other religions; a changed attitude to Judaism was particularly important. Social justice was another concern that was urgently addressed. In the chapter on "Socio-Economic Life" of the *Pastoral Constitution on the Church in the Modern World* (*Gaudium et Spes*, 1965), the bishops wrote that justice demanded vigorous efforts "to remove as quickly as possible the immense economic inequalities which now exist."[37] Such teachings reinforced and enlivened an already strong Catholic commitment to improving urban life, and encouraged Catholics to work together with other Christians in addressing problems of the city.

Meanwhile many Catholics, whose families had often experienced the prejudices of a Protestant establishment, were entering into the mainstream of American life. Enjoying increasing affluence, and wider acceptance perhaps influenced by the election in 1960 of the first Catholic president, many Catholic families joined the move to the suburbs. This required new suburban churches, and also weakened the congregations, parochial schools, and parish finances of the inner-city churches.[38]

A striking phenomenon of the period beginning about 1961 was the rise of *church-based urban training*, or action training centers, documented in George Younger's fine study.[39] Twenty-seven centers were set up in

37. Walter M. Abbott, ed., *The Documents of Vatican II* (New York: American Press, 1966), pp. 271ff.

38. Hudson, p. 417.

39. Younger, *From New Creation to Urban Crisis.* The title is suggestive, the first part

19

twenty-two cities, the Urban Training Center in Chicago and the Metropolitan Urban Service Training (MUST) program in New York being only two of the best known. These centers were supported by fifteen national church agencies, including white and black Protestants, Roman Catholics, and some smaller bodies.[40] An indication of the breadth and intensity of this training is that "one center alone records 4,000 participants in 100 training programs over a five year period. Dozens of cadres emerged as training staff for these centers, and hundreds of clergy now working in cities across the country gained conceptual and practical tools for their ministry in urban areas."[41] The rapid emergence of these training centers and programs is as striking as the fact that most of them flourished and died in about fifteen years, though several such centers still exist today.

Community organizing emerged as a widespread strategy for addressing urban ills. Inspired by Saul Alinsky's methods, organizing was essentially a strategy of politically empowering communities to solve their own problems.[42] It worked not through conventional party and electoral politics, but through generating conflicts and winning battles with government and business institutions over neighborhood issues like housing, schools, jobs, health, public safety, and so on. If churches previously — and still — put most of their social ministry energies into various forms of *service,* Alinsky defined the pursuit of community well-being in terms of *power.* In this he was parallel to Reinhold Niebuhr's insistence that power was a crucial ingredient in every societal transaction, and that its use was unavoidable in every movement seeking social justice. The tactics of confrontation in which Alinsky trained his disciples were controversial in middle-class quarters, including, of course, the church. But many urban church workers came to discover the effectiveness of Alinsky's organizing tactics and began to reflect theologically on the issues it posed for their previous understandings of the gospel, the church, and Christian ethics.

The story of churches and community organizing has two stages. While clergy and professional lay organizers saw their causes and battles as mandated by the Bible and Christian ethics, *in the first stage* of the move-

---

alluding hopefully to Gibson Winter's *The New Creation as Metropolis* (New York: Macmillan, 1963), the latter to the deepening urban crisis of America's cities in the 1980s and 1990s.

40. Church of God (Anderson, Indiana), Evangelical and United Brethren, Reformed Church in America, Brethren, Mennonites, Moravians, Disciples of Christ.

41. George Todd in Younger, *From New Creation to Urban Crisis,* p. ii.

42. Saul Alinsky, *Reveille for Radicals* (New York: Random House, 1969; first published in 1946).

ment they were themselves frequently organized — or co-opted — to the initiatives of others. More recently *the second stage, church-based community organizing,* has emerged.[43] Here the initiative is taken by coalitions of neighborhood churches, and congregations have found that they can grow and be transformed by this form of mission in their communities.

Urban training and *community organizing* were two of the most widely used strategies. But there were many others, and they will recur frequently in the following chapters. A sampling follows.[44]

- *group urban ministry,* of which the East Harlem Protestant Parish is the best-known example
- *church planning* both of new congregation development and of strategic efforts to engage metropolitan structures and forces
- creation of *ecumenical metropolitan coalitions and church federations*
- creating *special staff positions* with names like minister of metropolitan mission and metropolitan mission coordinator
- *industrial mission*[45]
- *ecumenical metropolitan experiments and projects* such as Metropolitan Associates of Philadelphia to mobilize laity along vocational lines and the Los Angeles Regional Goals Project to involve churches in city planning
- creation of *national institutes, centers, and committees* as agencies for cooperation by denominations, such as the Joint Strategy and Action Committee, the Institute on the Church in Urban-Industrial Society, and the Interfaith Center for Corporate Responsibility

The forty years following World War II saw major changes in American urban life. The northern migration of African Americans (and migra-

43. See, for example, Dick Simpson and Clinton Stockwell, *Congregations and Community Organizing* (Chicago: ICUIS, 1987); Gregory F. Pierce, *Activism That Makes Sense: Congregations and Community Organization* (New York: Paulist Press, 1984).

44. See also the summaries at the beginning of chapter 12.

45. This was concerned with industry, factories, and business, and at its height had thirteen sites in cities such as Detroit and Boston. According to leading participants there were two main emphases: making the workplace more humane (e.g., in assembly line situations), more team based, and less authoritarian; and emphasizing ethics as an intrinsic part of the business process. In contrast to many cities today where former city plants are idle, or manufacturing has moved overseas, in the earlier postwar years factories were common urban phenomena and industry was a normal component of urban life. Hence the frequent pairing of "urban" and "industrial" as in "urban industrial mission" and Institute on the Church in Urban Industrial Society (ICUIS).

tion into the cities of other ethnic groups, especially Hispanics), the phenomenal growth of suburbs, the impact of government low-income housing policies and "urban renewal," the growth of the black middle class, the reduction of industrial production and manufacturing generally, the impact of the Cold War on government spending priorities — these are some of the chief factors that have made our cities what they now are and thus shaped the context of urban ministry. The following chapters analyze how churches have engaged urban life. They document an impressive devotion to urban community on the part of many Christians. They also show how the postwar period involves both increasing attention, staff, funding, and imagination up through the sixties, and the decline of these efforts in the last two decades. They provide ample evidence for reflecting on the analytical questions that spurred the study, which will be taken up again in chapter 12. Equally important, they will stimulate everyone concerned about the vital role the church can play in the renewal of America's cities.

• 2 •

"Not by Might, nor by Power": Urban Ministry in American Baptist Churches

GEORGE D. YOUNGER

Introduction

Churches and leaders associated with American Baptist Churches took a leading role in city mission work in the United States during the latter half of the nineteenth and the first half of the twentieth century. Walter Rauschenbusch, Samuel Zane Batten, and other Baptist pastors were active in forming the Brotherhood of the Kingdom, which was one of the seedbeds of the Social Gospel and furnished support to this group in their service in city churches.[1] Edward Judson, a son of overseas mission pioneer Adoniram Judson, was responsible for organizing Judson Memorial Church in Greenwich Village in New York City, which was one of the first institutional churches and became a model for others.[2] Charles Hatch Sears, executive secretary of the New York Baptist City Society, was a leading theoretician and strategist for city mission who saw city problems growing out of the "immaturity" of a social system in its "adolescence" rather than

---

1. For a description of the Brotherhood of the Kingdom, see Charles Howard Hopkins, *The Rise of the Social Gospel in American Protestantism, 1865-1915* (New Haven: Yale University Press, 1940, 1967), pp. 131-34.

2. For accounts of Edward Judson's work in establishing Judson Memorial Church, see Charles Hatch Sears, *Edward Judson: Interpreter of God* (Philadelphia: Griffith and Rowland Press, 1917), and Joan Jacob Brumberg, *Mission for Life: The Story of the Family of Adoniram Judson* (New York: Free Press, 1980).

out of "depravity," although he did locate the source of urban poverty in commercial greed.[3]

By the end of World War II the legacy of over eighty years of city mission work was carried forward in the Department of Cities of the American Baptist Home Mission Society (working together with the Woman's American Baptist Home Mission Society [WABHMS]). The style and scope of that work can be seen in the following activities reported in 1948:[4] 233 bilingual churches (mostly European languages, but including 31 Spanish-speaking); forty-seven Christian centers (religious settlement houses); ten educational centers working with "Negro" church leaders; thirty-three church extension projects; and eleven Christian Friendliness missionaries[5] supported by WABHMS to work (along with six thousand women volunteers) with displaced persons and race relations. All of these activities had been part of American Baptist city church strategy since before the organization of the Northern Baptist Convention in 1907. The only addition was the Juvenile Protection Program, which had begun out of concern for wartime juvenile delinquency among youth.

The other denominational body that had an interest in urban policy issues was the Council on Christian Social Progress, organized in 1941 to address the economic issues facing labor and working people. Through the years the scope of its resolutions and other pronouncements expanded to include other social, political, and economic issues. In 1973 the staff and program of this agency were incorporated into the home mission board.

I. Postwar Emphasis on Church Extension

The major feature of the policy of American Baptist home missions after World War II was its emphasis on church extension in the burgeoning suburbs. During the war the American Baptist Home Mission Society had shared in development of new ministries to people in housing areas related

3. Charles Hatch Sears, *The Redemption of the City* (Philadelphia: Griffith and Rowland Press, 1911), and *The Crowded Ways* (New York: Council of Women for Home Missions and Missionary Education Movement, 1929).

4. The "116th Report of American Baptist Home Mission Society, 1948"; and "71st Report of Woman's American Baptist Home Mission Society, 1948."

5. "Christian Friendliness" was originally established as the "Christian Americanization" program to work with immigrant women and teach them English literacy and homemaking skills.

to war industries or military bases.[6] They had also had a significant relationship with Japanese who had been relocated from the West Coast to detention camps inland. In the first decade after the war, funds from a special capital campaign, the World Mission Crusade, were used by the home mission boards to finance new church starts in the automobile suburbs, which differed both in location and population from the railroad suburbs of the 1870s on, which depended on rail transportation to commute to the city. In 1954 Lincoln B. Wadsworth, who had been secretary of the Department of Cities, moved to become secretary of a newly organized Department of Church Extension to support development of new churches. In 1954 a denomination-wide capital funds campaign, Churches for New Frontiers, was conducted to raise both program and property funds for church extension.

Other changes in home mission strategy in 1954 and shortly afterward were also to have an influence on urban ministry. In the field of bilingual ministry, which was a major share of the projects in which the national boards participated, most of the churches had begun to hold services in English for second- and third-generation Americans, with decreasing attendance at the language services by those in the first generation or who had been postwar immigrants. Therefore, a goal was set for every bilingual church to "be self-supporting or will have united with a self-supporting American Baptist church" by 1956. However, American Baptists had only recently begun in 1951 to stress their work with Spanish American churches in the continental United States. For this reason it was not too long afterwards that Spanish American work was exempted from this policy change. In 1954 the national Christian Friendliness program moved to a major emphasis on race relations, in keeping with both National Council of Churches and American Baptist resolutions that sought "a non-segregated church in a non-segregated society."

Prior to the mid-1950s the major attention in resolutions voted at the annual conventions was on economic issues like jobs and housing, on race relations, on public education, and on traditional moral issues like alcohol, gambling, and prostitution.[7] Nothing was said specifically about

6. Principal sources for this historical survey are in the annual reports of American Baptist Home Mission Society and Woman's American Baptist Home Mission Society to the American Baptist Convention.

7. Texts of all resolutions are included in the annual minutes of the Northern Baptist Convention, succeeded by the American Baptist Convention, and then American Baptist Churches in the U.S.A.

urban issues or ministry in cities, except for a unique resolution on "Sectionalism" adopted by the Northern Baptist Convention at the acrimonious meeting in 1946 that asked the national body "to create greater understanding between churches in city and country and in different parts of the nation." In the field of race relations, the resolutions were principally directed against segregation and discrimination in society, asking for permanent Fair Employment Practices Commissions at the federal and state levels, and for an end to the poll tax, as well as an end to discrimination in employment, education, armed services, and housing. Only in a resolution adopted in 1954, after the Supreme Court decision in the *Brown v. Board of Education* case abolished segregation in public schools, was there explicit recognition of the same issues in the churches. This resolution said in part:

> We affirm our belief that God is no respecter of persons, that every individual is of infinite worth in His sight, and that it is His will that the law of Christian love operate in all human relationships. We urge American Baptists to increase their opposition to other areas of segregation — housing, employment, recreation, church participation. We urge local churches to carry forward educational programs dealing with this issue, and we propose cooperation with other Christian bodies of like mind.

Integration in both church and society continued to be the major emphasis in race relations for the next decade.

II. Beginning of a New Urban Strategy

A new urban strategy began to develop after 1954 when Rev. Paul O. Madsen, who had been pastor of First Baptist Church of Boulder, Colorado, took over as secretary of the Department of Cities. By 1958 the work of this department had been expanded to include all local church mission strategy except for church extension, and its name had been changed to the Division of Church Missions. Although many of the previous urban strategies continued, the national body devoted itself to conducting community surveys, sharing information about programs and resources, and sponsoring training for pastors in both rural ("town and country") and urban churches.

In 1957 Rev. E. B. Hicks was employed as a national staff person to relate to the historic black denominations. Rev. J. C. Herrin, a white staff member, began work in the South in 1961. This constituted a reentry of

American Baptists into the heartland of the Southern Baptist Convention (SBC), which they had left by agreement in 1894, and led to the formation of a new region, American Baptist Churches of the South, composed primarily of churches dually aligned with the major black denominations, along with a few that were also members of SBC.

One other organizational change in this period that affected urban strategy was the merger in 1959 of the Juvenile Protection Program, which was working principally with juvenile delinquency programs in urban areas, with the Christian center program under the title of "neighborhood action."

Along with other mainline white Protestant denominations who belonged to the National Council of Churches and participated in the Department of the City Church, American Baptists held an Urban Convocation on October 29-31, 1957. In preparation for this event, Rev. James A. Scott, a black staff member, developed an urban fact book, *American Baptists Today,* in consultation with the National Council of Churches, Home Mission Societies staff, and the state and city secretaries of the American Baptist Convention.[8] Using a national study of the distribution of churches in the United States on a countywide basis, he developed a set of analyses that showed the following facts about American Baptist churches and membership in 1955:

- Fifty-six and one-tenth percent of the 1,491,048 members of American Baptist congregations were located in "urban" municipalities (over ten thousand population), even though only 28.1 percent of the churches were in those locations and could be called "urban."
- The highest proportions of urban members were in the Pacific Coast and West (73.3 percent), New England (60.2 percent), and the Great Lakes (57.7 percent). The other two sections of the country were also close to one-half "urban" in membership — Central and Rocky Mountain (48.6 percent) and Middle Atlantic (47.1 percent).
- Three hundred thirty-three American Baptist churches were aligned with another Baptist group, and 264 of the churches reporting were primarily serving minority ethnic groups.
- Between 1950 and 1955 American Baptists lost a total of 308 member churches and an average of 10,473 members per year.

8. James A. Scott and Edward D. Rapp, *American Baptists Today/Urban Fact Book* (New York: American Baptist Home Mission Societies, 1957).

Paul O. Madsen, who headed the national efforts, summarized the challenge of urban ministry in this way:

> The evangelization of the city is a primary call to American Baptists. In urban America, if this call is not heeded and met, then American Baptists will inevitably decrease. The majority of the people of the United States are increasingly living in our cities. Here the church must find the way to minister in the name of Jesus Christ, who is Lord and Master of all.[9]

Three groups in different sections of the country prepared study papers for the convocation on the nature, the needs, and the strategy of the urban church. Discussion groups brought the 291 participants together to look at these themes, as well as at three different types of urban church situations — downtown, transitional, and neighborhood churches. Most of the leaders and participants were white, as were all but two of the 15 members of the Urban Commission appointed to follow up the work of the convocation.

Although there had been talk of continuing convocations on urban concerns, only two more national meetings were held by the Division of Church Missions. In 1961 they broadened the focus to be a Convocation on the Mission of the Church.[10] In 1965 they joined with city and state organizations, through the Associated Home Agencies, to hold a Workshop on the City Church. The background paper for this second gathering was entitled "Needed . . . A Strategy for Mission," which underscored the fact that eight years of planning, study, discussion, and joint effort had not yet produced a unified strategy for American Baptists in the field of urban ministry.

Another form of follow-up to the 1957 Urban Convocation was the promise of continued publication of facts about urban churches, and the conduct of strategy studies with local churches, as well as associations, city societies, and state conventions. In 1960 Rev. James A. Scott conducted an American Baptist census to update and extend the findings of the 1955 survey. A series of monographs based on the census were published between 1962 and 1964. An important finding of this study was that the major products of a decade and a half of church extension were slow-growing churches. Of the 437 churches established between 1950 and 1959, 277 reported fewer than 150 members. If American Baptists at the time of the

9. Paul O. Madsen, foreword to *American Baptists Today/Urban Fact Book*, p. 4.
10. The Convocation on the Mission of the Church was reported in Paul O. Madsen, ed., *Leaven* (Valley Forge, Pa.: American Home Baptist Mission Societies, 1962).

census were not primarily a suburban denomination, neither were they a big-city denomination. The largest number of urban churches and membership were concentrated in cities over ten thousand but under five hundred thousand in population.[11] This kind of regular reporting on church characteristics resulted at a later time in the Congregational Profile System, which keeps track of statistics, community characteristics, and program emphases of member churches in the American Baptist Churches in the U.S.A. (ABC/USA).

From 1964 through 1966 the Church Strategy Program in the national board produced a series of "action guides" designed to help local churches deal with a variety of issues such as urban renewal, public housing, planning and strategy, and congregational organization. Training for urban pastors was provided for a time at the American Baptist Assembly in Green Lake, Wisconsin, under the leadership of Rev. Robert T. Frerichs, who had already established there a training center for town and country pastors. A resource library for urban church work was also maintained at the training center.

During the 1950s a few urban churches and their pastors (who were principally white males) were featured in denominational meetings and publications, and helped to draw attention and give leadership to the work of city churches — Judson Memorial Church (Rev. Robert W. Spike and Rev. Howard E. Moody) and Mariners Temple Baptist Church (Rev. George D. Younger) in New York City; First Baptist Church (Rev. Jitsuo Morikawa and Rev. Charles R. Andrews) in Chicago; First Baptist Church (Rev. Harold Geisweit) in Oakland; and First Baptist Church (Rev. Gene E. Bartlett and Rev. John H. Townsend) in Los Angeles.

The next developments in urban ministry for American Baptists did not come from those persons and structures with direct responsibility for city churches. Rather, they were the result of significant changes in the work of what later became National Ministries, especially in the Department of Evangelism, and pressures from the churches and wider community. Because of these developments in the 1960s and 1970s, ABC/USA had become a different denomination by the mid-1980s, with more to offer in ministry to metropolitan areas.

11. "Strategy and the Urban Church," in James A. Scott, *Implications of American Baptist Census for Strategy Development* (Valley Forge, Pa.: American Baptist Home Mission Societies, May 1964), bulletin no. 8, pp. 241ff.

III. National Activity — The View from Above

In 1956 Jitsuo Morikawa was asked by the American Baptist Home Mission Society to come to the national staff as secretary of the Department of Evangelism.[12] After growing up in British Columbia, and being educated at the Bible Institute of Los Angeles, the University of California at Los Angeles, and Southern Baptist Theological Seminary, Morikawa had worked as youth director for Japanese churches in the Los Angeles area. In 1942 he and his family were removed by executive order to a detention camp in Poston, Arizona. After being relocated to Chicago in 1943, he was called first as assistant minister of First Baptist Church and later became the church's senior minister, the only pastor of Japanese ancestry serving an interracial congregation.

Morikawa inherited a commitment by American Baptists to join other Baptist bodies in North America in a five-year program, the Baptist Jubilee Advance, from 1959 through 1964, culminating in the celebration of the 150th anniversary of the formation of a Baptist missionary convention to support the missionary work of Adoniram and Ann Judson in Burma. He called together a group of pastors and seminary professors to serve as an advisory committee to do basic thinking and planning. His rationale for this kind of preparation was that "any significant evangelism must arise out of the best corporate thinking of the denomination." The result of this study was a paper on the meaning and task of evangelism, which gave the following definition of evangelism:

> Evangelism is the proclamation of God's Good News (the Evangel) in Jesus Christ (the chief Evangelist), revealed in the Scripture by the Holy Spirit, to every people and generation, that they may acknowledge Christ as Lord and Savior in faith and obedience, enter the fellowship of His church, and thus become a part of the Church in its suffering.[13]

When Morikawa came to the evangelism post, the principal emphasis of that department had been on visitation evangelism and evangelistic

---

12. The biography of Jitsuo Morikawa is Hazel Takii Morikawa's *Footprints. One Man's Pilgrimage: A Biography of Jitsuo Morikawa* (Berkeley, Calif.: Jennings Associates, 1990). His own testimony is given in Jitsuo Morikawa, "My Spiritual Pilgrimage," an address to the annual luncheon of the Ministers and Missionaries Benefit Board of American Baptist Churches in the U.S.A., in Lincoln, Nebraska, on May 23, 1973.

13. "Called to Be Witnesses" (New York: American Baptist Home Mission Societies, 1958).

preaching. He gathered a staff of people — F. Lenore Kruse, Rev. Donald F. Thomas, Rev. Joseph D. Ban, Rev. Harvey G. Cox, Rev. Paul L. Stagg, and Rev. Richard M. Jones — all of whom were committed to broadening the understanding of evangelism and assisting the churches to witness in a secularized, urbanized society. Cox and Jones were placed in academic settings in Boston and Berkeley, in order to be in dialogue with both theological seminaries and university faculty.

This was also a time of serious inquiry concerning the meaning of evangelism and mission in the world Christian community. Morikawa worked with Hans Hoekendijk in the Department of Evangelism of the World Council of Churches. He also served on the ecumenical committee that was responsible for the study "The Missionary Structure of the Congregation," initiated at the New Delhi Assembly of the World Council of Churches in 1961. A significant venture in the Baptist Jubilee Advance program developed for American Baptists was an emphasis during the third year (1961-62) on lay witness in society.

When the Baptist Jubilee Advance was completed, Morikawa turned his attention to the organization of Metropolitan Associates of Philadelphia (MAP) as an ecumenical experiment in missionary engagement on the frontiers of the modern metropolis. The prospectus for MAP declared in 1965:

> Evangelism in the modern metropolis is a central issue of the contemporary church. Witness in the public world of a secularized, industrialized society constitutes the peculiar, perplexing missionary frontier of the modern world.[14]

Jitsuo Morikawa and two other American Baptists from the staff of the Department of Evangelism, Rev. Richard M. Jones and Rev. Richard E. Broholm, helped staff the program, along with others from the United Church of Christ, Society of Friends, United Presbyterian Church, and Lutheran Church — Missouri Synod. Both the Episcopal Church and the United Methodist Church participated in sponsorship and were represented on the Board of Managers. Dr. Thomas Wieser, who had worked with the World Council study on missionary structure and was on the staff of the National Council of Churches, assisted with theological reflection and evaluation. From the beginning MAP was totally ecumenical within white Protestant Christianity.

---

14. This and other quotations are from papers produced by Metropolitan Associates of Philadelphia (MAP), available in the archives of the Board of National Ministries, American Baptist Churches in the U.S.A., Valley Forge, Pa.

Theologically, MAP felt that it was proceeding on the basis of an ecumenical consensus on mission and evangelism that included the following elements:

1. Concern for how local congregations "might become more authentically missionary congregations ministering in the midst of the complexities of an urban technological, industrial society."
2. Using the "nature of missionary action in the world" to determine the shape of the local congregation.
3. Understanding the call to "disciple the nations" to include "new nations" of an industrial society, such as the world of politics and government, industry and daily work, education and the arts, leisure and recreation, residential and private life.
4. Seeing the membership of congregations present in all the social structures of the world "bearing witness and influence in these structures," and asking the following "critical questions": "What is the character of the witness borne by the laymen [sic] in these structures?" "What is the nature of Christian witness in a world of technological revolution and nuclear crisis?" "What does it mean to participate with Jesus Christ in His renewal of the metropolis?"
5. The need to test theological data on the calling of the church and the witness of the laity "in the crucible of experimental missionary involvement."
6. The call to renewal and new ways of missionary obedience for both clergy and laity "willing to surrender certain securities of traditional ways, and venture out on the risks of new patterns of Christian service."

Sociologically, MAP adopted a typology developed by Robert C. Hoover, chairman of the Graduate Department of Urban Planning at the University of Cincinnati. This scheme saw the life of metropolis to be divided into sectors of human institutions and services — art, education, health, social organizations, politics and government, business and industry, and physical development. Because it was located close to American Baptist headquarters in Valley Forge, Philadelphia was to be used as the base for MAP's efforts. The project relied on three categories of persons: worker-ministers, who would be theologically competent clergy and take secular jobs; lay associates, who would be theologically sensitive laypersons already involved in secular occupations and representing all the laity present in the whole spectrum of the city's life; and urban agents, who would be theologically competent clergy or laity serving as reporters or researchers to become identified with significant events in the sectors and seek to understand them from within. The style of MAP was planned to be action-research, with a trained researcher on the staff and the whole staff functioning as a research team. During the 1966-67 academic year Robert C. Hoover joined the staff while on sabbatical in order to develop further a model that he called "logo-structural involvement research." Built upon Victor Frankl's concept of meaning, this form of analysis was intended to aid the institutional subsystems of a metropolis to come to an understanding of their true meaning by studying the institution's myths, norms, and beliefs and those historically decisive events that call into question or radically alter those subsystems. Hoover developed a style manual for this action-research process that was far too complex for MAP's staff and lay associates to use, so it was simplified to include three principal instruments: a situation inventory as "a social science tool for reflection and observation" to examine existing policies in a subsystem, an evaluation guide as "a social ethics tool for goal evaluation" to examine emerging critical issues in terms of value categories, and an action planner as "a social practice tool for implementation of new policy into action." Thus, the emphasis on action-research began to move toward missionary action informed by the categories of strategic planning.

From the organization of MAP in 1965 Morikawa, Jones, and Broholm were not only the core of the staff for the MAP program in Philadelphia but remained on the staff of the Division of Evangelism of the American Baptist Home Mission Societies (ABHMS), of which Morikawa was also director. That staff included other members who worked on program materials for congregations, as well as another member, Rev. George D. Younger, who remained in New York City, where he was working on issues of housing and redevelopment, and helping with the evaluation of MUST (Metropolitan Urban Service Training), an action training program sponsored by the United Methodist Church. It was intended that these involvements in Philadelphia and New York City would help to feed into the evangelism strategy of the denomination following the Baptist Jubilee Advance.

At the same time that MAP was being started in Philadelphia, significant changes were occurring in ABHMS, where the evangelism staff was based. James A. Christison, a layman who had been treasurer since 1959, was elected as the new executive secretary succeeding William H. Rhoades, another layman who had served in that position since 1957 after previously being treasurer. As treasurer Christison worked with Rhoades on a series

33

of actions to gain more leverage for the invested funds of the societies. In church extension ABHMS moved to holding first mortgages on church properties. Funds that had been invested in New York City real estate were moved into federally sponsored low-income housing. When Christison took over as executive secretary, ABHMS within a short period of time had formed three wholly owned corporations to finance various areas of mission work — American Baptist Extension Corporation for church extension, American Baptist Service Corporation for institutions, and American Baptist Management Corporation (ABMAC) for housing. In addition, funds were pulled back from the direct subsidy of local projects, and national staff were to be used principally as consultants.

Christison asked Morikawa and his staff to assist the national mission organization in its planning. A Policy and Program Committee of the ABHMS Board was studying how to structure the societies' program in the future. They asked the staff members of the Division of Evangelism and the Church Strategy Program to look at two issues: how to relate to other denominations and how to handle the multiplicity of programs in urban areas that were scattered across the various program divisions. The Urban Study Group, consisting of Younger, Hoover, and Rev. Lawrence H. Janssen, suggested that in a matrix style of administration, as it was already developing in ABHMS, it did not matter where programs were placed administratively, but that planning and strategy would have greater relevance if they tried to view the wider society through the lens of the six MAP sectors (arts and education, health, social organizations, politics and government, business and industry, physical development) rather than through the program areas that had developed historically. This suggestion was immediately taken up by the board and Christison, and Morikawa had another hat — director of the Office of Planning — added to the two he was already wearing for the Division of Evangelism and for MAP.

In 1969 the programs of National Ministries (a new name given to the home mission boards in a denominational reorganization in 1973 to parallel International and Educational Ministries) were divided into two divisions, Parish Development and Social Action. Programs that had been associated with the old Department of Cities were now divided between the two. Inner City Program (by which was meant relationships with black churches) and Parish Witness (the former Christian Friendliness program) were placed with Parish Development, while Christian centers, Neighborhood Action programs, and Juvenile Protection were with Social Action. Low-income housing through ABMAC was a freestanding entity.

Strategic planning began that same year with a look at assumptions, followed by a study of trends.[15] During 1971 two staff task forces were organized to look at areas identified by the study of trends — growing concern for the environment and continuing situations of injustice in society. Each group came back with strong evidence that both the values of the Christian faith and the need for social change justified National Ministries in giving major attention both to environmental concerns and justice issues. As a result, a new term, "ecojustice," was coined to symbolize an approach that would not allow concern for the natural world and the environment (ecology) to take away from issues of social justice in society, including economic and racial justice. By 1974 the MAP experiment was closed, and all evangelism staff members were working once again at Valley Forge. In that same year a new emphasis on evangelistic lifestyle, making use of some of the insights gained from board and staff planning sessions, was introduced throughout the denomination. The use of strategic planning and corporate goals lasted past Morikawa's retirement in 1976 and Christison's replacement by Rev. William K. Cober. However, the new staff in the Division of Evangelism shifted the emphasis in that area from lay witness, and a total concept of mission and evangelism, to an emphasis on church growth. By the end of the 1980s concern for denominational survival, and increased witness to new language and nationality groups, had resulted in greater attention once again to "new church development" (formerly called "church extension"). The only explicit concern for urban ministry and city churches was carried by a single staff person for "urban strategy." Between 1978 and 1989 this post was filled successively by two women — Judy Claude, a black laywoman trained in economics and politics, and Rev. Yamina Apolinaris, a Puerto Rican pastor who had received her theological education in the continental United States. Christian centers, Neighborhood Action programs, and Parish Witness continued their activity as before, only with fewer dollars and staff.

From the 1960s onwards, resolutions voted by delegates at the annual conventions took on a sharper tone and addressed many urban issues without saying much about urbanization itself. A general statement on "The Mission of the Church in Our World Today" in 1965 included "urbanization" as one of eight contemporary questions for which individual members, churches, and national agencies were urged "to seek earnestly and

---

15. These developments are documented in planning papers of American Baptist Home Mission Societies and Board of National Ministries of ABC/USA collected by Richard M. Jones. Originals are available in the archives of the Board of National Ministries, American Baptist Churches in the U.S.A., Valley Forge, Pa.

prayerfully the guidance of the Holy Spirit in creative thinking to do the will of God" and have the courage "to face honestly." A parallel statement on "Theological Foundations" affirmed that "God speaks through His Word and that He works creatively in our perilous times through pagan forces and nations as well as through the Church." American Baptists were called to "be aware of the areas of human need and to become personally involved in the frontiers of transformation" in order to "bear with God the suffering and tragedy of human injustice and loneliness and be a part of the continuing redemptive work of our Lord Jesus Christ through the Holy Spirit."

Continuing resolutions on race relations spoke both to segregation and discrimination in the church and in the wider society. A 1964 resolution supported participating in demonstrations and programs of nonviolent direct action. A 1963 resolution on "Status of Women" championed full participation of women in public and economic life, while also calling for increased opportunities. The latter theme was applied both to public life and to church life in a 1969 resolution, "Increased Opportunities for Women." In 1968 urban issues came quickly to the fore, as a result of the urban rebellions by blacks and other minorities. Although the resolution "Violence and Civil Disorder" adopted that year said, "A spirit of unrest, violence, and revolution pervades our society partly through the failure of religious, political, economic, and social institutions to meet changing social needs," the actions that were urged upon churches and church members focused on reform in law enforcement agencies, changes in court procedures, and improvements in the welfare system. The rationale given for this attention to police, courts, and welfare rather than larger systemic injustices was a conviction that "violence in our city streets and social institutions reflects our commitment to the solution of our problems by violent means." By 1970 the city streets had been forgotten, and a resolution on "Crisis in the Nation" was concerned with unrest on campuses and called for dialogue with youth.

One other development in the national denomination that affected urban ministry was denominational reorganization. A vital part of urban strategy for American Baptists from the end of the nineteenth century had been the organization of city societies as separate entities for the conduct of mission in metropolitan areas. Concern about the cost of duplicated administrative structures and the difficulty of spanning large stretches of the country that had smaller numbers of American Baptist congregations led to a Study of Administrative Areas and Relationships (SAAR) in 1968. As a result of this study, several state conventions and city societies were merged into larger regions.

The relationship between the national program boards and American Baptist Churches in the U.S.A. was made more explicit by changes recommended by the Study Commission on Denominational Structure (SCODS) in 1972. An even more significant development was the shift of policy-making for the whole denomination to a representative body, the General Board, rather than by the delegates to annual conventions, who had been the "members" of the national societies. The General Board members were assigned to the three program boards — International Ministries, National Ministries, and Educational Ministries. This centralization in a representative body for the whole denomination both lessened the influence of the city societies and left the biennial conventions of delegates from the churches with very little decision-making power. In 1978, as a result of further recommendations from the Study Commission on Regions (SCOR), ties between regions, state conventions, and city societies, and the national structure were also strengthened. By the end of this series of steps, there were only nine city societies left in the ABC/USA — Chicago, Cleveland, Indianapolis, Los Angeles, Metropolitan New York, Niagara Frontier, Philadelphia, Pittsburgh, and Rochester/Genesee — and several of these shared interlocking relationships with the state conventions or regions in which they were located.

IV. The Forces from Underneath

Although the official responses of the national mission organization and the national denominational structure were longer on words than accomplishments in the postwar period, it is not the nature of Baptist polity to depend on national bodies and middle judicatories as is characteristic of most other mainline Protestant denominations in the United States. Instead, Baptist emphasis on the autonomy of the local congregation and voluntary cooperation through the associational principle places the principal emphasis in the neighborhoods and municipalities where those congregations are located. At times this has been considered a weakness because it does not result in an overall strategy. But it is also able to produce, by the calculus of hundreds of local efforts, a result that is far more effective than the highly visible activity of wider church bodies. A striking example of this occurred in the late 1960s when the Central Baptist Church of Wayne, Pennsylvania, remortgaged its building and gave the resulting funds to an urban redevelopment project in central Philadelphia; this one local congregation produced more direct funds than were immediately available through all of the national "urban crisis funds" that were then being planned by the mainline denominations in response to the civil disorders in the nation's cities.

The continuing presence of these local congregations in the cities of the nation was an underlying fact of American Baptist life, no matter what was being said or done at regional or national levels. A few downtown congregations that were predominantly white moved from their historic locations to the suburbs. Many more downtown and neighborhood churches that were not able to adapt to racial change in their area closed, merged, or sold their buildings to minority congregations, many of which were also Baptist. But the greater number of city churches held on in their neighborhoods. They have been joined by black Baptist churches and other ethnic and language congregations, so that the percentage of churches and church members who are Baptist (although not all of them American Baptist) in the urban areas of the United States is greater now than it was at the end of World War II.

Two city congregations, one on each coast, representing both older white downtown and neighborhood churches, and black Baptist churches, can serve as examples of the creative responses made locally to urban change in the period following World War II. Judson Memorial Church in New York City and Allen Temple Baptist Church in Oakland, California, have both been models in their own metropolitan areas and throughout the country.

Judson Memorial Church had been established in Greenwich Village in New York City by Edward Judson as a church to serve a neighborhood of Italian and other European immigrants. With facilities for athletic and club programs, as well as a large sanctuary, the church's ministry was in need of reexamination and overhaul when Rev. Robert W. Spike came as pastor in 1949. Along with Rev. Dean R. Wright, who served as campus minister to the downtown campus of New York University, Spike began a program of out-reach to gang youth in the old Italian community at the same time the church began to relate to the writers and artists who were coming to the Village in great numbers. These program emphases continued and were expanded by Spike's successor as pastor, Rev. Howard R. Moody, when he arrived in 1956.

Judson's art program featured a gallery that displayed graphic artists who were not yet accepted in the commercial galleries and museums. The gymnasium and church sanctuary were used by modern dance artists for recitals of new works and pieces of performance art ("happenings"). After starting to open up the church's space for other groups to stage dramatic productions, the church sponsored the Judson Poets' Theater, which became a strong power in off-off-Broadway theater. Rev. Al Carmines, a gifted

38

composer and songwriter, joined the church staff and was responsible for many of the musical plays that were produced. In time the discipline and rehearsal that went into theater were also given to the church's own services of worship as many of the artists and performers became participants in the congregation.

Both through the pastors and the members of Judson, there has been a continuing involvement in politics and issues of public policy. Starting with opposition to the machine politics of Tammany Hall, concerns expanded to issues of narcotics treatment, civil rights, legalized abortion, prostitution, and opposition to the Vietnam War. In many cases Judson Church developed ministries with those for whom they were advocating — counseling for women with problem pregnancies, a holistic health center dispensing medical information by phone, and an outreach program to street prostitutes.

Judson Memorial Church, under the leadership of Spike and Moody, became a church that was not only located in the city but was truly of the city. The congregation has moved from doing ministry for and with the community to taking the community fully into its own life as a church. Unlike many urban churches that sponsor or carry on programs for the community, every aspect of Judson's fellowship, including worship and membership, has been influenced by its community and the ministry to which it has been called.

On July 19, 1981, Moody preached a sermon that looked at the heritage of Judson Memorial Church and its creative urban ministry over the twenty years that Carmines had been on the ministerial staff. He found the following themes running through that ministry: being holistic, being pluralistic, having the willingness to be experimental and ad hoc, and being organic and evolutionary. He ended his examination with this summary:

> This church, in spite of the ups and downs of history, the partial eclipses of its congregation as protestants fled to the suburbs, is rooted and anchored in an exciting and fascinating history; we need to value it, but without living in the past. The *themes* that run like a thread through the fabric of our existence have enabled us to be free and unbounded, and at times by coincidence, sometimes by the leading of the Spirit, always by the grace of God, to be on the cutting edge of new ministries of the church in the service of the world. What those programs and services happen to be in any period are not nearly so important as our faithfulness and obedience to God's mission in the world.[16]

16. Howard Moody, "The Judson Experience: A Thematic Church in a Changing World," sermon preached July 19, 1981 (mimeographed).

Allen Temple Baptist Church is a historic congregation serving Oakland's African American community since its organization in 1919. When Rev. J. Alfred Smith Sr. became pastor in 1970, he came with a strong commitment to having a seven-day-a-week program and a powerful witness in the community. Although he has also continued graduate study followed by service as a professor in the Graduate Theological Union in Berkeley, his major effort has been concentrated on serving as pastor of Allen Temple and shaping its ministry.

When the Black Panther Party was organized in Oakland, Smith moved the church's ministry to the streets where both the Black Panthers and other disaffected youth were trying to face head-on the problems of being black and poor in America. Allen Temple's largely middle-class congregation supported this ministry and grew in its ability not only to advocate for youth and the Black Panthers, but for the whole African American community in Oakland and the Bay Area.

While continuing to be a congregation that supported the usual church programs of worship, music, Christian education, fellowship groups, Bible study, prayer, and counseling, Allen Temple moved with the perception that there could not be a healthy church in a sick community. The pastor and members became active in local politics and advocacy on community issues. Professionals in the congregation — teachers and school administrators, social workers, health workers and doctors, government employees — saw their own vocation as a place to exercise their Christian calling and found in Allen Temple a strong support base for their ministry.

A recent example of the way Allen Temple not only reaches out to its community but draws the community into its own life is in the growing ministry with persons living with AIDS and others who are HIV-positive. Although members had all the usual fears for their own safety, people with AIDS have been welcomed into the worship services and church fellowship, and been made a special prayer concern of the congregation. Church officers and members have been specially trained to visit in the hospitals, as well as to provide concrete personal support. The majority of those with AIDS have contracted it from narcotics abuse or sexual activity, but the church has reached out to them without passing judgment on their past behavior. This has strengthened the diaconal ministry of Allen Temple.

Allen Temple Baptist Church is an urban congregation that has fully accepted and embraced the community in which it has been placed and where its members live. The church has chosen to make its own fellowship a part of the community, and has been willing to open up its own fellowship to take the community fully into the congregation.

Although there were fewer city societies as American Baptist organizations, those that have remained expanded their membership to include many dually aligned black Baptist congregations, and adapted their ministry to concentrate more on the sharing of resources among churches and their leaders, rather than on the use of their finances to start new churches and support struggling congregations. The SAAR study had increased pressure to merge as many city societies as possible into the state or regional body in which they were located. But this only increased the desire of many of those city societies to remain in existence for the sake of urban ministry and mission.

On February 6, 1971, representatives of seven of the nine city societies, along with those from four urban states and regions, met with staff members of American Baptist Home Mission Societies to call for formation of an "urban team" and to ask for staff assistance from the national organization. For the next four years, after writing many papers and holding hearings in several metropolitan areas, a report was developed for the National Staff Council. It called for increased emphasis on urban ministry. The only immediate results of this effort were the employment by National Ministries of a staff member for urban strategy and the adoption by the General Board of a Policy Statement on Metropolitan Ministries in June 1979:

> It shall be the policy of American Baptist Churches to minister in the name and in the spirit of our Lord in the metropolitan areas of the U.S.A. in ways which are consonant with our biblical heritage and which are directed toward the needs which our resources best equip us to serve. We shall develop appropriate ministries upon the basis of adequate research which shall take cognizance of the ethnic and racial pluralism and the urgent needs of our many metropolitan areas. Such ministries shall be directed toward bringing and sharing an effective Christian witness in and through the ecclesiastical, political and economic sectors of such areas, ministering to the personal, social, and structural needs of metropolitan U.S.A.[17]

After almost a decade of struggle American Baptist churches still did not have the "urban team" that had been requested by the urban executives. A new Metropolitan Ministry Task Force was established in June 1980 to

17. "Policy Statement on Metropolitan Ministries." The term "metropolitan ministries" was adopted because "urban" was felt to mean "inner city" to many people following the civil disorders of the 1960s.

follow through on the concept of a Metro Team. The strategy developed was to hold an Urban-Metropolitan Ministry conference in Philadelphia on March 21-23, 1982. Registrants included a mix of national and regional executives, representative urban pastors and staff workers, and representatives of all the ethnic caucuses of ABC/USA. The conferees voted to support the formation of an American Baptist Metropolitan Ministry Team, to be composed of practitioners — urban pastors, staff members, and lay leaders — and denominational executives at both regional and national levels. It would also remain in close contact with the American Baptist ethnic caucuses.

Beginning with the biennial meeting in Cleveland in 1983, the American Baptist Metropolitan Ministry Team established a pattern of annual meetings in conjunction with the SCUPE (Seminary Consortium for Urban Pastoral Education) Congress in Chicago and meetings every other year during the biennial. With assistance from Rev. James Stallings of National Ministries and the Cleveland Baptist Association, a one-day Pre-Biennial Urban Experience was held for seventy-five registrants. Although a major part of the experience was success stories from local congregations and a field trip to churches and neighborhoods in Cleveland, the group also heard from Rev. Donald Benedict, a founder of the East Harlem Protestant Parish and retired director of Chicago's Community Renewal Society, and Dr. Edward A. McKinney, professor of social service at Cleveland State University.

With assistance from the staff of National Ministries and supported by representatives from regions, the Metro Ministry Team continued to meet and hold gatherings through the biennial meeting in Milwaukee in June 1989, when Rev. Yamina Apolinaris resigned as the staff member of National Ministries for urban strategy and became executive minister for the Baptist Churches of Puerto Rico. Over a five-year period the team had worked hard to create a Steering Committee and Board of Representatives to plan and carry out its national meetings. It had developed a model for regional-based units that would bring together urban practitioners in various parts of the country, but this was never put into effect. In addition, the team produced a set of printed resources and a newsletter that were mailed to all interested pastors and other urban workers in the denomination, and provided financial support for regional projects and scholarships for specific training events and continuing education experiences. Its interests are continued only in the occasional meetings of the executives of the city societies who worked so hard to bring it into being.

The civil rights movement played a major role in changing the stance of American Baptist Churches in urban ministry. Although some black Baptist churches had historically been connected with associations and state bodies related to the Northern Baptist Convention, most congregations were members of the two major historic black denominations, the National Baptist Convention of America and the National Baptist Convention, U.S.A., Inc. In the period immediately after World War II, the commitment of American Baptists to "work for a non-segregated church and a non-segregated community," following the lead of the declaration by the National Council of the Churches of Christ in 1952, seemed to place them in opposition to the continuation of all-black congregations. Much of the urban strategy was devoted to assisting all-white congregations in areas of racial transition to become interracial churches. Although many cities saw close cooperation between white and black Baptist churches on social, political, and economic issues, this did not result in ecclesiastical equality. Black Baptist congregations shared many characteristics in common with their Euro-American brothers and sisters, but they also had a separate line of historical development. In fact, these differences were more a question of mutual recognition of faith and order than of asking black Baptists out of their African American tradition to "come home" to their parents.

From the beginning of the civil rights movement, American Baptists maintained close contact with the Southern Christian Leadership Conference and its heavily Baptist leadership. American Baptists took part in civil rights demonstrations in the South as well as in the northern and western cities. Both Dr. Martin Luther King Jr. and Dr. Ralph Abernathy were serving churches that joined in dual alignment with American Baptist Churches, as did most of the congregations that left the National Baptist Convention, U.S.A., Inc., to form the Progressive National Baptist Convention (PNBC). From the early years of the 1960s an increasing number of black churches, especially in the cities, became dually aligned with American Baptist Churches.

When the American Baptist Churches met for their convention in Boston in 1968, a group of black American Baptist pastors, who had been active in civil rights and were aware of the continuing pattern of white control of the denomination, held a meeting to confront Dr. Edwin H. Tuller, general secretary, and other leaders of the denomination with what they felt was a pattern of indifference and refusal to use the leadership of black American Baptists. The result of this meeting was an invitation to greater participation and leadership within the denomination. The group organized as Black American Baptists, the first of several caucuses in the denomination. They studied the structure and leadership of ABC/USA and made their recommendations for changes. Within two years Dr. Thomas Kilgore Jr., pastor of Second Baptist Church, Los Angeles, and a past president of the PNBC, was elected as president of American Baptist Churches. In 1971 ABC/USA voted to join the PNBC in raising the Fund of Renewal, which was not only like the "urban crisis" funds of other mainline denominations but included a large program of intercultural education to expand the racial consciousness, sensitivity, and sophistication of all American Baptists, especially those in all-white congregations. Since 1968 American Baptists have had vastly expanded African American leadership at all levels. This has had the effect of increasing the urban consciousness of the denomination and giving a greater leadership role to urban pastors and laypersons.

A particular flowering from the civil rights movement was the development of a new American Baptist region in the South, which had traditionally been the stronghold of the Southern Baptist Convention. Out of the work of E. B. Hicks and J. C. Herrin on the Home Mission Societies staff, American Baptist Churches of the South (ABCOTS) was organized in 1970 with Hicks as its first executive minister. From the beginning ABCOTS has been a region composed largely of African American congregations along with some dually aligned Southern Baptist churches, and now with a growing number of new church starts, Hispanic and Haitian churches in Florida. Its membership is almost completely located in cities and metropolitan areas of the Southeast, Gulf States, and Texas.

Increased ethnic consciousness and feminism also resulted in changes in the composition and approach of American Baptists to the issues of urban society. Hispanics, Asian Americans, and Native Americans, following the lead of African Americans, also asked for increased representation in leadership and for attention by the national denomination to their issues. Hispanics were aware of their growing proportion in the general population, as well as in the cities. They asked for greater attention to Hispanic new church development and for more Christian education materials in the Spanish language. Asian Americans were a more diverse group, including Chinese Americans, Japanese Americans, Filipinos, and Vietnamese. They were concerned for leadership development and relations with countries around the Pacific Rim. Native Americans, who had been the subject of home mission efforts from the earliest days of the national denomination, still had white pastors in most of their churches and missions. They demanded theological training for their own candidates and leadership training for laypersons. Hispanics and Asian Americans each formed recognized caucuses, and have received at-large representation on the General Board as "underrepresented groups."

Growing immigration into the United States has brought large numbers of people, many of whom had been Baptists in their native country, into the cities and metropolitan areas. Hispanic ministry has increased on the basis of continuing immigration from Puerto Rico and Mexico, from Cuba after Castro's takeover, and in more recent years from Central and South America, especially Nicaragua and El Salvador, both of which have strong Baptist conventions in fellowship with American Baptists. Continuing political unrest and poverty in Haiti has brought Haitian Baptists to the cities, where they have organized churches and related to ABC/USA. And the Asian American population has become increasingly diverse with immigrants from the Indian subcontinent, Burma (home of the oldest overseas Baptist convention in fellowship with American Baptists), Korea, and other Asian countries. In most cases these new immigrants have trained pastors and church leaders from among their numbers who have assisted in organizing missions and churches that have become part of the urban mix of American Baptist life.

Increased attention to women's issues has also been occurring since the 1970s. National Ministries organized the FACT (Feminism and the Church Today) program in 1976 with L. Faye Ignatius as its first staff person. Working with laywomen, including American Baptist Women, the denominational women's organization, and with key women staff members and ordained women, this program has expanded women's representation in all phases of American Baptist life. American Baptist Women has served as the denominational "women's caucus."

V. A Different Denomination

Out of the interaction of official national policy and programs, and the forces from underneath, coming out of a changing population in the United States and the resulting changes in American Baptist congregations, American Baptist Churches had become a significantly different denomination by the mid-1980s from what it had been at midcentury. An increased percentage of its church members were located in the metropolitan areas of the country, not only around the major cities and megalopolises but also in the smaller cities of the nation. There was an increased number of black and interracial (multicultural) congregations, and a greatly increased percentage of black members, principally in dually aligned African American congregations. Current denominational statistics show that American Baptist Churches in the U.S.A. has a total of 5,286 member churches divided as follows: white, 4,314; black, 1,070; Hispanic, 297; Asian, 60; Native American, 25; other, 60.[18] This quiet change was more the result of personal and congregational decisions than of a grand denominational strategy. Once more the prophetic word has been fulfilled: "Not by might, nor by power, but by my Spirit, says the LORD of hosts" (Zechariah 4:6, RSV).

According to a study made by the Congregational Profile System of the denomination, these changes in the ethnic composition of American Baptist Churches should continue into the next century when the majority of the churches' membership will no longer be white, principally because of increases in urban churches that are black, Hispanic, and Asian American. The tables on pages 47 and 48 show trends in numbers of churches and resident membership by ethnicity from 1971 through 1991, with a projection for the year 2000.[19]

The national strategy, while placing far less emphasis on urban ministry, represented a new commitment to evangelism and church growth. This included the entire constituency, and much of the innovation in church programming came from churches located in metropolitan areas, where the majority of American Baptists lived. Starting with some of the regions that were located in areas of explosive population change and growth, ABC/USA began once again to emphasize "new church development," but no longer in the suburbs as was true after World War II. The new church starts included new African American congregations and churches with an ethnic constituency, especially Hispanic.[20] Provision was also made in this strategy for "restarts" in urban neighborhoods with churches whose constituency had moved or become older while a new population had moved in around them.

Unfortunately, the more explicit efforts to make the "urban church" or "metropolitan ministry" a denominational priority have not been as successful in capturing denominational attention and resources. Since 1988 when Rev. Yamina Apolinaris left the staff of National Ministries, the position that was designed to work with urban strategy has gone unfilled. The

18. "Summary of Denominational Statistics for the Year Ended December 31, 1992," prepared by the Congregational Profile System, National Ministries ABC/USA.

19. From an unpublished paper on trends in ABC/USA membership, prepared for the Regional Executive Ministers Council in December 1992, by Norman M. Green Jr., director, Congregational Profile System.

20. An analysis of the 504 new church starts organized between 1989 and 1994 shows the following ethnic breakdown: 35% Anglo, 34% Hispanic, 13% Afro American, 9% Asian, 4% Haitian, 2% Portuguese, 1% Native American, 2% Other; see "The Harvest Is Ripe" (ABC/USA, 1995).

Table 1

Trend of Resident Membership by Ethnicity for ABC/USA
with Projection for Year 2000

Year	White	%	Black	%	Hispanic	%	Asian	%	Nat. Am.	%	Other	%	Total
1971	970,836	74.9	301,380	23.3	17,352	1.3	2,600	0.2	1,081	0.1	2,343	0.2	1,295,611
1976	922,036	70.9	352,012	27.1	20,697	1.6	2,916	0.2	1,018	0.1	2,366	0.2	1,301,045
1981	849,983	64.7	431,773	32.9	23,885	1.8	3,899	0.3	889	0.1	2,329	0.2	1,312,758
1986	754,576	60.9	446,726	36.1	28,089	2.3	4,987	0.4	1,113	0.1	2,608	0.2	1,238,099
1991	684,491	56.9	473,236	39.4	31,994	2.7	7,106	0.6	1,185	0.1	4,304	0.4	1,202,316
2000	535,000	45.7	575,000	49.1	40,000	3.4	12,000	1.0	1,200	0.1	7,000	0.6	1,170,200

Table 2

Trend in Number of Churches by Ethnicity for ABC/USA with Projection for Year 2000

Year	White	%	Black	%	Hispanic	%	Asian	%	Nat. Am.	%	Other	%	Total
1971	5,078	85.6	631	10.6	151	2.5	16	0.3	24	0.4	34	0.6	5,934
1976	4,858	83.1	742	12.7	169	2.9	20	0.3	24	0.4	31	0.5	5,844
1981	4,639	79.5	914	15.7	201	3.4	29	0.5	23	0.4	32	0.5	5,838
1986	4,459	77.6	976	17.0	215	3.7	38	0.7	25	0.4	35	0.6	5,748
1991	4,350	74.4	1,066	18.2	289	4.9	58	1.0	24	0.4	56	1.0	5,843
2000	4,000	68.0	1,300	22.1	375	6.4	100	1.7	25	0.4	80	1.4	5,880

American Baptist Metropolitan Ministry Team, which was organized in 1983 after over a decade of planning and concerted effort, was not able to catch the full support and attention of urban pastors and other practitioners, and has not met since the spring of 1988.

The attention of the General Board of ABC/USA has been given to the development of broad policy statements on key areas of society, and resolutions have been directed to the issues of the moment, many of them arising out of the increasing complexity of life in an urbanized and urbanizing society. Now that such declarations on issues from the perspective of the Christian faith are made by the General Board, which meets twice a year as a representative body, "Statements of Concern" at biennial meetings are directed to a more limited range of issues. Those brought by petition from the constituency have increasingly become expressions of constituency discontent, particularly on issues like abortion and homosexuality, rather than new issues from underneath.

Conclusion

Unlike many other mainline Protestant denominations during the same period, American Baptist Churches in the U.S.A. has remained and even grown in the cities and metropolitan areas of the nation. There are three major reasons for this continued commitment: (1) working-class and middle-class whites who make up the vast majority of American Baptist membership did not move out, especially if they were elderly; (2) the denomination has been invigorated by the addition of a large number of urban black American Baptist congregations, which retain dual alignment with the historic black Baptist denominations; and (3) new immigrants, many of them coming from churches related to Baptist bodies in other parts of the world, have formed missions and churches that have related to ABC/USA.

American Baptist theologians and writers have contributed several large visions for urban policy that have been influential beyond the denomination. Harvey Cox wrote *The Secular City* in 1965, which became a rallying point for many Protestants and other Christians who desired to have a positive effect on the life of the emerging metropolitan society. Jitsuo Morikawa developed the sector approach to urban policymakers through Metropolitan Associates of Philadelphia (MAP), which later came to govern the entire home mission strategy of the denomination in National Ministries. "Ecojustice," a concept and a label that originated in that strategic

49

planning process, has become a valid paradigm for understanding the interaction of environmental and social factors in the urbanized society of the latter half of the twentieth century.

Although American Baptists shared, through the National Council of Churches and the Joint Strategy and Action Committee (JSAC), in the development and execution of earlier ecumenical strategies, they did not possess the staff and financial resources to try to match the larger mainline Protestant denominations. Responding to the changes in U.S. society and their own changing membership, American Baptists have moved back to predominantly denominational and pan-Baptist strategies. This has brought greater attention to African American, Hispanic, Asian American, and other ethnic groups of Baptist churches, but it has left them with few national ties to the rest of the Protestant community, let alone to Roman Catholics and other faiths.

The picture at the metropolitan and more local level is quite different. American Baptists continue to be strong participants in local and regional ecumenical efforts, and work with a wide variety of religious and secular groups in seeking to deal with urban problems. There have been many notable achievements and significant programs in local churches, neighborhoods, communities, and metropolitan areas. However, in common with most other Protestant denominations, and even the Roman Catholic Church, this has failed to produce a coherent national strategy for urban ministry or for dealing with metropolitan issues and problems.

To close this survey, let me try to sketch the outlines of what seems to be the future direction for American Baptists in urban ministry and in dealing with the policy issues that shape (and distort) urban life in our nation. The future for American Baptist Churches in the U.S.A. will be with a more holistic approach to urban ministry. It will not talk about "city churches" and "suburban churches," but churches that are part of a metropolitan society that is not limited to national borders.

However, the approach for Baptists and ABC/USA will continue to be based in local congregations. This is not only because of the form of Baptist polity. It is also because the infinitely complex society that has developed in the late twentieth century, although governed by multi-national corporations and larger collectivities, including national and state governments, has multiple effects on the lives of people, many of them unintended by the overall policies and plans that are developed. Therefore, to respond, to fight back, to adapt at the local level is to be truly "at the center of the action." American Baptists have already made some major changes since World War II and should continue to make a positive witness for Jesus Christ in metropolitan areas in the coming decades.

If the major locus of action is to be with local congregations, then the national denomination, including National Ministries, the traditional focus for national strategy in urban ministry, and regions can no longer claim to be a rallying center. Rather, they will need to serve as a resource to strategies and programs that are carried out in many parts of the nation by local churches and their allies.

There will be a continuing role for thinkers and theologians, for writers and theorists — and American Baptists should be expected to make their contribution to this part of the churches' strategy. But their work will need to be more biblically and theologically based in the future. God is not done with the church, and God is not done with the urban-metropolitan society. We need to take time to discover where God is leading in the days ahead.

• 3 •

To Be Untrammeled and Free: The Urban Ministry Work of the CME Church: 1944-90

LUTHER E. SMITH JR.

World War II: A Defining Crisis

Soldiers often speak of war as a crisis that raises questions about the ultimate meaning of life and their capabilities to respond to challenges. The willingness to kill and risk being killed forces people to probe the deepest recesses of commitment and character. In a similar way, war is a defining event for the nation. As a country tries to justify the demands placed upon its citizens, it will refer to the nation's founding principles, spirit, and pride. At such a time, more than the honorable resolve of a nation is made manifest — a nation's flaws also become evident.

Near the end of World War II, Colored Methodist Episcopal (CME)[1] annual conferences drafted and adopted reports that expressed how the war exacerbated frustrations over the plight of African Americans. A report from the 1944 meeting of the Southeast Missouri and Illinois Annual Conference stated:

> The American Negro has proved his loyalty to the Stars and Stripes through the centuries in times of peace and in war alike — even though the Stars and Stripes seemed indifferent as to the Negro's welfare. The Negro's daring deeds on and off the battlefield; his patience, fortitude

---

1. In 1954 the Colored Methodist Episcopal Church changed its name to Christian Methodist Episcopal Church.

and unflagging devotion to America's interests, democratic ideals of Justice, fair play and opportunity, are beyond doubt marvels of this age.

We deplore deeply and inexpressibly the apparent disinterestedness shown by those in authority as to the discriminations that are daily practiced in devious, yet effective, ways against Negroes.

The report continues with a severe conclusion:

There are some among us who, having been driven to hopelessness and desparation [sic], believe that some American White People, if they must choose between conquering Hitler and giving the Negro Equality of Opportunity, would prefer to have Hitler win the war![2]

In the same year, a statement from Central Texas Annual Conference reiterates this feeling that the nation is guilty of hypocrisy and betrayal:

How may America save her face in the eyes of the world by daring to talk about Law and Order ABROAD and still permit lynching of human beings here AT HOME without doing anything about it? O Democracy! If such as we observe here is Democracy, may God deliver us from it![3]

These reports contain a long list of grievances that demand redress. Discrimination in employment practices and in the armed forces, the failure of the federal government to pursue aggressively the passage of the Fair Employment Practices Act, the absence of government action when violence has been perpetrated against black persons, failure to enact into law a federal anti-lynching bill "with teeth in it," local political indifference to the civil rights of black people, and justice in the courts are the primary issues outlined by the conferences. The call to arms inspired the church to proclaim once again a call for justice.

Two other reports indicate the social concern of these church meetings: "Getting Children off the Streets" and "Keep Your Job." Taken together, the above issues of civil rights, economic opportunity, political accountability to black people, justice in the courts, and social welfare programs not only identify the principal social concerns of 1944, but also the issues

2. "Special Report of the Committee on State of the Country," which was unanimously adopted at the Southeast Missouri and Illinois Annual Conference. *Annual Conference Year Book of the Second Episcopal District, Colored Methodist Episcopal Church,* 1944, pp. 44-45.
3. "Special Statement to the Country by the Special Committee on State of the Country," prepared at the Central Texas Annual Conference. *Annual Conference Year Book, Second Episcopal District,* 1944, p. 236.

that would dominate the social witness of the CME Church for the next forty-five years.

I. The Making of an Urban Identity

The CME Church was organized in 1870. This new denomination came into being after black and white leaders of the Methodist Episcopal (M.E.) Church, South, worked together to fulfill the desires of its black members for a separate and independent black denomination. Black people's recent emancipation from slavery fueled the passion to be free and to exercise authority and power in all aspects of their lives — and this included their participation in the church. The establishment of the CME Church enabled the ex-slaves, who were members of the M.E. Church, South, and who chose to join the new denomination, to address the religious and social needs of black people without the constraints of petitioning a church structure controlled by white people. The CME Church began and grew as a church of the rural South. By 1900, thirty years after its founding, over 90 percent of its 150,731 members lived in southern states and Texas. The rest were in the midwestern states of Kansas, Missouri, Illinois, Oklahoma, and Kentucky. During this time 72 percent of the black population was also in the rural South.[4]

The massive migration of the black population to cities and the North is well documented. The church's awareness of these changes was evident in the Central Texas Conference's 1944 resolution "regarding the great migration of C.M.E.'s to California and the Pacific Northwest in general." The resolution spoke of "several thousands of our most loyal members" having left Texas for the West. Church leaders were then implored to assess the possibilities for CME Church expansion into the West.[5] This concern for expansion prevailed throughout the denomination. The North and West were the new mission fields.

Interest in expansion was driven by two concerns. First, the CME Church was concerned about losing its members who were part of the migration. The denomination sought to establish churches that would reunite persons who were loyal to the CME Church. And second, the emphasis upon mission could provide new members for the denomination.

---

4. Othal Hawthorne Lakey, *The History of the CME Church* (Memphis: CME Publishing House, 1985), p. 489.

5. *Annual Conference Year Book, Second Episcopal District,* 1944, pp. 231, 232.

Membership stability (with migrating CMEs) and membership growth were not just matters of institutional vitality. Church leaders believed that establishing new churches was essential to providing places of Christian nurture and witness. They had a deep conviction that individuals and families needed CME churches for their spiritual growth.

The migration of the black population, and the consequent expansion of the CME Church, was primarily to cities. African Americans moved from the rural South to southern and northern cities. This pattern was also true for the CME Church. Bishop Othal Hawthorne Lakey, in his history of the CME Church, entitled this transition "a rural church goes to the city."[6] The changing demographics of the black population had drastically transformed the geographical identity of the CME Church.

CME churches were not only places of Christian nurture, they were also institutions for urban socialization. Most black people migrated to attain better employment opportunities. Even when they were successful, the adjustment to city life could be difficult. An improved economic life did not necessarily translate into a richer social, personal, and spiritual life.

The church served as a place of orientation, introduction, and association for the newly arrived urban citizens. Churches emphasized being an institutional "family." Persons were welcomed and embraced into fellowships of caring. They were known by name, invited to offer their talents to the ongoing work of the church, visited when sick, consoled when in grief, and recognized as significant contributors to the welfare of the fellowship.

This pastoral role of the CME churches was a critical urban ministry. It offered relationships where the individual was respected. Although the larger society failed to acknowledge this status, the church was one of the few places where black people were affirmed as first-class members of their social order.

Urban socialization also occurred as pastors often provided members referrals to employment opportunities in the community. Pastors cultivated relationships with both black and white businesses, and then used these connections to help their unemployed members. In cooperation with the Urban League, churches sponsored workshops on grooming, skill development, interviewing, and work habits for employment.

Churches sometimes served as referral institutions for black professionals (i.e., doctors, lawyers, morticians) who depended upon the support of local church members to launch their businesses. Pastors and in-

6. See Lakey, pp. 487-95.

fluential laity would intervene for members who had difficulty with welfare, health care, and government systems.

This community orientation of many CME pastors in the postwar years is apparent in such leadership roles as that of Rev. A. R. Davis, who was elected president of the West Side Human Relations Council in Detroit; the council sponsored youth, neighborhood improvement, and race relations programs.[7] In 1947, Rev. J. Claude Allen was appointed to the Board of Education of Gary, Indiana. Rev. U. Z. McKinnon was honored by the Omega Psi Phi fraternity as the most civic-minded and responsible citizen of Jackson, Tennessee, during 1948.[8] And Rev. Jasper M. Pettigrew was elected president of the St. Louis Branch National Association for the Advancement of Colored People (NAACP) in 1949.[9]

On a national level, in 1945 Channing H. Tobias, as secretary of the Social Welfare Commission of the CME Church, testified about the necessity for the Fair Employment Practices Act before the U.S. Senate Committee on Education and Labor.[10] The CME Church contributed financial support and endorsed the programs of the NAACP and Urban League. The church also participated in the Fraternal Council of Negro Churches as it spoke out against racial discrimination and injustice.

In these early postwar years the CME Church responded to urban realities with strategies that continue to characterize the denomination's urban ministry witness. CME clergy and laity joined with national religious, civil rights, and employment organizations to protest social and economic injustice. Cooperation with these organizations helped the denomination inform its members about social issues and the various tactics employed to address them. It also enabled the CME Church to be part of national campaigns to educate the public, influence civic leaders, and lobby political representatives. The national organizations, through this cooperative arrangement, increased their membership and support base. The CME Church provided a constituency that gave these organizations more visibility and clout as they sought to represent the oppressed masses.

The denomination depended upon the initiative and resourcefulness of local congregations to address urban needs. No national church bureaucracy existed as a resource for local churches or urban communities.

7. *Christian Index*, February 1, 1945, p. 6.
8. *Christian Index*, January 20, 1949, p. 9.
9. *Christian Index*, February 10, 1949, p. 4.
10. *Christian Index*, April 5, 1945, p. 5.

The Church's Social Welfare Commission and Social Relations Commission analyzed issues and made resolutions, but they did not have an implementing staff. Perhaps more than anything, the work of these commissions signaled to the local church that the denomination had a public commitment to issues of justice and social welfare. Therefore, as a local church responded to community needs, it felt in line with denominational policy.

The denomination implemented the strategy of establishing local congregations in communities with increasing numbers of black residents. Although it was not a condition for establishing these missions, such churches often became fellowships of identity, care, socialization, and social activism. The extent of a church's community witness relied upon the commitment and creativity of pastoral leadership and the expectations and support of laity. Consequently, the CME Church's expansion into urban areas did not always result in the church serving a wide range of community needs. Pastors were not appointed to develop community centers, but to plant thriving churches. Even where the CME Church had already established a congregation in a community, pastoral appointments were usually made in the attempt to match the abilities of the minister with the needs of the congregation, rather than the needs of the larger community.

Still, these churches were important centers of meaning for their membership, and some were centers of social activism for their community. Both roles would enable them to make a significant contribution to the impending pivotal period of social transformation: the era of the civil rights movement.

II. Civil Rights: Emancipation in a New Era

The identity of the denomination was shaped by population shifts to the cities, especially of the North and West. The increasing urban identity of the CME Church during the 1950s is appraised by Bishop Lakey as follows:

> Whereas the [CME] conferences of the South were composed of a large number of small circuits and congregations, the conferences of the North consisted of very large local congregations. Local churches in Chicago, St. Louis, Cleveland, Los Angeles, and Detroit were reporting memberships in excess of a thousand members, while only two or three local CME churches in the entire South were reporting over 500 members — and there is some evidence that the two largest of such churches in Dallas

and Houston had their numbers increased on paper by the bishop to show some competition with the larger northern churches. We conclude that even though a majority of CME members still remained in the rural South, the Christian Methodist Episcopal Church had, by 1960, become an urban denomination as its largest and most prestigious congregations were located in the cities, and its style of worship and polity were influenced by the values of the rising Black middle class.[11]

As Lakey observes, it was not just the numerical shift to cities that shaped this newly formed urban identity, it was also the establishment of large and financially strong congregations that symbolized institutional success. The achievements of such churches served as paradigms for membership growth and church programming throughout the denomination.

In 1960, the urban identity of the denomination is also evident in "A Statement to the Christian Methodist Episcopal Church" issued by the College of Bishops. The "Statement" comments upon domestic social issues, civil rights, housing, urban renewal, and capital and labor. The urban mind-set of the church leaders was evident in their concern for housing:

> The [housing] problem is a complex one, but not so great that it cannot be predicted that it will not become more prominent as millions of our people migrate from the South to the North and West, and from farm to the cities, and thus increase a congestion that has already brought a host of ills in its train. Low-cost housing, whether by Federal or other governments, cannot fill the gap for there is a demand for better housing among our folk who are economically able to afford better homes in less congested areas. Neither class must be neglected, but we call upon the authorities to devote a particular energy to this development which promises to make segregation more prominent and hardened than previously.[12]

The plight of city dwellers dominates the "Statement." The urban context is foremost in the identity of the denomination.

In cities, CME churches exercised their urban identity by continuing to offer their resources for community needs. The church remained a place of personal meaning where individuals experienced worship, programs, and fellowship that affirmed their worth as people of God. It was a place of social meaning where the economic, social, and political issues that affected

11. Lakey, p. 491.
12. *Christian Index,* August 4, 1960, p. 6.

black people were defined and where protest actions were developed. Churches were also dependable sources of emergency food, clothing, and money to members and nonmembers alike.

A most crucial role of CME churches was that of being a place of meeting. Church facilities were frequently used by social and political groups for meetings, exhibits, rallies, and fund-raising events. During a time when black people were prohibited from renting meeting space at hotels and conference centers, either because of discriminatory policies or cost, black churches made their sanctuaries and educational halls available. Churches became centers for community life — a role also of many CME churches. Various groups (fraternities, sororities, neighborhood organizations, political committees, community advocates, Boy and Girl Scouts, civil rights organizations, professional guilds, etc.) would depend upon the churches for their activities. As community centers, churches contributed to the social, economic, and political achievements of community groups.

In 1956, the denomination relocated its Collins Chapel Hospital in Memphis, Tennessee, to a new building that cost $500,000 ($200,000 from the CME Church and $300,000 from the Memphis community). This service and expenditure represented the CME Church's commitment to health care for the black community. It was an alternative to health care facilities that either refused to serve black people or served black people only under a segregated arrangement. By no means was this meant to be a denominational facility to which all CME members would travel for medical treatment. Nor did the denomination have the resources to develop hospitals all over the country. But it did demonstrate its conviction within a particular urban community. Collins Chapel Hospital was a sign of the denomination's witness to the concern for and importance of health care.[13]

CME pastors and laity continued to give leadership on issues that affected the quality of urban life. The following examples are but a sampling of such leadership during the 1950s. In 1953 Irvin C. Millison, a CME member and the first African American appointed as a federal judge, organized pastors to enact civil rights laws in western states.[14] In that same year a CME pastor in Texarkana, Texas, was recognized for his community service with an interracial ministerial alliance, Crippled Children's Hospital, the YMCA Board, Red Cross, and Community Chest work.[15] Channing H. Tobias (mentioned above as secretary of the Social Welfare Commission),

13. *Christian Index,* May 14, 1976, pp. 3-4, 15.
14. *Christian Index,* April 9, 1953, p. 10.
15. *Christian Index,* July 16, 1953.

in his capacity as chairman of the board of the NAACP in 1954, met with President Dwight D. Eisenhower during a Freedom Fulfillment Conference.[16] In 1959 Rev. Henry C. Bunton ran for the school board of Memphis.[17] Rev. Jasper M. Pettigrew was reelected president of the Chicago Interdenominational Ministerial Alliance, and he continued serving as vice president of the Chicago Metropolitan Church Federation.[18] Another major involvement of CME leadership was with the civil rights movement that emerged from the Montgomery bus boycott and the leadership of Dr. Martin Luther King Jr. Many organizations and individuals participated in civil rights activities long before the Montgomery events. But the ability of King and other leaders to create the sense of a "movement" (i.e., dramatic activities that persisted as matters of public concern and policy debate) ushered in a new era for civil rights protests.[19]

In the fifties and sixties, CME clergy and laity were significant leaders in the movement. Early in the life of the Southern Christian Leadership Conference (SCLC), Rev. Henry C. Bunton served on its board of directors and its executive board. As pastor of a CME church in Memphis, he was involved in numerous civil rights activities. Bishop B. Julian Smith (Memphis), Rev. J. W. Bonner (Montgomery), Rev. Jesse L. Douglas (Montgomery), and Rev. Nathaniel Linsey (Birmingham) worked closely with King and the movement in their cities. Rev. R. B. Shorts, a CME pastor in Atlanta, Georgia, served as president of the Ministerial Association. He led boycotts against Coca-Cola and K-Mart until they agreed to hire more black employees. Shorts pressured the Atlanta Police Department to hire its first black officers. And he organized to ensure domestic workers (usually black women) the right to be free of requirements to work on the first Sunday of the month (which meant missing their churches' Communion services). Attorney Donald L. Hollowell, an active CME layman in Atlanta, "was legal counsel for the vast number of Civil Rights demonstrators and protesters, including Martin Luther King, Jr. in the late 50's and 60's."[20]

Throughout the fifties and sixties, the denomination endorsed and

16. Lakey, p. 587
17. Lakey, p. 566.
18. *Christian Index,* September 3, 1959, p. 2.
19. The advent of television as a common appliance in the American home has been interpreted as a major factor in giving birth to the civil rights movement. The network news reporters captured the drama of protest, police brutality, racial violence, and civil unrest with visual images that stirred the nation's conscience.
20. Much of the information on this list of leadership in the civil rights movement is from Lakey, pp. 581-84.

provided financial support for the Urban League, NAACP, and SCLC. The leaders of these organizations addressed the Church's general conferences. The College of Bishops, general conferences, and annual conferences passed resolutions encouraging churches to support these organizations at the local level. CME pastors, in northern, western, and southern cities, served as presidents of the local NAACP chapters. CME laity were involved with the local boards and activities of these organizations. Some pastors worked to integrate public facilities and end discrimination without necessarily working through an established civil rights organization.

The denomination's position regarding the importance of actively supporting civil rights causes was strongly stated through its pronouncements, funding, and involvement of clergy and lay members. Participation in the civil rights struggle was not only a matter of social justice, but throughout the denomination it was understood as a religious calling for the institutional church and its members.

In 1962, the College of Bishops sponsored a national conference on civil rights for CME clergy and laity. In addition to furthering the objectives of the civil rights movement, the conference was organized to counteract rioting and other destructive acts within the black community. Many were concerned that if black communities were destroyed by riots, then gains in civil rights would be lost.

Dr. Mance Jackson recalls working in 1966 with the Black Panthers in Berkeley, California, while pastoring a CME church. He sought to redirect their energies from violence, and to address the Panthers' complaints of police brutality through police/community relations task forces. Bishop Dotcy I. Isom Jr. tells of working in the mid-1960s to keep communities in East St. Louis, Illinois, from being burned down by black radicals. These events were omens of forthcoming issues of dissent within the black community that would challenge traditional civil rights strategies and shape new forms of community involvement for the churches.[21]

---

21. Information for this essay, and especially for the period of the 1960s to the present, was gathered through interviews with Mrs. Sarah Allen, Bishop Richard O. Bass, Rev. Lymell Carter, Rev. Tyrone Davis, Bishop Joseph C. Coles Jr., Bishop Marshall Gilmore, Bishop Dotcy I. Isom Jr., Dr. Mance Jackson, Bishop Othal Hawthorne Lakey, and Bishop Peter Randolph Shy. Ms. Juliana C. Smith provided research assistance. Rev. Lawrence L. Reddick III and Rev. Helen B. Pearson made helpful comments for revising the manuscript.

III. Black Power: Protest and Policy-Making

In the sixties and seventies the aforementioned ministries of socialization, personal nurture, meeting place, social service, and protest against civil rights abuses continued in local churches. Now CME churches were not dealing with massive migration from the rural South so much as with transition in their neighborhoods.

Many urban CME churches had their origins in transitional communities that were changing from a predominantly white to black population. Their growth depended upon black migration to the city and the relocation of black people who sought better housing in racially changing communities. But after a period of stability, these communities continued in transition. Some communities changed from middle-class to lower-income populations. Others changed from residential to blighted or commercial areas. In both cases, CME churches discovered that their immediate neighborhoods no longer contained many of their members. This created an identity crisis for many CME churches regarding their community ministry.

With more members commuting from other neighborhoods (especially suburban), churches often felt estranged from their communities. In Bishop Joseph A. Johnson's 1970 Episcopal Address he reported:

> Many churches stand on the corner as formidable institutions formed out of brick and mortar with huge doors and large locks, and the tragedy is that except for occasional services during the week and Sunday they remain on the corner of the street as silent fortresses with closed doors, stained glasses, and dark auditoriums.[22]

However, to the credit of these congregations, almost all of these churches remained in their communities. Rediscovering their community role was not always easy or successful, but they stayed. And some of these congregations began to reconnect with their communities after receiving dedicated and creative pastoral leadership.

CME leadership was either appointed or elected to major positions in the governmental and social service sectors of society during the sixties and seventies. Rather than only protesting the system from the outside,

22. "Minutes of the Twenty-seventh General Conference and the Twenty-sixth Quadrennial Session and Centennial Celebration of the Christian Methodist Episcopal Church," May 6-17, 1970, Appendix, p. 28.

these leaders accepted positions that gave them decision-making authority from inside the system.

Examples of such leadership would be: Rev. Kelsey A. Jones and Dr. Joseph W. Rucker were members of the Health and Welfare Planning Council in Jackson, Michigan;[23] Rev. J. Lorenza Key was appointed to the administrative staff of the Housing and Urban Renewal Agency of Macon, Georgia;[24] Rev. David Cunningham was elected chairman of the War on Poverty Committee of Memphis;[25] Rev. Joseph C. Coles Jr. was elected to Cleveland's Board of Education; Rev. Amos Ryce II was elected to the St. Louis Board of Education and was president of the St. Louis Metropolitan Church Federation; Rev. James L. Cummings was a member of the zoning board and the city council in Indianapolis, was elected to the St. Louis Board of Education, and was appointed to the East-West Gateway Coordinating Council (the major economic development agency for the metropolitan area); Rev. William R. Johnson Jr. was a commissioner for the Community Relations Commission of Memphis; Rev. Marshall Gilmore was president of Dayton, Ohio's Commission on Human Relations, which dealt with complaints in employment and discrimination issues in city government; and attorney George Haley (a CME layman) was elected a state senator in Kansas. This emphasis upon transforming systems from the inside was an outgrowth of the civil rights movement that sought both changed policies and greater representation in decision making from the black community. The emphasis also grew from the emergence of "black power" as a philosophy of social transformation.

In the public controversy that sometimes pitted the Student Nonviolent Coordinating Committee (SNCC) against the strategies of the SCLC, it would appear that SNCC's shouts for black power were a denunciation of the reconciliation strategies of SCLC and its generation of activists. While there is some truth to this conclusion, there is also more agreement than disagreement between the two approaches. In his book *Where Do We Go from Here: Chaos or Community?* Martin Luther King Jr. argued more against the strategic wisdom of using the phrase "black power" than against the concept and objectives of black power. Radical elements of the Black Power movement demanded that society be restructured so that black people could have *complete* control over their economic, political, and social destiny. But the Black Power message, embraced by the majority of people

23. *Christian Index*, June 29, 1961.
24. *Christian Index*, August 10, 1961, p. 4.
25. *Christian Index*, March 3, 1966.

in the black community, asserted that black people should have *substantially more* control over their destiny.

CME pastors were active in supporting political candidates who represented the interests of the black community. In Chicago, Rev. Dotcy I. Isom Jr. of St. Paul CME Church worked with other CME churches to successfully elect Bennett Stewart (a CME layman) as an alderman, and later to elect him to the U.S. Congress. Yvonne Brathwaite Burke, a CME laywoman, received CME support in her successful elections to the California House of Representatives and the U.S. Congress. In Dayton, Rev. Marshall Gilmore participated with the Interdenominational Ministers Alliance that endorsed and supported political candidates. Throughout the denomination, pastors frequently allowed political candidates to speak to their congregations during Sunday morning worship services. Pastors were not reticent about expressing political judgments and indicating how the welfare of the black community was dependent upon the victory of particular candidates.[26] CME churches cooperated with the Opportunities Industrialization Centers (OIC), which provided job skills training for black youth. In Chicago, CME churches supported Operation Breadbasket (later to become Operation PUSH), which conducted feeding, civil rights advocacy, and employment programs. Linking with local organizations that attempted to effect systemic change was a common strategy of CME churches in urban areas.

In the 1970 Episcopal Address, Bishop Johnson stressed the legitimacy of current voices that advocated the importance of blackness in history, theology, and participation in decisions. He then identified four areas for CME involvement in urban ministry. Three dealt with the CME Church needing to help persons find meaning in their lives through commitment to Jesus Christ and Christian discipleship. A fourth focused on social structures:

> . . . we must provide a ministry of confrontation of the social evils in our world. Every minister in our Church should be involved in

26. Many black pastors are now disillusioned about politicians (black and white) being the hope for urban black people. In part, pastors have seen black and white politicians use power in ways that benefit only the politician or business interests, but not the masses of urban black people. Pastors and black politicians committed to helping the black community have also come to realize that political power does not always translate into influencing economic interests that are essential to urban vitality. This has led some black pastors to be less enthusiastic about using the worship hour to promote a political candidate. In addition, whereas only one black candidate used to run for a particular office, now an office may have several black candidates seeking election. This makes it difficult for a pastor to identify a single candidate as the one who best represents the interests of the congregation.

supporting the other agencies in the community which serve human welfare. This means that the minister must find time to serve on Commissions of Human Relations, Mental Health Association Boards, The Society for Crippled and Abandoned Children, Welfare Agencies and other Boards in the community which are designed for the social and personal uplift.[27]

Cooperation with social service and justice organizations was being advocated as a necessary strategy for CME churches in mission.

Another major strategy employed by CME churches was to either house or operate community programs. Dr. Mance Jackson, former executive secretary for the CME General Board of Social Concerns, says many CME churches were operating day care centers before the federal government got involved with financial support. Churches were also conducting programs that provided fellowship and recreational opportunities for senior citizens and youth, food and clothing closets for the needy, tutoring for youth, and pastoral care ministries to prisoners.

CME pastors worked through ministerial alliances and interdenominational church organizations to protest segregation in schools, police brutality, the inadequacy of public welfare payments, and discrimination in employment and social services. While these might have been the issues of the immediate neighborhoods in which CME churches were located, the urban outreach of CME clergy and laity extended to metropolitan-wide boundaries. More often than not, citywide and national issues were a greater priority to CME leadership than neighborhood issues. The symptoms of oppression were evident in one's neighborhood, but the causes were in the governments, businesses, and agencies of the larger community.

The prevalence of this spirit of social involvement can be observed in the resolutions from various structures of the church. The previously mentioned 1960 College of Bishops "Statement" called the CME membership to action:

> We call upon our membership to acquaint themselves with this problem [housing], to the end that they may not only seek after improvement in homes and housing, but that they may also join forces with individuals and movements which seek an amicable, Christian solution to the vexing problem. It is a problem of the body, of the soul and spirit — of which the latter two must be untrammeled and free.

27. "Minutes of the Twenty-seventh General Conference and Twenty-sixth Quadrennial Session and Centennial Celebration," Appendix, p. 29.

The bishops then noted the governmental venture in urban renewal where slums were demolished for new housing and business. They warned:

> Instances are known where such renewed areas are later sold to, and occupied by, other races, with Negroes excluded. Under the conditions, our folk view urban renewal as a masquerade — as just a new device to remove and to segregate them in less desirable areas, if indeed it attempts to settle them at all.
>
> We call upon the authorities to review such practices, to assess the effect upon our people. We call upon our people to acquaint themselves with the probable effects of such movements, and to prepare to enter into discussion and conference with associations and authorities who seek to minimize the effect upon displaced minorities.[28]

This statement patterned the denominational approach to addressing urban issues. The critical nature of the issue was pronounced, the impact upon the constituency of the CME Church was clarified, and members were encouraged to participate in coalitions that challenged oppressive policies. There were no church general boards or staff assigned to be resources for local congregations in dealing with social concerns.[29]

Still, the procedure of making resolutions enabled the church to articulate its commitment, and it may have inspired significant ministries that materialized at the local church level. Districts, annual conferences, and general conferences continued to give their energies to stating the church's relationship to urban realities.

In 1966 the general conference of the CME Church adopted its first "Social Creed." The "Theological Perspective" of the creed is insightful for understanding the denomination's religious identity:

> We believe that the Christian Methodist Episcopal Church is a part of the body of Christ, and that it must express itself in the world in the light of the life and teachings of Jesus Christ. Jesus taught us many things both by word and example — to be concerned for the welfare and well-being of others, to love our neighbors as ourselves, to be concerned for justice. For the Church to be silent in the face of need, injustice and exploitation is to deny the Lord of the Church. . . .
>
> We believe that whatever is of interest and concern to people —

28. *Christian Index*, August 4, 1960, p. 6.
29. In the CME Church, general boards have a status analogous to that of departments in other denominations.

66

physical, intellectual, social, economic and political — should also be of interest and concern to the Church. The purpose of our worship is to prepare the participants for their divinely ordained redemptive witness in every place and circumstance.[30]

The creed continues by indicating the CME position on various issues: economic life, inflation, health services, wages and working conditions, automation, poverty and unemployment, urban life, Christian vocation, the United Nations, military service, alcohol, crime, gambling, sexuality, and human rights. On urban life the statement reads: "We believe the inner city to be a mission field crying out for bold, new creative ways of witness. Therefore, we call our urban congregations to a deeper involvement in neighborhood life."[31] Again, the concern is put forth without strategies of action that address the issues.

In 1969, Rev. C. D. Coleman, who was general secretary for the General Board of Christian Education, organized a national conference for CME youth and young adults entitled "Beyond Blackness to Destiny." Speakers at the conference spoke to the importance of the black power message and black pride, and the significance of Christian witness with an awareness of one's racial identity. The "beyond" concept in the title did not denounce blackness but sought to stress that Christian identity was the ground from which racial identity took its meaning.

The study guide on the theme had articles on violence, racism, and the legitimacy and necessity for black power. Clearly, the General Board of Christian Education was seeking to speak relevantly to the current debate on racial consciousness and the appropriate methods of social transformation for black people. It provided resource materials for a denomination-wide exploration of race and power.

The Commission of Social Concerns was established in 1974 by the general conference. The commission articulated the church's position on community issues, but it did not have a staff to promote strategies throughout the church and help congregations with implementing programs.

The 1978 General Conference passed Social Concerns resolutions on public education, scientific research, capital punishment, housing, family life, euthanasia, abortion, homosexuality, the Equal Rights Amendment, and South

30. *Denominational Statements on Issues of Social Concern: The Christian Methodist Episcopal Church* (General Board of Social Concerns, n.d., n.p.).
31. *Denominational Statements.*

Africa. All of these statements contained a theological perspective, analysis, and recommendations that tended to be rather general. It is impossible to assess whether these statements motivated increased involvement of CME churches with these issues. The denomination did not sponsor programs or designate staff or funds to empower CME churches' participation in actions related to the resolutions. These resolutions seemed to express more the social and political orientation of the denomination than its willingness, or ability, to commit funds, personnel, and organizing energies to the issues.

Throughout the sixties and seventies the denomination generated significant statements about urban concerns. A Social Creed and Commission on Social Concerns came into being. And CME pastors and congregations were a prophetic witness to a wide range of urban issues. They marched, conducted sit-ins, supported political candidates, participated in the decision-making structures of systems, and established programs for their communities. Not until the first general conference of the eighties would the denomination establish a General Board of Social Concerns that had a paid staff member to coordinate strategies of social witness. Ironically, the church's lack of steadfast support for this general board has raised more questions than answers about the church's interest in a national office for its social commitment.

IV. Structuring Hope

The 1982 General Conference terminated its Commission for Social Concerns and made a deeper commitment to social ministries by establishing the General Board of Social Concerns. Four years later, at the 1986 General Conference, the general board was discontinued. Many in the CME Church took pride in having the only full-time staff member for social concerns among the black Methodist denominations. It was a sign of the denomination's commitment that social issues were integral to its identity. The pride and the general board were short-lived. The general board had only one staff member (the executive secretary). This limited number of administrative personnel is the situation for almost all of the church's general boards. Except for secretarial assistance, they are one-person operations. Theoretically, the bishops will assume responsibility for national goals being implemented within their episcopal districts. Often a bishop relies upon episcopal district, annual conference, or district committees to help national goals become programs for the local church. Sometimes national program goals are not emphasized by the leadership of the episcopal district.

Dr. Mance Jackson, the general secretary for social concerns, created a handbook that sought to organize social concerns boards and directors at the episcopal district, annual conference, district, and local church levels. He organized denominational conferences on social concerns. And he was a resource to annual conferences and local churches when invited. The impact of this work is difficult to measure. His time and budget were limited. His initial efforts were to develop the foundation upon which a national program might be built.

The demise of the General Board of Social Concerns occurred through a denominational "restructuring" plan for national boards. The position taken by many church leaders was that Social Concerns was not being dropped, but was only being integrated with other CME commitments. The restructuring plan merged the three General Boards of Social Concerns, Missions, and Evangelism into a single general board. A theological rationale was given that distinctions among these three activities should not be encouraged. Evangelism, missions, and social concerns go hand in hand wherever the church is faithful to the whole person.

However, the new General Board of Evangelism, Missions, and Human Concerns was not given funds for three staff persons. The author has not heard anyone in the denomination express the conviction that single-staff administration was adequate for any one of these three boards. Yet, the three were reduced to the portfolio of a single general secretary. This has led many to the conclusion that restructuring was really a guise for cutting budget expenses.

Although the church's commitment to national coordination of its social witness wavered, the commitment of its local pastors and churches to outreach remained strong. Pastors continued in leadership positions with the NAACP, Urban League, OIC, and SCLC. In 1991 Rev. Henry Williamson in Chicago became the national president of Operation PUSH. Participation in ministerial alliances, interdenominational organizations, and coalitions with community organizations persisted as a major strategy for engaging systemic issues. Churches addressed systemic issues through involvement in various community development programs. For example: Hopps Memorial CME in Syracuse has built (with other churches) ten low-cost houses; St. Luke CME in Nashville constructed and now manages forty-eight apartments for the elderly and handicapped; Trinity CME in Augusta built and manages a one-hundred-apartment complex for low-income families; Brown Memorial CME in Louisville has since 1986 placed over fifteen hundred youth in summer jobs.

Today, CME churches operate feeding programs for the homeless and

poor, conduct voter registration drives, operate and house preschool programs, and sponsor programs for the elderly. The 1980s brought an increase
in church programs that focused on drug abuse, teen pregnancy, single-
parent families, and the problems confronting black males. A first strategy
of churches is to sponsor forums about such issues. But churches have
developed ongoing programs of counseling, support groups, mentoring
relationships, and cooperation with social service agencies.[32]

In 1978 the Congress of National Black Churches was established as
an ecumenical organization to strengthen programs of the six participating
denominations. The CME Church is a participating member and helps in
funding the organization. The congress has four programmatic emphases:
(1) an internship program with community agencies for young pastors to
understand community realities, and to explore the possibilities for creative
ministries that address community needs; (2) the Black Family Program,
an after-school program that works with children and their parents on
tutoring, parenting, self-esteem, and affirming one's African American heritage; (3) a drug education program that works through ministerial associations; and (4) an economic development program that seeks to explore
possibilities for the denominations to participate in banking, insurance,
and publication ventures together.

CME pastors participate in the internship program, and CME
churches are active in the black family and drug education programs. The
congress is beginning to gain experience and influence. CME bishops have
expressed hope that the congress will be an important investment that
furthers the urban ministries of local congregations. Its promise, as a resource for churches nationwide, speaks to the need for both ecumenical
cooperation and national administration in dealing with complex social
issues.

The congress has a greater capacity for researching issues, securing
foundation and government grants for programs, and giving staff time to
local organizing than did the single-administrator General Board of Social
Concerns. However, while local congregations may work ecumenically on
local issues, they frequently have a difficult time identifying with a national
ecumenical body that tries to empower their ministry. To date, the denomination has not initiated programs to help congregations work effectively
with such national ecumenical efforts. The involvement of four CME bishops on the congress's thirty-member board of directors is a substantial

32. See Luther E. Smith Jr., ed., *Pan-Methodist Social Witness Resource Book* (Nashville:
African Methodist Episcopal Publishing House, 1991).

commitment and indication of support from the denomination. Only time will tell whether the congress is an adequate substitute for a strictly denominational agency for social concerns.

V. Conclusion

If a "strategy" is an intentional method of decision making, organization, and action to arrive at specific goals, then one would be hard pressed to conclude that the CME Church had a strategy for urban ministry. The importance of resolutions about social injustices is evident. CME structures made prophetic pronouncements that challenged the social order, government, and the churches. But the denomination rarely provided strategies for local churches to implement its concerns for urban ministry.

The financial limitations of the denomination may be the major cause for the absence of denominational strategies. The denomination could not underwrite the urban ministry initiatives of its congregations. The church did not have the funds to hire staff, develop programs, and make grants that would address its urban concerns. Bishop Joseph C. Coles Jr., reflecting on his ministry in Harlem, regretted that he could not initiate more programs for his community. His inability stemmed not from a lack of interest but from a lack of resources. He saw and appreciated what churches with strong denominational resources could do. But he knew that the CME Church was "impoverished to give funds and personnel," and that it was struggling to survive economically.

This conclusion does not intend to suggest that the CME Church should have redirected its resources to establish denominational agencies that would engage in urban issues on behalf of congregations. The congregational base of CME urban ministries is a strong foundation for addressing urban realities. It involves clergy and laity in direct interaction with the people and issues of their communities. But the denomination could have given more energy to developing strategies that would help congregations implement its resolutions on social concerns.

Throughout this history, the leadership of CME clergy has been a prominent force in the church's urban witness. This is because the denominational authority structure is hierarchical. Laity give considerable authority to pastors in leading the congregation, and pastors submit to the leadership of bishops. As in all hierarchical structures, the higher positioned leader usually sets the agenda and expects loyalty to his or her leadership. And leaders are held accountable to acceptable standards of behavior. In CME

71

churches this has meant that pastors are the key individuals for an outreach ministry. Even if the pastor does not initiate the idea of a ministry, and is not active in conducting it, very few ministries will survive without the pastor's tacit approval. Urban ministry is pastor dependent. If a church has a civic-minded minister, then this approach can involve a congregation that might ordinarily be complacent toward its community. If a minister is not interested in the community, however, the enthusiasm of laity for outreach can be greatly diminished, if not extinguished.

Another consequence of the hierarchical structure has been for some pastors to become their church's outreach ministry, rather than leading their membership into ministry. This limits the fuller involvement of the Christian community in acts of caring.

On the positive side, some pastors do utilize their leadership position to enable membership involvement. They commit their churches to bold ventures because they accept the authority and respect their laity have for them. This capability to commit the church has been crucial in planning protests that could not wait for churches to go through an extensive decision-making process. The most educated ministerial leadership in the CME Church would usually be in urban churches. The city churches were the largest and most prestigious of the denomination, and therefore became the choice appointments for well-educated and effective clergy. The urban context had some of the best-trained and best-tested pastoral leadership that the denomination had to offer.[33]

Since the urban churches symbolized leadership capabilities, and could financially support the involvement of their pastors in denominational meetings, they provided the majority of candidates that sought and attained the episcopacy. The hierarchical structure therefore had episcopal leaders who were sensitive to urban realities and the necessity for prophetic witness to these realities. The bishops who directed the church had an urban consciousness and commitment that guided denominational pronouncements and influenced their appointments to urban churches.

This analysis of hierarchy should not be interpreted as a dismissal of the importance of laity to urban ministry. In CME churches, many of the outreach programs require lay volunteers and donations. CME laity are leaders in civic and social organizations that cooperate with local churches

---

33. Rev. Lawrence L. Reddick III (editor of the *Christian Index*), in his comments on a draft of this essay, makes the important observation that many well-educated CME clergy chose to serve the needs of smaller southern communities. He appropriately warns against a conclusion that only urban areas had educated clergy.

to address urban needs. Their involvement through such organizations as the NAACP, the Urban League, SCLC, black fraternities and sororities, and black Masonic lodges has been vital to activities of protest and social services. CME churches have supported CME lay members who have been candidates for public office. The Women's Missionary Societies of local CME congregations have become more involved in working with urban youth and providing emergency assistance to the indigent. And many a CME pastor has been pushed into community activity because of the commitment of laity.

Not all urban CME churches are community oriented. In fact, frequently the two or three largest CME churches in a city will be the only ones of the denomination with pastoral or congregational leadership involved with urban ministry issues. Pastors of the smaller churches may find it necessary to work in a secular job in order to have an adequate income; their availability for community activities is therefore restricted. Some CME clergy, even in the larger churches, have personalities or ecclesiologies that are not comfortable with community conflict. Still, the record of CME involvement in urban issues is impressive.

Over the years, Collins Chapel Hospital has been the major denominational investment in an institutional ministry to urban needs. The facility has an emergency outpatient clinic, as well as rooms for long-term care. It offers radiology, eye care, and diagnostic laboratory and dental services. The First Episcopal District financed and operates the John Madison Exum Towers (named after a CME bishop), which has over 240 apartment units for the handicapped.

The denomination spends large sums of its resources in supporting four colleges and a seminary. Although not usually defined as an urban ministry, this commitment to higher education is related to urban realities. These schools prepare the black leadership that will hopefully offer creative solutions to urban needs. Many of the students would not be able to receive a higher education were it not for these church-supported institutions. The commitment to higher education drains the denomination's limited resources, but it is a credit to the CME Church that its dedication to these institutions has remained steadfast.

Since World War II higher education has received the largest allocation of the denominational budget, between 27 and 40 percent. Because the purposes of higher education are broader than resolving immediate crises within the urban life, the support of colleges is not normally considered a "strategy" of urban ministry. However, higher education has such a positive impact on what happens in urban settings that this commitment of the CME Church needs to be credited as an important contribution to urban life.

Rather than having a systematic plan to transform the urban context, the CME Church may have looked to the past for its direction. In 1879, Bishop Lucius H. Holsey (a founder of the CME Church), in the opening editorial of the *Gospel Trumpet,* stated that the periodical's purpose would be to "discuss without hesitation, any phase of the civic, social, and those economic and political questions that may affect the well-being of the Church and the race."[34] The CME Church has understood social issues to be central to its religious witness. For the CME Church to continue as a faithful witness to this heritage, it will need to become more intentional about developing strategies that give life to its urban commitment and prophetic proclamations.

VI. Recommendations for Future Strategies

The following recommendations are made recognizing the limited denominational funding for urban ministry programs. These recommendations would not require expensive departments or personnel for implementation. They build upon the procedures and traditions of the CME Church.

1. The CME Church needs to be more *intentional* in preparing pastors for urban ministry. The increasing complexity of urban issues will require clergy who are not only called to congregations, but who are also called to the congregations' communities. The church could help pastors to acquire experiences that would identify significant issues of community outreach, and enable them to assess options for ministry.

This intentional preparation could take the form of establishing a conference on urban ministry that addresses specific issues for CME churches in the urban context. The conference could be conducted as a national event, or it might be sponsored in episcopal districts or annual conferences. Pastors who are new to the urban context could be required to participate in an urban conference. Such a conference need not be sponsored by the CME Church. CME pastors could attend urban ministry events sponsored by other denominations or seminaries, and they could take urban studies courses from local colleges.

The purpose of this recommendation is to provide clergy with concepts that will prepare them to understand and communicate with their

---

34. This comment is in *Denominational Statements.*

congregations, communities, and policy-makers about the forces effecting their context. The church should also encourage laity to participate in such educational experiences. The recommendation's emphasis upon pastors acknowledges their pivotal role in approving or initiating urban ministries.

2. Most CME churches, even with memberships over five hundred, have only one minister, who must be pastor, social worker, business manager, program coordinator, etc., for the congregation. More creative possibilities for organizing local congregations for mission might occur with multistaff leadership.

Churches could begin to explore the possibilities for funding additional staff. Or they might examine models of lay leadership that equip laity to perform essential functions that are usually reserved for the pastor. Before this, however, congregations will probably need help in understanding how they have come to assume that having only one minister for congregational leadership should be the accepted norm. The denomination should consider the merits of a program that would assess the feasibility and benefits of multistaff churches, and ways to empower lay leadership in congregations.

The Methodist polity of annual pastoral appointments to churches makes the development of lay leadership crucial to urban ministry. Every year Methodist pastors face the possibility of being appointed to a different church. If a church is overly dependent upon its pastor for urban ministry, then its urban witness is jeopardized by this annual process. Strong lay leadership is needed if a church's outreach is to have continuity.

3. The annual conference is the central meeting for pastors and laity to understand the commitments of their episcopal leader. Bishops might emphasize the importance of the urban witness of churches by requesting mission information as a part of each pastor's annual report to the conference. This would signal to clergy and laity that outreach is as crucial as financial achievements and increases in membership.

4. Urban CME churches need a networking mechanism that would enable them to learn from one another. Many are involved in outreach ministries without an awareness of how other CME churches are engaged in similar efforts. Perhaps a newsletter twice a year would be sufficient. But some publicity on issues, programs, and resources could be both inspirational and instructive. The *Christian Index*, the official publication of the church, does this to some extent, but only if churches take the initiative to send articles; and such articles are often highlighting multiple achievements of a church. A newsletter that focused on urban ministry would be a more effective instrument for urban churches.

5. The necessity for a national coordinating organization for social concerns should not be ignored. If the Congress of National Black Churches fulfills this need, then greater effort should be made to connect local churches with the work of the congress. If the congress does not prove adequate to the analysis and resource development needs for urban ministry, then the denomination should reconsider establishing a general board that addresses social concerns.

In 1990 the CME general conference theme was "Christian Methodism: A Goodly Heritage, a Formidable Challenge, a Biblical Response." When the last forty-five years are assessed, the theme characterizes the CME Church's involvement in urban ministry. The church has called upon its heritage to meet urban challenges. If it takes seriously the biblical mandate to commit its life to God regardless of the consequences, then necessary institutional restructuring will not be precluded by fears of institutional survival. Jesus' obedience to God led to his death, and no less a risk is required of all who claim to be his disciples. Without this commitment, the CME Church may continue to serve urban needs, but it will retreat from issues that seem too threatening or demanding. With this commitment, it will be untrammeled and free to work miracles.

• 4 •

"My Soul Says Yes": The Urban Ministry of the Church of God in Christ

ROBERT MICHAEL FRANKLIN

Introduction

In 1895, black America's most influential spokesperson and Tuskegee Institute's young president, Booker T. Washington, urged recently emancipated black Southerners to resist the understandable temptation to migrate northward. "Cast down your buckets where you are," he bellowed to southern blacks in the racially mixed audience of the Cotton States and International Exposition in Atlanta.[1]

His words were forceful but futile. Washington did not live long enough to see the dramatic urbanization of the black population that followed 1915. With the combined incentives of expanded employment opportunities created by the world wars, intensifying racial oppression in the South, and more available public relief during the Depression, by 1965 three-fourths of the black population was living in cities, and half of it in the urban North.[2] By 1980, New York had the largest black population of any city (1.7 million), followed by Chicago (1.2 million), Detroit (758,939), Philadelphia (638,878), and Los Angeles (505,210).[3] Census data for the

1. Louis R. Harlan, "Booker T. Washington and the Politics of Accommodation," in *Black Leaders of the Twentieth Century*, ed. John Hope Franklin and August Meier (Urbana: University of Illinois Press, 1982).

2. Sydney E. Ahlstrom, *A Religious History of the American People* (Garden City, N.Y.: Image Books, 1975), 2:572.

3. "America's Black Population," Bureau of the Census, p. 1.

1980s indicate that over 52 percent of African Americans now reside in the South, confirming a reverse migration trend from northern to southern cities. The earlier massive migration of rural blacks to southern and northern cities is a fascinating drama that has received brilliant treatment by some of America's finest artists, including Langston Hughes, Zora Neale Hurston, Richard Wright, James Baldwin, and Gloria Naylor. These and other writers have portrayed with humor and pathos the arduous process of uprooting and resettling. As Zora Neale Hurston commented in her first novel, *Jonah's Gourd Vine* (1934), "Railroads, hardroads, dirt roads, side roads, roads were in the minds of the black South and all roads led North."[4]

The urbanization of black Christianity was not altogether a twentieth-century phenomenon. During the earliest years of U.S. history, there were independent black churches founded by free blacks in northern cities. For instance, Richard Allen established the Bethel Chapel African Methodist Episcopal Church in Philadelphia in 1794. Nevertheless, with the rapid migration and urbanization of southern blacks, a new chapter of black church urbanization was opened. For the first time, the churches faced the challenge of resettling and reorienting hundreds of thousands of newcomers, not unlike the churches that welcomed European immigrants. This "ministry of resettlement" was performed vigorously both by mainstream, "middle-class," institutional churches such as Bethel Chapel AME and the Abyssinian Baptist Church of Harlem, and by the numerous storefront churches, then typical of the rapidly urbanizing Church of God in Christ (COGIC).

Suggestive for understanding the plight of black people migrating from the rural South to the cities is a paradigm developed by anthropologist Victor Turner. In *The Ritual Process* he suggests that whether a person is moving from childhood to adolescence, or from civilian to soldier, there are distinct structural and dynamic features common to all ritual processes. He suggests that the ritual process involves three phases: (1) a beginning state of relative stability and familiarity (stasis); (2) a transitional period that is fluid, normless, and threatening (liminality); and (3) a time for rejoining the community with a new status (reincorporation).[5]

In light of Turner's categories, it seems to me that the church was

4. Zora Neale Hurston, *Jonah's Gourd Vine* (New York: Harper and Row Publishers, Perennial Library, 1934), p. 151.

5. Victor Turner, *The Ritual Process* (New York: Cornell University Press, 1969). Turner admits his theoretical indebtedness to University of Chicago anthropologist Arnold van Gennep.

instrumental in each phase of migration and urbanization. As the "institutional center" of the black community, it constituted the stasis of pre-migration life. It became an extended family away from home *(communitas)* for thousands of unemployed, hungry, and bewildered new arrivals. However, this was also a period during which many black people left the institutional church, seeking to redefine themselves in more secular terms. And the urban church, similar to its role in the rural South, became the "surrogate world" for all who sought religious support for their resocialization into a new black civil society.[6]

In this chapter, my focus is upon the development of the urban ministry of the Church of God in Christ, the youngest and fastest growing of America's black denominations.[7] Although the denomination is now a fixture in every large American city (over one hundred thousand population), most people are unaware of its origins. Therefore, I begin with a brief historical sketch of the church, followed by a discussion of five features of its urban ministry that may offer clues to all who seek to enhance inner-city ministry. In the third section I provide a biographical sketch of the current presiding bishop, Louis Henry Ford, along with an analysis of his significant contributions to the denomination's vision of urban ministry.

I. Urban Origins of the Church of God in Christ

The denomination is one of many spiritual offspring born of the dynamic urban ministry of the Reverend William J. Seymour, a black evangelist and pastor, who conducted the famous "Azusa Street revival" in Los Angeles from 1906 to 1909. Leonard Lovett, Church of God in Christ pastor and theologian, describes the centrifugal dynamism of Seymour's ministry in these terms: "Without instruments of music, no choir, no collection or financial arrangement, no bills posted to advertise the meeting, without any organized church support, individuals from some thirty-five nations heard the message of Pentecost during this three-year revival and returned to initiate the movement in their own nations."[8]

Among the many pilgrims who crossed the globe in order to partake

6. The concepts of "institutional center" and "surrogate world" were coined by C. Eric Lincoln and Peter Paris, respectively.

7. This claim is documented in C. Eric Lincoln and Lawrence Mamiya, *The Black Church in the African American Experience* (Durham, N.C.: Duke University Press, 1990).

8. Leonard Lovett, "Perspective on the Black Origins of the Contemporary Pentecostal Movement," *Journal of the Interdenominational Theological Center* 1 (Fall 1973): 36-49.

of Seymour's charismatic ministry was Charles Harrison Mason (1866-1961), the former Baptist preacher who founded the Church of God in Christ. The first incarnation (pre-Seymour) of the denomination appeared in 1897 when Mason departed the Baptist church in order to establish a more satisfying religious community. This move was inspired by Wesleyan preachers of the nineteenth-century Holiness Movement who emphasized the sanctifying work of the Holy Spirit, and occasionally espoused social justice themes. Following Mason's Holy Spirit baptism, he returned to the South and reorganized the denomination (post-Seymour) around a revitalized doctrine of the supernatural ministries of the Holy Spirit.

Mason himself was an extraordinary person, and was perceived to be a saint endowed with a variety of charismatic gifts, especially of teaching, healing, and prophecy. He was known for his intense prayers and his quiet, inscrutable but charming manner. Bedecked in his trademark dark suit and bow tie, he often appeared in the pulpit with rocks, tree roots, and other natural paraphernalia donated to him by church members who were impressed by his teaching concerning God's signs and wonders revealed in nature. These became object lessons for his simple, unadorned, expository sermons.

Soon, members of the denomination adopted the biblical title "saints" to represent themselves. Today, the saints recognize 1907 as the official founding date (sacred time) and Memphis as the headquarters city (sacred space) of the predominantly black, Holiness-Pentecostal, international denomination of 3.7 million people.

The attachment to the city of Memphis is worthy of note. Memphis was Mason's ministerial base of operations for more than half a century. He was well known to the city officials of Memphis, and even to the FBI, which monitored his activities during World War I following his prophetic indictments of the American government's proclivity for war.

Memphis is also home of the Charles Harrison Mason Temple, spiritual headquarters of the organization. The denomination manifests considerable pride over the Temple, which was constructed, amazingly, during World War II when materials were scarce. In part, this pride flows from a collective sense of ownership resulting from the personal investment of money, materials, and actual construction assistance by many members who are alive today. When constructed, it was the largest black-owned auditorium in America, a sort of ecclesial counterpart to Booker T. Washington's Tuskegee experiment; "concrete" proof that black people could build, own, and operate their own nationally recognized institutions. Although this fact is widely misreported, the Temple is also nationally recognized because Dr. King gave his last speech ("I've Been to the Mountain-top") from its pulpit on April 3, 1968.[9]

Precisely when Booker T. Washington was urging blacks to remain in the South, Charles H. Mason was sending his disciples to the North to evangelize the transplanted masses. Clearly, he anticipated the future urbanization of African Americans and planned carefully to be in the thick of Christian witness and service in the burgeoning cities. C. Eric Lincoln and Lawrence Mamiya observe in their significant study:

> Among Bishop Mason's strengths was his ability to cultivate leadership and delegate responsibility. His strategy of sending evangelists to accompany the northerly migration of African Americans and of charging bishops with the establishment of new jurisdictions in such metropolitan areas as New York, Philadelphia, Detroit, and Chicago resulted in COGIC becoming a predominantly urban church.[10]

By the time of World War II, there were major COGIC congregations, led by exceptionally gifted ministers, in all of America's largest cities: Bishop Otha M. Kelly, Brooklyn; Bishop O. T. Jones Sr., Philadelphia; Bishop William Roberts, Chicago; Bishop Samuel Crouch, Los Angeles; Bishop I. S. Stafford, Detroit; Bishop E. M. Driver, Houston.

Although most of the prominent names associated with the development of the denomination's urban phase are male, members of the denomination are aware of the pivotal role played by women. At least three leaders must be mentioned in this regard: Mother Lizzie Woods Robinson (supervisor of the Women's Department); Mother Lillian Brooks Coffey (national evangelist who succeeded Mother Robinson); and Dr. Arenia C. Mallory (president of Saints Industrial and Literary School, Lexington, Mississippi). Dr. Mallory's impact upon an entire generation of post–World War II COGIC leaders who lived in cities is an impressive saga. One of her prized pupils was Louis Henry Ford, a young man from Clarksdale, Mississippi, who became presiding bishop of the denomination in 1990.

In a fascinating study of the impact of African American women upon the religious culture of black people, scholars Jualyne E. Dodson and Cheryl Townsend Gilkes indicate that Mason

recruited educated women to work in the building of the denomination and

---

9. Most sources report that King's "Been to the Mountaintop" speech was delivered at a Masonic temple.

10. Lincoln and Mamiya, p. 82.

the educational ministries. These women developed a "women's work" that came to be known as the "women's department." It was the women who were migrating to the cities who carried the movement to urban areas, preaching revivals, "digging out" new works, and then writing "home" for a pastor.[11]

Such women helped to establish, within every congregation, the biblical office of "praying and mourning women of the church" who functioned as the backbone of the institutional church.

In the absence of opportunities for ordained pastoral leadership, these women developed and sustained organizations devoted to nurturing children (Sunshine Band), young adults (Purity Class, Sunday School and Young People's Willing Workers), and inner-city outreach ministries (Prayer and Bible Band, Missionaries, Home and Foreign Missions); and fortifying the spiritual ethos of the congregation (Sewing Circle, Deaconess Board, Mothers Board, etc.). Although these ministries were developed in the rural South, when the great urban migrations occurred they were transplanted to northern cities and thereby helped preserve the intimate mood of congregational life with which people were familiar.

Following the death of Bishop Mason on November 17, 1961, the church entered a period described by its official historians as "the wilderness wanderings," referring to the dispute concerning Mason's successor. The existing seven-person executive committee was expanded to twelve, and Bishop O. T. Jones Sr. was "honored as the Ceremonial Head of the Church with the title 'Senior Bishop.'"[12] But the dispute intensified and found its way to the Chancery Court of Shelby County, Tennessee, where church leaders were admonished to follow the existing denominational constitution, and to convene a constitutional convention in January 1968. Bishop James O. Patterson emerged as the new presiding bishop, was reelected in five subsequent quadrennial elections, and served for twenty-one years. During those years, Patterson orchestrated the denomination's redefinition from a small sectarian organization to an international body on a par with its older black church counterparts.[13]

---

11. Jualyne E. Dodson and Cheryl Townsend Gilkes, "Something Within: Social Change and Collective Endurance in the Sacred World of Black Christian Women," in *Women and Religion in America*, vol. 3, ed. Rosemary Reuther and R. Keller (San Francisco: Harper & Row, 1986), pp. 80-130.

12. The Reverend German R. Ross, Bishop J. O. Patterson, and Mrs. Julia Mason Atkins, eds., *History and the Formative Years of the Church of God in Christ* (Memphis: COGIC Publishing House, 1969), p. 77.

13. Evidence suggests that patterns of growth changed under Patterson. Whereas

Compared with other denominations in this volume, the Church of God in Christ is a tender bud on the tree of American Christianity. The story of the women and men who surrounded Bishop Mason remains to be told. But clearly the modern history of America's great cities cannot ignore the humanizing contributions of the financially poor but spiritually rich and energetic "saints" of the Church of God in Christ.

II. Humanizing the City: Five Dimensions of Urban Ministry

In this section, I present five features of the church's approach to urban ministry. Its principal urban mission is to *humanize the impersonal, individualized, and materialistic character of modern city life* through a kaleidoscopic variety of ministries that can be organized under the categories of *renewal, empowerment, preservation, resistance, and celebration.*

1. Renewal

COGIC congregations sought to renew the spiritual vitality of Christianity in the United States vis-à-vis the onslaughts of materialism, cultural alienation, and racism. Mason, like other black religious virtuosi, lambasted the racist and exploitative misuse of the Bible and the church by hypocritical white church leaders. He believed that Pentecostalism represented an effective spiritual avenue for transforming race relations based upon white domination of the black population. The presence of Seymour presiding over a mixed racial revival seemed emblematic of the possibility of new social realities inaugurated by the coming of the Spirit. It is a little-known fact that the contemporary Assembly of God denomination is an institutional offspring of COGIC, one of the rare occasions in American church history when a black denomination gave rise to a white one and both continued to thrive.[14]

Bishop Mason welcomed the wholesale entry of scores of existing congregations with similar doctrines into the denomination, Patterson eschewed it. Bishop Ford is said to be open to the mass model of expansion. This will be interesting to monitor, particularly since large numbers of female pastors are waiting for official signals regarding their status and prospects for affiliating with the church. COGIC ordains women for certain specialized ministries (chaplaincy), but does not presently condone female pastors.

14. See Vinson Synan, *The Holiness/Pentecostal Movement in the United States* (Grand Rapids: William B. Eerdmans, 1971); this is also documented in official publications of the Assemblies of God.

In addition to the significant theological claim that Pentecostalism might hold the key to racial reconciliation and ecumenism, Mason, through his emphasis upon a theology of the Holy Spirit, critiqued his own black Baptist and Methodist/Holiness roots. As black people sought to assimilate the dominant culture, there was a tendency to exchange African-oriented religious practices for those of Euro-Anglo Christians. By stridently reintroducing drums, spontaneous song celebrations, call-response preaching, dancing, and emotionally liberating worship, Mason sought to *re-Africanize black churches*.[15] He was leading American churches back to Jerusalem by way of Africa.

Hence, COGIC's urban mission entailed the spiritual revitalization and cultural renewal of American churches. Mason perceived the subtle *tendency in industrial, urban culture to devalue the nonmaterial dimension of life*. To white Christians his message was, "Open yourselves to the work of the Holy Ghost." To black Christians he said, "Accept and celebrate who you are as God's African children." In humble storefront buildings, COGIC members carried on their heroic work of humanizing city life through spiritual renewal.

2. Empowerment

Through its practices, the denomination proclaimed a gospel of *empowerment through the acquisition of economic goods* such as land, property, and wealth. Most urban COGIC churches during the World War II years were storefront buildings. The denomination sought to empower poor black people by encouraging them to move from those modest buildings into the impressive cathedrals and synagogues coming available due to white suburban flight. When they could not buy, they built. I would underscore that this understanding of economic empowerment was indebted to Booker T. Washington's reigning ideology at the time of Mason's early years. The denomination translated this idea into "concrete" reality with the completion of Mason Temple in 1945 at a cost of $400,000. Notwithstanding this achievement, Mason prophesied that there would not be a building anywhere capable of accommodating the saints.

By directing church and personal funds, Mason was instrumental in

15. This "re-Africanization thesis" has been discussed by COGIC theologians Ithiel Clemmons, Leonard Lovett, David Daniels, and Alonzo Johnson in conversations with the author.

helping his urban disciples move into larger, more impressive facilities. Soon mortgage-burning ceremonies became commonplace but elaborate occasions for exhibiting the power of collective economic behavior. I have personal memories of my financially marginal grandmother, Martha McCann, shedding tears on the day our congregation burned its mortgage. Like most middle-class people, today I can only imagine the depth of community pride and self-affirmation that arose from the labors of poor people like her.

Sociologist Joseph R. Washington Jr. has observed that black sects and cults engage in a form of material power acquisition under the guise of promoting spiritual rejuvenation and cultural pride.[16] Although his claim has some merit here, it would be a mistake to overlook the significant theological foundation of the economic empowerment motif.

For Church of God in Christ members, Mason Temple was more than an expansive, awe-inspiring building. Mason Temple, like their own local houses of refuge and worship, was what happened inside — near the altar, under the sound of Bishop Mason's prayers, or when touched by the anointed hands of the praying women. That is, the Temple was a place in which the holy could be encountered and felt. It was that safe place wherein the terrible and awesome power of the numinous could be directly consulted.[17] It was an expression of the ancient and apparently universal human quest to discover one's true self at the intersection of the sacred and profane. The Temple became the kingdom of God. During Mason's life, evidence of divine healing (canes, crutches, wheelchairs) were hung on the walls around the building. Today the body of Bishop Mason is enshrined in a room open to pilgrims and visitors, reinforcing the Temple's sacred and central significance for the denomination's members.

Mere ownership of a church building was not, per se, an act of empowerment and humanization. Rather, it was the denomination's effort to promote a more holistic understanding of prosperity than was evident in modern culture. Church leaders sought to remind the rich and famous that human beings do not live by bread alone, and that it would profit them little to gain the whole world while losing their souls. The cornerstone biblical verse of Bishop Patterson's theology of stewardship was 3 John 2: "Beloved, I wish

16. Joseph R. Washington Jr., *Black Sects and Cults* (Lanham, Md.: University Press of America, 1972), p. 13. Washington observes that "Black cults are most difficult to analyze because their creeds generally hide their deeds; the religious language more often than not distorts the secular or power undercurrent. The black cult-type is not merely a religious movement."

17. Rudolph Otto, *The Idea of the Holy* (London: Oxford University Press, 1923).

above all things that thou mayest prosper and be in health, even as thy soul prospereth" (KJV). It was an act of defiance and humanization both to challenge affluent people not to put their trust in material things and to encourage economically marginal people who were exploited and devalued in the labor market to claim their entitlement within the capitalistic economy they helped sustain. At the state jurisdictional level, local bishops cosigned on loans to congregations seeking to purchase property. Although a growing segment of the denomination is moving into the middle class (annual family income between $24,000 and $50,000), and many clergy are affluent (over $50,000) with all of the accoutrements of conspicuous consumption, they struggle to possess these goods without being obsessed with them.

3. Preservation

A third feature of urban ministry was the deliberate effort to *preserve the humane culture of agrarian life* by transplanting to northern cities certain elements of the southern legacy, especially attitudes toward time, the social significance of dining together, and the emphasis on interpersonal intimacy.

A visit to Tuskegee University's George Washington Carver National Museum reveals that the school's former chemistry professor and scientific genius produced not only hundreds of inventions, but also a vast array of spiritual reflections on the character of agrarian life. Carver, like theologian Howard Thurman and scores of other spiritually sensitive black Southerners, apprehended beauty and coherence in nature. Carver understood this to be continuous with the deep and pervasive spiritualism of the African cultures from which African Americans were removed.

The most obvious feature of the agrarian legacy of the church is the phenomenon of the annual November Holy Convocation. Its scheduling was a function of the harvest calendar for southern sharecroppers and independent farmers. After the hard work was completed, the saints looked forward to spending an extended time of worship and fellowship in Memphis. Each year, as the sap drained from the trees and the leaves turned gold and red, to paraphrase Hurston, "roads were in the minds of the saints and all roads led to Memphis." For several decades, the convocation lasted for "twenty days and twenty nights."[18] As an accommodation to the pace and demands of modern

18. Conversation with historian Alphonso Westbrook, April 3, 1991. I express warm appreciation to Mr. Westbrook for his informed and generous help with research for this chapter.

life, it has been tailored to a week-long meeting, thereby increasing attendance. For northern blacks who owned little or no land, the annual pilgrimage to the South reminded them of days past when they lived closer to the land and interacted with it daily. The convocation also carried symbolic value for black people who were not members of the denomination. Many people attended to experience directly the power of the worship and fellowship.

As a local analogue to the long convocation, COGIC worship services have been noted for their length. Three-hour to four-hour services are common, hour-long sermons are the norm. Historians of religion note that poor and traditional communities often manifest a different attitude toward time than do people who participate in modern, industrial culture. When people on the economic margin of society gather for worship, there is no reason to rush the ritual process because there is nothing more important for them to do anyway. As one scholar has noted, "the cows don't have to be milked at exactly 4:02, but the assembly line worker has to do something at 4:02 or the whole factory shuts down."[19]

Although I have a diminished appreciation for needlessly long services, especially when children are being kept away from studies or from rest for the next day at school, I have come to appreciate the social function of the congregation for marginal people. For people who reside in dangerous housing projects or otherwise dehumanizing environments, going to church and remaining in church all day is therapeutic. Better the children sleep safely during services than roam city streets unsupervised.

In addition to long worship services in which people encounter the holy through imaginative, morally serious preaching, liberating music, and empowering prayer, typically churches prepare a full meal to be served, and usually sold, after worship. The consumption of food is sacramental, a time when Christ's redemptive presence is experienced. In the context of breaking bread together, the process of fellowship unfolds. During these times, older members who feel isolated in nursing homes have an opportunity to visit with people who respect them. Young people have an opportunity to bond with friends who share their values. Single mothers have access to a large support network of other mothers. And everyone enjoys the benefits and burdens of being an extended family in the inner city. Similar to southern agrarian culture, this kind of community humanizes city life by acknowledging the inviolable dignity of every person. Every person's name is known, personal gifts are expressed, and people begin to experience the reality behind the metaphor, body of Christ.

19. Conversation with Professor David D. Daniels II, April 3, 1991.

On a personal note, some of these preserved "southernisms" are illustrated in the ministry of my grandmother, Mother Martha McCann. As president of the deaconess board at Chicago's St. Paul Church of God in Christ, she regularly visited sick people in their homes. Typically, her house visits included the delivery of a huge pot of collard greens and a bag of clean clothing gleaned from the family's closets. My bewildered brother and I did not fully understand this gesture of Christian love, but we always enjoyed the boundless joy exhibited by the elderly sick woman and her many grandchildren when our car stopped in front of their apartment building. Little did I realize that my theological education was underway.

4. Resistance

A fourth dimension entails expressing *resistance to urban pathologies* such as institutional racism, the gratuitous use of violence, the pervasive and seductive allure of the narcotics subculture, and the escapist addiction to sensual pleasures. The churches do this by empowering believers to defy the claims of a secular, morally confused culture. The ministry of resistance takes a variety of forms.

According to Philadelphia's Bishop O. T. Jones Jr., a probable successor to the current presiding bishop, the impact of the church's urban ministry is rooted in the theology of Luke 4:18. In that passage Jesus proclaims that the Holy Spirit anoints and empowers ministries directed toward the poor and brokenhearted. Jones believes the church's message is especially appealing to the urban underclass because it treats evil and sin as tangible realities, and offers "deliverance from the power if not the presence of sickness and evil." Because there are no incurable conditions or unredeemable states, the church offers hope to everyone, even those who choose not to attend Sunday services.

The Church of God in Christ tends to view the city as contested turf that properly belongs to God, but has fallen under the province of evil. The ministry of resistance is combative without being militaristic. Power is kept in check by love. Pacifism is not an option in the face of the war in the streets. War must be waged against the forces of unrighteousness to win back the territory and "lift high the blood-stained banner." But it must be a just war. Bishop Jones's invocation of the concept of "deliverance" is an apt way to name this spiritual contest. Deliverance is that transformation which enables fallen humanity to move from the bondage of sin through conversion into the new community of saints. Deliverance entails setting free the captives of whom Jesus spoke. It is evidence of an authentic liberation theology. Temporally, the deliverance process may occur suddenly or over an extended period of time. Spatially, it most frequently unfolds within the context of a revival or worship service, but it may also be initiated during a house visit or other mode of personal evangelism.

Denominational historian David D. Daniels observes that the phenomenon of deliverance and receiving the Holy Spirit blessing can be understood as more than a linear process (sin to conversion to sanctification). Rather, deliverance possesses a dialectical character in which the alternating rhythms of "holding on" (to the presence of Christ's Spirit) and "letting go" (of the claims of the world) are common. Daniels suggests that, rather than being confusing and contradictory moral imperatives, the two messages are situationally appropriate to the complexity of the unfolding spiritual passage.[20]

Armed with biblical warrants for preaching deliverance to captives, and with a sophisticated sense of the psychodynamics of conversion, church members enter threatening inner-city spaces to bear witness to the power of the Spirit to break the chains of sin. The Home and Foreign Missions Board and Missionaries Board send people into housing projects to teach young parents home economics skills and to care for the children of incarcerated parents. Outdoor worship services and door-to-door neighborhood canvassing are designed to take the fight to the trenches and to challenge the hegemony of the narcotics subculture in its own front yard.

As I noted in the case of Mother McCann, the saints fed the hungry, clothed the naked, housed the homeless, and visited the incarcerated long before mainstream congregations decided to join the struggle. And, even when many white congregations enter direct urban ministry of this sort, the liberal theological frame of reference does not authorize a "wartime" deliverance approach to ministry, preferring instead to focus upon institutional, systemic change. To their credit, black churches have sought to sustain an emphasis upon both personal and social transformation.[21] However, in general and regrettably, the two traditions have been slow to learn from one another in order to combine the commitments to both personal evangelism and social justice.

20. David D. Daniels (McCormick Theological Seminary, Chicago), lecture delivered to COGIC "Holy Ghost Conference," Birmingham, Alabama, January 16, 1990.

21. I elaborate upon how this dual emphasis is present in the moral reflections of Booker T. Washington, W. E. B. Du Bois, Malcolm X, and Martin Luther King Jr. in my book *Liberating Visions: Human Fulfillment and Social Justice in African American Thought* (Minneapolis: Augsburg Fortress Press, 1990).

Following the lead of black Baptist and Methodist denominations, the church has begun to shed the stereotype of apoliticism and anti-intellectualism. Since the emergence of the modern civil rights movement (1954), the denomination has cautiously entered the fray of electoral politics and established its own educational institutions. Analysts remind us that the two commitments are mutually reinforcing, since higher levels of educational attainment translate into increased political activism, and such activism calls for greater access to data, more sophisticated analysis, and alternative action strategies. Both Bishop Patterson and Bishop Ford have been influential in placing these concerns on the front burner of the denomination. In March 1970, the C. H. Mason Theological Seminary was established as a formal component of the Interdenominational Theological Center in Atlanta, directed first by Dr. Leonard Lovett and now by Dean Oliver Haney.

More than any other church official, Bishop Ford has sought to raise the political profile of the church as a potential force in municipal and national politics. The church supported James O. Patterson Jr. in his unsuccessful bid to become the mayor of Memphis. During Jesse Jackson's presidential campaigns, COGIC officials were prominent in his state organizations, and he was invited to address a record-breaking convocation crowd in 1983.

5. Celebration

In 1982, the church published its first hymnal, *Yes, Lord!*, titled after Bishop Mason's most popular praise chant. Often, this chant was used to prepare people for worship, but just as often to bring calm and stability to a highly charged service. From the beginning, Mason marked the liturgy of COGIC with an emphasis upon the joyful, spirited praise of God. Music, preaching, testifying, and prayer were often woven together in a smooth, flowing garment of worship, making it impossible to know precisely when one stopped and the other began. This was part of the genius of Mason's spontaneous, spirit-centered worship.

"Yes, Lord" also reflects the dominant attitude of the saints toward the unfolding will of God, and the future outcome of the war against evil. Soldiers in the army of the Lord are authorized to celebrate Christ as the victor who makes our lives possible.

In recent years, the church's "Yes, Lord!" spirit has been contagious within, and beyond, the black church community. COGIC musical artists have exposed other non-Pentecostal traditions to the attitude and therapeutic power of Mason's spirit. Some have gone on to become major commercial successes (Andrae Crouch, The Hawkins, Winans, Clark Sisters, etc.), often to the chagrin of more conservative saints. Both ecumenicity and respectability have been enhanced by the musical non-elite. And more importantly, many unchurched inner-city people have been intrigued by the joy and music and fellowship of COGIC services. Such services have succeeded in incorporating and transforming elements of the entertainment-driven popular culture. For instance, holy dance that is full of action, sensuality, and audiovisual stimulation is a common, albeit declining, feature of COGIC worship. Its decline, like so many other elements of the southern legacy, is in direct proportion to the denomination's quest for mainstream respectability.

Having identified at least five prominent dimensions of the church's approach to urban ministry, I now turn to consider the person and urban contributions of the current presiding bishop, the Church of God in Christ's urban theologian.

III. Politicizing Urban Ministry: Bishop Louis Henry Ford

Every organization has a person who places it on the map in a memorable way. Through Malcolm X, the Nation of Islam moved from the margin to the center of the civil rights movement. Similarly, Bishop L. H. Ford placed the Church of God in Christ firmly in the public square at the intersection of religion and politics. More than any other leader of the church, he has raised the political profile of the denomination to new dimensions, and he exemplifies a political approach to urban ministry that is attractive to younger clergy. Nevertheless, many people feel that his eclectic and situational public theology has allowed him to get more involved in politics than prudence recommends.

Louis Henry Ford was born in Clarksdale, Mississippi, on May 23, 1914. When he was called to the ministry in 1926, he reports that his father did not support his participation in the Pentecostal church. Although his mother was proud of his call to ministry, she died when he was thirteen. In 1927 he attended the Saints Junior College in Lexington, Mississippi, coming under the tutelage and maternal care of Dr. Arenia C. Mallory.

Like scores of other young blacks, Ford went to Chicago during the Depression and preached on the street corners of the Windy City. Although there were numerous established congregations in the city, he founded St.

Paul Church of God in Christ in 1936. Today, the church building and related ministries occupy an entire city block on the south side of Chicago.

In a fascinating and fortuitous turn of events, he seized the opportunity to purchase Chicago's oldest house (Widow Clark's house). This fact alone raised his public visibility several notches in a city with so many distinguished black religious and political leaders that it could afford to be stingy in its attention to newcomers. In a wonderful gesture of humanizing this revered Chicago symbol that had fallen into disrepair, he renovated the house and conducted early Sunday morning training sessions (the Breakfast Club) where children, myself included, were drilled in Scripture memorization, current events, black history, mathematics, etiquette, and personal hygiene. It was a stroke of vision, genius, and audacity to think that he could make leaders out of ghetto kids. But we followed him from city hall to the county jail to the golf course, listening and learning all the way. Vicariously, we received a small dose of what he had learned from Dr. Mallory.

In 1946, he was appointed national public relations director and in 1955, one of the bishops of Illinois. That was the year the bus boycott in Montgomery, Alabama, was being orchestrated by Dr. King. King, along with other progressive black Baptist pastors, was beginning to initiate the civil rights movement that flowed out of an urban political theology well developed in black Baptist and Methodist circles. King, like the rest of the nation, was shocked by the brutal murder of young Emmett Till. Till was a member of Roberts Temple Church of God in Christ, and Ford was invited by the family to preside over the funeral. Photographs that recorded the event captured Ford comforting Till's mother. His public presence in the civil rights arena made space for other black Pentecostal clergy who seemed more inclined to ignore rather than engage "worldly" political realities.

Whereas King represented a prophetic challenge to the political status quo, Ford's outlook was more accommodating. Ford believed that more economic goods and jobs could be attained by working with the establishment. Now that many of America's largest cities have black mayors who depend upon the black church for support, Ford's political style seems to be well suited for the times. During the 1970s and 1980s, this boss-client approach to politics and ministry had been rejected by younger, more progressive clergy in COGIC and elsewhere, in part because it placed black leaders in the humiliating posture of cutting unattractive deals with white ethnic politicians. Even then, Ford maintained that as long as there is a legitimate city government, religious communities need to be able to deal with it in a productive manner. When King came to Chicago in order to

focus national attention on residential hyper-segregation and discriminatory housing practices, Ford was among the clergy who supported the goal
of open housing but opposed the presence of a young outsider seeking to
lead the Chicago movement.

In later years, Ford endeared himself to Mayor Richard Daley Sr. and
became one of Daley's race relations advisors and power brokers. He par-
layed city hall connections into access to National Democratic Party leaders.
His photo collection contains pictures of him with President Lyndon Johnson, several senators, governors, and celebrities. Although most church
members were not ready to embrace the secular city with Ford's gusto,
because of his profound and unquestioned loyalty to Bishop Mason they
tolerated his enthusiasm for civic affairs and his attraction to the good life.

Even while ascending the ladder of political power in the church
(elected to the executive board of twelve bishops after Mason's death), he
remained active in Chicago electoral politics and in civil rights movement
activities, becoming an Executive Committee member of the NAACP in
1966. During these years, Ford was responsible for the Civic Night programs
at the Holy Convocation in Memphis. Each year, a significant national
politician addressed the delegates. This platform worked in both directions.
The civic status of COGIC delegates was validated by a worldly VIP, and
the politicians were brought face to face with tens of thousands of potential
supporters. Politicians always got the message; the Church of God in Christ
constituted a noteworthy voting bloc. Bishop Ford deserves credit for this
well-choreographed performance, although he was criticized for permitting
politicians of questionable repute to occupy the sacred pulpit at the Holy
Convocation. Many people believed that he needed to be reminded that it
was a *holy* meeting. But it is precisely Ford's understanding of the civic,
public realm as a religiously significant arena that places him in a unique
category relative to most other COGIC leaders.

Ford's public theology is eclectic and situational. He draws from a
vast diversity of sources for developing warrants for urban, public ministry.
He has been known to quote Roman Catholic bishops and successful entrepreneurs, his favorite being Mr. Marriott of hotel chain notoriety. Anyone
who is working to inspire and uplift humanity is a friend to the Christian
cause. His pragmatic action plans are calculated to maximize whatever good
can be achieved in the immediate situation. Broad principles and long-
range goals seem to be secondary to achieving immediate results.

Ford's principal contribution to our discussion on urban ministry lies
in the skill with which he maintained practices designed to humanize urban
life, while politicizing a growing denomination through consciousness rais-

ing at national meetings, and providing a concrete model of political urban ministry. He has helped to broaden the black Pentecostal tradition's view of ministry in the city from direct acts of charity to infusing the arena of public policy-making with a humanizing, moral perspective.

Bishop Ford has always understood the city to be a place filled with opportunities for God's redemptive action. He refers to Jesus' time in Jerusalem as an example of a holy man who was not afraid of city realities. He practices Paul's injunctions to pray for those in political authority, and dismisses world-rejecting theology as an heretical, selfish escape from serious public engagement.

St. Paul Church is located in the shadow of the largest housing project in the world, the Robert Taylor Homes. Ford has seized upon this fact by designing a vast array of programs to minister to the 160,000 residents of the homes. Although he sold Chicago's oldest house back to the city for a handsome profit, the Breakfast Club continues. The congregation operates the Chaney Ford Day Care Center (named in honor of his mother), is constructing a Senior Citizen Home Complex, and has an enormous kitchen that serves free meals and distributes free clothing to anyone in need. For six years, Ford was a commissioner for the Cook County Department of Corrections. He was instrumental in having dilapidated prison facilities demolished and rebuilt, and initiating educational programs for offenders. Also, he conducted annual Christmas Day services, delivering home-cooked soul food to several hundred female inmates. His connections to city and county government also provide him with access to numerous jobs usually filled by college students during the summer. With these he rewards personal sacrifice and affirms the value of higher education.

Bishop Ford's leadership style has been characterized as authoritarian and aggressive, more suited to behind-the-scenes, heavy political action than delicate, diplomatic public governance. From 1976 until 1989, he was Bishop Patterson's assistant and received high marks for his vice presidential performance. But he declares that he is destined to occupy the office of presiding bishop, so it remains to be seen how he will make the transition to denominational spokesperson and institutional symbol.

IV. Conclusion

Now that we have examined the history, vision of urban ministry, and most influential representative of the Church of God in Christ, what may others learn about ministry in the city?

94

The COGIC story reminds us that black people who migrated to the cities were economically poor but spiritually rich. It was precisely this alternative culture and community that reinforced their sense of dignity, beauty, creativity, and collective power in the midst of racism, classism, sexism, and other forms of oppression. Urban ministry in the future must take seriously how human selves may be affirmed and sustained amidst the assaults of impersonalism, individualism, and materialism. The COGIC story is a story of humanizing modern city life through spiritual renewal, economic empowerment, cultural preservation, collective resistance, and existential celebration.

In my judgment, one of the downsides of COGIC's approach to urban ministry is that it assumes widespread familiarity with the language and symbols of evangelical Christianity. Many preachers and parishioners assume that ministry consists in proclaiming the gospel in traditional terms, and when people fail to respond, they restate the message at twice the volume. Too little attention is given to the difficult work of reinterpretation and adaptation to modern sensibilities, especially the domination of consciousness by television-induced consumer desires.

Religious pluralism is the new reality that will be the context of future ministry in the city.[22] This represents a new challenge for black churches that have exercised almost hegemonic influence on the symbolic life of the community. Now, there are thirty-year-old grandmothers who have never been to church and are not products of the wisdom tradition of black church culture. There are alienated young men who know nothing meaningful about the Exodus motif or the symbols of the cross, resurrection, communion, and baptism. The church must now seek to *reconstitute a shared symbolic life for a diverse community* in ways that respect nonconformity with the Christian tradition. One place to begin is to reflect upon our common plight as human beings who struggle with what the philosopher Cornel West has characterized as the existential challenges of death, despair, depression, and dread.[23] Then, churches should seek to offer Christian interpretations of that plight and possibilities for thriving within and beyond it. I am persuaded that a theology of reconciliation that emphasizes God's irreversible covenant with humanity is a promising hermeneutical beginning.

Through its urban emphasis upon lively, contagious worship and

22. Lincoln and Mamiya discuss this in terms of the challenge of Islam for the future of black church ministries.

23. Cornel West, *Prophesy Deliverance* (Philadelphia: Westminster Press, 1982).

deliverance-oriented evangelism, the Church of God in Christ illustrates the urban genius of black church culture. Despite the enormous challenges faced by all Christian churches in the city, the spirituality and ministry of the Church of God in Christ remind us that the liberating power of Christ can transform the present hopelessness in our inner cities. As the Church of God in Christ marches ahead hopefully, one hears the voice of Bishop Mason singing, "My soul says yes, yes, yes, to my Lord."

Seeking to Hear and to Heed in the Cities: Urban Ministry in the Postwar Episcopal Church

NORMAN FARAMELLI, EDWARD RODMAN,
AND ANNE SCHEIBNER

I. Introduction

Addressing a topic as elusive and broad as urban ministry in a denomination as complex and diverse as the Episcopal Church is a task to approach with much fear and trembling.[1] Certainly the last fifty years have seen a wide variety of responses, pilot projects, and new initiatives on all three levels of our corporate life, that is, congregational, diocesan, and national. Our task is to explore this rich history by decade, attempting in the process to encompass highlights from each of these levels of ministry. In addition, we will highlight individuals and groups who were instrumental in advocating for urban ministry at critical times during this period.

Several preliminary observations may be helpful in order to appreciate the unique context that the Episcopal Church provides for the development and implementation of major social ministry. Because we are a sacramental church, form and symbol have particular meaning. Thus, concepts such as pilot projects often have more significance than they might in some denominations. Similarly, our penchant for "decency and order,"

---

1. This chapter is dedicated to the memory of the late Joseph Pelham, who served as executive director of the Episcopal City Mission in Boston for over ten years.

combined with our hierarchical structure, gives particular importance to the national church programs. Supporting such projects has consistently provided the focus for advocates of urban ministry when seeking both legitimation and funding from the national church.

At the same time, the vast majority of resources needed to carry out any ministry in our church is to be found at the congregational level. In the case of urban ministry, this is especially true because of the varied circumstances that different cities provide for urban ministry. This has profound implications since it is the diocesan structure that mediates these resources, normally through annual diocesan conventions. Urban ministry is therefore in a vulnerable position, since most large cities are in dioceses controlled by wealthy suburban churches. For us, the concept of "the suburban captivity of the church" has real meaning and consequences. A diocesan power structure dominated by white suburban churches reveals why race and class are such critical determinants of attitudes and priorities of the overall church system. This factor, probably more than any other, gives greater importance to efforts aimed at national recognition for urban ministry.

Any view of this period must also take into account the profound impact of the civil rights movement, urban unrest, the emergence of the counterculture, and the greater availability and use of controlled substances (drugs). Certainly, within our denomination the urban church has been the constant battleground between those who wish to engage these issues and seek societal remedies, and those who prefer to ignore them and keep things the way they were. Indeed, many of our urban churches have become white elephants, as declining membership, changing demographic patterns, and urban violence have negatively affected center-city parishes. At the same time, a resurgence of ethnically oriented ministries and creative responses to these challenges have spelled renewal for other parishes. As we approach the end of this century, the jury is still out on whether the Episcopal Church has a promising future in urban ministry.

One final set of preliminary observations needs to be made regarding urban ministry in the Episcopal Church. The image of the Episcopal Church historically has been that of the Tory/Republican Party at prayer. In many instances the image has been and remains true. But it is important to note that in most of our large urban centers, especially on the East Coast and in the Midwest, blue-collar and ethnic congregations have always been numerous. Indeed, the class consciousness of the nineteenth century became the church planning strategy for many urban areas and, when coupled with the Anglican concept of parish as a geographical entity, led to the proliferation of congregations without any policy to maintain them.

Simply put, most large urban churches were built by wealthy merchants, bankers, etc., who were the proprietors of the church. This was usually exemplified by the purchasing of pews, which provided both the capital to construct these great buildings and also the endowments to maintain them in their later years as the original founders passed on. These same people also built "chapels" in the working-class neighborhoods so that the blue-collar congregants would not have to rub shoulders with their managers. The existence of these buildings provided a convenient focus for ethnic and racial segregation of urban churches as the populations in these working-class neighborhoods changed. Unlike their downtown counterparts, these chapels were not provided for in perpetuity by the original benefactors, and the American Episcopal Church abandoned the notion of parish as a geographical entity, because private resources were not sufficient to support an establishment mentality and were antithetical to the separation of church and state as it came to be understood in this country. Thus, any discussion of urban ministry that does not acknowledge issues of deferred maintenance, capital expenses, and alternative uses of church buildings is not realistic. These are the bottom-line issues that many of our congregations have been facing for the past several decades.

In what follows, then, we will attempt to explore the interrelationship of these various factors in the chronicle of urban ministry within the Episcopal Church over the past four decades. We assume full responsibility for the contents, and only hope that the picture we paint is as broad and colorful as the reality it depicts.

II. Historical Sketch

The religious boom in the period following World War II occurred when the character of American metropolitan areas was dramatically changing. First, there was migration of large numbers of blacks from the rural South to the urban North. This was true when the cities seemed to offer greater opportunities, while southern farms were becoming mechanized.

In the 1940s, the Episcopal Church recognized the importance of work in race relations by establishing a national staff position to oversee its development. Rev. Tollie Caution, a black clergyman and prominent rector from Philadelphia, was the longest-tenured and best-known incumbent in this position. Fr. Caution's role was to work with the black congregations. His office provided a voice for black congregations, and had the effect of creating a central jurisdiction for the black parishes.

While trends toward suburbanization did not begin in the late 1940s and 1950s, they were clearly accelerated during that period. The booming suburbs grew in part because of the use of massive amounts of federal funds for both housing and highways. Housing mortgages enabled many people to purchase their first homes, particularly in the new suburbs. Extensive highway construction connected the cities to outlying areas in new ways.

1. The 1950s

Throughout the 1950s, the distinguishing feature of the church was not urban ministry but the suburbanization of the church, with a corresponding abandonment of the city by white Episcopalians — especially in large inner-city areas. While Episcopalians moved to the suburbs in large numbers, suburbs were seen to be the wave of the future — offering single-family dwelling units on a plot of ground with a yard — a great place to raise the children! Suburbs were also places where white people with similar incomes could live with others of the same race, since the suburbs were seldom integrated racially.

In the 1950s, the new model for the local congregation was identified with the characteristics of the suburban congregation. The suburban parishes were numbers oriented — number of parishioners, number of children in church school, number of new churches constructed, and so on; in contrast, many urban parishes — especially in the city neighborhoods — were struggling with declining memberships. Many urban congregations longed for the good old days when the pews were full and the church school was filled with children.

The ethos of the church as a whole was clearly suburban — the yardstick for successful ministries and successful parishes was suburban. For young clergy, the path to successful ministries was to build and develop one of those growing suburban congregations. Even the educational program materials that were innovative (such as the Seabury Series) were clearly suburban in orientation and did not respond to the needs of people in urban parishes, nor to the needs of many new, unchurched residents of the city. This period was captured vividly by Gibson Winter's book *The Suburban Captivity of the Churches*.[2]

2. Gibson Winter, *The Suburban Captivity of the Churches* (New York: Macmillan, 1962).

The urban churches in the Northeast and Midwest began to feel the impact of southern blacks. The Episcopal Church experienced a double dose of immigration with the advent of growing numbers of West Indians, especially in eastern cities. This led to the transition from white to black congregations in many urban parishes that augmented the presence of the historic black congregations that dated back to the Revolutionary War.

While ethnic ministry within the Episcopal Church has increasingly gained acceptance during the period under review, urban ministry has been traditionally linked with black ministry. The recent emergence of Hispanics and Asians in large numbers indicates an important role for various ethnically based congregations in the future. But it has been the black church that has historically chosen to remain in the city. There are four kinds of black churches that continue to exist to this day, and each has played a role on the urban scene.

The Historic Black Church. As a result of the attempt to segregate the free black members of Saint George's Methodist Church in Philadelphia, Richard Allen and Absalom Jones refused to submit to this indignity and led the other free blacks out of the church. They formed the "Free African Society," which did many good works in that community, especially during the yellow fever epidemic. Besides creating a burial society and founding the second lodge of the order of Prince Hall Masons, Allen and Jones founded the Saint Thomas' African Episcopal Church. While both men favored affiliating with the Methodists, the majority of members desired to affiliate with the Episcopal Church. Jones acceded to the wishes of the majority and facilitated the affiliation with the Episcopal Diocese of Pennsylvania, under the name Saint Thomas' African Episcopal Church. Richard Allen, though supporting the efforts of Saint Thomas', chose to found Bethel African Methodist Episcopal Church, and became the first bishop of the new denomination. Jones was ordained deacon, and later priest in the Episcopal Church, but because the congregation was determined that Jones serve as their rector, they had to forgo participation in the diocesan convention for many years.[3] As a result of these events, throughout the nineteenth century these historic churches emerged in urban centers where free blacks had developed large communities. Among Episcopalians these would include Saint Philip's Church, Harlem, and Saint James', Baltimore.

Historic Black Missions. While the former category of parishes were noted for their independent status, and therefore freedom to innovate and

---

3. See George Freeman Bragg, *History of the Afro-American Group of the Episcopal Church* (1922; reprint, New York: Johnson Reprints, 1968), pp. 47ff.

protest, a larger number of black congregations, particularly in the South and the Midwest, were creations of the diocese. This put them under the direct control of the bishop with respect both to budget and choice of clerical leadership. Unfortunately, this model of dependency has been perpetuated in both rural and small-town areas to this day. Often these missions have had white clergy who have been unable to provide the leadership in the community that is expected from the black church. It is also fair to say that this ready-made model of dependency and therefore control has been offered to many Hispanic and Asian American congregations in their formative stages.

Post–World War II West Indian Parishes. Throughout the Northeast and Florida, and scattered about other parts of the country, the post–World War II migration of West Indians has had a profound impact on the Episcopal Church in many urban areas. Indeed, it is calculated that nearly a third of the black congregations and clergy in the United States are rooted in this influx of ready-made Anglicans. Most of the fast-growing black parishes owe their success to this reality. Following the traditional model of the church as a cultural womb for new immigrants, these parishes have assumed their rightful place in the front lines of urban ministry.

Cross-Cultural Parishes. This is the new term for former white parishes that have gone through a membership transformation brought on by changing demographics, but that managed to stabilize with a combination of white, black, Hispanic, or other minorities in some kind of balance. While the majority of neighborhood churches experienced the phenomenon of "white flight" and simply went from white to black, these notable exceptions have been beacons of hope for the vision of racially diverse parishes. Some of these were St. Stephen's, Boston; St. Stephen's and the Incarnation, Washington, D.C.; St. Paul's, New Haven; St. Mark's in the Bowery, New York; and Trinity, Chicago.

During this religious boom the city was not totally forgotten. In the Episcopal Church there were some major urban ministry efforts in the 1950s. In fact, many of the models on the local congregational level occurred before there was widespread activity on the national level. New styles and new energy for urban ministry were displayed by people such as Rev. Kilmer Myers working with the gangs on the Lower East Side of New York City; Rev. Paul Moore and Jenny Moore in Jersey City, New Jersey; the work in Harlem, Roxbury in Boston, San Francisco, East Los Angeles, Watts, and other cities.[4] This was a time when upper middle-class white clergy lived and worked for a period of their careers in poor neighborhoods. Unfor-

---

4. See E. Paul Moore Jr., *The Church Reclaims the City* (New York: Seabury, 1964); C. Kilmer Myers, *Light the Dark Streets* (New York: Seabury, 1957).

tunately, many of the efforts were the exceptions and not the norm in urban parishes. In each case the work was done under charismatic leadership, which often proved difficult to sustain after the departure of the leader.

On the whole these efforts were not widely supported by national programs. Nevertheless, some national staff people, such as Rev. Tollie Caution and Rev. Paul Musselman, held up the need for urban work and tried to refocus the church on city issues during the time of the suburban boom.[5]

Where there was involvement in urban issues, the focus was primarily on presence and service — the institutional and racial components of urban ministry were just beginning to be understood. The dimensions of class were slow to be recognized in the Episcopal Church, but it was clear that there was a new awareness of the extent of poverty in both urban and rural areas.

2. The 1960s

The 1960s were a time of optimism and vision. Unlike the 1950s, there was less social complacency. Racial justice was more of an issue and there was a mood that things could be changed. The Kennedy years led to the call to service for the country in the Peace Corps, VISTA, and other areas, as well as a new awareness of the civil rights struggle. Harvey Cox's *The Secular City*[6] offered a new metaphor of the promise of the city, and captured the spirit of the sixties. The city was seen by many as a place of hope and possibility. Michael Harrington's *The Other America*[7] documented the extent of rural and urban poverty. And the links between poverty and race were becoming clearer.

At first the Episcopal Church, with the exception of many of the black congregations, was not heavily involved in the civil rights struggle, but specific individuals were. The Episcopal Society for Racial and Cultural Unity (ESCRU), founded by two white clergymen — Cornelius Tarplee of the national staff and John Morris, a southern pastor — helped prod the church to become engaged in the struggle for racial justice. Through national staff, the issue of racial justice began to surface and be addressed. ESCRU was one of the first groups to question and challenge national church policy on important social issues. It became clear in the 1960s that the issues of race and racial justice were critical for any commitment to urban ministry in U.S. cities.

5. G. Paul Musselman, *The Church on the Urban Frontier* (New York: Seabury, 1960).
6. Harvey Cox, *The Secular City* (New York: Macmillan, 1965).
7. Subtitled *Poverty in the United States,* it was published by Macmillan in 1963.

At the 1961 General Convention, the rectors of large city parishes and deans of some of the urban cathedrals promoted an effort on urban mission, a program that was to be jointly undertaken by all departments of the Executive Council. This group became known as the Church and City Conference. It began with some white rectors and cathedral deans such as Revs. John Heuss (Trinity, New York City), Paul Moore (Christ Church Cathedral, Indianapolis), Kilmer Myers (Intercession Chapel, New York City); it later became more inclusive with the addition of black clergy such as Nathan Wright (Boston, then Newark), Joseph Nicholson (St. Louis), St. Julian Simpkins (Rochester, New York), Van Samuel Bird and Jesse Anderson Sr. (Philadelphia), and Moran Weston (Harlem, New York City). Two observations need to be made about these early years: first, the cathedral church or the large downtown church building emerged as a significant center for urban presence; second, some of the deans of these cathedrals later became prominent bishops in the Episcopal Church.

From 1961 to 1964, under the leadership of Rev. Jim Morton, and later Rev. Jack Woodard, the national church undertook the Joint Urban Program, which had three major components. The first was raising the consciousness of the church to urban issues through conferences referred to as "Metabagdad." "Metabagdad" was a symbol of the growing metropolitan areas — cities and suburbs throughout the United States. These conferences represented a major effort of the national church to shift the consciousness of the entire church, and introduced many to people who were engaged in exciting forms of urban ministry, such as Rev. Robert Castle from Jersey City. "Metabagdad" conferences recruited persons with city planning and social-science skills, such as Dr. Perry Norton of New York University, to address urban issues.

The conferences also focused on the need to divide metropolitan dioceses into pie-shaped slices, so each subregion could have a mixture of suburban and urban parishes to engage more effectively the metropolitan realities on a shared basis.

The second component of the Joint Urban Program was the designation of twelve dioceses to serve as "pilot dioceses." The hope was that these dioceses would serve as replicable models for the rest of the church.

The third component was the development of training programs for urban ministry, the best known of which was the Urban Training Center for Christian Mission in Chicago.[8]

The ambitions of the Joint Urban Program might have seemed gran-

8. See "Report of the Standing Commission on the Church in Metropolitan Areas," *The Blue Book of the General Convention*, 1982, pp. 168-74.

diose, but this program exposed many people to the social and economic issues in urban-industrialized society, which was a major departure for a pastorally centered church. The program was useful, but it was limited, even though it was a major effort to shift the church's view of the urban arena. During that time there were local models (Boston, Jersey City, New York), and some were supported by the national church while others were highlighted and publicized by the national church and shared with others.

The 1960s saw the development of the industrial mission network in the United States, first patterned after the models in England spearheaded by Rev. E. R. Wickham. The industrial mission movement grew to address a range of issues in urban-industrial society, such as problems in the workplace and the influence of economic institutions in shaping society. The Episcopal Church played a major role in the development of the network via the leadership of Rev. Hugh White in Detroit, Rev. Scott Paradise, and others who staffed the industrial missions.[9] Industrial mission posed a challenge to the church to engage in areas of ministry that were not accessible to the parish structure. Although it had its exciting moments and did some excellent work in highlighting some issues of economic justice, industrial mission did little to shift the focus of the church to new forms of ministry. Industrial mission came to America in the late fifties, flourished in the sixties, and began to phase out in the seventies.

At the 1964 General Convention several decisions were made that had a significant bearing on urban ministry. Bishop John Hines was elected as presiding bishop, replacing Bishop Arthur Lichtenberger. Bishop Hines was to be a surprise. It was not expected that a bishop from West Texas would become a crusader for racial and urban justice. The convention also voted to continue the Joint Urban Program as a top priority. In 1964 the Episcopal Church Women (ECW) voted to dedicate substantial funding from the United Thank Offering to the urban program. These monies were used to support experimental urban ministries as well as a new publication, *Church in Metropolis*. This was just one of the many examples where the ECW empowered program initiatives and provided a lead for the general convention. This ECW leadership pattern has continued, even though women, since 1970, are now also a major force in the deputations to the general convention itself.

9. Hugh C. White, "Detroit Industrial Mission Faces the World of Work," *Witness* (Ambler, Pa.) 46, no. 25 (August 20, 1959): 7-11; Hugh C. White and Robert C. Batchelder, "Mission to Metropolis," *International Review of Missions* 54, no. 214 (April 1965): 161-72; Scott I. Paradise, *Detroit Industrial Mission: A Personal Narrative* (New York: Harper and Row, 1963).

The Episcopal Church also participated with other denominations in the development of the Urban Training Center in Chicago and played a major role in its evolution. The activity on the national level was reassuring to many working in local urban congregations, even if it often seemed remote.

The national church became increasingly supportive of the civil rights struggles. Through the efforts of Rev. Arthur Walmsley in the Division of Christian Citizenship, the national church began to support individuals and organizations that were fighting racial segregation; it provided finances, technical support, educational resources, and moral support. With the passage of the Civil Rights Act of 1964 and the Voting Rights Act in 1965 the future looked promising. Racism, however, turned out to be much deeper and much more pernicious than many had thought. Racism was embodied in the fabric of white-controlled institutions and functioned automatically, even without malicious intent.

Despite the progress on the legislative front, there was much despair and anger in many of the black communities throughout the nation. Hence, the sixties became a time of urban unrest, uprisings, and burning cities. It was clear that the right to vote had to be coupled with the need to have something to vote for. It was a time of confusion as the nation moved from the "Negro problem" to white racism. Even the widely heralded "Kerner Report" in 1968, although identifying "white racism" as the basic problem affecting our society (one of the first times it was diagnosed that way), proceeded to list a variety of things that the black community should do, instead of looking at what white-controlled institutions needed to do.[10]

Amidst the urban crisis, Presiding Bishop John Hines convened a special task force in 1967 to develop an appropriate response. This turned out to be a major effort in community empowerment. The presiding bishop wanted the church to stand beside and support "the dispossessed and oppressed people of this country for the healing of our national life."[11] The result was the General Convention Special Program (GCSP). According to Hines, GCSP was to "bring people in ghettos into areas of decision-making by which their destiny is influenced. It will determine the use of political and economic power to support justice and self-determination for all." GCSP was to accomplish this by providing skilled personnel assistance and making relatively large sums of money available to community organizations involved in the improvement of depressed urban areas. It was an exciting and bold venture.

10. Commission on Disorders in American Cities, 1969.
11. "Address to the General Convention," *Journal of the General Convention*, 1967.

In the urban ministry models referred to previously there was a common thread — leadership in the community and standing up in an advocacy role for issues of social justice. Most of the church programs developed at the national level were designed to provide programmatic support to this type of urban and ethnic ministry. The one exception was GCSP, which chose to ignore and bypass this important segment of the church's life.

Conceived by Bishop Hines as a bold new initiative in response to urban unrest, GCSP was doomed to fail from its inception, primarily because it interpreted the important concept of community empowerment in a narrow ideological context. Rather than exploring the wide variety of community-based initiatives that flowered in the late 1960s, such as the founding of the Freedom National Bank in Harlem, GCSP chose to champion black nationalism as the only valid organizing principle. Not only was this foreign to most of the black churches who still embraced integration and equality as important goals; it was anathema to the broader church, who could not understand its ideology and linked it with the rhetoric of Malcolm X.

The Spike Lee movie *Malcolm X* ended with his assassination and the founding of the African American Unity organization. That group quickly splintered with Malcolm's demise, and many organizations, most of them local or grass-roots, espoused their own versions of Malcolm's original idea of pro-blackness as distinct from anti-whiteness. This subtle distinction was lost on the majority population and, when coupled with the continued rhetoric that suggested that violent confrontation was an acceptable strategy, provided ample concern that these groups could not be trusted, and should by no means be given legitimacy, especially through church grants. The most notable example of this phenomenon was the Black Manifesto promulgated by Jim Forman and the Black Economic Development Committee. It was this group that seized the microphone at the 1969 Special General Convention of the Episcopal Church and created a yearlong debate about whether the church should respond to the demand for reparations. This entire episode came to a climax at the regular general convention in Houston in 1970, at the same time as the aforementioned fears regarding the grant-making strategy of GCSP were reaching their full force.

Another reason GCSP never gained acceptance was that it failed to utilize its high visibility and familiarity with the turbulent inner city as an educational and interpretive vehicle for the rest of the church and society. This self-imposed isolation insured that no broad-based constituency of support would be developed. Finally, by choosing to fund perceived radical groups, often over the objection of the local diocesan bishop, GCSP generated many enemies in high places. (Since there was a desire not to have grants to community groups vetoed by some bishops, the approval of the diocesan bishop was not required for making GCSP grants in the diocese.) Thus, GCSP bypassed the dioceses and the local congregations. To some advocates of empowerment on the GCSP model, the diocese and local congregations were not solutions but impediments to the urban crisis. This effort also intentionally ignored the black Episcopal Church and its leadership, and proved to be the occasion for the termination of Dr. Caution and his office, as the mood seemed to turn away from the local congregation and the black church and toward community empowerment and black consciousness.

These events precipitated a serious reaction from many leading black clergy, including Bishop Burgess of Massachusetts, and culminated in a major personal confrontation with Bishop Hines. This group gained no satisfaction from their protest and in turn issued the call that led to the formation of the Union of Black Clergy and Laity (UBCL) in Raleigh, North Carolina, in 1968. The UBCL, which became the Union of Black Episcopalians (UBE), burst upon the national church scene at the Special Convention at Notre Dame in 1969, where the church was confronted with the Black Manifesto and the issue of "reparations." Over the years, UBE has served as a conscience to the church on matters of race and urban ministry.

At the 1969 General Convention GCSP was the major item of business. Although the church supported it, there were signs of tension and strain. Even some of its proponents were concerned about strengthening it by utilizing the learnings from the Joint Urban Program, and the necessity of including the church on the diocesan and local levels, which clearly did not happen in the GCSP program.[12]

There was a severe backlash against GCSP, but it was not accompanied by new efforts and models of urban ministry. The trend toward further suburbanization of the church continued. The ethos of the church remained clearly suburban. Despite the mood of the times and the furor that enveloped some parishes, many congregations in both the suburbs and the cities were not dramatically affected by the events of the 1960s.

12. See Robert E. Hood, *Social Teachings in the Episcopal Church: A Source Book* (Wilton, Conn.: Morehouse Publishing, 1990), pp. 120-33, for a discussion of the GCSP.

3. The 1970s

Many of the supporters of the GCSP effort were surprised to see a dramatic shift from a focus on civil rights and racial justice to black cultural nationalism. The slogan "black power" shocked the church, which never understood it. Because of the opposition to GCSP and due to a limitation of resources, the 1970 convention in Houston severely limited the GCSP funding. This convention also voted a 50 percent reduction in the national staff. GCSP funding was terminated in 1973, officially ended by the general convention in Louisville.

At Louisville, a new presiding bishop was also elected when Bishop John Allin of Mississippi succeeded Bishop Hines. Bishop Allin was in many ways the antithesis of John Hines, since he was the most conservative of the candidates who were nominated. This election occurred at the same time that the ordination of women was narrowly rejected by the convention.

One of Bishop Allin's first charges, after consultation with the Union of Black Episcopalians and others, was to establish a special committee to plan for new outreach ministries. This committee, chaired by Bishop Moore and Dr. Charles Lawrence, recommended the establishment of the ethnic desks and the formation of a new body that later became known as the Coalition for Human Needs (CHN). CHN was really a substitute for GCSP as a way to address ethnic diversity and community development. Over the years CHN has been able to address many of the community empowerment issues that were part of the original GCSP program, but it is much lower key and has had improved lines of accountability to the bishops of the dioceses. For example, no CHN grant can be administered in a region over the objections of the bishop. Over the past fifteen years CHN has been making annual grants totalling $500,000 to $1 million.

During the 1970s some of the exciting urban ministries begun in the fifties and sixties continued. The work of Rev. Paul Washington at the Church of the Advocate in North Philadelphia is one example. Fr. Washington was well known throughout the church for his staunch commitment to the gospel and his keen pastoral sensitivities. He embodied a sense of the new black consciousness but always functioned effectively with all kinds of people, and served as a model of leadership in the church and society; he was particularly effective in influencing the power structures of Philadelphia. Washington in many ways established a "climate of opinion" about the role of the church in the inner city. The Church of the Advocate has been truly a beacon in Philadelphia and to the wider church.

In the late 1960s and in the 1970s, the war in Vietnam and the emphasis on women's ordination siphoned off human resources and energy from urban ministry. But it would be inaccurate to say that the lack of interest in urban ministry was primarily the result of antiwar and women's ordination efforts. It was also during the 1970s that one could see new trends of gentrification in the cities as white people began to move back just at the time when, in some cities, middle-class blacks began moving to suburban areas.

During the early 1970s the Episcopal Church was preoccupied with the women's ordination issue. The defeat of women's ordination at the Louisville convention in 1973 soon led to the irregular ordination of eleven white women priests hosted by Rev. Paul Washington and the Church of the Advocate in North Philadelphia in July 1974. The Church of the Advocate remains a magnificent structure in the middle of a deteriorating neighborhood. The symbolism of that ordination in that place was significant as the issues of racial, economic, and gender justice were joined at least momentarily. Women's ordination was finally approved at the general convention in Minneapolis in 1976.

The election of Bishop John Allin in 1973 was the sign of a major symbolic and programmatic shift in the national church's commitments. By 1976 the need for a focus and a locus for those involved in justice ministries was painfully clear. Bishop Allin in turn saw the church as divided by the social action initiatives of the Hines era, and by the internal battles over the Prayer Book revisions and women's ordination. He drew the analogy between these issues and the divisions in the first-century church over issues such as the mission to the Gentiles and whether baptized males could remain uncircumcised. Unity then was symbolized by sending money for famine relief to Jerusalem for distribution.

At the 1976 convention Bishop Allin called for a major $100-million capital funds campaign to be administered by the national church. The focus of this campaign, called Venture in Mission (VIM), was to be on overseas mission work. The unspoken assumption was that the need for mission activity was not in the United States but abroad. The idea of having major funds raised in their dioceses for such an effort was not a happy one to many bishops, especially those from dioceses with major urban centers.

At the Minneapolis convention, Bishop John Walker of Washington, D.C., convened a group of urban bishops, many of whom were active in the Church and City Conference. The group became known as the Urban Bishops Coalition (UBC). The coalition's intention was to refocus the church's agenda on the pressing needs of the cities. How could the issues of urban ministry best be brought to light? The coalition initiated two major activities during the next three years, each of which had immediate impact. The first was a series of urban hearings in seven selected North American cities, with an additional hearing in Colon, Panama, and a national hearing in Washington, D.C., which culminated the process. The result was the publication *To Hear and to Heed,* a compilation of the findings elicited by the hearings, authored by Rev. Joseph Pelham, a black clergyman who was then dean of students at Bexley Hall, Colgate Rochester Seminary. Some of the themes that were expressed are worth noting:

> . . . we must decide that we will be for the poor. We must decide to act in such a way that will dispel the widely held perception of the church as the chaplaincy service to the Establishment. This will mean "taking sides" and in that sense, ceasing to attempt to be all things to all people. . . .
>
> . . . we must make a commitment to a struggle which has no foreseeable end. This requires deciding in favor of staying power against faddism. It means a willingness on the part of the church to stay in the cities and to engage in what Gibson Winter referred to as a "pilgrimage" rather than a "crusade."[13]

By 1978, partly due to the urban hearing process, the bishops had regained control of the Venture in Mission program. Portions of the money raised were indeed sent to New York headquarters for distribution, but the decision making and the bulk of the money remained in the dioceses. Since the total monies raised exceeded the $100-million goal, the presiding bishop also saved face. The UBC failed to adopt a major recommendation in the Pelham draft that stated that no major fund-raising be done until the church had come to grips with perhaps the major finding of the hearings, namely, that people on the front lines in the cities were not asking for money or new programs but for a commitment that the church would stay and be a presence in their struggle for dignity and life. The opportunity to shape a fund-raising effort in response to such a discernment process was lost.

Another initial effort of the coalition was a series of educational events know as the North-South Institutes. These seminars brought together experts from a variety of fields to discuss the shape of the social, political, and economic forces at work in the world. A basic assumption of these sessions was that the East-West split known as the Cold War was being replaced by a North-South split in which the industrialized nations of the Northern Hemi-

---

13. *To Hear and to Heed: The Episcopal Church Listens and Acts in the City* (Cincinnati: Forward Movement Publications, 1978), p. 51.

sphere would struggle jointly for continued dominance over the emerging nations of the Southern Hemisphere. This effort led to the publication of the Urban Bishops Pastoral letter on the state of the economy on Labor Day 1979 (publicized in the *New York Times*) and served as the call to the ecumenical community to take seriously the issues of poverty, race, and class.

The urban hearings in turn led to the formation of the Episcopal Urban Caucus (EUC). In February 1980 the EUC emerged on the national church scene as the logical synthesis of its parent organizations, the Church and City Conference and the UBC. Emerging as it did in the sixth year of the twelve-year term of incumbent Presiding Bishop John Allin, EUC was many things to many people. The initial assembly, held in Indianapolis, was organized by Rev. Hugh White and Rev. Natlia Beck, with help from the seconded staff of the UBC, which was fresh from the urban hearings process and the first North-South Institute.

At its inception, the caucus combined several strands of unhappiness and a sense of alienation from the national church that had gradually developed during Allin's tenure. The more than six hundred people who attended its first meeting included:

1. Those who felt a need for an interracial and culturally diverse forum for interaction on a wide range of social issues and practical urban ministry concerns. The EUC filled a void that had been felt ever since ESCRU's demise a decade earlier.
2. Those who felt disaffected with the slow pace of change in the church, e.g., on issues like inclusive language, liturgical reform, clergy deployment, and the institutional church in general.
3. Those who brought a keen interest in a particular social policy issue such as nuclear war, economic justice, the energy crisis, and gentrification, and who felt that the institutional structures were not responsive either educationally or programmatically to their concerns.
4. Those participants in the urban hearings who were anxious to see what the follow-up would be to the issues raised in *To Hear and to Heed*.
5. Recipients of the church's social ministry who were specifically recruited so that the voices of the poor and the marginalized would be present and participating.

Needless to say, such a diverse gathering was unable to define a single focus and chose to try to do it all. In retrospect, the fact that this organization has been able to achieve a significant number of changes in the church's programmatic emphasis is a minor miracle, given its diffuse and trendy constituency. It did, however, produce several publications that expressed concerns of different parts of the diverse constituency, such as those pieces on nuclear war and parish revitalization.

The caucus meets annually, and its membership and range of interests have changed over time. Not only did the first assembly focus on the poor and the oppressed, it also touched a wide range of issues related to urban-industrial society such as the arms race, ecology, energy, gentrification, reindustrialization, economic justice, and the revitalization of urban parishes. In the earlier assemblies, the focus was as grandiose as building a national church movement in parallel to the national church. Later it became clear that the caucus should be a prod to the national church. As the years have progressed, the caucus has focused largely on the issues of race and poverty, which were defined by Bishop Burgess at one of the earlier gatherings as the twin issues in urban America. The caucus has also kept its focus on the revitalization of urban parishes.

Today the caucus stands as a major national vehicle, especially for minorities, to voice concerns about the urban church, the use of national church resources, and how the gospel is proclaimed in an urban setting. The caucus continued the task of monitoring this process and seeks ways to keep the original vision of a strong advocacy program alive on all levels of the church. EUC also maintains its own advocacy, but with a sharper definition with regard to racism, economic justice, and urban issues. Its annual assemblies remain the only open and accessible forum for discussing social policy and urban ministry issues by all orders in the church's life, and a place where the often lonely practitioners of urban ministry can gather for mutual support and refreshment.

4. The 1980s

In the 1980s the need to support parishes directly involved in urban ministry and mission led to the development of the Jubilee program. Jubilee was approved at the 1982 General Convention in New Orleans. It was developed by the newly revived Standing Commission of the Church in Metropolitan Areas during the 1979 to 1982 triennium. The commission was charged by the 1979 General Convention in Denver to "develop recommendations and strategies which will be of concrete assistance to the Church in metropolitan areas, in shaping new patterns of mission and ministry," and specifically to "devise an action strategy for consideration by the 1982 General Convention in regard to the role of the general convention and Executive Council in the implementation of a program of urban mission and evangelism in urban and other deprived areas, with primary focus on local congregations."[14] Commission members who participated in the first three assemblies of the EUC engaged in ongoing dialogue with various dioceses, the EUC, and the Church and City Conference.

In their report to the 1982 convention, the commission stated that "the issues which most recently informed the General Convention Special Program still press the Church to action." But in an effort to show that lessons had been learned from GCSP, the commission called the church to "new methods of mission and ministry" that would share learning from "effective styles of mission to serve as resources" for others and to "affirm and be solidly based in the diocesan and especially the parish structure of the Episcopal Church, recognizing that it is the local parish which ought to be the chief vehicle for the Episcopal Church's strategy for mission and ministry."[15]

The theme underlying Jubilee was the year of Jubilee highlighted in Leviticus 25, anticipating a time when the inequities in society would be ended and land would be returned to its rightful owners. The programmatic content of Jubilee Ministry was to include consciousness raising to "challenge and confront the members of the Episcopal Church to understand the facts of poverty and injustice, leading them to an active role in meeting the needs of poor and oppressed people and in the struggle against the causes of such suffering."[16]

Jubilee Center designation has been given to congregations and other church-based agencies involved with poor and oppressed persons. The idea was to lift up models of ministry that could be an inspiration to others and also serve as training sites. Some 130 centers have been designated since the program's inception. A human resources bank that would assist parishes in locating persons with needed skills and training that involved an internship program was also envisioned. There was also a research and evaluation component, the latter developed as a peer evaluation process for Jubilee Centers. A quarterly magazine called *Jubilee* was published sporadically over the years but eliminated in 1989 because of the reallocation of communication funds. A Public Policy Network developed separately from Jubilee Ministries. A Jubilee Ministry Grants program has provided some $600,000

---

14. "Resolutions on Church in Metropolitan Areas, 1979," *Journal of the General Convention,* 1979.

15. "Report of the Standing Commission."

16. "Report of the Standing Commission."

between 1988 and 1991 to parishes and local groups. The Jubilee grants program is administered by the Coalition for Human Needs, which has since its inception provided ongoing support for community groups as well as church-related, parish-based efforts like Jubilee.

In its effort to garner support for the program in 1982, the commission opted for declaring that "The Jubilee Ministry draws no distinctions between 'domestic' and 'overseas' or 'world' mission, or between rural, suburban or urban mission." They cited Presiding Bishop Lichtenberger's 1964 statement at his last general convention that:

> The most distant places in the consciousness of most of us are the slums and ghettos in our cities. We must consider them as mission frontiers every bit as compelling as the most remote place geographically on the face of the earth. There is no longer a distinction between foreign and domestic mission. It is all one.[17]

It is important to reflect on whether that assumption has proved to be strategically correct. Certainly the groups appointed to the Jubilee Ministry oversight committee have usefully included the Appalachian People's Service Organization (APSO), Episcopal Urban Caucus, and the Church and City Conference, as well as representatives from the various ethnic desks of the national office. And it is certainly true that most Jubilee Centers are in urban areas. But it is also true that the ethos of the Jubilee Ministry program is not specifically urban. What Jubilee Ministry has succeeded in doing is identifying with parish-based ministry. At the 1988 General Convention in Detroit, the Standing Commission urged a continuation of the program and an extension of Jubilee into the area of advocacy to complement the efforts of parish-based mission that were largely service oriented. This was approved, but reductions in funding have impaired all Jubilee programs.

As originally conceived, Jubilee was the organizing principle for several key components for what became a new focus for urban and rural ministry throughout the church. Simply stated, these included the creation of a proactive Washington Office of the Episcopal Church that could lobby national social policy and international peace concerns. This was a departure from the Chaplaincy to Congress model many in the church supported.[18]

17. "Presiding Bishop's Address," *Journal of the General Convention*, 1964.
18. "To Build a Just Society: Episcopal Church Public Policy Network — A Ministry of Advocacy," Public Policy Network, Episcopal Church Center, New York, 1986 (rev. ed. 1988).

The central office of Jubilee was envisioned as the coordinator of the key social ministry and advocacy programs. Internally, it focused on identifying and supporting Jubilee Centers, the Jubilee interns, and the Jubilee officers group. Externally, it related to the Social Policy Office, the Washington Office, the *Jubilee Journal*, and the Jubilee grants program. As conceived, this coherent and coordinated mechanism would become the fulcrum of the national church domestic program. Unfortunately, the inability to hire staff in a timely manner meant that these various components were broken up and for the most part subsumed under preexisting agencies within the church.

At the 1982 convention the development of a public policy network was seen as an integral part of the Jubilee concept. The service aspect of Jubilee was seen as politically correct by the Allin administration. Advocacy, especially in the arena of national government, was a cause for ambivalence or outright rejection by those who thought the church should not meddle in such matters.

Jubilee has been effective but has not become "the leaven in the lump" the designers hoped for. Is it possible for a national program to support parish-based ministry? This question in some ways is still unanswered. The vision of the commission was that local congregations would be the base for diocesan strategy, and that the same process among dioceses "would create a new and dynamic national mission strategy." Jubilee Ministry began as presence that led to service but later began to move toward advocacy. The cutbacks experienced recently by Jubilee and other national mission efforts would indicate that this dream remains unfulfilled.

In 1987 eighty bishops of the Urban Bishops Coalition released a paper called "Economic Justice and the Christian Conscience." Many denominations had developed economic justice position papers during the 1980s in response to what was perceived to be a widening gap between the rich and the poor. The urban bishops' paper was adopted as a study document by the House of Bishops, which urged the dioceses to develop proposals for action to submit to the 1988 General Convention in Detroit. The Diocese of Michigan responded. Under the leadership of Bishop Coleman McGehee, Rev. Hugh White staffed the effort that studied both local Detroit projects and drew on people and models from around the country.

A key part of the development of what became known as the "Michigan Plan" was played by a congregation in an economically depressed Detroit neighborhood. Rev. Ron Spann and the Church of the Messiah were deeply involved in attempting to respond to the neighborhood housing and employment crises. The parish had become involved in housing cooperatives because the members discovered that their well-meaning effort to rehabilitate an apartment building across the street resulted in an adversarial landlord-tenant relationship. People changed in many ways. The rector ended up becoming a part-time member of a worker-owned cooperative engaged in housing rehabilitation because a parishioner, Ron Horning, returned from seminary and turned his private construction business into a cooperative.

It was another of Messiah's parishioners, James Perkinson, who developed the paper "Taking Action for Economic Justice: A Theological Assessment." He developed the idea that cooperative activity was needed to overcome the divisions between rich and poor and allow people to respond to God's call to "stand in the breach before me for the land, that it should not be destroyed" (Ezekiel 22:29-30). The document focused on four models: cooperative housing, worker-owned enterprises, community land trusts, and community credit unions — that is, an access to shelter, jobs, land, and capital. As Perkinson explained:

> Cooperation, as either a process or structure, is by no means infallible. It is subject to manipulation and co-optation by the self-interested and the powerful as is any other system of getting things done. What it does provide for, however, that many other systems do not, is a structure of mutual vulnerability. It can allow rich and poor to come into relationship with each other without immediate colonization or instant passive aggressive sabotage.[19]

Since the Diocese of Michigan was hosting the 1988 General Convention, the diocese provided tours of the industrial and urban devastation afflicting Detroit as well as visits to cooperative projects.

Following the unanimous adoption by the 1988 General Convention of "Taking Action for Economic Justice," a national implementation committee was formed. The committee was balanced according to geography, laity and clergy, and racial-ethnic considerations, but not according to urban, rural, and suburban categories. Like Jubilee Ministries, the perception in the church at large seems to be that these programs are urban focused. This perception is again due to the origin of the proposal and the fact that many of the projects funded through this initiative have in fact been urban. But the focus of the committee has been on institutional issues

19. James Perkinson, "Taking Action for Economic Justice: A Theological Assessment," report for the general convention, Detroit, Michigan, July 1988; Diocese of Michigan, Office of Public Affairs, Detroit, p. 12.

such as establishing the legal basis for doing alternative investments and loans with church funds and how to involve a diocese in the support of local projects. Unlike GCSP, the attempt has also been to develop a concept of equitable access to economic resources — land, jobs, and capital — rather than focusing on urban ministry as such. The debate in the committee has centered around the usefulness of the cooperative model, and whether the church's attempt was foisting the cooperative model inappropriately on the poor rather than being used for the conversion of both rich and poor to model a different way of living and working together.

Unlike in the 1960s, increasing shortages of funds for national church programs have caused a severe restriction on national staffing. The director of the national church's grants program was given administrative responsibility for economic justice in order to assure smooth coordination of grant-making efforts. However, that has meant the committee has had to rely on consultant services for various programmatic needs, such as producing a case study manual and running a series of regional workshops. A loan fund is now being developed with the $3.5 million of national funds set aside for community economic development. This fund will be used, in part, to assist the dioceses in establishing their own community investment funds to be used to enhance economic justice programs in all areas, but in major urban dioceses this will be especially helpful to cities.

The 1990 census showed a dramatic increase from 1980 in the number of Hispanics and Asians. These demographic changes became apparent to the Episcopal Church during the 1980s as new ministries with Hispanics and Asian Americans evolved. Most of these ministries are involved in congregational development, and few are financially self-sufficient. The problem of dependency over the long term is real for such ministries, and gives the Hispanics and Asian Americans a real opportunity to learn from the experiences of their black brothers and sisters.

III. Implications of Four Decades of Urban Ministry

What insights can be drawn from four decades of urban ministry in the Episcopal Church? Here are some preliminary observations:

1. One of the first issues is that the Episcopal Church has difficulty in calling a program "urban." Whether that resistance is a cultural bias or not is hard to determine. Certainly the many pockets of rural poverty must not be ignored. It is clear, however, that there are political problems in referring to a program as "urban," a legacy related to race and class, since

the term *urban* to middle-class and white Episcopalians conjures up images of race and poverty. But the aversion to the word is probably also related to a deeply rooted distrust of cities that has been part of the American tradition since the days of Thomas Jefferson.

2. The Episcopal Church has a very difficult time dealing with racism and class distinctions. The church has an easier time trying to abate poverty through direct service than dealing with issues of race and class, as causal factors. The concern for service always outstrips any programmatic effort for advocacy and other strategies that attempt to get to the systemic roots of social and economic problems.

3. The Anglican Communion is growing in Third World nations where the vast majority of the people are people of color. The demographic changes in the United States as seen in the 1990 census data indicate growth not only in the black population, but particularly in Hispanic and Asian populations. The prospects for ministering to new people are hampered by the still prevalent suburban mentality, and the fact that most seminary graduates are more prepared for a suburban parish than any other kind of ministry.

4. The shortage of black, Asian, and Hispanic clergy is serious. For example, among the black clergy, it appears that the new graduates and young priests will not offset the many retirements that are expected over the next decade. Similarly, there are very few Asians and Hispanics who are ordained or are preparing for ordination.

Nor is this problem being addressed by the large increase of women in seminary. As of September 1990, statistics from the General Convention Office indicate that 1,752 women are ordained as priests and deacons. Of these, 1,692 are European American, 46 are African American, 5 are Native American, 5 are Hispanic, and 4 are Asian. The overwhelming majority of women in seminary is white and middle class. Hence, given the new ethnic and racial groups in our cities, the Episcopal Church is not adequately training a new generation of clergy leadership. In a word, the Episcopal Church has yet to deal with the issue of inclusivity and the realities of a multicultural and multiracial world.

5. There has been an inability in the Episcopal Church to stick with a particular strategy for a long time. Our churches, like our society, are psyched up for short-term crusades, not long-term journeys or pilgrimages. We resonate with addressing problems that have immediate solutions. Urban ministry is by its very nature systemic and therefore resistant to quick fixes.

6. There is still confusion around a ministry of presence versus a

ministry that grapples with issues and advocacy. The object is to combine presence with advocacy, just as it is desirable to combine spirituality with social action. Nevertheless, it seems to be very difficult to include all of those elements in specific urban mission efforts.

7. Many of the church's programs have worked effectively and deserve to be continued. Some, like the Coalition for Human Needs since its inception in 1975, have effectively distributed large amounts of funds to various community groups. Jubilee Ministries has also been useful as a way to stimulate models for urban mission that are rooted in the local congregation.

8. It is important that the lessons from the GCSP program be learned. There should be innovative forms of ministry that go beyond the work of the local congregation, but the local congregation and the diocese should not be bypassed. The mission of the church only makes sense when the church is directly or indirectly involved and when the church has a sense of ownership of the mission program.

9. There are links between local congregations and the dioceses as well as between these and national efforts. The national church can support local efforts, but cannot be fully involved in them. Models of ministry developed via the national church can be supportive to those struggling in local parishes. One cannot, of course, design local strategies from a national office or even from a diocesan office. There has been an interesting dialectic or tension between the levels of the church, and those tensions have never been fully resolved.

10. Since the 1960s, the priorities in the church have changed. The financial surplus is gone, as seen in the demise of industrial mission and many urban-based projects. The first casualties of shrinking financial resources, unfortunately, were the ecumenical efforts, such as urban-industrial mission, since the "support your own first" mentality is still prevalent in the Episcopal Church as it is elsewhere. The second casualty is in giving beyond the local parish. Not only do parishes now see more local mission opportunities, but the mounting expenses — clergy salaries, property and medical insurance, building maintenance, fuel costs, etc. — have led to a ballooning of the local congregation's budget on in-house items.

11. We also need to distinguish between downtown churches and parishes in the urban neighborhood. It is the neighborhood parishes that seem to be in the most trouble. Some of the large downtown parishes are still in good shape financially, thanks to gentrification, endowments, and the attendance of suburbanites on Sunday.

12. In urban mission, effectiveness has depended more on the leader-

ship than on the structure. Very often effective models do not survive under new leadership. The leadership of the congregation, especially of the clergy, is determinative for effective urban ministry.

13. There are also serious problems associated with the "free enterprise" model of urban ministry. Unless a congregation is a special mission of the diocese that receives special funds, the parishes are on their own, using the free enterprise model. If a parish is located in a poor area, it simply does not have the resources to fund adequate program and staff. Hence, we see the "fractionated" clergy problem, working on a three-quarter, one-half, or even one-quarter time basis. This is particularly problematic in urban parishes, where rapid neighborhood turnover and change require some continuity of leadership and a full-time presence in order to build community in the midst of chaos.

14. The focus on single issues or single constituencies has hurt the church just as it has injured the body politic. No matter how valid the issue may be — such as abortion, gay rights, or the arms race — the focus on the single issue keeps us from remembering who we are as a people. Furthermore, the urban agenda cuts across many issues and cannot be reduced to any single issue. Urban mission is hurt by single-issue agendas.

15. The focus of the Episcopal Church on the local parish is healthy but scary. We need to recognize the parish as the major sociological unit in the church, but we need to define the possibilities and limits of the parish and develop and sustain alternate forms where and when needed. The demise of many of the experimental urban ministries and urban-industrial missions does not bode well for the ability of the church to engage in diverse forms of urban mission.

Where are the new efforts in urban-industrial ministry? Where are the new urban training centers?

16. The challenge of the 1990s is first to recognize where we are and to reflect on what we have learned over the past forty years. The suburban model is still the governing model, even if the suburbs are not growing as they did in the fifties and sixties. We need to recognize the trends and especially the slippage in urban ministry as the various levels of the church confront a financial crunch. There is a crying need for an urban parish strategy on all levels of the denomination.

17. There are limited human and especially financial resources, and there are also some limits on available energy. The Episcopal Church's tendency to proliferate programs without increasing the overall capability to respond is troubling. Changes in national priorities in the Episcopal Church have not highlighted the role of urban mission, although many are

related to urban work. Urban work and racism are often demoted on the priority list by the "hot" issue of the moment.

18. Finally, there is a clear need for increased ecumenical action on all levels with regard to urban ministry, especially on the diocesan and national levels. There are some good ecumenical models on the local level that need to be expanded and emulated. The "doing it alone" mentality seriously hampers our effectiveness in confronting the urban realities.

What has all this meant? Some good things have happened in urban ministry, but there is much to be done. The jury is still out on the overall effectiveness of the efforts in the Episcopal Church over the past forty years, and it is still not clear what directions urban ministry will take. The financial crunch facing many urban congregations, the deterioration of properties, the scarcity of clergy for Hispanic and minority ministries, and other factors do not bode well for the future. The problems that the Episcopal Church now faces with regard to inclusivity based on race, ethnicity, gender, and sexual orientation, coupled with the traditional problems of the rifts between spirituality and social action, or between mission and institutional maintenance, are not encouraging. Nevertheless, we proceed with faith and hope — faith in a just, loving, and forgiving God, and hope that through God's grace we may see glimpses of the kingdom here and now.

· 6 ·

Themes of Lutheran Urban Ministry, 1945-85

RICHARD LUECKE

WORLD WAR II PROVED a watershed for Lutherans in North America. They had fought as Americans, some against foes in former Lutheran homelands, and returned to unprecedented industrial and demographic developments in their cities. It was during the 1940s and 1950s that, as Franklin Clark Fry put it, Lutherans came out of the *Bierstube* into American life, and it was then that this president of the United Lutheran Church in America came to be called "Mr. Protestant."

More than other mainline Christian groups, Lutherans had sought to maintain inherited identities in an American society that was being pulled and pushed from the land to the cities and was wiring its offices to world cities. By the early 1960s more than a dozen Lutheran streams merged into three larger bodies of approximately two million adult communicants each. Our story will be about these people and will take us to the point of a larger merger that formed the Evangelical Lutheran Church in America in 1988.[1]

---

1. The Evangelical Lutheran Church in America (ELCA) united several Lutheran streams, all of which had themselves coalesced since World War II. The *Lutheran Church in America* (LCA) was formed in 1962 of four Lutheran bodies having German and Scandinavian backgrounds, some of whose Eastern roots reached far back into the eighteenth century. The *American Lutheran Church* (ALC) was composed in 1960 of four Lutheran bodies, largely Scandinavian and strong in the Midwest, which had been previously linked in the American Lutheran Conference. The *Association of Evangelical Lutheran Churches* (AELC) was a smaller, intentionally transitional body formed in 1976 by congregations that found themselves unable to continue in ministry with the leadership of the *Lutheran Church — Missouri Synod*

In addition to sharing the Bible and ecumenical creeds with Christendom, Lutherans reaffirm "confessions" of the gospel that were formed during the sixteenth-century reformation in Europe, of which the Augsburg Confession is best known. "Confession" is an operative term for Lutherans, referring first to these historical expressions, and then also to a current "confessing" needing to be done in the face of new idols and (some would say) new opportunities. This sets the scene for responses to emerging urban realities that are similar and yet contentious, in which parties are disposed to say "Here I stand!"

In *Mission in the Making* F. Dean Lueking described three formative sources of mission within a single Lutheran body in America — "American evangelicalism," "evangelical confessionalism," and "scholastic confessionalism" — and showed how these "criss-crossed again and again to weave a pattern of unexpected contrasts and unique blending."[2] The currents we will describe with respect to urban ministry in and among the various Lutheran bodies are similar to these. The three sections of this essay are organized not strictly as the stories of separate Lutheran church bodies, but according to three classical Lutheran theological themes that came to expression in those who led the way in urban ministries.

While all Lutherans affirm the confessional formula "justification by faith" and the distinction between law and gospel, this was pressed by urban missioners in three Trinitarian directions. Our sections will treat (1) "The Engraced City" — a theme of protagonists who drew from the experiential and societal attentiveness characteristic of an earlier "pietistic" movement and who now described divine grace as active in creation and in sustaining those who struggle with new problems and possibilities of civilization; (2) "Two Reigns of God in the City" — a traditional distinction now renewed and used by theologians, church commissions, and practitioners to produce the most developed Lutheran statements on societal issues and the most developed formulation of principles for parish ministry in the cities; and (3) "Christian Freedom in the City" — which gave charter to independent spirits who engaged in experimental and unofficial forms of ministry but also came together to influence the urban agenda of their church bodies and the constitution of the new Lutheran church. The first two sections will refer primarily to developments in Lutheran Church in America (LCA),

---

(LCMS), a denomination formed by German immigrants in the nineteenth century that had shared mission projects with smaller bodies in a Lutheran Synodical Conference.

2. F. Dean Lueking, *Mission in the Making: The Missionary Enterprise among Missouri Synod Lutherans, 1846-1963* (St. Louis: Concordia, 1964).

the third section primarily to those in Lutheran Church – Missouri Synod (LCMS), Association of Evangelical Lutheran Churches (AELC), and American Lutheran Church (ALC), but (as we shall see) there was "criss-crossing."

I. "The Word of God That Changes and Revives the Whole Earth": The Engraced City

That Lutherans brought a piety to America that included social action was a theme of settlers who established the first seminary at Gettysburg; some of them, alone among Lutherans, stood up to be counted against slavery. Near the close of World War II this claim was revitalized by the arrival in Gettysburg of Bertha Paulssen from the Confessing Church in Germany, who became the first sociology teacher (and first woman teacher) in a Lutheran seminary and a mentor most productive of early urban ministry heroes.[3]

It was Walter Kloetzli, a war-experienced student at Gettysburg and one of Bertha Paulssen's "wicked creatures" (as she called them), who from 1955 to 1965 issued the urban challenge to Lutheran bodies from his post as secretary for Urban Church Planning of the National Lutheran Council (NLC), an inter-Lutheran consultative agency (1918-66). Adapting research methods previously used by H. Paul Douglas of the Federal Council of Churches, Kloetzli initiated urban planning procedures of six to nine months' duration with church leaders in at least 150 of the 200 U.S. metropolitan statistical areas.

"The church should be concerned with urbanization," Kloetzli preached, lectured, and wrote, because "God's Word is meant for all nations and all creation" and is "not limited to a select group of privileged people." American Protestants had been fleeing "the seething turmoil of the modern city" and seeking refuge in a previous "rural frame of reference — a 'village' atmosphere." "Rural" implied primary group relationships characterized by affection, but neglected the emergent "urban" reality that demanded attention to relationships mediated through larger-scale programs and institutions. Some pastors were, in fact, trying to survive in changing urban communities by *not* mentioning these things.[4]

3. Theses guided by Paulssen from 1945 to 1965, including many by persons who will enter into our story, are listed in *Gettysburg Lutheran Theological Seminary Bulletin: Essays in Honor of Bertha Paulssen,* November 1965.

4. See Walter Kloetzli, *The Church and the Urban Challenge* (Philadelphia: Muhlenberg, 1961); see also his *Urban Church Planning,* written with Arthur Hillman (Philadelphia: Muhlenberg, 1958).

Against reactive claims of congregational autonomy Kloetzli mobilized studies combining sociologists, who documented familial and inward-turning characteristics of congregations, with church theologians.[5] While it was true that the Augsburg Confession criticized certain hierarchical structures and refused, in loyalty to the gospel of God, to absolutize structures of any kind, its very intent had been to keep the church bent on its mission — which might now become thwarted if congregations drew back into themselves.

Kloetzli called successfully for more sociology studies in seminaries; for revised national mission policies, including enlarged budgets for inner-city work; and for consultations on the urban church combining boards and commissions. It was this urban staffer who in the early 1960s, with Donald Benedict and Gibson Winter, conceived the idea of a national ecumenical Urban Training Center for Christian Mission (UTC).

From studies of changing cities Kloetzli showed that *housing* was a manifest arena of social displacement; hence a primary focus for church engagement should be "urban renewal" and new public housing programs. The information gathered with constituencies in Baltimore, Chicago, Milwaukee, and elsewhere was to inform them for advocacies that could help set public goals and hold government officials to high standards. Churches were to serve as partners in development projects by performing neglected analysis or auxiliary services, including relocation of displaced residents. Kloetzli was not ready, however, for what happened next — for community organizers in Chicago and elsewhere who described urban renewal programs as "negro removal" and used them as issues to mobilize city neighborhoods. Informed by sociologists who thought in terms of social equilibrium rather than conflicted change, and by a theology disposed to find divine purpose in technological developments, Kloetzli stayed with the consensual definition of community organization he had shared with Arthur Hillman in *Community Organization and Planning*,[6] repeating Hillman's repudiation of trade union tactics by neighborhoods. It was no part of urban mission, at least on his first view of the matter, to "rub raw

---

5. Kloetzli provided data for an NLC publication by Lutheran social scholar Gerhard Lenski and theologians entitled *Congregationalism as a Problem in the Exercise of Christian Social Responsibility within American Protestantism.* He also coordinated field work for an NCC "Effective City Church" study in which Charles Y. Glock described limiting stereotypes imposed on pastors and congregations. Parts of this are available in Kloetzli, *The City Church — Death or Renewal: A Study of Eight Urban Lutheran Churches* with an afterword by Glock (Philadelphia: Muhlenberg, 1961).

6. Walter Kloetzli, *Community Organizing and Planning* (New York: Macmillan, 1950).

the sores of discontent." He objected "not to the goals but the methods" of Saul Alinsky, and then also to the goals insofar as they seemed to endorse "quotas" in trying to stabilize communities. Failing to get a disavowal of Alinsky and discontinuation of an Alinsky presence at UTC, Kloetzli left its board.[7]

The Scope of Grace

When, in 1962, Walter Kloetzli convened a Lutheran consultation on the city at the old Sherry Hotel in Hyde Park, Chicago, some church dignitaries complained about dilapidated accommodations. The opening speaker chided them for a lack of empathy with city dwellers and warned them against a corresponding lack of imagination. That speaker was Joseph Sittler, a teacher at the University of Chicago Divinity School who had received his denominational training at Wittenberg College and Hamma Divinity School in Ohio, where faculty and constituencies had perpetuated the Lutheran piety that was moving westward from Gettysburg. It was to a legendary teacher at Hamma, John Olaf Evjen, an early expositor of Ernst Troeltsch and the historical and societal settings of belief and practice, that Sittler had dedicated an early book on the Word of God in Martin Luther that treated the "Word" as creative of historical forms and institutions.[8]

Sittler began at the Sherry by observing how the earliest Christian communities had been planted in great cities of the empire. Cities were "the fountains, the conservators and the propagators of culture, political forms, and laws." Since Abraham, the biblical heroes of faith had looked forward to a city of God "that has foundations" (Hebrews 11:10). The biblical vision of a fulfilled human society was not of any return to a garden but of a city that is to come.

7. Other church leaders agreed with this early interpretation of Alinsky, as did the editors of the *Christian Century* in Chicago. Ironically, as a regional administrator of U.S. Housing and Urban Development programs in Chicago and Kansas City, Kloetzli would conduct a major study of "citizen participation" and preside at the demolition of the Pruitt-Igoe public housing project in St. Louis. He later became director of program development for HUD in Washington, D.C.

8. Joseph Sittler, *The Doctrine of the Word: The Structure of Lutheran Theology* (Philadelphia: Muhlenberg, 1948). Hannah Arendt, in reclaiming authority for city communities in her book *On Revolution*, cited a similar Luther from *The Bondage of the Will*: "The most perpetual fortune of God's Word is that for its sake the world is put into uproar. For the sermon of God comes to change and revive the whole earth to the extent that it really gets through to it."

Sittler then pointed to emerging possibilities and perils in the public realm requiring faithful responses beyond those of keeping order. The gospel implied "an analytic and anticipatory function" that is alert to these. He warned against homogenizing and ruthless developments in the city that obstruct realization of humane possibilities, but added that human struggles with these are sustained by "grace." The Reformation-period focus on Christ and divine grace in individual lives through the forgiveness of sins had not been wrong — it had addressed an historical threat raised within the church to the sovereignty and initiative of the grace of God — "but restriction of the understanding and power, the meaning and scope of grace to that dimension does not reach to the everyday stuff of which our misery as social, economic, and political creatures is compounded." Without a broader understanding, contemporaries were likely to find themselves "ever deeper locked within that radical individualism from which it is the work of grace to release [them]." Sittler's question for Lutheran urban theology and ministry was this: "How do the powers of grace . . . bear upon [people] in their earthly nature and placement, in their neighborly context, in their tool-making and machine-making and economic-elaborating function?"[9]

This creation-grace stream of theologizing remains a muted theme among Lutherans. It is regarded by some church theologians as insufficiently attentive to the distinction between "two kingdoms," that is, the reign of God over people of faith through grace in the gospel and God's reign over everything else through the law.[10] Karl Hertz, an Ohio Lutheran seminary teacher remembered for pioneering work in contextual education, observed before his death in 1992 that Gettysburg-Ohio themes were still active in urban clergy in an "underground" way. At UTC in Chicago, Joseph Sittler was one theologian who could be invited back again and again — which raises a question whether Lutherans attending from many Lutheran bodies were not also "underground" or, as Sittler said of himself, "at the edge."[11]

9. Joseph Sittler, "Urban Fact and the Human Situation," in *Challenge and Response in the City*, ed. Walter Kloetzli (Rock Island, Ill.: Augustana, 1962).

10. This helps explain why Lutherans were less enthusiastic than others over Harvey Cox's *The Secular City* when it appeared in 1964. But a minority view, which refused to separate the grace of God in the forgiveness of sins from grace that sustains people in their engagement with technical and social possibilities in historical experience, found expression in the symposium "Secular City: Image for Lutherans?" in *Lutheran Quarterly* 18, no. 1 (February 1966), ed. by Frederick K. Wentz of Gettysburg.

11. Sittler required reading of an essay by Krister Stendahl, "The Apostle Paul and the Introspective Conscience of the West," *Harvard Theological Review* 56 (July 1963): 199-215, which argued that Lutherans had read their own inwardness, gained from Luther and

II. Law and Gospel: Two Reigns of God in the City

World War II put confessionally minded Lutherans back to work on their traditional distinctions between law and gospel and the "two kingdoms." They could no longer speak of a simple separation between "throne and altar" since earthly rulers had shown themselves massively and murderously subject to evil powers and trends. The task, as posed by William Lazareth, a new theologian at the Lutheran Seminary in Philadelphia, was "to put the church back under the Gospel of God and the state back under the Law of God."

Concern for the society could not remain a matter of indifference to believers, least of all in America where citizens bear a constitutional responsibility for community and public life.[12] The "two kingdoms" distinction was elaborated to include attention to social-economic institutions other than government (remembering sermons and tracts of Luther on family, schooling, and business). These were the "left-hand" work of God, or "masks" of God, through which God was doing the work of preservation and justice — *though not of justification*. Their function was to be distinguished from salvation, which is the work of the gospel alone, and the language used in taking them up was to be that of "natural reason" and "civil righteousness."

1. The Church and Community Organization

The process by which these characteristic understandings came to expression in urban ministry can be traced by sketching Lutheran responses to emerging local, mass-based community organizations in the cities. We have already noted, in Walter Kloetzli and others, a reluctance to support Alinsky-style confrontational community groups during the years 1955 to 1965.[13] From 1965 to 1975, pressed by urban events, Lutheran bodies made

---

Augustine, back on Paul and the New Testament. Richard Sennett suggests that an "introspective consciousness" from Augustine has confined the spirit of city architecture and city streets, in *The Conscience of the Eye: The Design and Social Life of Cities* (New York: Knopf, 1990).

12. A touchstone of postwar Lutheran social consciousness in America is a three-volume work entitled *Christian Social Responsibility*, ed. Harold Letts (Philadelphia: Fortress, 1957); see also Lloyd Svendsbye, "The History of a Developing Social Responsibility among Lutherans in America from 1930 to 1960, with Reference to the American Lutheran Church, the Augustana Lutheran Church, the Evangelical Lutheran Church, and the United Lutheran Church in America" (diss., New York: Union Theological Seminary, 1966).

simple no-strings-attached contributions to community organizations, including those served by Alinsky's Industrial Areas Foundation (IAF); and during a third decade, 1975 to 1985, Lutherans reasserted their historical distinctions in a disciplined formulation of doctrine and practice.

The largest of eight incorporated national boards of LCA at its outset in 1962 was the Board for American Missions (BAM). While the primary emphasis of this board was on establishing congregations in the growing suburbs, it also included a secretary for the urban church. The first of these, Orville Hartman, cooperated with more than twenty national denominations in establishing the Urban Training Center in Chicago. His successor, Richard Bartley, trained with the first year's group, then routinely recruited urban clergy for this training and also brought thirty-three synodical presidents to Chicago for a special program. Arnold Tiemeyer, a staffer for BAM in the Chicago area, met Saul Alinsky at UTC and moved to promote relations with community organizations nationally.

Clergy trainees, along with others at the Chicago center, were placed in community organizations where they were first to listen, then to cooperate as participant-observers, and finally (in the case of longer-term participants) to take part in developing community strategies and programs. Alinsky and the IAF afforded a particularly lively model of community organization, but by no means the only one. Alternatives were set forth, for example, Leopold Bernhard, then at First Lutheran in Columbus, Ohio, and by Milton Kotler of the Institute for Policy Studies in Washington, D.C., who made regular visits to UTC to describe projects being conceived in conjunction with a "neighborhood foundation" and "neighborhood constitution" in East Columbus Community Organization (ECCO).[14]

Prompted by Bartley and Tiemeyer, LCA now gave direct support to community organizations as different as Belmont-Craigen in Chicago, which was a scene of housing marches with Martin Luther King, and COPS

13. Kloetzli's enthusiasm for secular developments could and did attach to community organizations other than Alinsky's. He and his followers have said that community organizations may have a "saving" significance for people. "No people," e.g., people regarded by others as deviant or pathological, "become a people."

14. At UTC, housing programs and strategies for economic development were conceived in terms of community initiatives and compared in many settings. Richard Hauser of London described the internal dynamics of groups moving from apathy and violence, through catharsis and leadership development, to formation of socially creative institutions. Ivan Illich of Cuernavaca, Mexico, showed how intervening service institutions can produce disinvesting and debilitating effects, with implications for community planning and strategy. For UTC curriculum, see Richard Luecke, *Perchings* (Philadelphia: Fortress, 1972).

(Communities Organized for Public Service), which was being organized by Ernesto Cortés of IAF in San Antonio. From 1968 to 1970, moved by uprisings in many cities, LCA made a churchwide appeal for funds called ACT ("Act in Crisis Today"). Arnold Tiemeyer investigated possible uses of this $4-million fund and recommended direct grants to community organizations, including $125,000 to $150,000 annually to the Interdenominational Fund for Community Organization (IFCO).

City planning visits were still being conducted by Harold Foster and Eiichi Matsushita, former colleagues of Walter Kloetzli who were now at BAM; by now, however, these visits were only three to four weeks in duration and were often conducted through windshields in specific neighborhoods, with resulting proposals for special ministries, staffing, clusters, closings, and mergers.[15] In some cities, groups previously assembled for research and planning with Kloetzli were using that data to gain support for community organizations. In Milwaukee the information was taken up by an all-Lutheran group chaired by former mayor Frank Zeidler and then by an ecumenical organization directed by Fr. Pat Flood, whose housing marches drew participants from Chicago and elsewhere. Lutheran Urban Church Planning in Baltimore, under directors Jack White and Robert Hoyt, used the studies to document deprivation and powerlessness in city areas and to make a case for community mobilization. After the disorders of the late 1960s this Lutheran alliance worked with Roman Catholic and Presbyterian groups and the Greater Baltimore Association to support formation of five community organizations. These organizations moved from confrontational activities to development of twenty-three community-sponsored housing programs very different from "urban renewal." They became forerunners of the BUILD (Baltimorians United in Leadership Development) organization in Baltimore, which now addresses broader city issues including widely watched work in school reform.

Meanwhile congregational practices were growing up in some of the nation's most disinvested and devastated city areas that would lead to modified relations with community organizations and to the most developed official understanding of parish-based urban ministries in Lutheranism.

West Side, Chicago. Amid the flames and tanks of 1965, David Nelson and his sister Mary, offspring of missionaries, arrived at Bethel Church (LCA) with its German cornerstone and thirty-five white families, in an

15. New demographic data-gathering for church clients was taken up by an inter-Lutheran Center for Social Research for the Church (CenSRCH), developed by Victor Streufert at Concordia College, River Forest, Illinois.

area that had changed from thirty-five thousand whites to sixty thousand blacks in five years.

Though secularizing theories abounded during the 1960s, *they made it a point that worship would stay central at Bethel*. The Sunday service and weekly prayer meetings were to be "the glue, gas and guts" of what the people did, including some newly adopted activities through which "neighbors take care of neighbors." Later, 150 choir members would rock the old building and join their sound to that of Latinos in Mexico City (Bethel helped build squatter houses there), Native Americans at Turtle Mountain, and whites in Minneapolis — a "four-point parish."

When banks withheld dollars and three hundred homes became lost within a square mile in a single year, Bethel staff and volunteers purchased and rehabilitated one HUD-foreclosed three-flat by means of a pony-up purse and sweat labor. The next step proved crucial, that is, the formation of Bethel New Life, Inc., albeit with a volunteer staff and only $9,600 in the account. *Reinvestment would be a major strategy, and local people would be legally and corporately in charge of their own rebuilding.*

This legal body continued to work with church offices, colleges, and congregations (never limited to "partner" congregations), but was now also able to wring land and building concessions from the city, to package funds using limited partnerships as well as no-interest and low-interest housing programs (Jimmy and Rosalynn Carter came with a summer crew of Habitat for Humanity), and to win neighborhood loan agreements from a major Chicago bank seeking to open a branch in the area. By 1990 the corporation had built or restored 500 housing units with 700 more in the works, including a 114-unit building using $5.8 million in layered financing. Twenty-plus neighbor congregations, including independent Baptists, were cooperating in an "Isaiah" plan for new housing. Bethel acquired a failing hospital and adapted it for comprehensive programs with the elderly, day care, and cultural arts. It created cooperative enterprises in sewing, home care, and recycling, and an experimental Self-Sufficiency Program that converts welfare funds into grants for work with families, including procurement of employment and housing.

Here was a further learning: *community revitalization is not achieved through a housing project here, a new school principal there, a jobs program somewhere else. It begins to look like a circle of things.*

By 1990 Bethel New Life, Inc., was working with a budget of more than $6 million and employing almost five hundred workers.[16] The congregation had grown to seven hundred members and was self-supporting.

16. See Patrick Barry, *Rebuilding the Walls* (Chicago: Bethel New Life, 1989).

Its families, with very few college-educated members and an average income of $14,000.00, were contributing an average gift of $28.20 per week and were conscientiously refusing to think of themselves as "poor."

Brooklyn and South Bronx. When John Heinemeier came to St. John's congregation (LCMS) in Brooklyn as an associate pastor helping to free Richard John Neuhaus for broader engagements, he found three primary emphases that would stay with him.

1. *Use of the traditional liturgies* — this included a daily Mass. Though four services were held on Sunday in three languages, all participants were to see themselves as one congregation gathered around Word and Sacrament as though their very life depended on it — as it did.

2. *Social action in which church affiliation and role were always clearly signalled.* No press of daily rounds justified turning aside from programs of the Lutheran Human Relations Association, the civil rights movement, local school struggles (including those of Ocean Hill–Brownsville), or Clergy and Laity Concerned about the War in Vietnam.

3. *Local ecumenics with the Williamsburg Clergy Association.* This association sponsored seven hundred rental units under federal programs.

In 1976 Heinemeier moved to Risen Christ church in Brooklyn (also LCMS). At St. John's, he later said, he had performed "social ministry" but had not achieved "social change." Here he met IAF organizers, took the training, and came to assist with training.[17] Here was added an additional learning: *some professional or skilled assistance is highly desirable, even necessary, in organizing the broader community.*

Heinemeier became a convener of East Brooklyn Clergy. The "Nehemiah Project" initiated by this group began with sustained organizing of neighborhood people for the announced purpose of achieving not only shelter but power and stakes that would change their future. By 1990, twenty-three hundred units had been produced with the working poor, 40

---

17. Heinemeyer defended this style of organizing against critics of Alinsky in the church: "Powerlessness, when imposed, is not what Jesus wants for his people. *Voluntary* powerlessness, perhaps — in fact, that is one of the deepest forms of Gospel living. . . . For 99.9 percent of the people [here] it is imposed powerlessness, not voluntary." See "John Heinemeyer: Hope Blooming in the Urban Desert," *The Other Side*, May 1988. This pastor is also featured in the fiftieth anniversary booklet of the Industrial Areas Foundation.

To affirm voluntary poverty, Heinemeier joined Jesus Caritas, an association based on the life of the French Roman Catholic priest Charles de Foucald, a forebear and classic of urban ministry. Putting de Foucald and Alinsky together made for a dual understanding that cultivating internal congregational life and building a powerful neighborhood organization can go hand in hand. Membership, attendance, and offerings doubled.

percent of whom came from public housing. First organizing dollars were provided by the Atlantic District of LCMS. A development loan came from the Roman Catholic bishop in Brooklyn. The city was shamed into a tardy grant of $10,000 per unit, repayable if a house were sold for profit.

Communications were opened with city boards and officials. Stories live on. Mayor Koch, having missed the ground-breaking ceremony but catching the late news with a voice-over from the prophet Nehemiah about rebuilding the city, belatedly declared, "I am Nehemiah!" For a city hearing, neighborhood people occupied all the leather chairs around a horseshoe-shaped table, leaving the lonely spot down front for a late-arriving commissioner — who was their public servant.

In 1982 Heinemeier transferred to the LCA Metropolitan Synod of New York and moved to St. John's (LCA) in South Bronx, the most impoverished congressional district in the country just four miles from East Manhattan. Here he occupied a parsonage that had been vacant for thirteen years. In addition to strengthening Eucharistic worship and incorporating local contextual expressions, he helped reshape an all-Lutheran coalition into South Bronx Ministry,[18] which became the catalyst in establishing "South Bronx Churches" with forty congregations from nine denominations. Heinemeier reasserted the importance of *disciplined support groups of ministers among the poor and of ecumenism at the community level.*

The South Bronx Churches employed IAF in organizing the community, which moved to acquire rental and low-income housing. Grants included $100,000 annually from the ALC; this commitment was assumed by the Evangelical Lutheran Church in America (ELCA) after the merger of 1988. At its 1980 convention, LCA voted $500,000 for the South Bronx Churches and development in their area. It also moved to make church policy out of learnings by coalitions in settings like this.

In the mid-1960s Lutheran congregations remaining in inner Philadelphia (twenty-six of a former forty-six) formed a cooperative "Philadelphia Central City Lutheran Parish" for the purpose of adopting common disciplines and procedures and marshalling scarce resources. The LCA Board for American Missions at first refused to support this extraordinary development, but the local synod gave initial financial assistance of about $50,000 per year. Under the leadership of the first parish director, Robert Neumeyer, black

---

18. For a ground-level description of a day in the life of a South Bronx Lutheran congregation, 65 percent Hispanic, 35 percent black, by a gifted and exemplary pastor, see Heidi Neumark, "Transfiguration Lutheran Church," in *The Experience of Hope: Mission and Ministry in Changing Urban Communities*, ed. Wayne Stumme (Minneapolis: Fortress, 1991).

membership of the "parish" grew from five hundred to thirty-five hundred (from 7 percent to 80 percent of total membership). In 1978, when John Cochrane became parish director — he'd been a Bertha Paulssen student and is said to have baptized parish youth in the area swimming pool (in some versions with a fire hose) — ethnically diverse membership in the congregations was still growing even though the population of the area had declined.

In the course of this development, the BAM committee on urban mission, under its chair Franklin Fry of York, Pennsylvania, became supportive. The national church contributed subsidies and grants to this central city parish of more than $200,000 per year for a decade. (Total contributions from all sources over twenty-five years amounted to $15 million.) Responding to local experiences like this, the 1980 LCA convention in Seattle called for an urban ministry unit to work directly with its office of church extension — in the future, church development would not take place in a world apart from city congregations.[19] Director of the new unit was Harvey Peters, who had already organized a process to round up learnings and "put urban ministry at the center of the church's mission plans."[20]

2. Statements and Principles

To introduce this undertaking Peters set forth a list of previously tried but only minimally successful strategies for keeping congregations afloat in city areas: "withdrawal and preservation" (relocate or merge); "coexistence" (welcome community people to existing programs, open facilities to outside programs); "adaptation" (support extra-congregational activities or community organization); "cooperation" (cosponsor ecumenical agencies or street ministries); "specialized and experimental ministries" (form separate ministries for people of color or whose language is other than English, offer alternative forms of congregational life). All such measures had been going on in congregations, Peters said, *while* their membership was dispersing and declining. He offered a new word for the policy to be adopted, that is,

19. LCA Bishop Robert Marshall had now combined BAM with other boards in a new Division for Mission in North America (DMNA). This made for creative day-to-day collaboration. LCA social statements produced by the Office of Church and Society under William Lazareth at this time remain the most considered in the history of Lutheranism. See Christa R. Klein with Christian D. von Dehsen, *Politics and Policy: The Genesis and Theology of Social Statements in the Lutheran Church in America* (Minneapolis: Augsburg, 1989).

20. See Harvey Peters, "The Lutheran Church and Urban Ministry in North America: An Overview," chap. 2 in *The Experience of Hope.*

"re-rooting" congregations in ways that would achieve both new members and new behavior on the scene.

What "re-rooting" meant was expressed in a cooperatively formed manifesto entitled "The Parish as Place: Principles of Parish Ministry."[21] A preamble asked bishops to affirm these principles and expect them to be applied, asked seminaries to require them of field students and interns, and asked parishes to put them into day-to-day use. Synods, commissions, and agencies were to assign people and funds with an eye to putting these principles to work in particular settings.

Congregations would now be re-rooted in a "parish." "Parish" in this scheme took back its historical meaning as a geographical place and included all who inhabited a neighborhood area (as *oikoumene* originally referred not to churches but to the whole inhabited earth). "Parochial" (*para* plus *oikos*, dwelling next door, neighboring) then described congregations as sojourning, being "in but not of" their parish or neighborhood. Taken together, these terms would keep congregations from forgetting either their special identity or their surrounding community. Then came the "principles."

1. *Parish ministry demonstrates the fullness of God's mission.* "God's mission" is twofold, requiring a twofold practice: that of "the means of grace given exclusively to the church — the Word and the Sacraments of Baptism and the Eucharist," and that of participation in God's other work through participation in the life of the neighborhood.

2. *Parish ministry is geographical and integral to its setting.* The pastor lives there. So increasingly do the members. As the church occupies ground and is public, so the pastor would be visible and known by name beyond his flock. Members would know their neighbors and become directly involved in community organizations.

3. *Parish ministry is inclusive.* Congregations would intentionally reflect the racial-social-economic composition of the people in the parish. Ethnic Lutherans would increasingly become indigenous Lutherans. The traditional Christian liturgy would be used *and* there would be respect for "the symbols, music, and culture of the people in the neighborhood."

4. *Parish ministry is interdependent.* Arrangements would be made for mutual support and accountability among ministers of the Lutheran churches in the area, including common study, prayer, and consolation, and they would consciously represent the entire denomination.

5. *Parish ministry is catholic.* Pastor and people would seek ways to show

---

21. Reproduced as an appendix in *The Experience of Hope.*

unity and share responsibility "with all other congregations of the one holy catholic apostolic church that are located in the same parish."
6. *Parish ministry is intentional.* Regular one-on-one calls would be made to households. Exactly because they were *not* looking for an extra-congregational "clientele," invitations would always be made to all participants in whatever activity to take up full participation in the congregation and the means of grace.

This stance was also adopted by the Division for Service and Mission of the American Lutheran Church in 1982. In the new Lutheran church, formed in 1988, the Division of Outreach adopted this paper as a statement of policy. With the merger, the number of "urban coalitions" grew from nine to forty-five. Directors still came together from the cities and several rural areas, including Appalachia. The "principles" were duly read, marked, learned, and inwardly digested within the order.[22]

During the decade of the 1980s, it should be noted, the Philadelphia Central City Parish suffered losses. Four congregations closed, and few were offering assurances that all the rest would survive into the next century. On one new sober assessment, the accomplishment of this coalition and its spin-off, Northwest Philadelphia Lutheran Parish, had been to "give Lutherans an extra decade, at most two, in the city." Proximate causes of this decline, and that of some other city coalitions, may be sought by looking to realities both in the churches and the neighborhoods.

In 1990 the Philadelphia parish included 5,332 African Americans, but turnover had been rapid and these were by no means the same people who had adopted coalition disciplines in the previous decades. All congregations had not been equally active in the parish; all were not equal recipients of funds. Moreover, total funds available from the larger church diminished in the early 1980s and were further reduced after the merger in 1988. In the Milwaukee coalition this led to shared practices with respect to funding applications and allocations. In the Bronx it led to John Heinemeier's suggestion that there may be something to learn from the economics of independent congregations in the inner city — "if Lutherans are not to be priced out of the inner city."

22. They are expounded in operational terms by Thomas G. Sinnott, *Mission and Ministry: A Training Manual* (Northfield, Minn.: Editorial Avance Luterano, 1989). Sinnott was assistant to Bishop Herluf Jensen of the LCA New Jersey Synod, who was himself a relentless advocate for urban ministry. A summary of meetings of coalition directors from 1980 to 1989 is included by Sinnott in a tenth-year report of the Hudson County Lutheran parish (83 Wayne Street, Jersey City, NJ 07302).

In many inner cities there was now a rapidly increasing proliferation of racial and religious groups. In his coalition-oriented manual, *Mission and Ministry,* Thomas Sinnott described "obstacles" to urban ministry including new sensibilities required on the part of both pastors and people with respect to black and white styles, Puerto Rican family practices, West Indian ceremonies, and much more.[23] In some cities congregations were now marching week by week to stand and pray at crack houses. In only a few coalition areas was there a professionally served community organization of the kind that was found indispensable by John Heinemeier in the Bronx and that was being used and defended by Paul Santmire even in the "smaller big city" of Hartford.[24]

While the "principles" had directed attention to the comparatively small investments made by the church in inner-city congregations, they made no reference to the hemorrhaging disinvestment that was causing the downward spiral in parish areas or to any broader strategies of reinvestment and community economic development.

III. "The Freedom of the Christian": Free Spirits in the City[25]

"Scholastic confessionalism" is Dean Lueking's phrase for a third Lutheran mission style, one that gives much attention to "pure doctrine" and to teaching people who already believe, and that may therefore extend to

---

23. Sinnott, pp. 75f.

24. Santmire defended church cooperation with community organizations during a time of widespread controversy and chagrin over the confrontational tactics of a clergy-led group in Pittsburgh, the Denominational Ministry Strategy, which was protesting against corporation practices as a cause of local unemployment; see "Getting Where the Action Is," *Lutheran Partners,* July 17-24, 1985. (Cf. Paul Johnson, "Clairton, U.S.A.," *Christian Century,* July 17-24, 1985.)

When Santmire arrived at Grace church, Hartford, in 1980, the congregation had survived a loss of four hundred communicants and was beginning to reconstitute a mixed constituency of blacks, Hispanics, and young professionals. "Handles" were found for local problems through formation of the Asylum Hill Organizing Project, a multi-issue neighborhood association employing five organizers and program staff and using a subsidiary corporation for contractual dealings. Seed dollars from LCA leveraged a start-up grant. Training was supplied by an agency for community organization supported by the Roman Catholic archdiocese. The "circle of things" began to emerge: jobs, economic development, education, and safety.

25. In a tract of 1520, *The Freedom of the Christian,* Martin Luther defended two propositions: "The Christian is a perfectly free Lord of all, subject to none and a perfectly dutiful servant of all, subject of all." Voluntary associations of Lutherans, not least those arising in LCMS, exemplified both sides of this.

138

people ill taught at other altars. A church body focused in this way leaves large space for unofficial initiatives on the part of individuals and groups who see a need or hear a call and respond to it. It then becomes a question what will happen when these voluntary missioners, who are closest to people who differ or are caught in the wheels of change, get together.[26]

Missouri Synod work with African Americans began in southern segregated cities like New Orleans, Charlotte, and Greensboro, and rural communities like Selma, Alabama, where the first missionaries were a seaport preacher and an enterprising circuit rider. In Selma and Greensboro a segregated school and seminary were established that, by an irony and providence of history, later supplied pastoral leadership and helped fill congregations in northern cities.[27] In the North an entrepreneurial black preacher, Marmaduke Carter, charmed Midwest congregations with German sermons and hustled his own support to form the first LCMS congregation headed by a black clergyman. All other early black congregations were headed by white clergy and all were called "St. Philip's."[28] Not until the 1950s, when every week for an entire decade a thousand people were getting off trains from the South in cities like Chicago, would other black clergy come to shepherd LCMS flocks in the North.[29]

The story of interracial change and urban mission in this church body cannot be told apart from that of a soft-spoken, lifelong reformer, Andrew Schulze.[30] As a white shepherd of St. Philip's in St. Louis, and later as a

---

26. The story of voluntary social ministries in the Lutheran Church — Missouri Synod is told best by F. Dean Lueking in *Mission in the Making* (see n. 2) and *A Century of Caring, 1868-1968* (St. Louis: LCMS Board of Social Ministry, 1968). Not until the 1950s was a churchwide board of social welfare established by this body. Lueking comments: "They [the missionaries] fought their way into the synodical framework. Once in, they were not sure this was a good idea."

27. Grace Church in Hartford, for example, received a stream of African American Lutherans from LCMS missions and schools in Alabama. See n. 24 above.

28. Say "St. Philip's" and everybody knew. Karl Lutze, a director of Lutheran Human Relations Association in America, explains: "The first St. Philip was successful with a black eunuch — and white churches were most comfortable in accepting non-whites when they were deprived of their full humanity."

29. Moses Dickinson in Chicago, Clemens Sabourin in New York City, William Scheibel in Washington, D.C., and Paul Lehman in Los Angeles begin the list of African American pastors who then conducted an interracial and urban mission to the church itself.

30. See Andrew Schulze, *The Race against Time: The History of Race Relations in the Lutheran Church — Missouri Synod from the Perspective of the Author's Involvement, 1920-1970* (Valparaiso, Ind.: Lutheran Human Relations Association in America, 1972); see also Jeff G. Johnson, *Black Christians: The Untold Lutheran Story* (St. Louis: Concordia, 1971).

missionary in Chicago with a school in Ida B. Wells public housing, Schulze and his teachers fought continuing battles to gain admission of their students to other synodical schools. In 1936 St. Philip's of Chicago and St. Philip's of St. Louis (heretofore members of a looser Synodical Conference dominated by LCMS) sought formal admission to synodical membership on the national convention floor. In 1946, when the Federal Council of Churches was calling for "a non-segregated church in a non-segregated society," this resolution finally passed. In 1965 an African American delegate could say to the Missouri Synod in convention at Detroit, "Brothers, we are here!" That convention also proved explosive.

The Lutheran Human Relations Association of America (LHRAA) had begun in a voluntary way two decades before with Andrew Schulze in St. Louis. From 1953 annual meetings were held at Valparaiso University in Indiana, where President O. P. Kretzmann appointed Schulze to a part-time chair in the theology department, supported him when he was arrested with demonstrators in Albany, Georgia, and powerfully and poetically defended him in a state that had been a home to the Ku Klux Klan. Chapters grew in fifty-six cities, served by seventeen coordinators. For six consecutive years during the 1960s, with leadership from Karl Lutze, LHRAA conducted city training for professional church workers, including the graduates of seminaries and teachers colleges, using Chicago as a laboratory. During the 1970s it sponsored week-long workshops in changing neighborhoods to which seventy-plus local congregations would send participants including their pastors and officers.

To every LCMS convention from 1956 to 1977 came resolutions prepared by the annual meetings of LHRAA. To the 1965 Detroit assembly came ten resolutions calling for churchwide actions bearing on urban ministry.

- For open congregations and an end to "negro missions."
- For staying in changing communities.
- For fair housing and employment practices and removal of all restrictive clauses or tacit understandings in congregations and their communities.
- That all synodical schools and publications teach truths about race that accord with sound theology and science and that interracial education be supplied for pastors, teachers, and leaders.
- That districts anticipate and plan a community-based future with their inner-city parishes, and that all parochial schools be open to neighborhood children and be strengthened in areas of racial unrest.
- That seminary students be assigned for their experiential year to inner-city parishes.

- That cooperation with the poor, nonwhites, and Native Americans be made mission priorities and a focus of expenditures.
- That support be given to organizing efforts in minority communities.
- That members who have engaged in demonstrations for furthering racial justice be commended and encouraged.
- That church schools and church publications adopt this stand, and that these resolutions be implemented by those in authority at every level.

That year LHRAA shared a booth with proponents of six "Mission Affirmations" drawn from a paper commissioned by the mission board and prepared by Martin Kretzmann of the India field and seminary. Conventioneers lined up in very nearly the same way on both sets of resolutions.[31]

To write off such resolutions, once passed, as the perfunctory side of convention proceedings is to underestimate Lutheran respect for "what is written." A new synod president, Oliver Harms, convened special conferences on race as required in 1965 and 1967. He was made a one-term president by a reconstituted convention in 1969. When, in the course of controversy with the succeeding president, the Concordia Seminary faculty marched out to become a "seminary in exile" (Seminex), the difference was waged as one over scriptural interpretation. Reuben Schmidt of the LCMS mission board was one of many who said, "It wasn't just texts, it was mission."

Neither individuals nor congregations in this synod escaped the tide of urban social history. When William Griffin came from segregated training at Selma and Greensboro to the Lutheran Church of Christ the King (not St. Philip's) founded by Andrew Schulze in Chicago, he was able to "cut his eye teeth" (as he put it) with other clergy at UTC, where they met black leaders and "found out that what they were doing was OK." A young staff member at the local community organization he chaired was Jesse Jackson, then a fellow at UTC. A new day had arrived for African Americans in the Missouri Synod, according to Griffin, when, on the seventy-fifth anniversary of St. Philip's in Chicago, founded by Marmaduke Carter, it seemed every African American Lutheran from Milwaukee to Gary wanted to be present.

Congregations, too, tell stories of interracial development that retain a Missouri flavor.

---

31. The ten overtures on racism were published together with the six mission affirmations by LCMS and LHRAA as "Human Relations: Resolutions of the Lutheran Church — Missouri Synod" (1965). This is now a collector's item.

First Immanuel Lutheran Church, Chicago. At its centennial in 1960, this congregation on the near west side, which had grown from three hundred to three thousand in the late nineteenth century and was now back to three hundred, faced a racially changed neighborhood that was being further altered by an expanding University of Illinois medical center. With Ralph Moellering this became the first Chicago LCMS congregation to accept African Americans and other minorities into a formerly white fold.

During the Chicago civil rights movement, with Donald Becker as pastor, this congregation opened its doors to a Martin Luther King rally by a painful, racially divided margin of one vote. It also voted funds to the Blackstone Rangers and Disciples, well-known street organizations, in response to an appeal from John Fry of First Presbyterian Church in Woodlawn. During the 1970s, with six other inner-city parishes of the various Lutheran bodies, it called on twenty-five outer-ring and suburban congregations to join in forming Lutheran Congregations for Career Development, a program that assists city youth to good vocations. Immanuel gave its kitchen to a youth-owned cooperative bakery of this program. Young trainees in production, marketing, and bookkeeping carried bread to the Eucharist in suburban congregations and then stayed to tell their story and conduct a sale.

In the 1970s and 1980s, even with a clear black majority, Immanuel church did not vote with other congregations to leave LCMS because, the pastor explained, "Blacks did not want to hurt whites with whom they had lived through these years. Experience makes a difference."

1. Lutheranism's Voluntary Protestants

The Scandinavian and German Lutherans who merged and remerged to form the American Lutheran Church (ALC) in 1960 remained, in the view of many, an alliance rather than a union of churches. These were Wobegone Lutherans whose "mission" combined Protestant individualism with evangelical preaching and singing found on the American scene. It was independent Norwegian laity in Chicago who founded Lutheran Rescue Mission on West Monroe Street in a building said to have been owned by the Mafia. This later became Lutheran Family Mission and moved to the north side where, in 1980, it came to be led by Alvin Bergh, who was partly supported by a regional church office. It was individuals who initiated Plymouth Youth Center in St. Paul, Minnesota, where juniors of Luther Theological Seminary (including Alvin Bergh) gained street-level experience. To celebrate the 1960 merger, a new national office helped establish Holy Family Mission on the grounds of Chicago Public Housing at Cabrini Green. But it was congregations all by themselves that established a youth ministry and shelter at Lakeview Lutheran Church near Wrigley Field.

During the mid-1960s the ALC Department of American Missions was fostering new suburban starts with most of its $2.5-million budget, about $50,000 going to a desk for Metropolitan Mission that supported inner-city programs. In 1968 city-oriented ALC clergy and laity formed an unofficial Conference on Inner City Ministries (CICM) to "name urban realities," achieve church identification with the poor, recruit black clergy, get people of color on denominational boards, and "de-colonialize" modes of ministry with new populations. In 1970 the ALC church convention at Omaha responded to the Report of the National Advisory Commission on Civil Disorders ("Kerner Report") by authorizing an unprecedented urban crisis fund, to be dispersed by a Coordinating Committee on the National Crisis that included grass-roots leaders. This became Development Assistance Program (DAP), which conveyed about $600,000 each year for fifteen years to organizations including those of Native Americans, Appalachians, blacks, and Hispanics in the cities.

Former leaders, with whom urban missioners had chafed, were now off the scene. A new Division for Service and Mission in America added a program for "urban and ethnic ministries" that came to be conducted by Warren Sorteberg. "That's when CICM should have gone out of business," said Sorteberg. But it didn't. While the new division was looking over to LCA for "principles of urban ministry," CICM was looking around for other free spirits with whom to discern or invent unofficial quarklike signs of the city that is to come.

In 1969 James Siefkes moved from a stewardship office in California to the ALC Division of Social Concerns in Minneapolis. From a desk for "Mission Discovery," Siefkes now conducted programs called "Matrix" — two to five days with congregations helping them listen to voices of people caught or engaged in social change. Carloads came from Detroit and Milwaukee for days in Minneapolis, from Phoenix for days in Denver. Congregations in Houston spent time with city blacks. Church constituencies in other cities opened communications with AFDC mothers (Aid to Families with Dependent Children), youth gangs, and persons in the criminal justice system.

Siefkes also became a supporter in the 1970s and 1980s of activist individuals who conducted "probes" on problematic topics. As many as forty would be probing at the same time. Susan Ruehle assembled "Urban and Ethnic Resources for Churches," thereby facilitating communication among the congregations that produced them. "Peace and non-violence" filled one of the transitions in the ministry of John Schramm, who moved from UTC to form a socially engaged house church in Washington, D.C., and later served as assistant for social ministries to the bishop of Minnesota. "Faith and Fantasy" became a traveling troop of clowns with Floyd Schaeffer. Problems of media were treated in Mexico City. A "dialogue on investment," conducted in light of the international debt crisis, produced a 175-page report by clergy and laity in Brazil. Joseph Barndt returned after nine months at UTC to an urban ministry in Oakland where he wrote the first of two books on "white racism," then moved to Hell's Kitchen in New York and St. Peter's in the Bronx where he created a newsletter called *New Wine Exchange* and staged events that "gave people a place to go." Siefkes had worried that venturesome city activists would become lost to the church. Instead, they found their way to one another and produced combined effects on the new Lutheran church.

Inter-Lutheran cooperation took place in the cities even before the merger, and intensified during the movement out of LCMS. In Milwaukee, pastor Joe Ellwanger and Cross Lutheran Church (LCMS — formerly a white congregation of twenty-five hundred members, now an African American plus Laotian congregation of six hundred) were working creatively with the Milwaukee Lutheran Coalition, and its action organization Milwaukee Inner-City Churches Allied for Hope, in programs of economic development, housing, education, and responses to drugs and crime. In Detroit, congregations of all three pre-ELCA bodies — St. Mark (AELC), Grace (ALC), and St. Luke (LCA) — formed a three-point parish and sold lots to the Detroit school board to acquire the site of Eastern High School. Here, with the cooperation of city Baptists and the mayor and in spite of wary contractors, they built the first new church building in Detroit in many years. Renamed Genesis Lutheran Church, this group participated in the formation of a neighborhood development corporation as well as in advocacies with welfare mothers and programs with street youth. It afforded a training ground for seminarians and also for community-experienced candidates preparing for ministry through a program called ARTOS (Alternate Route to Ordained Service).

Individual congregations were now playing significant roles in the life of their cities and inviting others to join them. Martin Luther Place in Washington, D.C., recruited a national service corps for its own and other cities.[32] Among hundreds of multiservice agencies, two may be noted for

32. When John Steinbruck began here in 1969 after a term at UTC, the block on which his church stood housed three brothels and a palm reader. Today it is the site of "N Street Village," where the city's first church-based shelter was established in 1973. To this have been

bringing Lutherans of all three bodies together before the merger, for joining city and suburban congregations, and for combining service with advocacy.

Metropolitan Lutheran Ministry (MLM), Kansas City, Missouri. Three
separate organizations formed by congregations of the various Lutheran
bodies during the 1960s came together in 1971 under prompting by Walter
Kloetzli, then a regional administrator for HUD in Kansas City. Members
of all three groups met to follow up a city study produced by Victor
Streufert, an LCMS sociologist with the Lutheran Council in the United
States of America (LCUSA). A new MLM, with leadership by Luther Johnson, came to comprise forty-five congregations organizing volunteer services, communicating with other metropolitan agencies, and serving as a
community-based ministry among the poor.

In 1980 William Pape, a founder of CICM, came to this agency from
Avondale Lutheran Church in Denver.[33] MLM continued to offer "Team
Aid" for dealing with multiple problems of family life, centers for emergency help, assistance to homeless people including host homes, housing
counseling, employment services, and work with the elderly. In 1985 its
constituents formed "Lutherans for Justice and Peace," a city-suburban
group that performs research and education in public issues, conducts
hearings, offers training for citizen participation, and equips people for
discussion and action with advocacy groups.

Lutheran Metropolitan Ministry Association (LMMA), Cleveland. Following the 1960s upheaval in the Huff neighborhood, Cleveland pastors
called on LHRAA to assist with interpretation and response. Karl Lutze
recruited Richard Sering, pastor of a black congregation, to spend a summer
with Cleveland Lutherans. Sering helped develop the plan for a metropoli-

---

added 35,000 square feet of transitional housing, group homes, a clinic, family center, and
town houses for resident volunteers. A national volunteer corps places college students in
Washington, D.C., and other cities (sixty-one in 1990-91). Programs are supported by ten
thousand private donors. Advocacies, just five blocks from the White House, may take the
form of demonstrations, as in a Good Friday reduction to ashes of what seemed an anti-urban,
anti-people federal budget, performed over a cemetery for the homeless at the foot of the
Luther statue.

33. This former ALC parish is noted for its city-deeded property in a renewal area; for its
constituency of white, black, Hispanic, Asian, and Native American people and use of their
various motifs; for active participation by persons bearing "physically disabled" and "mentally
retarded" labels (also in the choir); for its "Tuesday schools" with seventy-plus street youth
speaking English, Spanish, Chinese, and Hmung; for vacation schools conducted in housing
projects; for visits by the "clown ministry"; and for participation in an Alinsky-style organization.

tan Lutheran organization and later returned to put it to work. An early task was formation of a "truth squad" to churches after a shoot-out in the Glenville community.

Today LMMA, governed by a board including five members of LCMS, five of ELCA, and five persons at large, works with a $3.3-million annual budget, of which a third comes from public contracts. A community reentry program, begun after Attica, resettles ex-offenders by building on their capacities and that of the communities in which they live. This was the first program to place work-release inmates in paying posts (hospitals, hunger centers, senior homes, youth centers), and it is helping to shape criminal justice practice in Ohio.[34]

George Hrbek, who came to Cleveland by way of "the Mansion," an LCMS ministry in Kenwood-Oakland community of Chicago, designed a County Ombudsman Program and was appointed by county commissioners to mediate complaints for all services in a five-county area. He organized a coalition of the homeless and, citing recorded complaints, proposed structural changes in policies and programs. Advocacies have resulted in legislation for nursing home reforms and housing for persons with disabilities.

Both suburban and city congregations are engaged in these projects (439 volunteers in 1990). They see themselves as pursuing a justice ministry including advocacy and social action.

2. The Spirits Converge

During events of the 1980s many of these urban "spirits" came on stage or brought their organizational skills to work backstage. James Mayer, who spent post-India and post-Missouri days conducting an unofficial exchange called "Partners in Mission," which enabled people active in social ministries to make themselves known to prospective supporters without going over any synodical desks, became the convener of an unofficial working group on "justice agendas." Just as there was a formal constitutional Committee for the New Lutheran Church (CNLC), chaired by William Lazareth, there would

34. This "community reentry" program is described in *Inner City Crime Control* (Washington, D.C.: Police Foundation, 1990), pp. 35-40. It has received foundation, community service, bar association, and mayoral awards and has been featured both on local TV and in a documentary of the ABC television network. A Mosaic Film produced for ELCA is available from Lutheran Metropolitan Ministry Association, 1468 W. 25th Street, Cleveland, OH 44113.

now also be an informal committee for Justice in the New Lutheran Church (JNLC). To JNLC came people from many urban posts and voluntary associations, including those previously linked through the *New Wine Exchange*.

Members of the Cleveland staff were chosen to manage a campaign that would provide monitors and advocates during the constituting process. Others we've met along the way, led by Mary Nelson of Bethel in Chicago, became never-failing shepherds in the precincts of the CNLC offering clerical assistance, information, and counsel to members of minorities for the purpose of achieving constitutional representation for people of color, laity, and women in all church assemblies and committees. Having achieved this in the draft constitution, the campaign shifted to the scene of three conventions conducted simultaneously by the merging bodies, where it opened booths, created events, and mounted posters: "Here's the church and here's the steeple — open the door and see ALL the people!"

With new church procedures in place, it might seem a time for JNLC to "go out of business." Some new bishops made this suggestion. But old and new participants formed an independent "City Lutherans in Action" with local and national conferences in strategic city places. Its newsletter, entitled *Just Cities*, provided a continuing exchange among ministries in major cities.

3. A Merger for Ministry

The story of urban ministry since World War II is rich in vitalities and ironies, and Lutherans have produced their share of both. Those who spoke of approximating the City of God in the earthly city were seen by others as compromising both the gospel and the secular. Those who were most intent on rightly distinguishing law and gospel, church and society, saw their budgets, their enthusiasm, and even their ideas for urban work arise in response to those already present in the broader society and just as responsively fall with them. Those Lutheran bodies who were least ecumenical in intent and least officially focused on issues of the wider society produced freely obedient spirits who found their own way to urban engagements and to one another and influenced beyond their numbers the formation of the Evangelical Lutheran Church in America.

Thematic differences, if they do not harden into opposition, can prove enriching. People who assert the interpretive principle of law and gospel (which few Lutherans wish to deny) could find in that very distinction — i.e., between adherence to the gospel of Christ by all members of the church and prudential judgments in social matters on which they may conscientiously differ — grounds for welcoming free spirits and voluntary initiatives in urban matters. They might also be led to ask a question of meaning and scope concerning the grace of God they wish to defend from compromise: Can beings who are by nature social be saved alone? Can there be a divine "adoption" of human sons and daughters without adopting their characteristic artifact and milieu — the city? A next step, perhaps, is to bring the full biblical story and vision, and the full mystery of the Holy Trinity, to illumine the problem that the city presents for faith — not only for the sake of strategy but for the sake of faith itself.

Urban ministries during the past decades in no way invalidated traditional Lutheran distinctions, but the use of these became more complicated and practical. The distinction between church and society is now elaborated by the presence of many new parties, languages, and customs on both sides. The issue for Lutherans is whether they will be available to new city immigrants of color in the future as they were to Europeans of the past. If not, this church will become in the great cities an officiant for last rites to members declining in numbers and age. A question arises whether that would still be a "confessing" church — in the sense of bearing living witness to the gospel that creates a congregation "from every nation, from all tribes and peoples and tongues" (Revelation 7:9, RSV).

The law-gospel distinction serves powerfully in urban ministry, but it less than ever divides neatly to the two sides of society and church. In the debate over arrangements for a new church organization, some protagonists cited a Luther dictum that no "ought" is necessary for people who live by the gospel. Constitutional provisions for multiracial representation could then be described as "legalistic," as imposing a law where no law is needed; a claim could be made that the Spirit enables any delegate to think and act in place of all others, including minorities. Such assumptions are subject to review on the basis of the evidence supplied during the past years, and perhaps also on the basis of another Luther dictum about being "at once sinners and saints." In matters of race the churches were notoriously slow in seeing what they "ought" to do.[35]

---

35. "Forced love" was the complaint raised by a pastor in Deerfield, Illinois, birthplace of the phrase "Not in My Backyard." Black Lutherans are asking white Lutherans to consider not only that they were comparatively slow in matters of racial justice but also that their characteristic individualism may be derived from the culture rather than the gospel. See essays in Albert Pero and Ambrose Moyo, eds., *Theology and the Black Experience: The Lutheran Heritage Interpreted by African and African-American Theologians* (Minneapolis: Augsburg, 1988).

It was a post–World War II confessional emphasis in America that God has interests on both sides of the church-world distinction and that "masks of God" are to be found in more places than government. This might lead us to expect in the next years increased concentration on secular institutions, programs, and practices bearing on finance, reinvestment, and economic redevelopment in dispossessed neighborhoods — measures that enable families and communities to gain stakes. (This was a theme of Torah, but it can also be argued on grounds of civic reason.) Community organizers would then work less in terms of "needs assessments" and more in terms of "capacity surveys" that facilitate community and multiply resources. John Heinemeier cautions against the very phrase "urban mission" if that is conceived in terms of "service" to passive recipients or of general "downtown" development.

The very word *urban* lends itself to uses by administrators and service purveyors rather than to citizen initiatives.[36] "We are more urbanized than citified," says Daniel Elazar. Future manuals for ministry, if they not only face urban trends but also remember civic traditions, will not define cities in spatial and pathological terms or treat urban systems as facts of life without also describing the city as communication among citizens and its systems and programs as common goods or "common wealth" to communicate about. If social utopianism is a theological error, as Lutherans are disposed to think, then it is an equal error to fail to use the inventive civic capacities that belong to all human beings as such.

A church for which "confession" is both a noun and a verb, which is both "reformed and reforming," will respond in the future as it has in the past to societal developments that constitute a threat to participation in the gospel. In an address to ELCA planners in 1989, Ivan Illich pointed to a modern substantizing of "life" (regarded in faith traditions as a gift or presence of God) that now threatens to replace the notion of "person" in which both gospel life and Western civilization have been anchored. Such a horror could arise unnoticed, he said, not only alongside the modern search for basic physical elements or beside medical procedures attending the beginning and ending of human lives; it could also arise alongside "manpower planning" and "managed life" in human society. The space of the city's poor has been described by persons who know it firsthand as an

---

36. Our words for city have two sources in Latin: *urbs* (space, grid, economic foundations) and *civitas* (communications among citizens). Augustine wrote a *Civitas Dei;* city planners or managers might write an *Urbs Dei.* The idea, of course, is to keep these in interaction.

"airtight cage," a cage that expands into a massive incarceration. Gustavo Gutiérrez has asserted the utter unacceptability on gospel grounds of societal structures that create "non-persons" or "non-agents." There will be stands to take.

When, in the early 1990s, Lutheran respondents convened in open conferences under the banner "Called to Faithfulness," the urban ministry people who had stirred the churches during previous decades were for the most part not there. It would have proved difficult, in fact, to find any seminary teacher or student or pastor who still brought personal experience of, say, labor struggles or the organization of an industrial area in the city. There was now no single groan over the "suburban captivity" of the church. There were many sighs of relief over release from "captivity to human social agendas."

This time the urbanists had the Constitution on their side, at least with respect to provisions for cultural minorities and women in the councils of the church. But the future of urban ministry in Lutheranism will depend on whether and how the new streams mingle. A creative "criss-cross and unique blending" (Dean Lueking's phrase) would put to rest lingering questions: Why should a church focused on the living gospel of God be thereby rendered dull? Why are the societal actions of faithful people not more inventive and more enduring?

It remains to be seen whether Lutheran parties will come to a parting of the ways or combine their confession and action for a new parting of the waters.

• 7 •

Presbyterian Ministry
in Urban America, 1945-80

GEORGE E. TODD

FROM THE FOUNDING of Presbyterianism in the sixteenth century in Geneva, Reformed theology and practice have strongly emphasized the responsibility of the church to shape the civic order of society. Faith in a sovereign God actively at work creating, governing, judging, and redeeming society in and through civic institutions impelled a response by the church to the issues of urban life. Calvin's theocratic democracy replaced ecclesiastical autocracy, and he drew up a constitution, a system of church and civil governance. This precedent led Presbyterians to be active in shaping American institutions; many Presbyterians were signers of the American Constitution. Commitment to shaping the civil order guided by this theological vision is at the basis of the Presbyterian approach to urban ministry.

This chapter will trace the main activities of the Presbyterian Church (U.S.A.) in its work of ministry in American cities from the perspective of the "northern stream" of the Presbyterian church.[1]

Presbyterian urban ministry in the postwar period has roots in the previous century. In the late nineteenth century Presbyterians built city churches with community centers to serve children and low-income families. Prophetic pastors like Charles Parkhurst exposed the evils of labor

---

1. The Presbyterian Church U.S.A. was the northern branch after the split during the Civil War. It merged in 1958 with the United Presbyterian Church (a union of several smaller Presbyterian bodies located mainly in the North) to form the United Presbyterian Church U.S.A. This body and the southern church (the Presbyterian Church, U.S.) united in 1982 to form the Presbyterian Church (U.S.A.).

exploitation and slum poverty. In 1907 the national church created its Office of Immigrant and Industrial Work, which ministered to immigrants, especially Reformed Christians from eastern and southern Europe; "ethnic" churches served Waldensians, Hussites, Hungarians, Chinese, and Japanese. Presbyterians were active in the settlement house movement and, by founding schools and hospitals, were leaders in urban education and public health, helping to lay foundations for the public systems that emerged. To serve the struggling labor movement in the face of opposition, the Presbyterian Mission Board in 1914 built the Labor Temple in New York City to provide office and meeting space for newly organizing unions.[2] And most important, black Presbyterians, who had been trained in schools, colleges, and seminaries the "northern" church had built in the South after the church split during the Civil War, migrated to northern cities where they became pioneers in urban ministry.

I. The 1940s and 1950s

We can date the beginnings of postwar Presbyterian urban ministry with the foundation of the Presbyterian Institute of Industrial Relations (PIIR) in 1944. Marshal Scott was deeply impressed by the gulf between the historic Protestant churches and the masses of industrial workers. He had read R. H. Tawney's *Religion and the Rise of Capitalism*[3] in seminary. As a Presbyterian, he believed that his church should include working people in its membership and participate in the struggle of American workers for just wages and working conditions. He persuaded the Board of National Missions to sponsor his study at Ohio State University, where he won graduate degrees in education and labor economics. He then persuaded the national church to support him in establishing the Institute of Industrial Relations, located first in Pittsburgh and later at Labor Temple in New York. By 1951 it had settled on the campus of McCormick Theological Seminary in Chicago, where it continued its work until January of 1991.

Several times each year the institute gathered thirty to forty clergy for three-week seminars that gave them intense exposure to industry. They visited factories and working-class neighborhoods. They learned from union leaders, managers, economists, public officials, and community or-

2. See James S. Armstrong, "The Labor Temple, 1910-1957: A Social Gospel in Action in the Presbyterian Church" (Ph.D. diss., University of Wisconsin, 1974).

3. R. H. Tawney, *Religion and the Rise of Capitalism* (New York: Harcourt Brace, 1952).

ganizers. Their biblical and theological reflection was laced with stiff doses of social and economic analysis that enabled them to explore the strengths and weaknesses of their church tradition while participating in working-class congregations. Seminary students spent ten weeks in factory jobs in the summers. When Marshal Scott became president of McCormick Seminary in 1971, over four thousand of the nine thousand clergy serving the United Presbyterian Church had participated in programs of the institute. These formed the basis of the denomination's urban ministry initiatives in the 1960s.

Over time the institute broadened its program to include exposure to urban issues such as housing, public education, racism, and urban government. In 1968 the World Council of Churches designated PIIR as its global repository for documentation on urban ministry. Under the leadership of Bobbie Wells Hargleroad the institute published a monthly *Abstract Service*[4] with case histories and documentation about urban ministries across the United States and in sixty other countries. Marshal Scott kept in active touch with PIIR alumni through a quarterly newsletter and mobilized them during major strikes and gave perspective on such labor legislation as the Taft-Hartley Bill. The Presbyterian Church, U.S., the southern wing of the tradition, became a PIIR sponsor in the 1960s. In the early 1970s the institute became ecumenical with a board representing six national churches — American Baptist, Episcopal, Lutheran Church in America, Presbyterian, United Church of Church, and United Methodist — and changed its name to the Institute on the Church in Urban Industrial Society (ICUIS).

A second development, of great importance for Presbyterian urban ministry, was the massive migration of southern blacks to northern cities during World War II and the postwar years. In some cities this was accompanied by the arrival of tens of thousands of Puerto Ricans and Mexicans.[5] Drastic demographic shifts took place in the northern industrial cities as previously all-white neighborhoods reacted to the arrival of African Americans.

Of course, there had been a few black Presbyterian congregations in

4. This is available on microfilm at the University of Chicago, Circle Campus, Department of Urban Studies; copies of the publication itself are available in various theological libraries including Lancaster Theological Seminary, United Theological Seminary (Dayton), McCormick Theological Seminary, and others.

5. These migrations have been thoroughly documented, most recently in Nicholas Lemann's *The Promised Land: The Great Black Migration and How It Changed America* (New York: Knopf, 1991).

northern cities since the nineteenth century. However, with the new migration a number of new and distinguished pastorates were undertaken. Younger black clergy, nurtured in strong Presbyterian congregations and well trained at church-related schools in the South, were recruited to organize congregations in buildings abandoned by white congregations that had relocated to other neighborhoods or to the suburbs. During the next forty years, many of these congregations became cornerstones of their communities. They provided direct service for children, youth, and families; helped new immigrants survive; and played a strong political role in advocating for the needs and rights of the people of their communities. They put the Presbyterian church in the midst of the suffering and violence that are the legacy of racial injustice. Such names as James Robinson, Edler Hawkins, Eugene and Thelma Adair, Eugene Houston, Jimmy Joe Robinson, Shelton Waters, Kermit Overton, Bryant George, Jim McDaniel, Metz Rollins, Ed Ward, and Leon Faniel come to mind among a number of others.

In the immediate postwar period, the Presbyterian church focused on establishing new congregations in the rapidly growing suburbs. Large amounts of money were assembled and administered for acquiring "choice sites," building "first units," and employing "organizing pastors." The church was eager to reproduce itself in classic patterns of ministry in white, middle-class neighborhoods in the new and growing suburbs. What was going on in the new black communities and in "changing" communities, to say nothing of increasingly deteriorating inner-city slums, was peripheral to this central thrust for new church development.

"Church planning" emerged as a development tool of urban mission under the auspices of new church development. For some church planners, analysis of demographic census data was the major tool for defining church strategy in cities. Presbyterians produced many volumes of such data, providing detailed statistical projections of ethnic composition, age, and economic and educational levels of people living in urban neighborhoods. These data were meant to show presbyteries where they could find good Presbyterian prospects for church membership. Congregations were relocated, merged, or dissolved, and new congregations were founded accordingly. Certain heavily populated communities were determined not suitable for Presbyterian ministries, because the populations were not of Presbyterian background.

At the same time dozens of long-established congregations across northern cities were struggling with their identities and their futures, as their immediate neighborhoods changed and their traditional white, affluent members dispersed to other parts of the city and to the suburbs.

Intense struggles of conscience marked the experience of most of these urban congregations as unrecognized racism became very visible when white congregations found themselves surrounded by new black and Hispanic neighbors.

However, relocation or dissolution, following adamant resistance to welcoming new neighbors, were not the only responses. During the 1950s, a number of efforts were made to build "integrated," or "multi-ethnic" congregations. Some of these congregations played important roles in organizing to "stabilize" changing communities, with the conviction that Christian faith calls for building neighborhoods where people of all races and nationalities can live side by side. The experience of most of these congregations, however, was to witness the transition of a neighborhood from white to black; the congregation, if it survived, became predominantly black.

Where a white congregation survived, it was sometimes because of its success in recruiting upwardly mobile black members who accommodated themselves to traditional Presbyterian modes of congregational life. It was through such experiences, including the effectiveness of the all-black congregations in northern cities, that Presbyterians began to recognize that *integration* would not necessarily be a criterion for success in ministry in the city. Increasingly, the contribution of black urban Presbyterian members to shaping denominational mission policy, strategy, and program came out of the experience in black congregations, and from the growing solidarity of black Presbyterians through the formation of local and national black Presbyterian organizations.[6]

By 1958, Presbyterians were ready to make a major policy statement on urban ministry.[7] The focus was on the *inner city*. Concerned with the flight of the church from the inner city, those recommendations urged that

> each church accept the responsibility to minister to its immediate total community, that each church be inclusive in its service and membership, seeking full fellowship and communion with all, without distinction of race, color or worldly condition; [further, if a church relocates to a different community] care be taken to ensure that an adequate Christian ministry is maintained in the community from which the church relo-

6. The planning strategy, born to serve the New Church Development effort, had to be modified to serve inner-city issues, and also had to be "supplemented" by new approaches.

7. See "Study of the Inner City" by the Special Committee on the Study of the Inner City, Board of National Missions, Division of Church Strategy and Development, United Presbyterian Church in the U.S.A.

cates, and that requirements for that ministry have primary claim on facilities hitherto available.

Policies like these emerged from the experience of a new breed of black activist pastors working in urban ghettos, and from a cadre of young, white pastors; some of them were World War II combat veterans who had experienced a strong sense of vocational calling to minister at points of greatest crisis and need in American society. This action by the national church governing body put brakes on the accelerating relocation of Presbyterian churches to the suburbs. Presbyteries implementing these policies refused to allow relocating congregations to sell their buildings or to transfer their assets from ministry in the inner city.

Often independent of national, regional, and local Presbyterian institutional structures, policy-making, and programs, several forces were at work — not least the movement of the Holy Spirit — to create a context for active response of Presbyterians to the needs of the city. There had now been a generation of clergy formed in the midst of unusual ferment, theological and biblical scholarship, and seminary training. Postwar urban ministry was a theological movement; its leadership was comprised of men and women who had their basic theological formation during the 1940s and 1950s. That formation was marked by Barth's emphasis on the sovereignty of God and the centrality of the Word. Other important influences came from the Niebuhrs, Berdyaev, Tillich, Bonhoeffer, Ellul, and Gollwitzer. Reinhold Niebuhr gave students practice in the political skills of discerning the signs of the times, along with the strongest kind of resistance to absolutizing any party, ideology, or strategy within history. H. Richard Niebuhr taught an ethic of response, equipping Christians to define their vocations in response to a God known to be acting in every event as creator, governor, and redeemer. Berdyaev deepened the sense of God being revealed in struggle, in the groaning of nature and history to bring creation into the fullness of God's intentions for its being. Tillich attacked the Protestant idolatry of churches that had become captive to class and nation; he nurtured sensitivity to a Holy Spirit alive in autonomous culture and in history, creating new forms of the church for the future. Bonhoeffer held up a vision of the possibilities of community in his *Life Together* and the demands for risk-taking engagement in his development of the themes "being for others" and "the church for others." Jacques Ellul, in *The Presence of the Kingdom*,[8] held together the absolute character of the Barthian transcendent Word of

8. Jacques Ellul, *The Presence of the Kingdom* (Philadelphia: Westminster Press, 1951).

God over against the world with the excitement of the mystery of that Word precisely present and powerful in the midst of human events. Gollwitzer, coming from prison camps, was making the Marxist tools available to Christians as gifts of God for realizing fuller justice within the political and economic structures.

Study of the Bible also figured large in the formation of the people who were to assume leadership in urban mission. They were taught by such biblical scholars as James Muilenberg, Paul Minear, and G. Ernest Wright. For many, the emphasis of the World Student Christian Federation on group Bible study, and particularly the methods of Suzanne de Dietrich, were important influences.

In the later 1940s and early 1950s, a number of experimental communities of Christian mission and action came into being in Europe and North America. There was much interchange both of persons and correspondence among these groups. In Europe the most influential communities were: the Iona Community, the Taize Community, the Sheffield Industrial Mission, the Gossner Mission, the French worker priests, the German Evangelical Academies, and the Mission de Paris. Abbé Georges Michonneau's book *Revolution in a City Parish*[9] and Bishop E. R. Wickham's *Church and People in an Industrial City*[10] were very influential. In the United States, the work of the East Harlem Protestant Parish and the Detroit Industrial Mission had begun.

The generation of missionaries produced in North America and in Europe through this biblical and theological renewal were impelled to take the world around them, right where they were, with deadly seriousness. The God who judges those who dwell secure in their power and privileges, and who offers promise and hope to those in poverty, in despair and bondage — the God of the Magnificat, of the Beatitudes, and of Exodus — was the one calling them into mission in the cities and industrial areas of their own countries.

These missionaries often found themselves at odds with the established structures of the churches. They rejected as idolatry the absolutizing of church, creed, and Bible as objects of worship rather than as instruments of revelation about God's action in the world. They set themselves against the apostasy that describes as "evangelism" various rites of initiation into the cults of those idolatries. They celebrated their experience of meeting

9. Georges Michonneau, *Revolution in a City Parish* (London: Blackfriars, 1949).

10. E. R. Wickham, *Church and People in an Industrial City* (London: Lutterworth, 1957).

and being blessed and renewed by God at those points where they found themselves present with poor and exploited urban dwellers and at the points where the issues of our time were joined.

Critics warned these urban mission activists that their efforts would wither if their work went on too much apart from the sustaining strength of the traditional and historic community of the Christian church, that is, the established congregations of the established churches. Yet, for many engaged in urban mission, traditional congregational life had served neither as a community of nurture and mutual support, nor as a source of helpful guidance and correction through traditional doctrine and practice. The resources of communal study of Scripture, and of a sacramental and liturgical community, were simply not available in many congregations of established Presbyterian churches. Many of those engaged in urban mission were impelled, because of their experiences of engagement with the world, to seek new forms of Christian community.

A World Council of Churches mission report expresses this well when it talks about "the church we are seeking."

> We are seeking the true community of Christ which works and suffers for his Kingdom. We seek the charismatic church which activates energies for salvation (I Cor. 12). We seek the church which initiates actions of liberation and supports the work of other liberating groups without calculating self-interest. We seek a church which is a catalyst of God's saving work in the world, a church which is not merely the refuge of the saved, but a community serving the world in the love of Christ.[11]

The East Harlem Protestant Parish, with its group ministry and storefront churches, was one of dozens of experimental inner-city initiatives taken by young clergy working across denominational lines. The organizing of the Detroit Industrial Mission, followed by the formation of industrial missions in a dozen other American cities, was another example of the search for new shapes for the church's ministry in cities.

To summarize: through the fifties, strong black Presbyterian congregations in a number of metropolitan areas had well-trained and experienced leadership carrying on service programs and giving leadership in their communities. A growing number of white men and women clergy had gained extensive experience as pastors with congregations in "transitional communities" and in the inner city. Many of them had an intense sense of

11. "Report of the Commission on World Mission and Evangelism (CWME)," Bangkok Assembly, 1973.

vocation, carrying the conviction that God had called them to exercise their ministries in arenas of urban crisis, suffering, and exploitation. These urban pastors, black and white, had experience with deteriorated housing, absentee landlords, substandard schools, police violence, drugs, family disintegration, racism, unemployment, lack of decent health care, and the dynamics of urban politics. New Presbyterian national policies on inner-city ministry had braked the flight of Presbyterian congregations to the suburbs; presbyteries were enjoined to find new ways to minister among populations in changing urban communities. On this foundation, the 1960s became for Presbyterians a period of vigorous action and experimentation in the response of the church to the city.

II. The 1960s

Here are some of the principal approaches followed during the 1960s.

1. Ethnic Identity and Black Power within Presbyterianism

Dr. Gayraud Wilmore, who headed the denomination's Church and Race Division during this period, chided those who sustained "nostalgia for racial integration" over against the emerging strength of black congregations and black leadership within presbyteries and the general assembly. There was widespread consciousness, especially among ethnic Presbyterians, that integration goals had most often served to accommodate themselves to mainstream, white, historical patterns of ministry and congregational life. Nationally and within presbyteries, strong ethnic caucuses were formed among black and Hispanic Presbyterians, and eventually Asians as well. Power exerted by these groups as well as by some strong individual leaders was to bring about, by the end of the decade, many changes in the way presbyteries and general assembly employed staff and developed and administered funds and programs.

2. Cadre Building

By the early sixties, forty presbyteries located in major metropolitan areas had created staff positions for developing and coordinating Presbyterian mission in the city. Many of these new professional staff, in addition to their theological training, had graduate degrees in social work, urban sociology, or urban planning. They worked with Urban Mission Committees that had become a standard part of presbytery structures. This was part of the radical expansion of presbytery staffs during the early sixties. Some twelve hundred "National Missionaries" had been employees of the Board of National Missions, staffing community centers, inner-city congregations, and other nationally designed programs. When in 1960 Dr. Kenneth Neigh came from the Detroit Presbytery to be secretary of the board a major change in strategy, from national hegemony to local and regional initiative, took place. Neigh believed strongly that presbyteries should define the mission of the church in their own areas, supported by national funds. In the urban presbyteries this change of strategy and structure provided strong impetus for expansion and experimentation as programs in their areas, traditionally administered from New York, became their own direct responsibility, with nationally funded local staffing.

Drawn from these people staffing the newly created local presbytery urban mission offices, a national group of "urban specialists" began to come together two or three times a year. When added to men and women from selected local urban mission projects, the group comprised about a hundred people. They met to share experience across metropolitan and regional lines, and to help shape national strategy, policy, and program. Excitement and urgency characterized those meetings as participants recounted to one another the stories of their successes and difficulties in responding to what they called the "crisis in the cities."

Among the participants in the urban specialist meetings were the six or seven post-seminary interns who were selected each year from graduating classes to work for a year under the supervision of expert urban pastors. Most of these interns went on to many years of service in Presbyterian urban mission programs. These urban specialists played a sustained role in developing denominational response to the turmoil in cities during the sixties; they also shaped the church's response to federal legislation, especially that emerging from the newly created Department of Housing and Urban Development and from President Johnson's War on Poverty. High on the agenda of urban specialists was incorporating the "maximum feasible participation" clause into the poverty legislation, and implementing in their local areas the provision that those who were to be served by government poverty programs should be involved in their design and administration. (These were insights learned from church community-organizing experience.)

3. Training Programs

Concern for equipping clergy and laity with skills for urban ministry led to a number of ecumenically sponsored training programs. Alongside the twenty-year-old Presbyterian Institute of Industrial Relations mentioned above, the Urban Training Center for Christian Ministry was established in Chicago with sponsorship from some ten national church bodies. Hundreds of seminarians, men and women clergy, and laypeople received intensive training in urban mission skills.[12] The center also served as an arena for reflection and for the development of common policies and strategies among the participating denominations. Students who came from a number of different confessional backgrounds were exposed to common methodologies. During each of three years the center received $300,000 to $400,000 grants from the Ford Foundation for the training of black clergy. This provided an important meeting place for strategizing for black clergy from all parts of the country, and afforded white students a unique opportunity to meet significant numbers of outstanding black church leaders. Jesse Jackson was an active part of UTC's training programs at that time.

Another large training effort in which Presbyterians participated was initiated by the Methodist church in New York City. Methodist Urban Church Training (later Metropolitan Urban Service Training — MUST) provided a New York counterpart to the Chicago program. Presbyterians participated actively in establishing several other ecumenical training centers as well: Atlanta Training Center, a Southeast training center based in Raleigh, a training center in Cleveland, and the Alban Institute in Washington, D.C.

During this period, theological seminaries also began to include courses on urban ministry in their curricula, and to provide urban ministry field experience for their students. In Washington, D.C., an ecumenical seminary called InterMet was created with a curriculum built around practical involvement of students in varieties of urban ministries. McCormick Seminary in Chicago found increased enrollment in its program offering a joint graduate degree in theology and social work. However, by the end of the seventies most of the courses specializing in urban ministry had disappeared from seminary curricula.

---

12. This history is fully documented in George Younger's study *From New Creation to Urban Crisis* (1987).

4. Ecumenical Structures for Urban Mission

Locally and nationally, Presbyterians had affirmed in their policy statements their commitment to ecumenical approaches to ministry in the city. In city after city, new interchurch and interfaith structures were created to facilitate response of the churches to the people and issues of the city. By 1967, Grace Goodman, doing research and documentation for the Presbyterian Board of National Missions, produced a study describing such structures in more than thirty-five cities.[13] Typically, urban mission activists found the established councils of churches uninterested and ineffective. Membership of these councils was usually made up of local *congregations* from all parts of the city and from all denominations. Since unity was a high priority for councils, controversial issues and work in situations of confrontation were seldom possible. The new urban ministry coalitions were structures representing *denominational* governing bodies, and these new organizations were usually formed by the urban ministry offices of these metropolitan jurisdictions. Unity was found in the common commitment of the activists to create church responses to human need and injustice in cities.

Nationally, the Presbyterians found that the Episcopal Church and the United Church of Christ, with whom they had participated in developing (1) urban training centers, in sponsoring (2) industrial mission, and in supporting (3) the new urban church coalitions, had also formed (4) national urban mission cadre groups. The three denominations came to recognize that their national urban mission offices were pursuing very similar agendas in support of action on housing, poverty, public education, local urban coalitions, urban training, and community organization.

A Department of Urban Church had existed since the mid-fifties in the National Council of Churches (NCC). This office provided a useful function in allowing the staffs of urban church offices of member churches to become acquainted. From time to time joint projects would be developed with support from the participating denominations. However, there was growing tension at that table as the urban mission activists of the United Church of Christ, the Episcopal Church, and the Presbyterian church across the country found themselves increasingly in the midst of controversial, prophetic programs supported by their national offices. This was especially true in relation to increasing support for community organization. At the

---

13. *New Forms of Ecumenical Cooperation for Mission in Metropolitan Areas* (New York: Division of Church Strategy and Development, Board of National Missions, United Presbyterian Church, U.S.A., August 1967).

NCC "Urban Church" table there was strong criticism and sometimes opposition to some of those forms of urban ministry.

By the mid-sixties, the three national groups of urban specialists — Episcopal, Presbyterian, United Church of Christ — had begun to hold concurrent and joint meetings. With the backing of these local leadership constituencies, the national staff people (with approval of their respective boards) brought into being the Joint Strategy and Action Committee (JSAC). For a brief period of two or three years, JSAC was an instrument through which the national staff, with a well-organized body of denominational leaders in the major metropolitan areas of the country, developed common program and funding allowing for fast and flexible response to critical events and needs in particular cities around the nation. A high degree of respect and trust had been generated among the national staffs of these three denominations and among the local urban ministry leaders across the country who had been coming together two or three times a year over a period of several years.

The quarterly publication of the Episcopal Church, *Church in Metropolis,* became a publication shared by the three denominations. The earlier Episcopal issues, along with those of the three years under JSAC editorial direction, provide perhaps the best and most readily accessible reporting on urban mission programs and concepts of the later 1960s.

JSAC, although it survived as an organization for more than twenty years, continued in its original form and purposes for less than three years. Church planners quickly saw it as a useful model for exchanging information among middle-level church administrators with functional program responsibility. Soon ten national denominations became members of a JSAC that, in addition to urban ministry, had expanded to include seven other programmatic areas. The original urban action agenda of the three founding denominational urban offices was almost completely dissipated. By that time, denominations were also beginning to back away from their high-priority commitment to urban agendas.

5. Response to Urban Revolts, Riots, and Police Violence

In city after city during the mid-sixties, ghetto residents took to the streets. General unrest provoked by bad housing, exploitive landlords, oppressive criminal justice systems, continuing racism, deteriorating schools, and pervasive poverty would be triggered through some incident. Often reaction to excessive use of police power would erupt into mass demonstrations with vandalism, fires, and pitched battles brutally repressed. The congregations whose members were residents in these communities became important advocates for programs dealing with the causes of unrest, and important mediators and brokers in bringing about truces with reparations committed for reconstruction and advocacy for new and more just relationships with urban power centers. The story of involvement of the churches in the disturbances in New York, Jersey City, Philadelphia, Kansas City, Detroit, Chicago, Los Angeles, and other cities needs a book of its own.

6. Community Organizing

For many church workers in the 1960s, community organizing became the single most important strategy for church urban mission. Community organizing was recognized as a new form of ministry that carried forward the long line of the church's service in urban communities. Whereas in the nineteenth and early twentieth century the church had pioneered in establishing schools, hospitals, community centers, and other forms of social service, community organizing represented a transformation of church thinking from service to *empowerment*. This was based on the insight that a major problem for people of deprived communities in urban society was the lack of power to participate in shaping the conditions of their own communities. Community organization was seen as a way to create institutions to empower low-income neighborhoods, and through which residents could define issues and could participate in bringing about change. A Presbyterian policy statement of 1968 said:

> The Church's traditional patterns of service in the city are undergoing drastic evaluation. As public and private secular resources, often partly due to church urging, assume larger responsibilities for social welfare the Church is relinquishing its traditional health, education, and welfare role to these auspices. Churches are recognizing the limitations of service projects developed outside a community and administered in behalf of residents. Community organization is providing a means by which powerless people are speaking and working to help themselves. . . .
>
> Church-sponsored social welfare agencies, as well as churches in low income communities, should be playing an active and growing role in initiating, supporting, and participating in neighborhood organizations. Church involvement in such organization is recognized as a vital dimension of metropolitan mission today. The Church is playing a major new

service role in its participation in and support of community organization. In a number of cities, churches have taken initiative to bring professional leadership to help people living in low income ghetto neighborhoods organize so that they may play a role in decisions about their own community life and in the processes through which decisions about their communities are made in the metropolis. This has become a significant way through which relatively affluent Christians have been able to respond to the growing gap between low income inner-city residents and the majority of Americans enjoying escalating wealth. . . .

Many Christians understand the limitations which their own isolation from the "culture of poverty" places on their ability to understand "what is good for the poor." Community organization enables persons alienated from an affluent culture to speak out and be heard across social, economic and cultural barriers. Christians and others, hearing and responding to these voices, enabled to speak by community organization, are served by a sorely needed check on the self-centeredness and sin which Christians should know infect all their most well meaning and charitable actions.[14]

The experience of the First Presbyterian Church in Chicago, with sponsorship of the presbytery and the national church, in helping to create the Woodlawn Organization served as an inspiration and a model to congregations across the country. This organizing effort, and the role of the churches in it, has been thoroughly documented in works such as Charles Silberman's *Crisis in Black and White*[15] and John Fish's *The Edge of the Ghetto*,[16] as well as numerous newspaper and magazine articles. The Industrial Areas Foundation (IAF), which grew out of the work of Saul Alinsky with mainly Roman Catholic congregations in the Chicago "Back of the Yard" neighborhood in the 1940s, provided major leadership and methodology.

At the time, churches were encouraged to take initiative in bringing together a broad base of labor unions, parents associations, block clubs, small business organizations, and social and athletic clubs to create an instrument through which a community could designate leadership and

14. *Guidelines for Development of Strategy for Metropolitan Mission* (New York: Division of Church Strategy and Development, Board of National Missions, United Presbyterian Church, U.S.A., 1967).

15. Charles Silberman, *Crisis in Black and White* (New York: Vintage Books, 1964).

16. John Fish, *The Edge of the Ghetto: A Study of Church Involvement in Community Organization* (New York: Seabury, 1966).

speak through a representative voice. In the Presbyterian church this has been a story of steadily growing experience and competence, as well as policy and strategy, since the early sixties. From 1963 through 1970 Saul Alinsky himself met annually with groups of thirty or forty mostly Presbyterian clergy for ten-day training sessions at the Asilomar YMCA camp near his summer residence at Carmel, California. Similar seminars were held during the year in other parts of the country. Each year three or four Presbyterians were supported in full-time professional training with IAF, entailing one year under the direct tutelage of Alinsky and the IAF staff in Chicago and one year of supervised internship with one of the IAF-related organizations around the country. Orientation to principles and skills of community organizing became a regular part of the metropolitan/urban mission training centers.

When Presbyterian congregations in such cities as Rochester, Buffalo, Kansas City, or San Francisco undertook to form organizing committees and to bring in professional organizers, intense controversy in both the church and the city always ensued. As the Presbyterian policy statement indicated, people comfortable with current urban power arrangements were not at all happy to hear new, heretofore excluded voices raised in criticism of traditional ways of running the city. As local congregations and the national church struggled to understand this new form of ministry, there was much soul-searching and theological reflection. Unaccustomed work had to be done by presbyteries in understanding the nature of power — what it is, and how it is held and used. Some of the biggest controversies came over the use by community organizations of abrasive and confrontational ways to assert their agendas when traditional channels proved unavailing.

Although it would be too much to say that community organizing has become a normal part of the urban mission agenda of Presbyterians, many congregations in major urban centers are actively involved, and there is a long and successful track record of including the voices of marginalized people in decision making about their communities. In recent years, community organizing has concentrated on church-based organizing, building dozens of strong organizations in cities throughout the country based on alliances of inner-city congregations. Well-known examples include COPS (Communities Organized for Public Service) in Texas where, in five cities, large, low-income Hispanic communities have been empowered to elect city council members, mayors, and state legislators; in New York City some two hundred congregations (fifteen of which are Presbyterian) participate in organizations in five communities — East Brooklyn Churches, Brooklyn

Ecumenical Council, South Bronx Churches, Harlem Churches for Community Improvement, and the Queens Citizens Organization. Among the variety of issues these organizations are tackling, they are generating several thousand units of housing affordable to the lowest income families. A national Presbyterian Office of Community Development each year helps support about twenty Presbyterian trainees in half a dozen different community organizing centers and, in conjunction with presbyteries, helps support Presbyterian congregational involvement in over fifty local organizing projects.

7. National and Local Political Action

Presbyterian urban cadres were especially active in the mid-sixties, through their ecumenical networks, in the campaign to create HUD as a new cabinet-level department in the federal government to focus on urban issues. As mentioned above, the churches were also involved in the Johnson administration's War on Poverty. Through active networking, pressure was exerted from a number of different metropolitan centers on crises in particular cities. Sometimes teams from several cities would come to the aid of the churches in a particular city facing local conflict. Urban missioners in Washington, D.C., were leaders in mobilizing the local churches to welcome the massive marches on the nation's capital during the sixties. They also helped with local logistics such as parade permits and police protection. Presbyterians played a major role in orchestrating the Chicago demonstrations during the 1968 Democratic convention where both racism and the Vietnam War raised passionate concern.

Another Presbyterian urban mission role in the sixties came through support of black communities in nominating and electing candidates for public office. Although it was usually not practical for the church to give direct support to particular candidates, through very active voter registration and get-out-the-vote programs Presbyterians, with other denominations, played significant roles that resulted in the election of black mayors in Cleveland, Gary, Newark, Los Angeles, Detroit, Washington, and other cities. Documenting the role of churches in the election of black mayors would be an interesting research project.

Three important national concerns on the urban mission agenda were affordable housing, public education, and national political action. In many localities, churches undertook campaigns for fair housing as part of their mission program, tightening legislation and compelling realtors to offer to

167

ethnic minorities rental and sale houses and apartments; pressuring banks and insurance companies to cease redlining, which made home purchase loans unavailable in low-income and minority communities; pressuring landlords to maintain buildings up to code; organizing tenants to fight for their rights; and initiating direct sponsorship for building moderate- and low-income nonprofit housing. Presbyterians, with other denominations and secular groups, founded the National Low Income Housing Coalition and the Low Income Housing Information Service to back up these programs. The Reverend Robert Johnson, who served as full-time national staff for housing concerns, played a major role in creating these organizations.

The scandalous condition of inner-city schools, both in physical plant and in quality of classroom instruction, also evoked many urban mission programs. Churches directly pressured districts and citywide school boards for increased budgets. Many churches supplemented public schools by providing study centers and tutoring programs. Working through the national Christian education divisions of several denominations, a National Ministry for Public Education was established in Washington, D.C.; it was staffed by the Reverend Douglas Still, who had come from a Presbyterian inner-city ministry in Chicago. That office lobbied for increased federal aid to public education and offered consulting assistance on programs to improve public education to churches in metropolitan centers.

National urban mission offices were pressed with increasing urgency by their local constituencies to find more effective ways to influence national legislation. In 1970 a center called IMPACT was created in Washington to provide local urban mission groups with regular information about legislation and to mobilize mission activists for quick action at crucial moments in the legislative process. IMPACT developed a computerized list of church members identified by congressional district and by commitments to act on particular social issues. During the next decade some fifteen state IMPACT organizations came into being.

8. Experimental Ministries

The national church encouraged creativity through designating some of its funds for experimental ministries. On a research and development model, three-to-five-year declining grants with built-in evaluation procedures were extended on the thesis that during that time the church could learn whether the experiment should become an ongoing program. Support for community organizing, local ecumenical structures, training programs, and clusters of congregations were among the continuing programs that gained validation through this process. Many varieties of ministry were developed with this experimental money: coffeehouse ministries, high-rise ministries, shopping center ministries, as well as ministries aimed at monitoring police practices, the administration of justice, and conditions in prisons. Presbyterians designed an ambitious experiment that supported and monitored urban ministries aimed at young adults in ten different cities. A Chicago-based "action-study" in 1966-68 did ground-breaking work in developing Christian education curricula for the inner city, including black history and special vacation church school materials.[17]

One of the most ambitious experimental efforts was the Los Angeles Regional Goals Project. Several denominations, through the NCC urban church office, joined to support a full-time clergy staff member for the Government Urban Planning office of the greater Los Angeles area. Calvin Hamilton, a Presbyterian layman who had earlier headed the urban planning office for Indianapolis, and who served on the oversight committee for Presbyterian urban mission programs, was the chief planner for Los Angeles. John Wagner left his post as director of the NCC urban church office to direct the project. Forty Los Angeles congregations became "centers of choice" where citizens came to look at the ways that goals, values, and visions for the city might shape concrete plans for the city's physical development. This project is documented in a full five-year study by John Wagner.[18]

Another major experimental program in which Presbyterians participated was initiated by the American Baptists. This was the Metropolitan Associates of Philadelphia (MAP), which was part of the World Council of Churches' Missionary Structure of the Congregation studies during the sixties. A team of clergy undertook to form "congregations" based vocationally rather than geographically — for example, people working in health care, in city government, in the legal profession, and so on. These groups, meeting in an office building in downtown Philadelphia, engaged in prayer and Bible study, created contexts for reflection on how they used their power within their secular callings, and explored ways of witness and service with the people among whom they worked. This is fully documented in the book

17. Edward White and Charles Yerkes, *Christian Education for the Powerless* (Board of Christian Education, United Presbyterian Church U.S.A., 1967). The board also published Louise White's *God Lives in the City*.

18. National Council of Churches, Department of Urban Church, "Report on the Los Angeles Regional Goals Project," 1970; see also "Summary Report of the Los Angeles Goals Council," November 1969.

edited by Dr. Thomas Wieser, *Planning for Mission*,[19] in his North American Studies on the mission structures of the congregation.

A third example was the involvement of national urban church offices in developing religious ministries in the large new town development that became Columbia, Maryland. The churches sponsored Dr. Stanley Hallett as a full-time member of the planning staff for the new town and pooled resources to build and staff a joint Protestant-Catholic religious center.

9. Internationalizing U.S. Mission

By the end of the sixties, it was obvious that the role of the United States in the world beyond its borders had a significant effect on what was happening in American cities. Links that had been established with the churches in Third World developing countries brought stories of exploitation of workers by U.S. corporations. At the same time, U.S. workers were experiencing dislocation and unemployment through the shift of domestic investment from the United States to manufacturing by cheap labor in other countries. In some cities, refugees and other immigrants began to appear with stories of their suffering under U.S.-supported Third World dictatorships. By the end of the sixties, the Presbyterian Urban Mission Office was helping to support more than thirty groups doing research on the impact of U.S. power on the welfare of people in Third World countries in southern Africa, Central America, and Asia. The North American Congress on Latin America and the Middle East Research and Information Service were originally supported in large part by urban ministry offices of the national denominations.

At the same time, people concerned with the global mission of the church recognized that the treatment of ethnic minorities in America and revolts in American cities were affecting the authenticity of American mission work abroad. From 1966 through 1968, recognizing that many U.S. missionaries had important experience in ministering in cross-cultural settings, the church brought back a large number of Presbyterian missionaries to the United States and assigned them to urban mission programs in racially intense situations. More than forty overseas churches with whom Presbyterians were related in mission were invited to send representatives

---

19. Thomas Wieser, ed., *Planning for Mission: A Report of U.S. Participation in the W.C.C. Missionary Structures of the Congregation Study* (New York: U.S. Conference for the World Council of Churches, 1966).

to help respond to the crisis in American cities. This experience became important not only in the direct services that were provided in many locations, but also in reshaping the Presbyterian church's understanding of the relationships between sending and receiving churches.

10. *Economics, Labor, and Urban Mission*

The work of the Presbyterian Institute of Industrial Relations (PIIR) since 1944 had consistently stimulated Presbyterian mission thinking about the situation of industrial workers and about the role of the corporations in the city. The Department of Church and Economic Life of the NCC and the National Religion and Labor Foundation had involved many urban mission people in study and dialogue.[20]

The sixties saw the emergence of a brilliant and dedicated group of clergy and laypeople in teams known as "Industrial Missions." This movement emerged from the studies in the early fifties on the theology of the laity. Two Presbyterian pastors influenced by PIIR were Jesse Chrisman and Jim Christiansen. After organizing a workers' church in the Detroit industrial suburb of Ecorse, they joined the team that became the Detroit Industrial Mission, initiated by the Episcopal priest, Rev. Hugh White. Presbyterians, along with several other denominations, sponsored industrial mission teams in a dozen or more American cities during the sixties and supported the National Industrial Mission, a coalition of these metropolitan-based teams. The industrial missioners did their work directly on the factory floors, and in labor union and corporation offices. They provided chaplaincies to workers on the shop floor and in offices as well as to corporation managers. They created cells and groups that studied the Bible and reflected on the dilemmas, frustrations, and possibilities of their lives in their workplaces. In many plants and offices they received a warm welcome as people tried to figure out as human beings and as Christians the roles they played as bosses and as employees.

Industrial missioners were particularly in demand to help corporations face the injustices of racial discrimination in both personal relationships and institutional patterns. They also became pioneers and experts in the field of organizational development, helping corporations discover how to build more humane conditions on the shop floor, in decision-making processes,

---

20. See the series of books produced by the NCC in the 1950s on Church and Economic Life, with participation of Reinhold Niebuhr, Walter Muelder, John Bennett, Liston Pope, John Ramsey, and others.

and in relationships between labor and management. Books by Scott Paradise, Norman Faramelli, Robert Batchelder, and others describe these programs.[21] The work is also thoroughly documented through minutes and reports kept by the individual ministries and by monitoring and evaluation carried on by the Episcopal Church. Major industrial mission efforts were undertaken in Detroit; Chicago; Cicero, Illinois; Cincinnati; New York City (Wall Street); and Boston.

Both through community-organizing activities in urban low-income communities and through the experiences of overseas missionaries and churches with U.S. corporations abroad, the Presbyterian church began to recognize that investing its financial assets in large corporations meant having some responsibility for the policies of these corporations. When Don Black, deputy general secretary of the Presbyterian Commission on Ecumenical Relations, went in 1966 to the annual stockholders meeting of the Kodak Corporation in Flemington, New Jersey, to vote Presbyterian Kodak shares in behalf of the members of the church-sponsored FIGHT organization in Rochester, Presbyterians found themselves at the forefront of a new corporate responsibility movement. Soon the denomination became one of the organizing sponsors of the Interfaith Center for Corporate Responsibility; much of the groundwork was done through the urban mission office. Through the center the churches monitored corporations in which they held investments, examining their performance in product quality; impact on the environment; employment practices, with particular attention to treatment of women and minorities; conduct of business in Third World countries; and relationships to communities where plants and offices were located.

Along with this, the denomination began to see how it could use its investments to assist community development enterprises, especially projects initiated by poor people to advance their own welfare. Out of this activity emerged the large Presbyterian Self-Development of People Program, the Presbyterian Economic Development Corporation, and the permanent Creative Investment Program; the latter earmarks a percentage of Presbyterian undesignated endowment funds for investment in affordable housing and other community development programs. A permanent denominational committee was also set up on Mission Responsibility through Investment (MRTI).

21. See Scott Paradise, *Detroit Industrial Mission* (New York: Harper and Row, 1966); Norman Faramelli, *Technethics: Christian Mission in an Age of Technology* (New York: Friendship Press, 1971); Robert C. Batchelder, *Men Who Build: Some Human Problems in the Construction Industry* (Detroit Industrial Mission Occasional Paper No. 5, 1963).

Ever since the first Presbyterian urban office was created as the Office of Immigrant and Industrial Work in 1907, through the 1960s when it was called the Office for Urban and Industrial Ministries, Presbyterians have been concerned about the condition of industrial employees in America and about the relationship of the churches with labor unions. However, by the end of the sixties, the NCC Department of Church and Economic Life had been closed, and the long-standing Religion and Labor Foundation had been dissolved. Several new Presbyterian labor initiatives emerged as the church moved into the 1970s. The National Urban Mission structures had collaborated with the NCC's National Migrant Ministry in support of the farm-workers organizing movement led by Cesar Chavez. Churches in cities throughout the country actively participated in organizing and carrying out the National Farm-Workers Union urban boycotts. The churches took great satisfaction in the success of those boycotts, helping to build the first strong national farm workers' union in America. The churches also supported the protracted struggle of the workers in the Farah clothing company, successfully boycotting Farah in a number of cities. Churches gave strong support in Kentucky and West Virginia to the struggle of coal miners against corruption within their union and in support of occupational health and safety measures in the fight against brown lung disease. At the end of the sixties, Presbyterian urban offices, along with other denominations, collaborated with the United Auto Workers in founding Southerners for Economic Justice. Staffed by Jim Sessions, who later became director of CORA (Commission on Religion in Appalachia), Southerners for Economic Justice worked with churches in a number of southern communities where union organizing was going on, helping the congregations understand and support the formation of labor unions.

III. The 1970s and 1980s

By the end of the sixties, opposition to the Vietnam War had upstaged the crisis in the cities, preoccupying the political attention of the churches and the nation. Fatigue began to overtake urban mission activists. The church and the nation were about to enter a period of reaction and retrenchment. The Presbyterian church went through a four-year period of structural reorganization and restaffing, culminating in 1972 in a new structure that merged its National Mission agency with its Education and Overseas Mission arms.

A number of observers reporting on the Presbyterian church during this period have described the reorganization as a reaction against elitist radicalism. They describe national staff as persons who administered church money to support programs chosen to implement their own radical agendas without accountability to the membership of the church at large. According to this thesis, the new structure was designed to restore accountability of the national church agencies to the constituent members of the church.

This writer takes sharp exception to such a version of events. It is possible to document that the 1960s represented the fullest expression and implementation of Presbyterian participatory and connectional polity and accountability to be seen in this century. Churches were impelled by the Holy Spirit to respond to the impact of the changes in the cities on their own institutional lives. A broad and vital engagement of clergy and church members in shaping presbytery and national church program was evoked. Traditional Presbyterian ways of doing business — often dominated by small groups of Presbyterian clergy and laity characterized by their social and economic power — were challenged through greatly increased participation of people who had hitherto been excluded, both at presbytery and national church decision-making levels. Records in city after city reveal greatly increased participation and vitality of presbytery committees taking on the challenge of the urban crisis. These committees brought programs and proposals, worked out through weeks and months of dedicated labor, to councils and presbyteries, where they were thoroughly debated. In many cases there was a significant increase in attendance and participation at presbytery meetings, stimulated by challenging and controversial proposals and debates about them. Again and again after such debate the proposals were adopted, often with strong majority votes. It was the frustration of displaced Presbyterian leadership, stymied in being unable to oppose these programs through customary exercise of their social and financial clout, that led to the backlash. These persons and groups were successful in redesigning the church in ways that would restore and reinforce their control. By the early seventies the political turning away from American commitment to government initiatives in addressing major critical social issues in housing, education, health, and poverty was accompanied by a drawing back of the Presbyterian church.

One significant element in the dynamics of these changes was that the time was overdue for progress in the emergence of racial and ethnic voice and power within the denomination. Almost all the national and presbytery urban mission staff members during the creative period of the sixties were white males. Since black empowerment, both within the church and within the society, was perhaps the *highest priority* in the agendas they pursued, success in realizing that goal necessarily meant their own displacement. It is understandable that black leadership, as its power grew through the formation of black caucuses, should view that white urban mission cadre with something between ambivalence and hostility.

By the mid-seventies, the entire group of Presbyterian urban specialists had been displaced. In many cases, they were replaced by blacks, Hispanics, or Asians, but in most cases the offices for urban mission had been entirely eliminated from presbytery structures in favor of offices on church and race, or on social welfare and social action. Black leadership in the denomination is certainly characterized by the prophetic and sometimes heroic ministries of black pastors in ghetto communities. In long-suffering and faithful struggles, black and Hispanic leaders subjected themselves to the disciplines of work within presbytery and general assembly bureaucratic structures, slowly changing them toward policies more supportive of ethnic Presbyterians. However, some ethnic leaders became effective in aligning with conservative forces of retrenchment. Those voices maintained that much of the Presbyterian urban agenda of the sixties had been inappropriately biased toward programs serving the people in the poorest urban communities. This line held that since most black Presbyterian churches were made up mainly of middle-class professional people, Presbyterian mission resources should go to support and strengthen those congregations and to form new congregations among the more affluent blacks. Conservative white leaders could demonstrate their commitment to black agendas by allying themselves with such black voices.

In the new denominational structure going into operation in 1972, there was no counterpart of the former Office for Urban and Industrial Ministries, which traced its history in the national structure back to 1907. In the development of a new structure that included offices on congregational life; church and race; self-development of people; and health, education, and welfare, some urban missioners hoped that urban-metropolitan concerns might inform the overall mission agenda. However, this turned out to be largely wishful thinking. The church became preoccupied with the processes leading to merger with the Atlanta-based Presbyterian Church, U.S., entailing yet another total restructuring and a decision to relocate the national church offices from Atlanta and New York to Louisville, Kentucky. The move itself was partly in reaction to what many considered an overly urbanized influence of church headquarters located in New York and Atlanta.

A number of persons who had been leaders in urban ministries during the 1960s did move into important executive positions in the new church.

Seven of the executives of the sixteen new synods and twelve presbytery executives had been involved with the Presbyterian urban mission cadre of the sixties.

In the 1970s and 1980s Presbyterian urban ministry agenda, both nationally and in presbyteries, refocused on the health and sickness of the local congregation. Many aging buildings in urban communities, which had been through transition in the fifties and sixties, housed congregations that lacked resources to maintain the buildings and support a pastor. Much attention was given to how these buildings might be used to serve their communities. Rental of church building space for government-supported day care and preschool programs became a common source of funds for building maintenance. Dr. Carl Dudley, based at McCormick Seminary and with significant financial support from the Lilly Endowment, developed extensive studies, consulting services, and funding for renewal in small urban congregations. Working with urban, suburban, and rural congregations, the Center for Church and Community Ministries sought to help congregations strengthen their Christian commitments to service and justice in active engagement with their communities.

The Presbyterian Self-Development of People program continued to stimulate presbyteries throughout the country to work with the poorest residents of their cities in designing economic development projects. Most of these projects supported small groups of low-income people who organized themselves for entrepreneurial manufacturing of salable products or the creation of marketable services. The Corporate Responsibility movement has continued to grow, as has the Creative Investment Program. The Presbyterian Health, Education and Welfare Association, originally founded in the fifties for Presbyterian professionals in social work, health delivery, and chaplaincy services, has grown considerably; it has become the arena where many of those who were known as urban specialists during the sixties have been able to communicate with one another and to have some voice in shaping programs of the denomination.

Presbyterian initiative has also been important in sustaining church involvement with labor. Although there has been no special national office with designated responsibility, during the seventies the church tried to respond to the crisis of widespread unemployment created by plant closings. Many Presbyterian congregations were directly affected. In Youngstown, Ohio, a major ecumenical effort was pursued to explore worker ownership of the closing steel mills there. In Pittsburgh and in Chicago the churches organized major programs of direct service to workers and families displaced by plant closings. Several denominations, with the participation of the presbyteries of Chicago, Cleveland, and Detroit, formed the Great Lakes Economic Displacement Project to study the effects of the relocation of industry from aging industrial cities to the Southwest and abroad. A new Religion and Labor Coalition was formed through which churches and labor unions actively collaborated to oppose U.S. corporations that were hampering union organizing in Asia and Latin America. William Phelps Thompson, then stated clerk for the United Presbyterian Church, chaired that coalition. More recently, Presbyterians have enlisted other denominations in forming the Washington-based Coalition for Workplace Fairness to support new legislation outlawing the replacement of striking workers.

In the eighties homelessness and affordable housing reemerged as major agenda items for the Presbyterian church. Hundreds of congregations have made their buildings available as shelters for the homeless. In almost every urban presbytery, ecumenical committees on homelessness and affordable housing are at work. The church has become a major provider of housing in urban areas through the use of federal legislation encouraging such sponsorship. New legislation in 1990 restored federal funding from a low of $6 billion at the end of the Reagan administration to the $28-billion level it had reached at the end of the Carter administration. Much of this legislation is aimed at encouraging nonprofit groups, including churches, to sponsor the building of low-income housing.

Urban community-organizing work has continued to grow over the past twenty years. Newly projected Presbyterian programs will reinforce this strategy as new policies give high priority to encouraging Presbyterians to reclaim their Reformed tradition of responsible participation in shaping a just society.

Is it possible to make projections about the character of Presbyterian urban ministry during the last years of the twentieth century? I find it risky to attempt generalization. The denomination has been very much absorbed in a series of reorganizations of its national administration since the early 1970s. It has just undergone a fourth or fifth restructuring in the last year. Much energy has been invested in the merger of the former United Presbyterian Church U.S.A. and the Presbyterian Church, U.S., leading to a relocation of national offices from New York and Atlanta to Louisville, Kentucky.

There has been heavy concentration on ways the national church can strengthen the local congregation to add new members and to nurture current membership. Some of this is designed to serve the particular needs of black, Hispanic, and Asian congregations. There is a general lack of commitment to ecumenical initiatives from the national church in relation to urban ministry.

At the same time, Presbyterians can be found among the leaders in every city across the country who initiate local coalitions of congregations and denominational governing bodies. These coalitions, often working outside the structures of local councils of churches, undergird a broad range of urban ministries, such as: responses to homelessness, work on affordable housing, ministries related to the AIDS epidemic, ministries in response to various dimensions of family crisis, and ministries with persons who are incarcerated or are ex-offenders.

For Presbyterians the role of its black congregations and its black membership in relation to this predominantly white, middle-class denomination remains an unsettled dynamic. Between 2 percent and 3 percent of Presbyterian membership is black. The extent to which the Presbyterian church will look to its own minority membership and to other blacks, Hispanics, and Asians for leadership in defining appropriate and faithful roles for the churches in the years ahead remains an unanswered and crucial question.

• 8 •

Roman Catholic Approaches
to Urban Ministry, 1945-85

FREDERICK J. PERELLA JR.

I. Foundations of Postwar Catholic Urban Ministry

Roman Catholic urban ministry in the post–World War II era was largely shaped by its foundations in the Catholic immigration period between 1840 and 1920, and by what has been called the "Golden Age of Catholic Social Action" during the Great Depression.[1] For Roman Catholics, parish and diocesan ministry *was* urban ministry because it concentrated in the industrial cities of the northeastern and northcentral states as waves of European immigrants, mostly poor and working-class, came seeking employment. Coming to a Protestant society and culture, they found support in urban Catholic parishes as they adjusted to the industrial capitalism of the United States and survived in a sometimes hostile nativist society where unskilled labor was frequently exploited and immigrants experienced the triple shock of emigration, urbanization, and industrialization. These rapid changes brought in train poverty, discrimination, overcrowded housing, poor health, and the social pathologies of fragmented families and substance addiction.

Prior to 1945, then, the experience of American Roman Catholicism

1. Special thanks is expressed to the following people for their generous help with this chapter: David O'Brien of Holy Cross College; Fr. Thomas Harvey of Catholic Charities U.S.A.; Msgr. Jack Egan of the Archdiocese of Chicago; Msgr. George Higgins of Catholic University; Fr. Philip Murnion and Harry Fagan of the National Pastoral Life Center; and Jerry Ernst of the National Catholic Conference for Interracial Justice.

179

was a story of urban ministry. But there was no distinctive concept of "urban ministry," a term that seems rooted in Protestant experience and suggested a dichotomy between ordinary Roman Catholic life and some specialized activity. At the beginning of the postwar period, Roman Catholic engagement of urban life can be viewed as four major "streams" or styles.[2]

1. Immigrant/Community Church

This stream is composed of local and parish-based organizations and institutions that embody the church's role as a worshipping, protective, and enabling community of faith and culture. The parish was and remains the primary center for pastoral care and development of people in the Catholic urban experience. Parishes and parish-based institutions were under the authority of the local pastor, who, while accountable to the local bishop, for the most part operated autonomously. There was little denominational or metropolitan policy or strategy, except to multiply parishes in order to provide these ministries to Catholics. Parishes were geographically defined, which meant that the clergy had pastoral responsibility for the care of all souls in their neighborhood. Therefore Catholic parishes and their institutions, while ethnocentric and creed centered, often extended their services to others in their area. In this immigrant-community stream could be found Catholic churches, elementary and secondary schools, and some local parish credit unions or small consumer cooperatives. In 1945 there were 7,493 parochial schools and 1,599 diocesan high schools in the United States, mostly in the cities.[3] In addition, the immigrant-community church created volunteer, self-help social services, such as emergency aid funds and volunteer mutual assistance groups like the St. Vincent de Paul Society.

2. Labor Organizing

Worker organizing, the second stream of Catholic urban ministry, began in ethnic neighborhoods and parishes. As unions grew large and national in scope, church involvement moved beyond the parish base to labor

---

2. These streams are loosely based upon the ideas of David J. O'Brien, who outlines three major styles in the U.S. Catholic Church's history of public life; see his *Public Catholicism* (New York: Macmillan, 1989), especially chap. 9, "Styles of Public Catholicism," pp. 230-52.

3. O'Brien, p. 23.

schools and leadership training networks, such as the Association for Catholic Trade Unionists. In 1945, there were one hundred Catholic labor schools or leadership institutes in the United States.[4] Little in the way of diocesan or national policy or organization-guided union organizing. The church's involvement was led by committed and charismatic individual clergy and laity. Union organizing and legislative work was a kind of informal "lay mission," integrated into the church through personal relationships. The labor schools maintained a loose network, as did the clergy who were active as advocates for labor; many convened periodically at conferences organized by the Social Action Department of the National Catholic Welfare Conference (the national social action agency and Washington representative for U.S. Catholic bishops) and the National Conference of Catholic Charities.

3. Establishment Church Services and Advocacy

This third stream grew from the huge expansion of the Catholic population between 1850 and 1920. Bishops and religious orders followed two main approaches to provide Catholic institutions to care for their own poor and dysfunctional people.

Health and Human Services. Hospitals, orphanages, homes for unwed mothers, colleges, and, especially after 1920, central professional social work and child welfare agencies were built under the auspices of religious orders or dioceses and provided intensive assistance to the poor, most of whom were Catholics. Initially supported by contributions to the bishop, gifts to religious orders, and individual fund-raising appeals, they later received funds from Community Chest movements and gradually became more dependent upon public, nonsectarian charitable monies. Between 1931 and 1985, professional diocesan Catholic Charities agencies grew from 30 to 160 in number. In 1945, there were 163 juvenile protective institutions serving over 20,000 residents and 373 orphanages with 48,000 residents; Catholic hospitals treated over 3.2 million patients.[5]

Reform Advocacy. Pro-labor and social welfare legislation was promoted by the Social Action Department of the National Catholic Welfare Conference, led by Msgr. John A. Ryan and Msgr. Raymond McGowan, and

4. Aaron Abell, *American Catholicism and Social Action: A Search for Social Justice, 1865-1950* (Garden City, N.Y.: Hanover House, 1960), pp. 275-76.

5. O'Brien, p. 212.

the National Conference of Catholic Charities, led by Msgr. John O'Grady. They did this in dialogue with supportive bishops, networks of labor priests and labor schools, Catholic lay leaders in unions and politics, and diocesan social work officials. This was the only form of national church policy and strategy for urban mission issues.

Fr. Charles Curran has described the operating theory behind these establishment church approaches as "Catholic Liberalism," which engaged in rational political advocacy at the national level and scientific casework and urban planning at the local level to achieve an ideal society.[6]

4. Prophetic Church Alternative Communities

The tragedy of the Great Depression prompted a tumultuous debate about the merits of industrial capitalism and gave birth to more prophetic, less political social movements. A network of hospitality houses and mutual-support centers grew from lay movements like Dorothy Day's Catholic Worker and Baroness Catherine de Hueck's Friendship House, both begun in New York City. They emphasized a radical commitment to communal sharing and presence among the poor. They withdrew from active engagement with mainstream social institutions and eschewed attempts to use government or legislative strategies to reform society. However, because of their independent prophetic approach, these movements could and did confront issues of race and war that other streams of Catholic social mission did not address. In 1939 there were over forty Catholic Worker houses or cell communities in over thirty cities.[7] Thousands of Catholic lay and clergy leaders were influenced by the Worker's commitment to social justice, service of the poor, and defense of the rights of labor. Friendship Houses, which engaged in somewhat more direct political advocacy and were more focused on interracial justice, extended to six cities between 1938 and 1948.[8]

The Catholic Worker, like the Friendship House network, was more a movement than an organization and had no systematic, theoretical framework. Rather, as Curran describes it, worker communities had a consistent *worldview:* pro-labor, pacifist, and opposed to racism and industrial society

6. Charles E. Curran, *American Social Ethics: Twentieth Century Approaches* (Notre Dame, Ind.: University of Notre Dame Press, 1984), pp. 164-65.

7. J. P. Dolan, *The American Catholic Experience* (Garden City, N.Y.: Doubleday, 1985), pp. 411-12.

8. Dolan, p. 413.

because they manipulated and depersonalized individuals. This stream was prophetic because it did not worry about political effectiveness or systemic reform, emphasizing rather change of the heart, individual witness, and a faithful way of life based upon a radical spiritual commitment.

II. Forces for Change, 1945-60

Roman Catholic urban ministry immediately after World War II essentially continued its pre-1945 streams. But significant changes in that period forced a gradual evolution in the Catholic urban experience. Like many mainline Protestants, Roman Catholics moved by the millions to the suburbs. Some diocesan ordinaries such as Cardinal Dougherty of Philadelphia and Cardinal Mundelein of Chicago had begun creating suburban parishes twenty years earlier. City parishes with reserve capital were asked to assist new parish development with inexpensive loans. Many dioceses also lent funds directly for suburban parish development. This suburbanization of the church and the concomitant postwar "baby boom" also led to the construction of thousands of new Catholic schools and convents as well, and to a less communal, middle-class church experience.

Ethnicity began to break down because the new parishes were composed of Catholics of many nationalities whose common bonds were education, income level, and status as military veterans. The inverse of this was the massive migration of southern blacks and of Hispanics to the northeastern and northcentral cities. In some areas, the locality-orientation of Roman Catholic parishes resulted in priests and staff reaching out to convert and welcome the new residents. Many in-migrating blacks accepted Catholicism partly because of the support they received from parishes and Catholic religious orders. But there were still more examples of exclusion and racial tension on the part of Catholic urban dwellers, priests, and institutions.

As some urban pastors began to involve themselves with the needs of the black and Hispanic parishioners and neighbors, and labor priests with minority unionists, some urban priests became more and more involved with issues of racial justice, housing, urban renewal, and employment discrimination. Although many white ethnic Catholics left the cities, the parishes stayed, and so did their schools. The archbishops of Washington, D.C., Chicago, New Orleans, and St. Louis stunned many Catholics as well as others by desegregating the churches and schools in the late 1940s and early 1950s.

In many city parishes, community life began to atrophy with the demographic shifts, and many of the parish-based ethnic and lay associations and mutual aid societies began to die out. Labor union development also slowed during this period as unions fought to consolidate and maintain the benefits they had won in the thirties and forties. The prophetic movements were quieted by the conservative, anticommunist, and prosperous American climate. The gradual shift of Catholic urban experience was contemporaneous with several small but influential movements of change in the church. First, associations of black Roman Catholics, religious order priests, and some progressive lay leaders had begun forming federations and councils seeking racial equality initially in the church, but also in civil society. The most prominent of these were the Catholic Interracial Councils led by the Jesuit John La Farge. By 1954 there were thirty-five such councils in the northern and southern United States.[9]

Second, lay apostolic movements flourished in certain sections of the nation during the forties and fifties. There was a cluster of associations that followed the methodology of the "Jocist" movements in Europe inspired by Père Joseph Cardijn. His approach centered on small groups of mostly lay members, meeting weekly to "see, judge, and act" upon their environment. A form of what was called the Catholic Action movement, the Jocist movements created a structure, process, and somewhat autonomous mode of operations for the lay apostolate. Groups such as the Young Christian Workers, Young Christian Students, and the Christian Family Movement, all centered at Notre Dame University and in Chicago, spread to over thirty-five cities in 1947. Priests, including Reynold Hillenbrand; Louis Putz, C.S.C.; and later, John Egan, all of the Chicago–northern Indiana area, were formed in a style of pastoral ministry that sought the empowerment of the laity to translate the church's social vision into societal realities.[10] Msgr. Hillenbrand, later rector of the Chicago seminary, influenced hundreds of priests in training. Fr. Putz organized Catholic students at Notre Dame who successfully pushed for the university to desegregate in the early 1940s.

In all of these small but powerful movements a new theology and idea of lay apostolate took form. Centered on Eucharistic and liturgical relevance and unity, and on the theological concept of the mystical body of Christ, these movements and others like them produced a generation of Catholic lay leaders who believed that they shared with the clergy in the mission and ministry of the church, particularly in the quest for social and

9. Dolan, p. 369.
10. Dolan, pp. 414-16.

racial justice. Also, they no longer considered themselves to be under clerical supervision. The unity to be spiritually and sacramentally achieved in Eucharist was also to be sought in society. The Eucharist therefore provided the power, and was the goal, for the social apostolate. In this era, Chicago was critically important, serving as the paradigm and creative source for urban Roman Catholics in the United States.

Third, major historical events brought all of these new spirits to the surface in the Catholic Church in the United States. The Second Vatican Council, convened by Pope John XXIII, marked an epochal opening of the Catholic Church to the world, which issued in rapid growth of lay involvement in the church's internal ministries as well as in the social apostolate, and in an explosion of ecumenical and interfaith collaboration for social reform. Another major event was the growing civil rights movement in the United States. Although there was no strong Catholic involvement in the southern civil rights campaign, a growing number of priests and laity in the North were aware of it and sympathetic to it. Catholic priests and students responded to the call for volunteers in the voter registration drives, freedom bus rides, and marches against segregation in the South. Finally, the election of John Kennedy, the first Roman Catholic to become president, signified for many Catholics not only that they had grown out of their immigrant and ethnic status, but that Catholics had the right and the duty to take responsibility for the nation's improvement. The problem was, it wasn't clear how being a Catholic should inform this new engagement. These mighty movements of society and of the Spirit unloosed a multiform and energetic social urban ministry in the 1960-85 period.

III. Streams of Urban Ministry, 1960-85

1. Urban Parish as Mission Outreach and Sign of Presence

The changing demographics of northern industrial cities and neighborhoods presented Catholic parishes with a struggle to define their mission and identity. In the 1945-60 period, many ethnic and national parishes steadfastly maintained their cultural and racial heritage, almost as a defense against the perception of lost gains as black and Hispanic in-migrants arrived looking for work. Others simply diminished in size and vitality. But a noteworthy number, motivated by the traditional Catholic notion of territorial parish as well as the belief that Catholicism was the true form of Christianity and universal in its mission to all peoples, engaged in sincere campaigns of proselytizing and service to the surrounding neighbors. Some parishes, such as St. Charles in Harlem and St. Elizabeth's in Philadelphia, became authentically black Catholic parishes, with a complete range of traditional Catholic societies and institutions, especially schools. Many blacks converted to Catholicism through the energetic outreach campaigns and instructional classes in these parishes. In some dioceses, black and Hispanic parishes were initiated along the lines of the old white ethnic or national parishes.

During the 1960s, a larger number of urban parishes became involved in the War on Poverty with its emphasis on local community action. The government desired the church's moral and social authority and support and, although public funds could not be used to fund the churches themselves, clergy frequently offered their churches as service centers where the social and educational needs of residents in the community could be met. Funding from local Community Action Programs (CAP) made possible efforts such as Project Head Start, which Catholic parishes hosted by the hundreds; remedial programs, which were staffed by suburban church volunteers and Catholic college and high school students; recreational programs for children; job training efforts; emergency food and clothing centers; and many others.

The involvement of Catholic parishes in these community service programs represented a different approach from that of the black or Hispanic "national" parish because the clergy and staff did not focus as much on building the congregation or seek participants to convert to Catholicism. In part because the CAP-sponsored programs were community and government sponsored, and in part because the ecumenical spirit of social mission put less importance on denominational identity, such parishes were less focused on building a worshipping congregation. Ministry was characterized by an openhandedness and respect for people's dignity and beliefs. The prevailing concept was that the church was called by the gospel of Christ to stand in loving service and to work for the dignity and the rights of the poor, so that a theology of presence and witness developed among such urban parish staff. Both the "ethnic parish" approach and the parish-as-mission-outreach approach represented continuations of the immigrant-community church stream from the prewar period. Social and educational services, funded by the War on Poverty, were community based and sprang up independently of Catholic Charities or other church establishment structures. "Hero" pastors such as Fr. James Groppi in Milwaukee and Fr. Geno Baroni in Washington, D.C., were known and respected because of their participation in the community and on ecumenical boards and councils, and because their churches were great human development centers.

Two major problems with the "mission outreach" model of urban church gradually surfaced. First, many of them did not have a strong political base, since they were not built on the kind of ethnic religious community typical of the urban Catholic parishes in the immigrant period. Simply put, many of the people they served did not come to church there, if anywhere. Second, the decline in paying membership — it was often considered wrong to ask for financial support from the community being served, as this would be seen as a sign of proselytizing and not of true charitable service — caused urban parishes to begin depending upon the dioceses for subsidy. The same applied to urban parochial schools. Great efforts were mounted in the 1960s and 1970s to keep parishes and schools open. Creative financial programs like the Interparish Sharing Fund in the Archdiocese of Detroit, the Cooperative Parish Sharing in the Archdiocese of Hartford, and the Christian Sharing Fund in the Archdiocese of St. Paul, as well as "twinning" or sister parish financial support relationships, generated millions of dollars of support by suburban churches for urban parishes and ministries. The twinning concept and program was begun in 1966 by Fr. John Egan of Chicago, whose Church of the Presentation in Lawndale began a people-to-people exchange with a well-to-do parish. This later evolved into a financial sharing program that was widely imitated elsewhere.

Subsidy relationships eventually began to cause dependency and resentment in some parishes, and increasing financial problems in dioceses in the 1970s and 1980s caused subsidy programs to shrink or be consolidated into other diocesan structures. From a religious point of view, traditionalists always distrusted this form of parish ministry because it was unorthodox and did not, in their view, fulfill the church's chief mission: the spread of faith in Jesus Christ through participation in the Roman Catholic Church. Traditionalist critics described this model of parish and pastor as "social activism," activity deemed less spiritual, and ephemeral. Here is an example of the conflict between inward orientation and public mission that arose during the transition from the immigrant period to the post-1960 period of the U.S. Catholic Church. In part, traditionalist criticism anticipated later reassessments of urban mission that examined the need for organized religious communities in urban society. The parish-as-mission-outreach stream assumed that the church institutions would provide the physical and manpower base upon which to build programs of service. It failed to produce the cultural, communal, and leadership power that only a vibrant faith community can. It is only fair to say, however, that this stream, present even now in thousands of locations in the United States, has provided millions of examples of Christian witness and charity and opportunities for middle-class Catholic laity, clergy, and sisters to find new expression of their desire to engage in ministry and service. And it has helped to educate and assist millions of poor and marginalized people, regardless of their faith.

2. Parish and Diocesan Housing Development

One of the primary issues encountered by urban clergy and staff in the 1950s was the need for decent, affordable housing. With the rapid immigration of blacks from the South and Hispanics from Puerto Rico and Mexico into the northern industrial centers, neighborhood tensions arose around integration and the phenomenon of block busting. Also, the 1950s saw a major urban government planning movement under the rubric of "urban renewal," which purported to tear down and reconstruct dilapidated neighborhoods and housing, but which more often disrupted old neighborhoods and divided sections of cities by racial and national lines. Government-subsidized housing construction, prompted by federal housing legislation in 1948 that promised a decent, affordable home for every American, took the form both of public housing developments and of privately sponsored but government-subsidized developments.

Roman Catholic priests and staff were conspicuous in these efforts. Often beginning as advocates for their parishioners and neighbors, clergy joined in planning and community action to fight unwanted urban reconstruction or to build public or subsidized housing according to community needs. Fighting wanton urban renewal gave birth to the community-organizing efforts described later. Many priests served on public housing commissions and initiated small housing developments and, later, housing development corporations. Between 1964 and 1974, for example, sixty-four Catholic dioceses participated in constructing over twenty-five thousand units of housing. Half of these were in urban areas, offered rental units to senior citizens, and were managed by independent agencies created or hired to do it. Many were the result of ecumenical and interfaith coalitions and corporations.

Such efforts led to development of large, highly sophisticated housing development and management organizations in dioceses such as St. Paul, Boston, Brooklyn, New Orleans, and St. Louis. Later, in the 1970s, through such networks as the Campaign for Human Development, Roman Catholic clergy and laity supported the development of housing cooperatives and other family-oriented, home ownership approaches, such as the Inter-Faith

188

Adopt-a-Building Sweat Equity Cooperatives in New York. These were alternatives to public housing that had so often been found wanting in human scale, manageable size, and a sense of community ownership. Also, private rental housing developments were not usually under the control of the occupants, so church networks turned to approaches emphasizing more participant control or to managing the rental development efforts themselves.

3. The Catholic Interracial Justice Movement and Diocesan Human Relations Offices

In 1958, the National Catholic Welfare Conference issued a pastoral "Statement on Discrimination and the Christian Conscience." Although it condemned racial discrimination and prejudice as a sinful violation of the church's assertion of basic human rights for all persons, it did not have a program of action and gained little attention from Catholic people. Organized Catholic action for racial justice issued from grass-roots networks such as the Catholic Interracial Councils, sixty of which federated in 1958 to form the National Catholic Conference for Interracial Justice (NCCIJ). Headed by Mathew Ahmann, a competent organizer, NCCIJ pulled together from around the country clergy and religious and lay activists who were engaged in racial justice work. These annual meetings became a seeding ground for new ideas about ministry and political action.

In January 1963, NCCIJ initiated the first major interfaith meeting, the National Conference on Religion and Race. This conference enlisted sponsorship from seventy national religious denominations and organizations. The conferees resolved to create conferences on religion and race in ten cities, aiming to build understanding and shared action agendas among various church and racial groups. Such interracial and interfaith groups appeared in far more than ten cities; it was a spontaneous phenomenon not attributable solely to NCCIJ's work, though its contribution was a major impetus. The commitment to interfaith action for racial justice also led NCCIJ to recruit Roman Catholics to participate in the March for Jobs and Freedom in August 1963, and the March to Selma in 1965, which saw over four hundred priests and many more Catholic sisters, brothers, and laity join forces with Protestants, Jews, and other advocates of civil rights.[11]

11. Philip Gleadon, ed., *Contemporary Catholicism in the United States* (Notre Dame, Ind.: University of Notre Dame Press, 1969); see chap. 7, "The Catholic Church and the Negro," pp. 147ff.

In addition, NCCIJ promoted local racial justice activities within Catholic circles: interracial home visits in cities around the nation were aimed at building understanding among the races; leadership training programs were offered in the black community; and remedial education projects provided tutoring and recreation programs that met in urban Catholic churches and were staffed by suburban and middle-class white Catholic volunteers. Three teams of religious sisters, headed by Sister Margaret Traxler, traveled around the country encouraging nuns to leave traditional apostolates in Catholic schools and other institutions and get involved in social action. This promoted one of the major personnel and ministry changes in Catholic urban ministry in the postwar period; as a side effect it also prompted talk of more collaborative decision making and independence by women professionals in the church, as women religious applied the theology and spirituality of social justice to their own context inside the institutional church. Women religious, as well as members of men's religious orders, played a major role in the development of new church and autonomous urban ministry movements in the 1960-85 period.

Finally, NCCIJ led the establishment of Project Equality in twenty dioceses. Project Equality fought for fair employment practices by organizing parishes to purchase products only from companies that did not discriminate in their hiring and promotion practices. It also encouraged church institutions to hire black and other minority persons. A grant of $522,200 from the Ford Foundation in 1968 spearheaded this effort.[12]

A major result of these NCCIJ training and action programs was the creation of human relations offices at the diocesan level. Professionally staffed church-funded offices, part of the bishop's chancery structure, were created in Detroit, St. Louis, and New Orleans. Much of the programmatic activity described above was then organized by human relations offices such as these, which became the prototypes for diocesan social action offices in many more cities later in the 1960s and 1970s. The human relations offices were led by priests, but were founded implicitly on the role of the laity in the work of social justice. Offices such as the one in Detroit, led by Father James Sheehan, created a huge urban-suburban network of individual volunteers through Project Commitment, where laity recruited directly from suburban parishes were trained to serve as allies in working on urban problems. Committees of lay leaders in 150 parishes were then organized around issues, selected by the activists in Project Commitment. The spiritual foundation for this was a commitment to the human rights vision of

12. Gleadon, pp. 147ff.

the church. The suburban parishes were not involved as organizational units but rather as recruiting grounds for the action committees. While the Detroit diocesan office worked hard to involve pastors and keep them informed, it was inevitable that the lay networks became semiautonomous, a kind of parallel structure, with pastors wondering whose agenda their own lay members were working for. The Project Commitment action committees were prototypes of the social action committees that sprang up across the country, and many had similar experiences of being a vehicle for lay mission and being very involved in social justice; but in many places they were marginal to parish institutional life, relating more closely to the diocesan office than to their own parishes.

Interfaith coalitions and ministries proliferated at the diocesan and local level to a much greater degree than at the national or regional level. These human relations offices effectively translated the Vatican Council's Decree on Ecumenism into action for racial and social justice because they could agree on these issues of human dignity without becoming ensnared in theological or ecclesiological disputes. But it was just such focus and freedom to act that, in many cases, also marginated them from the center of chancery and parish life.

4. Community Organization: Empowerment at the Local Level

In 1958, Cardinal Meyer of Chicago created an archdiocesan Office of Urban Affairs and appointed Monsignor John Egan to head it. Egan had served as archdiocesan moderator for the CANA Conference, a young adult ministry focused upon couples and young adults recently married. He was deeply involved in the Père Cardijn movement and sought in his ministry to integrate liturgy, social action, and the apostolate of the laity in society. He had also staffed the Cardinal's Conservation Commission in an early response to urban changes.

The Office of Urban Affairs continued the archdiocese's collaboration with the community organizer Saul Alinsky. Alinsky became famous in the late 1930s by creating a nonpartisan, church-union alliance in the "Back-of-the-Yards" stockyard worker neighborhoods of Chicago. Alinsky's theory was that urban problems adversely affecting the poor derived from their lack of social organization. To address urban poverty and social problems, the poor had to be enabled to analyze problems afflicting them, pinpoint the social institutions (and their leaders) who had power over the situation, develop an alternative vision of how these institutions could work with the community, and focus a campaign of political power to pressure those leaders and institutions to accede to the community organization's requests. This method was based upon the concept that most social problems resulted from a lack of political and social power among the poor, resulting in their inability to deal in the pluralistic interest group bargaining of the industrial city. Alinsky believed that a humane and democratic social order was built upon diverse organized communities able to bargain for their interests in the marketplace of economics, politics, and ideas. Protestant ministers, Catholic priests, and lay union leaders began to work together and rallied thousands of neighbors behind workplace and neighborhood improvement issues.

Alinsky and his associates were hired by the archdiocese to help address the growing racial tension and fragmentation of neighborhoods by urban renewal projects. Cardinals Stritch and Meyer wanted to encourage Chicago Catholics to stay in the city rather than to flee integration, to avoid the scandal of Catholics acting like bigots and the dissolution of city parishes.

The answer was to create a series of neighborhood community organizations drawing leadership and support from the churches. Alinsky believed that black, Hispanic, and white neighborhoods, organized separately but addressing similar issues, would form alliances for power and interact in a stable and mutually respectful manner. The training of priests as partners in organizing began in 1959. Between 1958 and 1964, three major community organizations were created in Chicago with much personal and financial support from Catholic parishes, pastors, and the archdiocese: the Organization of the Southwest Community (OSC), the Woodlawn Organization, and the Northwest Community Organization.[13]

Chicago's urban affairs office under Egan does not seem to have had a grand design for urban ministry or a systematic theory of the city. Its strategy was the *process* of community organizing. Church teachings about basic human rights, social participation, and the dignity of all peoples provided the theological underpinnings. The community-organization style of local decision making and practical political bargaining, based upon urban interest groups, was familiar to urban Catholics and clergy who had grown up with the immigrant tradition. Community organization was an American incarnation of the Roman Catholic social teaching about the right to participate in society, an extension of the immigrant/church and labor organizing streams.

13. A detailed history of the "Chicago Pattern" through the mid-1960s is available in P. David Finks, *The Radical Vision of Saul Alinsky* (New York: Paulist Press, 1984).

Given the church's affinity for urban neighborhood politics, it is not surprising that community organization spread rapidly in the U.S. Catholic urban ministry. Egan began to develop a cadre of clergy and religious interested in his approach to urban poverty when they convened at the annual NCCIJ conferences. Until that point human and civil rights work had not directly addressed urban poverty. After the initial urban riots occurred in 1964, Charles Silberman's book *Crisis in Black and White* broadcast the Chicago organizing story nationwide, and community organizing then became a major element in secular governmental theories of social renewal. It also grew in popularity among Protestant, Catholic, and Jewish advocates for racial and economic justice around the country.

"Urban affairs" was therefore a ministry waiting to happen, and by late 1965 similar offices had been created in the Archdioceses of Baltimore, Detroit, New York, St. Paul, and Washington, D.C., as well as the Dioceses of Dayton, Houston, and Omaha.[14] By 1968, more were added in Hartford, Milwaukee, and later in Cleveland, Syracuse, and Boston. These judicatory urban affairs offices, like the human relations offices before them, were prototypes of and forerunners of later diocesan social action offices. Most diocesan urban affairs operations focused upon organizing the poor and near poor to advocate for their own issues, especially Office of Economic Opportunity (OEO) antipoverty programs, urban renewal, and housing development. Diocesan office leaders participated personally in interfaith coalitions and programs, and fostered similar collaboration among congregations.

In 1967, the Reverend Edgar Chandler of the Chicago Church Federation, Rabbi Irving Rosenbaum of the Chicago Union of American Hebrew Congregations, and Monsignor Egan, the three principal leaders of the Interreligious Council on Urban Affairs in Chicago, joined Rabbi Marc Tannenbaum of New York in creating the Interreligious Foundation for Community Organizing (IFCO), an interfaith organization set up to promote, recruit personnel, and channel funding for community organization. In order to get a seat on the IFCO board, Egan had to organize a denominational group interested in community organizing. He therefore convened a small group of Roman Catholic priest-directors of other urban affairs offices, finally calling it the Catholic Committee on Urban Ministry (CCUM). CCUM, which began as a mutual support network, grew rapidly in the 1972-75 period into a diverse network of thousands of Roman Catholic social justice advocates — priests, sisters, and laity — engaged in

14. Joseph H. Fichter, S.J., "Chicago's Archdiocesan Office of Urban Affairs," *America Magazine*, October 23, 1965, p. 463.

all forms of social ministry, well beyond the initial urban focus. CCUM brought together hundreds of these advocates twice a year, once at an annual conference and again at a four-week summer training institute, both held at the University of Notre Dame. CCUM took up the convening and networking function that NCCIJ had performed in the 1960s. It became a gathering place for Roman Catholic radicals and reform activists, a school for thousands of new urban ministry personnel, and an advocate with the U.S. bishops for legitimization of urban and social ministry in the church.[15]

Community organization as a strategy spread even more rapidly in the 1970s because a national church program called the Campaign for Human Development (CHD; see below) was created in 1970. CHD provided national legitimization and, most importantly, funding, for thousands of community-based, *ecumenically sponsored* organizations, both urban and rural. In the mid-1970s, CHD was named by the Ford Foundation as the largest and most significant source of financial support for community organization in the United States, long after War on Poverty funds and VISTA had been curtailed under President Nixon's administration. Organizations like the UNO (United Neighborhood Organization) in Los Angeles, HART (Hartford Areas Rally Together) in Hartford, COPS (Communities Organized for Public Service) in San Antonio, SECO (Southeast Community Organization) in Baltimore, TCO (Twin Cities Organization) in St. Paul–Minneapolis, and many more were partly led by Roman Catholic priests and significantly funded by laity through their annual giving to the Campaign for Human Development.

Organizing still represents a major strategy in Roman Catholic urban ministry, but it has been limited by some major shortcomings. Although it was rationalized by principles in Catholic social doctrine, its process has rarely included an overt dimension of spirituality or evangelism. In addition, its method of social conflict leading to negotiation frightens many in the church. Consequently, organizing can appear to be a secular and even divisive activity to many bishops, and to even more priests and laity. More recently, attempts to address this problem and to engage congregations more completely have led to programs of church- or congregation-based organizing (see below).

A larger social-political problem was that power alliances were hard to form across urban-suburban lines, and some of the systemic issues facing low-income communities have not been addressed due to the organizations'

15. John J. Egan, Philip J. Murnion, and Peggy Roach, "Catholic Committee on Urban Ministry: Minister to the Ministers," *Review of Religious Research* 20, no. 3 (Summer 1979): 282-83.

lack of large-scale political influence and agendas. Larger historical trends in urban industrial communities are beyond the reach of community organizing. Trends such as the switch to service economies or the international movement of jobs and capital, which vitally affect low-income and working-class workers, are too large for traditional community organizing to tackle and require a clear political-economic theory that neither programmatic organizing nor Catholic public advocacy ever could develop.

In spite of these shortcomings, however, organizing and its sister strategy of community-based economic development represent social change approaches that undertake the transformation of culture and history envisioned in contemporary understandings of Christian social ministry.

5. Diocesan Social Action Offices

Judicatory-sponsored agencies like the human relations and urban affairs offices anticipated the widespread establishment of social action or justice and peace offices in large and middle-sized urban dioceses, as well as in predominantly rural dioceses. Between 1965 and 1980, such offices were created in over 100 of the 180-plus Roman Catholic judicatories in the United States. In some cases, these agencies succeeded or absorbed the earlier human rights or urban offices.

Diocesan social action offices are diverse in form, size, and strategy. About half were, or later became, departments of Catholic Charities, while the others were established independently of existing charities structures, usually as a department of the bishop's chancery staff. Competition and duplication of effort were frequent consequences of this. The social action offices had evolved separately as direct responses to the social and theological innovations of the 1960s and 1970s. Further, Catholic Charities institutions tended to be slow in undertaking parish or community-based social action, and in incorporating contemporary theology about social justice and transformation.

Diocesan social action offices pursued diverse program strategies, but most typical were: (1) parish-oriented social justice education about issues facing nonwhites and low-income persons; (2) participation in ecumenical and interfaith legislative and direct action coalitions; (3) provision of some assistance to parish and community-based social ministries in fund-raising and applying for government and foundation support. In many cases these offices also administered diocesan funds for support of urban ministry and parishes (described above in "Urban Parish as Mission Outreach and Sign of Presence") and served as local administrators for the national church's Campaign for Human Development.

This mix of activities increasingly grew to include public education and political action about international as well as domestic issues, since the growth of diocesan social action offices occurred simultaneously with the explosion of concern in the United States about military policy and U.S. imperialism in the Third World during the Vietnam War. The antiwar and international justice movements added a major area of concern to diocesan social action agendas, which resulted in enormously complex agendas being pursued by small staffs with limited resources. In spite of the growing focus on political policy, few of these offices maintained professional public policy lobbying staffs. Their actions were therefore aimed at generating awareness and direct action (boycotts, demonstrations), and issuing statements.

Developments like these, and the evolution of urban indigenous people's movements in debates over racial and ethnic empowerment, unfortunately drew many diocesan social action offices away from direct work with urban pastors or black and other nonwhite communities, and from direct sponsorship of local urban ministries of community organizations. Although a friendly and altruistic relationship has been maintained, and social policy advocacy and funding are still aimed to benefit people of color who are poor, the constituency of diocesan social action offices increasingly consists of liberal middle-class Catholics who believe in the issues of social justice. In the domestic field, their political agendas are not often set by the people they intend to benefit. This has allowed a certain fragmentation in Catholic urban ministry to continue, and led to suspicion by some that such offices are the creatures of liberal ideologues in the church.

However, the growth and institutional sponsorship of diocesan social action offices has marked official acceptance on the part of bishops in the United States that the educational and advocacy role of the church on issues of human rights and social justice is an essential and central aspect of church life. These offices have served as the agents of concrete interfaith and ecumenical relationships, able to focus upon practical agendas of common concern, rather than the more difficult ecclesial stumbling blocks of doctrine, worship, ritual, and intercommunion. In many dioceses, acceptance by clergy and church professionals of the congruence of social concern and spirituality has also been facilitated by these offices. Real accomplishments in interreligious legislative coalitions, community development, and community organizing have been achieved.

On the other hand, it is doubtful that diocesan social action offices can claim a large constituency among lay members of the church. Most lay members are unaware of their existence. Also, a tension between pastors and diocesan staffs has continued, because of implicit competition over the time and energies of parishioners. Diocesan agencies are often perceived as chancery agents, outside forces, that import programs and issues to the parish. The challenge of engendering a social mission agenda from within the parish base, and with it a larger constituency within the churches, still confronts diocesan offices. In part, the parish-based organizing and parish social ministry movements (see below) that evolved in the 1980s are meant to address this problem.

6. Empowerment Strategies

In the late 1960s popular movements examining the need for economic, political, and cultural power among nonwhites and the poor issued from the civil rights era. These movements, based upon growing critiques of Western, white-dominated capitalist sociocultural systems, were simultaneous with developments in church teaching that challenged the Western models of development and cultures. But the most important factor was a dramatic and dangerous rise in conflict between racial and ethnic groups in cities around the nation. These dynamics were caused in part by failed federal antipoverty programs, by political battles over control of War on Poverty funding and programs, and by a growing resentment by white urban dwellers of these programs and the civil disturbances occurring during that period.

For the first time in decades, black Catholic clergy convened nationally and formed the Black Clergy Caucus in 1965. The U.S. bishops appointed an Urban Task Force in 1968 with the assignment of (1) coordinating the activities of appropriate church agencies and organizations at the national level; and (2) providing the research, planning, communications, and field service support necessary to carry out an effective program without duplications.[16] The Social Action Department of the U.S. Catholic Conference (USCC) also recommended that "urban task forces" be created in every diocese to carry out similar activities at the local level and to collaborate with the national office. It recommended that these offices be

16. "The Church and the Urban Crisis," a report of the U.S. Catholic Conference Social Action Department, April 23, 1968. (The U.S. Catholic Conference is the national coordinating structure of the Catholic bishops, formerly known as the National Catholic Welfare Conference.)

staffed by full-time, professionally qualified staff.[17] The USCC's office was staffed by Fr. John McCarthy of Houston, Texas; Fr. Charles Burns, S.V.D., a black priest from Cleveland; and Fr. David Finks, the priest from Rochester, New York, who had headed the urban office for Bishop Fulton Sheen and spearheaded Catholic participation in the Saul Alinsky–led FIGHT organization.

After widespread consultations with church urban officials around the country, the task force reported in Fall 1969, calling for establishment of a National Office of Black Catholics; a much upgraded Division for the Spanish Speaking (an office already in existence at the USCC); a pastoral strategy to address the fears and similar needs of white ethnic populations coexisting in the cities with blacks, Hispanics, and others; and a national "annual collection for human development to be a concrete example of the way the nation can develop new priorities and new efforts in meeting the needs of society."[18] The Urban Task Force, inspired by Msgr. Geno Baroni's analysis of racial conflict, envisioned a coordinated strategy of national and local programs promoting community organization, economic development, and cultural identity. These efforts, to be engendered by indigenous communities through processes of self-determination, would hopefully yield a "New Coalition," which, though culturally pluralistic, would find common ground in seeking decent education, housing, employment, political representation, and recognition of the dignity of each culture. Only by consciously working to overcome the roots of racial divisiveness and polarization could the urban crisis be addressed.

The National Office of Black Catholics (NOBC). This office was created in 1970 and funded by an annual national church collection called "Black Catholics Concerned." The office served as a center for convening and educational training for people engaged in pastoral work among black Catholics. NOBC's history has frequently been troubled. Leaders were divided over whether to exist independently of the bishop's conference, or to be part of it. As a result it always had a kind of marginal status. Only about a third of the dioceses — those with a noticeable number of black Catholics — took the "Black Catholics Concerned" collection, so the office always struggled for funding. Because of its focus on racism and self-determination, NOBC's agenda centered on internal issues of culture and representation, fighting for more aggressive programs of recruitment of

17. "Church and the Urban Crisis."
18. "Task Force on Urban Problems Report," U.S. Catholic Conference, November 11, 1969; from U.S. Catholic Conference Archives.

black clergy and religious, for development of black and African liturgical and spiritual expression, for affirmative action in hiring church personnel, and for appointment of black bishops. Diocesan black apostolate offices were created in cities with large black Catholic populations, including Boston, New York, Philadelphia, Baltimore, Washington, New Orleans, Cincinnati, St. Louis, Chicago, and others.

Unfortunately, conflicts among leaders within the various associations led to estrangement of the Black Clergy Caucus, Black Sisters Conference, and Black Catholic Brothers network from NOBC, which was criticized in the 1980s for maintaining a self-perpetuating clique of lay leaders unrepresentative of wider lay circles. In the mid-1980s this led to the creation of a new movement by the priests and religious called the Black Catholic Congress, and in 1988 the first national Congress of Black Catholics in the twentieth century convened. The congress spawned a national pastoral plan and a series of training programs to address issues ranging from Afrocentric spirituality to strategies for strengthening the African American family and young men. The congress movement has been led by a caucus of black bishops, now twelve strong in the National Conference of Bishops, and has achieved the internal institutional status that NOBC never attained.

Secretariat for Hispanic Affairs. The Division for the Spanish Speaking was upgraded in an organizational restructuring at the USCC in the mid-1970s, and Hispanic layman Pablo Sedillo was named secretary for Hispanic affairs. From the beginning, the Hispanic secretariat possessed a more central position in the national church structure than did NOBC. Its programs have stressed development of prayer, spirituality, and leadership appropriate to the various Hispanic nationalities that belong to the church in the United States. From the appointment of the first Mexican American bishop in 1970, the number of Hispanic bishops has grown to twenty-one. Regional pastoral training centers that work in collaboration with the national secretariat were created in New York, Illinois, and California. These were inspired by the landmark Mexican American Cultural Center (MACC) in San Antonio. MACC served as a combination convening center, Hispanic CCUM, theology school, and pastoral training institute. Through MACC and other institutes, the Catholic liberation theology created by Latin American theologians was adapted and applied to North American pastoral formation in the Catholic Church. Hispanic networks of priests and sisters ("Los Padres" and "Las Hermanas"), similar to those organized among black Catholics, were created and have served as mutual support and advocacy vehicles for their members.

In 1975 and in 1977, the Hispanic secretariat convened national meetings to strengthen pastoral and religious education strategies. These led to a process of local, regional, and national consultations called "Encuentros," producing a national pastoral plan and training institutes. This process served as the model for the black congress process described above.

It can be debated how effectively the cultural empowerment offices have changed the church. In their early stages, the offices represented an effort at a kind of hospitality on the part of the white-European-immigrant-dominated church. The fundamental issue was: how can the church (we) make *them* feel less excluded, more like a part of the church? The hospitality approach is gradually being replaced by organizational efforts that are truly conscious of culture and are being led by indigenous leaders and theologians. This development is much stronger among Hispanics, particularly Mexicans, than African Americans. Because of their focus on internal issues of cultural inclusion, these movements in the church have not expressed themselves as often in political or social ministry. Thus, as they moved into the concerns of racism in the church, the gap widened between the urban ministry offices and the cultural empowerment offices. Moreover, neither has developed a strong evangelism strategy, a fact that may derive, particularly among African Americans, from the lack of indigenous clergy; from the lack of warm, emotive, supportive models of local congregations; and from the need for models of church that make it easy for laity to participate in leadership. The Hispanic movements have also been greatly strengthened by the demographic fact that Hispanics represent 17 percent of U.S. Catholics, a proportion that will increase greatly in the next twenty years.

7. Geno Baroni and the White Ethnic and Neighborhood Development Movement

Monsignor Geno Baroni of Washington, D.C., attempted to create a multifaceted "New Coalition," as proposed by the USCC Urban Task Force, but it failed because of the territorial distancing experienced by NOBC, the internal ecclesial orientation of both the Hispanic and the black programs, and the unwillingness of the bishops conference to back the white ethnic movement as part of the U.S. Catholic Conference structure. The bishops feared that the effort was unnecessary and would engender white racist activity. Therefore Baroni, with timely assistance from the Ford Foundation, created an independent National Office of Urban Ethnic Affairs in 1971.

Baroni's center evolved into a national resource and program center that focused upon ethnic cultural heritage development, neighborhood economic development, and the role of ethnic parishes in rejuvenating urban community. Ethnic festivals, ethnic heritage studies programs, housing development, small business economic development corporations, and neighborhood-controlled urban planning, as well as the rejuvenation of neighborhood credit unions, were the primary efforts to convene alliances between black and white ethnic coalitions, later also including Hispanics. These were promoted nationally, most notably in Gary, Indiana; in Detroit; and in Newark, New Jersey. Baroni's efforts won legislative support from both the Nixon and Carter administrations, and under President Carter Baroni ultimately joined HUD as assistant secretary with special responsibility for neighborhood housing and economic development.

Baroni's approach stressed partnership among government, private sector, and community institutions, a view that later won widespread acceptance among some policy-makers in the United States and was specifically promoted by the U.S. Bishops Pastoral Letter on the Economy in 1986.[19] The ethnicity movement was a national success in the 1970s. However, Baroni never achieved the sponsorship or inclusion in national church social ministry he originally sought. His programs were more strongly backed by political leaders and foundations. One major Baroni effort, the Catholic Conference for Ethnic and Neighborhood Affairs, aimed to organize a network of urban ethnic Roman Catholic clergy. It broke up partly because of a dispute with its coordinators and because Baroni was unable to pull the ethnic clergy, many of whom were independent and entrepreneurial, into a cohesive network.

Neighborhood economic and housing development, however, was widely adopted as an urban ministry strategy by many urban parishes and by some diocesan social action offices. Programs such as Interfaith Adopt-a-Building in New York City enabled low- and near-low-income Hispanic families to obtain vacant tenements, restore them with government-subsidized loans and Department of Labor trainees, and turn them into cooperative housing. A national network of community credit unions was organized and funded with special assistance from the National Credit Union Administration and technical support from Baroni's national center. Economic development corporations, supported both by start-up grants from the Ford Foundation and by the federal government, were fostered in many cities and assisted the launching or regeneration of small neighborhood businesses. Baroni's national

19. National Conference of Catholic Bishops, *Economic Justice for All* (Washington, D.C.: United States Catholic Conference, 1986).

center staff lobbied for the government and foundation funds and were supported by them in providing technical assistance to hundreds of such projects. Roman Catholic parishes and clergy were often central to the neighborhood leadership and coalitions that produced these programs. Many received critical staff and budget support from the U.S. bishops' Campaign for Human Development, and some got interest-free loans as well. After Baroni joined HUD, many of his key economic development ideas became policies at HUD between 1977 and 1981.

Baroni's strategic approach was a combination of cultural and economic empowerment, and was motivated by his analysis that racism and prejudice are greatly aided when racial or nationality groups lack a power base and property. The urban ethnic affairs movement attempted to continue or re-create the dynamics of social solidarity and neighborhood economic resource development that had worked for Catholic immigrants in previous decades. In this way, Baroni's approach was a methodological and conceptual extension of the immigrant-community church stream, but was more consciously based upon culture and community development than on the parish as service provider or social gathering place. Projects in this stream often were connected to and begun by community organizing, but frequently broke with organizing because development groups found that issue organizing and campaigns were too adversarial and that more collaborative modes of operation were needed to generate private investment and support by governmental agencies.

8. Political and Economic Empowerment: The Campaign for Human Development

The 1969 report of the U.S. Catholic Conference's Urban Task Force included a recommendation to create a special fund with a national church collection, which would support programs seeking self-determination of the poor, change of attitudes about race and poverty, and change of unjust social and economic structures. These concepts, first presented in the bishops' document "A Statement on the National Race Crisis: 1968," became the basis for the U.S. Catholic Conference's first national policy and program specifically addressing poverty and urban realities. Initially approved as a National Crusade against Poverty, it was re-billed the Campaign for Human Development (CHD). The creation of CHD marked several important developments with the U.S. Catholic hierarchy. First, the notion of working collaboratively with community leaders regardless of race or religion was a major step of solidarity with the poor and toward interfaith action. CHD funds could not be used for projects predominantly controlled by the church or the government. Its intention was, and is, to support the empowerment of people to name their own economic and social agenda. Second, the church assumed the responsibility to raise funds nationally and to distribute them through collaborative planning and action with diocesan bishops and staff. CHD was truly a national and diocesan policy. Third, the concepts of systemic injustice and social system reform, as central church strategies among the poor, were officially adopted for the first time in the U.S. Catholic Church. However, CHD never really had a theory or concept of social system reform. Rather, it stressed enabling participation in the system that exists, through self-help political and economic organizing.

The Campaign for Human Development has operated in diverse ways in the U.S. Catholic Church. In some dioceses it has functioned as a giving fund providing financial support for grass-roots groups; in others CHD has been the centerpiece of multifaceted metropolitan ministries that provide organizing, leadership training, funding, and political alliance to community-church coalitions. Partnerships of Catholic parishes with other denominational congregations, labor-based groups, and community-based groups extended Roman Catholic involvement in urban (and rural) development programs beyond providing cash to include their social, political, and investment capital resources. By 1985, after fifteen years, Roman Catholic involvement had supported over three thousand projects with over $80 million in grants, not counting the other forms of contribution. Over 75 percent of the money has gone to community-organizing projects. Also, housing development, urban consumer cooperatives, and rural producer cooperatives have received significant CHD support. CHD projects set a high priority on interracial understanding and collaboration. In 1985, 210 of its over 600 grants, or about 33 percent, went to projects in which there was close collaboration between Hispanics, African Americans, and whites. CHD's history has been to fund both urban and rural development efforts. By 1985, 30 percent of funded projects represented coalitions of *both* urban and rural communities.[20]

The Campaign for Human Development represents a convergent evolution of the immigrant church and labor-organizing streams that appeared in the pre-1945 Catholic urban strategies. Its theological basis is found in the classic Catholic human rights tradition, and the more con-

20. Data from U.S. Catholic Conference, *Daring to Seek Justice: People Working Together* (Washington, D.C., 1986).

temporary development about social justice (empowerment and liberation) and human development;[21] it also draws upon American self-interest pluralism.

In spite of the widespread effect of the CHD's efforts, major shortcomings can also be discerned. First, until 1985 or so, CHD projects were developed virtually on a track parallel to church pastoral strategies; there was little or no integration with pastoral planning and congregational development. CHD projects were, in effect, the fruits of qualitative church "outreach" into the community. Second, although many projects involved clergy and laity as leaders or members of their constituency, they rarely involved the parish faith communities as units. Such projects, therefore, were not often seen as expressions of evangelism or development of the community of faith. Overt effort to integrate prayer and spiritual reflection into the dynamics of the projects has been rare. As a result, many CHD projects have operated in a church organizational vacuum. Only in dioceses where the social action offices pursue a strong agenda of community organizing has this tendency been offset, and only since 1985 has the issue of integration into parish faith community development been addressed in movements toward congregational-based organizing (see below, "The Appearance of Other Strategies").

Nonetheless, CHD remains a major element of Catholic urban ministry strategy, which has been made a standing policy and program of the U.S. Catholic Conference.

9. Establishment-Church Strategies: Social Services and Social Reform; Catholic Charities and the 1972 "Cadre" Study

Catholic Social Services/Catholic Family Services (CSS/CFS). During the first twenty years after World War II, institutional human and social-service agencies under Catholic Family or Social Services maintained the basic patterns developed in the prewar era: professional social workers and counselors undertook casework, clinical psychological therapy, adoption, and other family-adjustment supports. In many larger dioceses, these services were complemented by providing relief in the form of food, clothing, and

---

21. In his 1967 encyclical letter *Populorum Progressio,* Pope Paul VI outlined for the first time in Catholic teaching a hierarchical progression of human and social development, beginning with fundamental personal growth and development. This concept of integral stages of human development includes the ability to own, produce, and participate in social and political decision making as central to human dignity.

emergency housing assistance, often supported by lay volunteer societies named after St. Vincent de Paul, Daughters of Charity, or Councils of Catholic Women. These lay organizations were independent, but many operated as lay auxiliaries of the local Catholic Charities structure, or as parish-based groups that effected a kind of liaison with local congregations. Agency funding came from community, nonsectarian sources, chiefly the Community Chest, later called the United Way, and from diocesan fund drives. Professionalization of social work, and the use of quasi-public funding sources, often had two effects. First, Catholic Social Services staff and program strategies became more secular and less tied to evangelistic or congregational developments. Second, in spite of the fact that many CSS/CFS agencies focused upon predominantly Roman Catholic constituencies in the years after the war, when public funding began to call for more community-oriented and nonsectarian services, CSS/CFS gradually increased their service to people of color and non-Catholic background. As of the late 1980s, a significant majority of Charities' services are provided to people of color and to the poor, regardless of religion. This development was embraced by theological perspectives that developed in the 1970s.

The turmoil during the 1960s, the War on Poverty programs and funding, and developments in Roman Catholic social doctrine converged to move leaders of the National Conference of Catholic Charities to undertake a strategic review of their missions and strategies. A two-year intensive study, known informally as the "Cadre Study" (after the fact that it was led by a cadre of key leaders), produced a report in 1972 entitled "Toward a Renewed Catholic Charities Movement." The basic thesis of the report was that if Catholic Charities wanted to change society into a more just social order, it must first change itself. In 1970, 140 dioceses had Catholic Charities operations, comprising over five hundred agencies and one thousand institutions. The report called for Charities to refocus and reemphasize social transformation as well as social amelioration approaches. Efforts for social reform, public policy lobbying, organizing and planning activities — the concerns of more classic Catholic social action — were called for, in addition to the traditional provision of services. Charities was to perform a role, not as a delegate or surrogate agency of charity, but as an enabler of communities and congregations. Its goal was to empower the poor and enable the Catholic people to act for change. The programmatic paradigm suggested was threefold: continuing commitment to service; advocacy for social reform; and convening the Christian community and other concerned people for education, consciousness raising, recruitment, and action.

The National Conference of Catholic Charities staff and structure were reorganized around these programs and began fifteen years of intensive efforts to support development of professional management and planning at the diocesan level, national involvement in key religious and human service legislative coalitions, and the development of national policy papers for use in local advocacy and education work. A major effort called Parish Outreach began in 1976. Its goal was to enable diocesan charities agencies to develop programs to convene and train parish social action committees in planning, social service, community organizing, and public policy work. Leadership training was stressed and, between 1976 and 1982, the number of diocesan charities operations that operated Parish Outreach offices grew from thirty-five to nearly sixty. In those dioceses, 39 percent of parishes (approximately thirty-five hundred) had Parish Outreach committees affiliated with or collaborating with the diocesan charities. These tended to develop more in the larger urban dioceses.

Catholic Charities frequently found themselves in internal turf conflicts with the diocesan social action offices that had evolved from the interracial relations and urban affairs movements. The staffs of the latter were often not professionally trained social workers and took more of a social witness approach to their advocacy, appearing to be more controversial. Many bishops experienced a huge proliferation of ministry offices and staffs after the Vatican Council era, and attempted to consolidate management and budget structures. Often, the social action offices were competing for budget with more conservative charities' agencies, and the more conservative chancery budget committees favored the institutional charities. Or, social action offices were placed under the management of Catholic Charities and experienced varying degrees of friction or constraint. In the late 1970s and early 1980s, there was a fair amount of competition between these diocesan church agencies for the attention of the bishops, for funds, and for collaboration with parishes. By the late 1980s this had been resolved in most dioceses through unified managements or clear delineations of responsibilities and collaborative arrangements.

It is fair to say that Catholic Charities has assumed the major role in diocesan social ministries in the United States. In fact, by 1990, Catholic Charities U.S.A. was the largest nonprofit human service organization in the United States. In 1990 over twelve hundred Catholic Charities agencies spent over $1.6 billion and reached over 8 million people.[22]

22. "Catholic Charities Judged as 'Most Efficient' Charity," *Pittsburgh Catholic*, December 13, 1991, p. 1.

10. Political Ministries

The involvement of church members in social justice and human rights advocacy at all levels evolved during the 1970s and 1980s into highly coordinated and more sophisticated political action programs. These programs were and are nonpartisan in their orientation, based upon a concept of Christian citizenship that calls church members to share in shaping social order so that it becomes more human and more conducive to full human development.

Independent coalitions and organizations of religious women and men were organized around national and regional peace and justice centers in the 1960s and 1970s. By far the most influential, particularly talking about issues of economic and international justice, has been NETWORK, a private membership organization of Catholic sisters, which developed a strong and professional lobbying presence at the U.S. Congress beginning in 1971. NETWORK bases its work on the church's teachings and concepts of biblical justice, but derives its positions from research and the opinions of its members. NETWORK also has presented qualitative training in legislative advocacy for anyone willing to attend its annual summer institute.

A number of diocesan social action offices developed skilled lobbying and legislative action operations as they matured from their early stages in the 1960s. Dioceses such as St. Paul, Cleveland, Rochester, Hartford, St. Louis, San Francisco, and Washington, D.C., either employed professional lobbyists to work with state and federal legislatures or developed closely coordinated working relationships with the state Catholic Conferences. Many diocesan offices also joined or organized interfaith and church/community legislative coalitions on housing, welfare reform, health care, jobs, and other issues affecting the poor. Catholic Charities' decision in the Cadre Study to renew its commitment to the public policy process led many diocesan and state networks of Catholic Charities institutions to form their own legislative offices or to resource the state Catholic Conference legislative agendas in a collaborative way. They also joined in human service agency coalitions with other religions as well as nonsectarian agencies at the state and national levels.

It has been rare that parishes as organizations have joined or supported the legislative networks on urban issues, although efforts have been made to develop a church public agenda including justice, right to life, and Catholic education issues.

These political ministries realized an involvement in public policy debate that was unprecedented in American Catholic experience and at times confused both Catholics and others about the boundaries of appropriate church-state relations. Also, they established strong precedents of ecumenical and interfaith collaboration on the issue of the social good of the society.

The U.S. Catholic Conference developed a large and capable policy staff in both domestic and international social development, and during the 1980s the USCC's Social Development and World Peace Department took the lead in the U.S. church in providing legitimacy for political ministry and developing pastoral teaching about social and urban issues; it produced major teaching statements on the U.S. economy, housing, race relations, and other urban issues. Together with the Roundtable, an association of diocesan social action directors, the USCC's Social Development Department instituted in the mid-1980s an annual conference that convened diocesan and religious social justice leaders, as well as the Campaign for Human Development network and others. They sponsor an annual summer institute to provide training for staff of diocesan social action offices. These efforts renewed the convening and mutual support function that the Catholic Committee on Urban Ministry (CCUM) provided Catholic social justice activists in the early 1970s. But the participants are more often the employees of institutional church social ministry offices than they were in the CCUM era.

An often-heard criticism of the political and social justice networks described here is that they do not include a representative number of African American, Hispanic, and other nonwhite, non-Anglo leaders or staff. This fact does not seem to be caused so much by unconscious racism as by the reality that Catholic urban and social justice ministries no longer have the urban constituency with which they began in the early civil rights era. They are led by sincere church staff and volunteers who are motivated by a vision of justice to speak on behalf of the poor in the United States and in the Third World. But this reflects the degree to which the social ministry networks have diverged from the needs and issues of urban pastors, parishioners, and residents. A renewed commitment to the organization and empowerment of urban pastors, parishes, and residents is necessary before the gap between the movements of indigenous church leaders and the professional social justice agencies can be closed.

11. The Appearance of Other Strategies

The Resurgence of Prophetic Grass-Roots Ministries. The years during and after the Vietnam War saw an explosion of witness communities that modeled alternative lifestyles and preached radical social change. These were often centered on a radical identification with the poor and a critique of Western and U.S. economic and international policies. They were rarely sponsored by or under the organizational aegis of dioceses or parishes, and were led by committed laity and members of women's and men's religious orders. Groups such as the Justice and Peace center in Milwaukee, Wisconsin, and the Community for Creative Non-Violence in Washington, D.C., developed effective educational and action efforts addressing U.S. government policies, corporate behavior, and direct relief assistance to the poor. They also integrated direct prophetic protest actions with a life of prayer and worship in communitarian organizations. These were more contemporary cousins of the Catholic Worker and Friendship Houses of the 1940s, adding radical political critique and political action to the earlier communities' practices of simple life and service to the poor.

With the deep recession of the early 1980s and the severe cutbacks in federal government aid programs initiated by the Reagan administration, soup kitchen and hospitality house ministries reappeared in large numbers. Some were organized after the model and network of the Catholic Worker, although with less of a pacifist focus. Others became full-fledged nonprofit agencies (such as homeless shelters and transitional houses), as homeless individuals and families, deinstitutionalized patients of mental hospitals, and substance abusers hit the streets in unprecedented numbers. Although many of the more professional shelters were organized by, or consolidated under, Catholic Charities, many still are autonomous and constitute a strong but unofficial urban ministry of Roman Catholic religious and laity.

Church-Based Community Organization. The shrinking of financial and political support from government and foundations for community organization and development, which resulted from Reagan administration policy changes in 1981, and the problems experienced by community organizing networks in connecting congregations' spiritual goals with the social justice activities of the diocesan and national church, prompted attempts to achieve a more integrated approach to community organization and development. Under the concept of congregation or parish-based organizing, networks such as the Industrial Areas Foundation and the Campaign for Human Development began to stress training and funding that make the parishes and churches in a community the constituency for an organization. Rather than merely sponsoring or physically hosting a neighborhood organizing project in which some parishioners and the pastor get involved, organizing strategies call for the entire parish to be interviewed and for an intensive program of leadership development to take place in each member parish. The entire life of the church can become the object for such organizations, so that church finances and youth ministry may become objectives as well as community affairs such as housing, crime, or jobs. Economic development is based on investment by parishioners and the parishes themselves, as they are helped to bargain with local banks and governments for partnerships.

Projects such as the East Brooklyn Churches, the Naugatuck Valley Project in Connecticut, BUILD in Baltimore, and UNO in Los Angeles (the last three organized by the Industrial Areas Foundation), not only developed their organizational bases within the religious congregations sponsoring them, but engaged significant investment of church members' and congregations' bank deposits and other capital to leverage larger investments from governments and banks in moderate-priced housing and worker-owned businesses proposed by their organizations. The agendas for these congregational organizing projects were developed in a process of consultations and prayer, which included theological and biblical reflection, about basic goals and values of the churches.

IV. Summary

Urban ministry in the Roman Catholic experience has taken a myriad of forms and occurred literally in thousands of combinations of the basic streams and strategies I have summarized above.

The four streams describe programmatic approaches to addressing the needs and realities of urban people: building faith communities that also provide services among the people in urban areas; working for governmental and societal action to reform laws and social institutions; operating service institutions that serve needy urban dwellers; empowering urban dwellers to become advocates and subjects of their own action; and modeling new communities or organizations that refuse to accept the logic and methods of the dominant society, and that test out alternative ways to address urban realities based upon a radical vision of social justice, equality, and human rights for all. These forms evolved greatly since 1945, but can be traced back to the forms prevalent at the end of the war period.

As the Roman Catholic community looks to the future of urban ministry, critical questions rise from its experience since World War II. Among them are the following:

1. Can the church develop a contemporary urban ministry strategy that integrates the missions of service and pursuit of social justice into the

building of faith communities? The strength of the church is in communities of belief, values, and mutually supportive action. Urban ministry that is not based on strong faith communities will be ephemeral or marginal, and possibly dependent upon the institutional church for ongoing financial support. While the church must always support ministries of charity, justice, and hospitality as a witness to the love of God and the dignity of people, ultimately these will not last without faith communities for whom urban mission proceeds from their worship and shared prayer life.

2. How can strong urban faith communities be developed without a strong program of evangelism, and how can this be done without competition among Christian denominations and congregations? Should the Roman Catholic experience of parish institution development be repeated with African Americans, Hispanics, and Asians? Should the model of the national parish, which allowed for pride of ownership and a sense of equality in the church, replace the practice of seeking shared or integrated parishes?

3. How can a strong evangelistic effort be mounted unless there is a strong commitment to development of indigenous leaders and ministers among those being evangelized? These in turn will need to be supported and empowered to create their own agenda for the transformation of their urban communities.

4. In order for the church to bring the power of its members to the work of urban ministry, partnerships must be created between congregations of urban and suburban dwellers, between whites and people of color. Issues of racism and cultural division will need to receive much more attention.

5. Can community organizing succeed in service to congregational development? And can it impact social-economic relations in the long run unless it leads people to a shared philosophy of social and political institutions?

6. What role shall the urban Catholic school play in future urban ministry efforts, especially in leadership development and the building of faith communities? How shall these be financed, and by whom?

7. What shall be the functions of ecumenical activities in maintaining or building a holistic approach to urban ministry in the future, especially if evangelism and faith community development are central aspects?

8. What shall be the role and stance of Roman Catholicism in public life, in working to build a just social order and to stand by the poor, when many of the poor are of different races and religious traditions? How will the Catholic people be educated, encouraged, and organized to support a church that is outwardly oriented in a pluralistic society, and in which a concept of the lay vocation in politics and in society has not evolved much?

• 9 •

Retreat, Reentry, and Retrenchment: Urban Ministry in the United Church of Christ, 1945-80

DONALD R. STEINLE

I. Deserting the City — Seeds of Re-creation: 1940-60

An infamous story is widely told of a conference minister in the United Church of Christ (UCC) who attended a church meeting and dinner in a small inner-city congregation. Its members were mostly descendants of German immigrants, and the church was in a changing neighborhood whose current population was largely Portuguese. After enjoying some of the German cuisine for which the church members were famous, the conference minister gave a brief speech. Following the speech, one of the officers of the congregation asked, "What do you think is the future of our church?" Without hesitation the conference minister responded, "You have no future!" Then he promptly packed up and departed.

Tragically, in the *informal* policy and practices of the United Church of Christ and its predecessor denominations, this has been the predominant attitude toward local churches in the city, especially in neighborhoods marked by rapid social, racial, and economic change. It has been somewhat less true of the Evangelical and Reformed tradition that combined with the Congregational Christian stream to form the United Church of Christ in 1957. On the Evangelical and Reformed side, there has been more emphasis on pouring resources and support into dwindling inner-city churches than on the Congregational Christian side. Still, the major emphasis of the whole denomination — officials, pastors, and laity — has been to foster new church development and support in those communities where its "natural constituencies" — white, European ethnic groups — were settling. "White flight" from America's large cities has been taken for granted by the denomination that also assumed local congregations should move to and be started in "high potential" areas, especially suburban areas adjacent to core cities. The Minutes of General Synod XII noted in 1979: "During the past twenty years, the number of U.C.C. churches in the ten largest cities has dropped from a total of 405 in 1957, to a total of 305 in 1977, a 25% decline."[1] Walter E. Ziegenhals observed in 1978 that the Chicago Metropolitan Association of the United Church of Christ had lost an average of a church a year in that city since 1900.[2] Thus, the burgeoning suburban communities that began to arise after World War II became fertile ground for new church development, and the movement of local congregations from city to suburb characterized all the predecessor denominations of the United Church of Christ. The "suburban captivity of the churches," to use Gibson Winter's famous phrase, was no stranger to the United Church of Christ, nor it to such bondage.

Some analysis of the contributory causes and reasons for the widespread desertion of our cities by local congregations of the United Church of Christ is appropriate. First, there is the well-documented theological and faith stance of most members of mainline Protestant denominations, including the United Church of Christ, commonly referred to as the "privatization" of the gospel. In this theology there is strong emphasis on personal salvation and individual moral virtue.[3] Such a faith stance leaves little room for concern about the "public" arenas of life, including the city as a form of social organization. Consequently, there seems little reason to maintain local church institutions in what seems to be a hostile environment.

A second and closely related attitude is a strong anti-urban bias that cuts through American society and is shared by most members in the United Church of Christ. John Lindsay, the former New York City mayor, has put it most bluntly:

> A strong anti-urban attitude runs consistently through the mainstream of American thinking. Much of the drive behind the settlement of Amer-

1. "Minutes of General Synod XII," United Church of Christ, p. 84.
2. Walter E. Ziegenhals, *Urban Churches in Transition* (New York: Pilgrim Press, 1978), p. 16.
3. David A. Roozen, William McKinney, and Jackson W. Carroll, *Varieties of Religious Presence* (New York: Pilgrim Press, 1984), pp. 9ff.

ica was in reaction to the conditions in European industrial centers, and much of the rhetoric behind the basis of freedom in America was linked directly to the perfectibility of man outside the corrupt impulses of the city.[4]

Such sentiments have been articulated by figures as diverse as Thomas Jefferson, Alexis de Tocqueville, and Jacques Ellul.

A third attitudinal factor contributing to the decline of UCC local congregations in the city is pervasive white racism — personal, social, and institutional. Unfortunately, members of the United Church of Christ are not immune to this ugly reality that infects so much of American life. Therefore, when the neighborhoods of these local churches began to include increasing numbers of African American and Latino families, many local churches of the United Church of Christ fled in fear and dismay.

Contributing to and undergirding these attitudinal factors were certain structural and organizational features of the United Church of Christ that led many local congregations to leave the city. Most local churches in the UCC tradition were organized assuming certain patterns and styles of life, above all a strong nuclear family, which were more true of rural and small-town existence than of rapidly changing metropolitan areas. An inability or unwillingness to change these structures of church organization contributed to declining membership and loss of financial strength.

Adding to this problem was a heavy denominational emphasis on increasing church membership and strengthening financial support for the national church. Because of this, the vast amount of national church resources and money from the end of World War II up to the present day has gone into building new churches in high growth potential areas.

The final element in the organizational dilemma facing the United Church of Christ is the extraordinarily strong emphasis on local church autonomy and independence. This is especially true of the Congregational Christian side of the tradition. Such local autonomy is guaranteed by Article Fifteen of the constitution of the United Church of Christ. Lyle Schaller has commented bluntly: "A pure congregational polity will eliminate the church from the inner city."[5]

Perhaps most damning of all, we in the United Church of Christ — from the top leadership of the denomination to the last person in the pew — simply have not expected much from our local congregations in the city.

---

4. John Lindsay, *The City* (New York: W. W. Norton, 1970), pp. 47f.
5. Lyle E. Schaller, "Organizing for Missions," *Home Missions*, September 1970.

Walter Ziegenhals reports a conversation with a local religion editor of a Chicago newspaper who said, "Nobody expects anything from the local church." Ziegenhals retorted in a moving way:

> Well, we differ on that point. I expect a great deal. I expect to find communities of faith and hope and charity. I expect to find communities of concerned people doing what they can to make their neighborhoods more human places in which to live. I still expect to find, even if not every day and on every issue, real passionate and prophetic concern for justice and equality.[6]

Though one side of the story of the presence, ministry, and mission of the United Church of Christ and its predecessor denominations on the urban scene is a tale of desertion, especially as viewed from the perspective of the traditional, local congregation, there is another and brighter part of the story. Countless efforts to find new strategies, forms, and structures for urban ministry and mission have grown out of or been supported by the United Church of Christ, many during the same post–World War II period.[7] Most of these ventures have been ecumenical in nature and spirit, so it would be most surprising not to find them also in other chapters of this book. Indeed, one of the strong marks of the United Church of Christ is its commitment to ecumenicity. As a denomination made up of four other Protestant traditions, and calling itself a "United and Uniting Church," it has sought to be part of cooperative efforts in all phases of its life and mission. Consequently, I will highlight those forms of urban ministry and mission where there is strong leadership, support, or origination from the United Church of Christ.

1. Cooperative Parishes

One cannot discuss new forms of church life in the city without reference to the East Harlem Protestant Parish (EHPP). Founded in 1948, it was one of the earliest, boldest, and most creative expressions of new structures for urban mission and ministry. Along with their families, three ordained clergy of the United Church of Christ were founders of EHPP, namely, George Webber, Don Benedict, and Archie Hargraves. They remain true giants of

---

6. Ziegenhals, p. 98.
7. Rüdiger Reitz, *The Church in Experimentation* (Nashville: Abingdon Press, 1969).

urban ministry in the denomination. The history of this important new venture in urban ministry is well documented elsewhere.[8] Though East Harlem Protestant Parish was ecumenical from the beginning, it is noteworthy that one of the first church executives to be approached about this idea was Truman Douglass. At the time he was executive vice president of the Board of Home Missions for Congregational Christian Churches and, after the 1957 merger, became head of the United Church Board for Homeland Ministries. The primary characteristics of East Harlem Protestant Parish were a strong emphasis on ministry in a particular geographical area, use of storefront church locations, a disciplined group ministry, a strong communal and worship life, and firm emphasis on a social action and justice agenda.

Several less-well-known cooperative parish ventures, which incorporated many of the themes of East Harlem Protestant Parish, were established in Cleveland, Buffalo, Chicago, and New Haven.

2. City Missionary Societies

On the Congregational side of the UCC tradition, the oldest structures designed to carry out urban missions were a host of city missionary societies formed in the nineteenth century. Only a handful remain as active mission structures, the most well known being the Community Renewal Society in Chicago, the City Mission Society of Boston, and the Christian Activities Council of Hartford. All were begun by Congregational laypeople — the Boston City Missionary Society in 1816, the Hartford City Missionary Society in 1851, and the Chicago City Missionary Society in 1882. Interestingly, all have had a change of name in their long histories. They have also followed remarkably similar journeys; these include setting up mission centers in city neighborhoods, supporting local urban congregations (many of them ethnic in character), sponsoring summer camps, and providing various other services. Each was established to serve the waves of poor immigrants settling in our cities during the nineteenth and early twentieth century.

Obviously, the Community Renewal Society, headed for many years by Don Benedict from the East Harlem Protestant Parish, is the largest and most influential of the remaining missionary societies, while the Christian

---

8. Don Benedict, *Born Again Radical* (New York: Pilgrim Press, 1982); George W. Webber, *God's Colony in Man's World* (Nashville: Abingdon Press, 1960).

Activities Council, operating in a smaller city, is quite small in comparison. In the following section, I offer a brief history of the Christian Activities Council as a case study since, in broad contours, its work has striking parallels to its Chicago and Boston counterparts.

Case Study: The Christian Activities Council (CAC)[9]

In 1850 several young Congregational men, concerned about the welfare of people in the inner city of Hartford, approached the Reverend Thomas Hopkins Gallaudet about what they might do to alleviate the suffering they had seen. He responded: "If I were a young man I would enlist the company of young men in some plan for the benefit of the destitute and stranger in this city." This became the springboard for forming the Hartford City Missionary Society in 1851. Throughout its long and successful history, its motivation and mandate have remained the same — to serve the needs of the poor, the oppressed, and the needy in the city of Hartford.

The structure of the society, renamed in 1945 the *Christian Activities Council,* consists of lay representatives from each of the sponsoring Congregational and UCC churches, along with several representatives at large. The organization has had at least one paid staff member, variously called a "city missioner" or executive director, since its earliest days.

Hartford, like most cities, especially in the Northeast, experienced successive waves of immigrants seeking the promise of a better way of life. Beginning in the mid-nineteenth century and continuing to the present day, the Irish, Italians, Germans, Russians, blacks, and Hispanics have found their way to an inner city that was ill equipped to meet their needs. Throughout its history the CAC has sought to serve those needs through a variety of strategies and approaches.

Street Ministry: A One-to-One Approach

The first city missionary hired in 1851 was David Hawley, a layman and farmer by trade. The primary focus of his ministry was personal visitation to individuals and families of immigrant groups. He brought spiritual, social, cultural, and economic relief to countless hundreds of poverty-

9. Information on the history of the CAC was gleaned from Robert A. Decker's history, *Hartford Immigrants: A History of the Christian Activities Council* (New York: United Church Press, 1987).

stricken people in Hartford. This dearly beloved man, dubbed "Father Hawley," served for nearly twenty-five years.

Mission Schools and Community Centers: An Institutional Approach

It soon became apparent that this individual, person-to-person approach was not enough. In 1852 the first mission center sponsored by the City Missionary Society opened on Morgan Street. Then followed the Pearl Street mission center in 1891 and the Village Street mission center in 1910. This attempt to provide for the religious, educational, and social needs of the people through settlement houses and community centers located in the midst of poverty areas has continued to the present day with the founding of the Inner City Exchange, the Robert G. Mack Center, the Stowe Village Community Center, and the Hill Center, most of which are still in existence.

A variation of the same strategy was establishing the "House in the Fields" as a fresh-air camp for unmarried women and their children. This was one of the signal accomplishments of the second city missionary, Mrs. Virginia Thrall Smith, an outstanding woman who concentrated her efforts on the needs of women and children. Though her work was sometimes controversial, Mrs. Smith was clearly one of the genuine pioneers in the rights of women and children, and her many accomplishments included founding the Connecticut Children's Aid Society.

Church Development: Working through Established Religious Institutions

The CAC helped start several ethnic churches (German, Italian, Swedish) and also had a hand in sponsoring Hartford's Warburton Community Church and the Flagg Road Church in West Hartford, both of which continue in existence today. In addition, during the 1940s and 1950s, the council established a specific strategy to work through existing congregations in the City of Hartford. Special efforts were made to strengthen the religious education program of Congregational churches as well as assisting in the outreach programs of these local congregations. During this period there were no community centers in operation under the aegis of the council.

218

Resource Development: Housing for the Elderly and Poor

In 1957, the CAC began to explore the possibility of sponsoring housing for the elderly in the Hartford area. It formed a spin-off nonprofit corporation called Church Homes, Inc., which built the Vine Court Apartments, the first independent living units for the elderly with Federal Housing Administration (FHA) insurance in the country. Since that time, Church Homes, Inc., has built a complex of facilities for the elderly known as Avery Heights, along with similar facilities in Meriden and Salisbury. It is now considered an outstanding provider of elderly care in the state of Connecticut.

During the late 1960s and early 1970s, the CAC decided to purchase and rehabilitate ten apartment buildings on Vine Street that became known as Horace Bushnell Apartments. At the time, this was the largest rehab project in Connecticut, and still provides low- and moderate-income apartments to residents of the area. In early 1980, the CAC sponsored the construction on Vine Street of a new congregate living facility for the elderly called Horace Bushnell Congregate Homes. This facility provides housing for sixty frail, minority residents. At the time, it was the only facility of its kind in Connecticut.

Structural Reform: Public Witness on Social Issues

During the 1980s, the organization took a greater role in public advocacy for the poor and oppressed. It established a "Public Witness Ministries" program with active political lobbying at the state and local levels on the issues of affordable housing, economic development and employment, child and maternal health, and public education.

In addition, the CAC has tried to develop more regional and metropolitan approaches to issues of poverty. One of these was providing home ownership opportunities in surrounding suburban communities for lower-income working families living in public housing in Hartford. Another was establishing, in 1987, the Metropolitan Training Institute, an instrument for urban mission education with laypeople throughout the metropolitan region.

The brevity of this history fails to do justice to the extraordinary variety of programs and people involved in the 140 years of effort by the CAC. Nor does it adequately portray the effect on the lives of countless thousands in the City of Hartford during this time. Nonetheless, certain consistent strengths and common themes emerge out of the rich heritage

219

of the organization, which are typical of City Missionary Societies throughout the United Church of Christ. Among them are heavy reliance on lay and volunteer leadership, the development of innovative models of ministry, and a willingness to change strategies as times and needs changed.

3. Settlement Houses

The settlement house movement in this country has a long and rich history and a national organization called the "National Federation of Settlements." The basic premises of settlement houses are these:

> 1. The programs were to be located near the people they served. 2. The participants were to be considered neighbors and not clients. 3. The programs were to be continuous and consistent. 4. The relationship between the staff and community was to be one of trust.[10]

This approach was the one most favored by the Evangelical and Reformed tradition before the formation of the United Church of Christ. Indeed, the E and R churches established a strong record of forming "Health and Welfare Institutions" such as hospitals and orphanages around the country. Strong settlement house institutions were established especially in St. Louis and Chicago.

In St. Louis, several "Neighborhood Houses" were started in 1913 as structures for serving the needs of those who were poor, sick, in prison, or suffering other forms of deprivation. There has always been an emphatic service and social-work component to settlement houses. On the other hand, in Louis Huber's remarkable little book *Songs of the Street*, it is clear that, at least in St. Louis, the service orientation of the neighborhood houses led to more fundamental and systemic justice issues. For instance, the neighborhood houses became deeply involved in helping to organize a rent strike in public housing in St. Louis during the 1960s. As frequently happens in the life of the church, a service orientation often leads people into the deeper mazes of systemic injustice and oppression.

In summary, then, the era from 1940 to 1960 was marked by a general retreat from city to suburb by congregations of the United Church of Christ and its predecessor denominations. Still, signs of hope and seeds of renewed zeal for ministry in the city were present during this same period. Coopera-

---

10. Louis V. Huber, *Songs of the Street* (Peace Institute Press, 1989).

tive parishes such as East Harlem Protestant Parish and others gave witness to the viability of local congregations as instruments to serve and empower the poor in the inner city, while the continued and expanded ministries of settlement houses and City Missionary Societies, which had their origins in earlier periods of history, bore testimony to the need for para-parochial structures to do what many local churches could not or would not do on the urban scene.

II. Renewed Commitment to Urban Mission: 1960-80

The turbulent social and racial upheavals that marked the decade of the sixties provoked a strong response from the United Church of Christ in terms of urban ministry and mission. As early as 1962 the Executive Council instructed the Department of the Urban Church of the Board for Homeland Ministries, in consultation with the Stewardship Council and the Office of the President of the church, to prepare a plan for a two-year emphasis on the church and urbanization.[11]

In the spring of 1963, the Executive Council formally recommended to the 1963 General Synod of the church that such an emphasis be pursued in the years 1964 and 1965.[12] The ensuing plan called for a strong emphasis on commitment and action throughout the whole church.

> The proposed emphasis is intended to aid the churches in a search for new ministries relevant to an urbanized world. Its purpose is to change the life and witness of the church radically enough to meet the impact of urban revolution. The proposal is to move beyond study and discussion to action programs which will engage the churches and their agencies with the forces shaping a new society.[13]

Several illustrations of such proposed actions were cited in the same advance report, including increased urban work by the Board for World Ministries across the globe, the establishment and expansion of the Ministers for Metropolitan Ministries programs, several community-organizing efforts, and the establishment of urban training centers.

At the general synod meeting on July 6, 1963, the assembled delegates of the United Church of Christ from across the country approved the

11. "Advance Reports," General Synod IV, p. 35.
12. "Advance Reports," General Synod IV, p. 41.
13. "Advance Reports," General Synod IV, p. 234.

proposed emphasis on church and urbanization. At least eight conferences proposed to extend the emphasis to a four-year period, but this was rejected. A key paragraph of the resolution noted:

> The objective is that the United Church of Christ as a whole and in all of its parts — its local churches, Associations, Conferences and Instrumentalities — shall become acutely perceptive of the impact of urbanization upon the world, and discover how, and where it is to minister in the name of Christ, for what ends, performing what functions, and through what structures.[14]

Don Benedict, then executive director of the Community Renewal Society in Chicago, was persuaded by Truman Douglass, the executive vice president of the United Church Board for Homeland Ministries, to take a year's leave of absence to direct this new urban emphasis. He established an office in New York to pursue this work, and describes his initial experience as follows:

> It was a staggering blow on my arrival in New York to be told by the Church's President, Ben Herbster, that there was to be no national fund drive for urban work. For years I had watched the church raise money for suburban church development, but now, when the needs of the city had come to the fore, the church had decided to cease all national fund efforts.[15]

Lacking major funding to implement the urban emphasis, Benedict decided to travel around the country meeting with boards of directors in state conferences to raise consciousness about the urban agenda. In his standard workshop format, he asked participants to list pressing urban problems in their area on one side of a sheet of newsprint and then to summarize current church programs and interests on the other side. Invariably there was a negative correlation.

In the meantime, Rev. Joseph W. Merchant, another key figure in urban church work in the United Church of Christ, used the urban emphasis to expand the work of his Department of the Urban Church within the United Church Board for Homeland Ministries. In the advance report to General Synod V he commented:

14. "Minutes of General Synod IV," p. 32.
15. Benedict, p. 32.

The decision of the 1962 General Synod to lift up the process of urbanization for special emphasis in the United Church has resulted, for the Department of the Urban Church, in the busiest and most productive years of its history — including that of its predecessor units. Urbanization has forced the church to turn toward the problems of the world. The turning has taken form in experimental ministries in numerous places.[16]

He went on to summarize a number of such efforts, indicating that urban department funds were at work in nearly one hundred different places. He also noted that increasingly the department sought to develop ecumenical means of carrying out its work.

In spite of Merchant's enthusiasm for the variety of efforts being pursued in urban ministry, he noted, much as Benedict had done, that the financial resources devoted by the United Church of Christ to this urban emphasis were wholly inadequate:

> The sum of a two-year emphasis on urbanization is an awakening with budget implications which truly reflect new life in the church. Lutherans, Episcopalians and Presbyterians are already placing a million dollars a year into their national urban work. The United Church of Christ has yet to reach one half of that figure. . . . We must, if we are to be faithful, find the financial means to support the vision so many now share.[17]

The following are the primary examples of the types of urban ministries mentioned in Merchant's 1965 report.

1. Ministers for Metropolitan Mission

This program of the United Church Board for Homeland Ministries began rather directly as a result of the new urban emphasis in 1963 under the leadership and supervision of Joe Merchant. Under this new program, an "urban missioner" was assigned to a local state conference and the costs of each position were shared by the national church and the conference itself. Each position was somewhat different, given unique local circumstances and varying strategies. Nonetheless, Merchant summarized the basic task as follows:

16. "Advance Report," General Synod V, 1965, p. 183.
17. "Advance Report," General Synod V, 1965, p. 185.

In addition to developing relevant urban strategy and assisting appropriate committees of Conferences, Associations and Congregations, these ministers assist in raising the right questions for the development of national strategy regarding the problems of the urban world of residence, work, leisure and public life. Through their involvement in local communities, we are sensing not so much how the old structures of the church must be reshaped, as that in practice, the new forms are already taking shape.[18]

By the end of 1965, Metropolitan Missioners were operating in eleven urban areas: Buffalo, Chicago, Cleveland, Detroit, Honolulu, Los Angeles, Louisville, Providence, San Francisco, Seattle, and Minneapolis–St. Paul. Again, however, the need for additional financial resources was an ever-present and haunting reality. Merchant reported: "With the request from Conferences for eight more, it is beyond our means to keep up with the demand."[19] By 1967 thirteen Metropolitan Missioners were employed, Milwaukee and New York having been added to the list of urban areas being served.[20]

In addition to the work in specific metropolitan areas and conferences, the "triple-M'rs," as they came to be known, met twice each year in the metropolitan area of one of the missioners to report and share insights about their common work.

In an important, unpublished address delivered to the assembled triple-M group on November 11, 1970, Joe Merchant outlined various themes that were critical to this whole program. He claimed that the Minister of Metropolitan Mission was to be a "catalytic agent of change." What needed to be changed were "systems that are oppressive," and community organization, he reported, was the method most often employed.[21] He also pointed out that the Minister of Metropolitan Mission cannot be "a lone ranger" and must maintain his relationship to the institutional church, both as a conference staff person and an "affiliate national staff member."

The triple-M program continued into the mid-1980s and included during that time a wide variety of persons and specific ministries. Among those who served, interestingly, were several clergy originally involved in the East Harlem Protestant Parish, including Don Benedict and Walter

18. "Advance Report," General Synod V, 1965, p. 184.
19. "Advance Report," General Synod V, 1965, p. 184.
20. "Advance Report," General Synod VI, p. 158.
21. Joseph W. Merchant, "The MMM and the Churches in the 1970's" (unpublished address delivered November 11, 1970).

Ziegenhals. The contributions, insights, and legacies left by the various Ministers for Metropolitan Mission have never been adequately reported, and the apparent loss of the files on this program at the Board of Homeland Ministries is a loss to the whole church.

2. Urban Training Centers

In Joe Merchant's advance report in 1965, he remarked:

> The Urban Training Center for Christian Mission finds the United Church deeply involved at all levels — faculty, Board of Directors, students. The Rev. Joseph W. Merchant is Chairman of the Board; a former staff member, the Rev. J. Archie Hargraves, served on the faculty. Qualified United Church ministers and laymen may attend without charge for room, board or tuition as a result of our participation in the membership of the center.[22]

In fact, training for urban ministry including clergy, seminarians, and laity became a burgeoning movement during the 1960s. George Younger, in his comprehensive study of what he called the "Action Training Movement," indicates that twenty-seven training centers were operating in twenty-two large U.S. cities, states, and regions.[23] As Younger points out, all were ecumenical, so I will concentrate on two where there was significant UCC initiative and leadership.

The forerunner of the urban training movement was the Urban Training Center for Christian Mission in Chicago. The driving force behind this concept was, again, Don Benedict at the Community Renewal Society. Benedict described his vision as follows:

> The Center is to be headquarters for study and demonstration, for reflection and involvement, for implementing the relationship between the gospel and urban culture. It is to be a demonstration school, an urban laboratory, concerned for injecting the Christian way of life into the urban community so that the church may fill its rightful role in this vast segment of contemporary society.[24]

22. "Advance Report," General Synod V, 1965, p. 184.
23. George D. Younger, *From New Creation to Urban Crisis* (Chicago: Center for the Scientific Study of Religion, 1987).
24. Younger, p. 41.

It began as early as 1961, but this Urban Training Center was actually launched in 1963. Again, it is significant that two people earlier involved in the East Harlem Protestant Parish were key figures, Don Benedict and Archie Hargraves. Of the various training centers established, the Chicago center was the only one conceived as a national model. Largely due to the withdrawal of denominational funding in the mid-1970s, this training center closed its doors in 1974. Its accomplishments and contributions are legion, and the life of the church will be affected far into the future by virtue of the training programs it implemented.[25]

The other training center to be mentioned here is MUST (Metropolitan Urban Service Training), located in New York. The original impetus and major funding for this came from the United Methodist Church, but its implementation and character were deeply impacted by George Webber, who became its first executive director in 1965. MUST always had a stronger focus on serving a particular metropolitan area, in distinction from the Chicago experiment, which was national in scope from the outset. It also developed a strong emphasis on combatting racism and encouraging minority empowerment through its work.[26]

It is significant that, although the urban or action training movement and the various centers that arose out of it did not survive long into the 1970s, three similar training efforts have begun in the 1980s, each in conjunction with a City Missionary Society. The Urban Academy in Chicago, the Urban Action Resource Center in Boston, and the Metropolitan Training Institute in Hartford were all started in this decade. The need for training in urban ministry is as acute today as it was during the earlier periods, and some within the United Church of Christ continue to respond.

3. Community Organization

The United Church of Christ has been a strong supporter of citizen empowerment and community-organizing efforts throughout the country. Not all community-organizing efforts are found in cities, but many are. As early as 1967, General Synod VI "endorsed the principle of community organization as an instrument of community action for the

25. Younger, pp. 51ff.
26. Younger, p. 71.

purpose of giving the powerless a voice in society."[27] In his report in 1967, Joe Merchant stated:

> Another high priority concern has been the support and encouragement of mass-based community organization among the poor, the powerless and racial minorities in urban ghettos. Through the techniques of community organization, the poor are being mobilized to gain the voice and power necessary for full participation in the life of our society, to influence the decisions that affect them, to grapple with their problems as identified by themselves and, otherwise, to have a chance at meaningful self-determination.[28]

He cites specific organizing projects in Buffalo; Beaumont, Texas; Cleveland; Chicago; Detroit; Gary, Indiana; Grand Rapids; New Albany, Indiana; Louisville; Rochester; and Washington, D.C. He also notes that about $359,000 was contributed by various United Church agencies to community organizations in 1966.

Much of the church support for community organizing was, as usual, interdenominational and ecumenical in nature. In fact, the United Church of Christ, along with the Episcopal Church and the United Presbyterian Church in the U.S.A., helped found the Interreligious Foundation for Community Organizing (IFCO) in 1966. Strong support for community organizing efforts remains a deep commitment of this denomination up to the present day, especially through the United Church Board for Homeland Ministries.

4. Churches in Transition

In discussing the church and urbanization, the issue of race is never far from the surface. I have already noted the preponderant tendency of churches within the United Church of Christ to close, merge, or move as their surrounding neighborhoods became African American or Latino. However, there are important exceptions to this, and the broader church began to take seriously its responsibility for "churches in transition," especially in the 1970s. Special concern about this issue was expressed by General Synod VIII in 1971.

One experiment that especially deserves attention is the churches-in-transition project, located in Chicago, and carried on throughout the 1970s.

27. "Minutes of General Synod VI," 1967; cited in "Minutes of General Synod XII," June 26, 1979, p. 87.
28. "Advance Reports," 1967, p. 158.

This project was launched by the Community Renewal Society in cooperation with the United Church of Christ and the United Church Board for Homeland Ministries. Its founder and director, Rev. Walter E. Ziegenhals, is an ordained United Church of Christ minister and again came out of East Harlem Protestant Parish and the Cleveland Inner City Protestant Parish. In his important book *Urban Churches in Transition*,[29] Ziegenhals analyzed the factors that contribute to community change and shared important insights in the experiences of predominantly white churches making the transition to African American or Latino congregations and leadership. It is essential to underline Ziegenhals's emphasis on the importance of broader denominational and ecumenical support if churches in transition are to be successful.

5. Cluster Development

Twenty years after the East Harlem Protestant Parish was established, Ted Erickson, serving under the auspices of the Division of Evangelism of the Board of Homeland Ministries, began working with some local congregations in urban settings in what was called a "cluster development" model. It had many similarities to the cooperative parish models, though it pulled together existing local congregations within a new cooperative venture. One of these efforts in the Asylum Hill neighborhood of Hartford, Connecticut, began in the fall of 1968 with two UCC congregations, Immanuel Church and Asylum Hill Church, taking major leadership roles. This planning process resulted in the formation of the "Asylum Hill Community Service Group," which later became the Asylum Hill Christian Community; this expanded to include Catholic, Lutheran, and Baptist parishes in the neighborhood ecumenical organization. Over the years, the Asylum Hill Christian Community has been responsible for sponsoring and forming the Asylum Hill Organizing Project (AHOP), probably the strongest community organization in Hartford, which later spun off Hill Housing, Inc., one of the major community development corporations in the city. I cite this illustration to point out the number of important new community institutions that can arise out of cooperative ecumenical ventures in the city.

Another cooperative model that has emerged in various metropolitan areas is some form of "urban-suburban" pairing or partnership between churches. Impressive among these is Horace Bushnell Church in Hartford,

---

29. Walter E. Ziegenhals, *Urban Churches in Transition* (New York: Pilgrim Press, 1978).

which has developed strong relationships with several suburban congregations and communities.[30]

6. Experimental Ministries

This is a "catch-all" category for a wide variety of ministries located in and serving segments of the population other than residential communities. Joe Merchant, in his report, mentioned a variety of specialized ministries in arts and culture, coffeehouses, street ministries, and so on.

Especially important, however, were several ministries in the "public sector." Those mentioned specifically were the Ecumenical Ministry to State Government in Detroit, the Human Environment Project in the Twin Cities, the Detroit Industrial Mission, the National Committee for Industrial Mission, and Metropolitan Associates of Philadelphia (MAP). In one way or another all these ventures tried to address issues and concerns having to do with vocational settings and vocational life. Few of them have endured as viable structures up to the present.

In 1977, after 14 years of burgeoning initiatives in UCC urban ministries spurred by the 1963 urban emphasis, General Synod XI of the United Church of Christ passed an overture called "Toward a New Urban Agenda."[31] It called for a renewal of urban mission within the United Church of Christ, and asked the Executive Council to authorize a two-year study under the direction of the Board for Homeland Ministries. The study was to do five things:

1. Review and evaluate all recent urban programs.
2. Analyze prospects and strategies for the survival of the church's presence in the city.
3. Review and consolidate all social policy positions relating to urbanization.
4. Prepare a theological statement on the responsibilities of the church in the city.
5. Make recommendations on the integration of future programs and priorities.[32]

30. See David S. King, *No Church Is an Island* (New York: Pilgrim Press, 1980).
31. "Minutes of General Synod XI," 1977, p. 74.
32. "Minutes of General Synod XI," 1977, p. 75.

This resulted in a major report to General Synod XII in 1979.[33] That report is probably the best brief summary of the mission of the United Church of Christ in urban settings to be found anywhere.

It begins with an historical survey of the development of urban life in America, along with observations on the role of the church in this process, and then sets out a theological basis for the continuing role of the church in the urban context. The report stresses five biblical themes — community, compassion, justice, liberation, and hope — that must undergird urban ministry in the United Church of Christ. The report then summarizes the various statements and social positions of the United Church of Christ on issues of employment, race, housing, health care, and public education as these impact the urban scene. Finally, the report refers back to the 1964-66 emphasis on the "Church and Urbanization" and cites a host of programmatic responses, nationally and locally, to this emphasis during the intervening years. The concluding recommendations call for an urban task force to prepare and present a pronouncement on the "Future of Urban Life in America" to General Synod XIII.

Analytically, what are we to make of this period from 1960 to 1980 when so much seemed to be happening in urban ministry within the United Church of Christ? Are there certain underlying themes, concepts, or strategies that undergirded and guided the development of urban ministry in this period?

First, it is apparent that those involved in shaping and implementing urban ministry and mission in this denomination were not primarily theoreticians — they were fundamentally activists deeply concerned about urban life, both its problems and possibilities. As Joe Merchant put it in his report in 1965:

> Through involvement in local communities we are sensing not so much how the old structures of the church must be re-shaped, as that in practice the new forms are already taking shape; we discover that the longed-for renewal of the life of the church comes *more in the doing* than in the study of what ought to be done.[34]

Nonetheless, some theoretical perspectives had direct practical and programmatic implications on urban ministry in the United Church of Christ. This is most vivid in the contrast between the 1963 proposal for an

33. "Minutes of General Synod XII," 1979, pp. 83ff.
34. "Advance Reports," General Synod V, 1965, p. 184; emphasis mine.

emphasis on the church and urbanization[35] and the report and recommendations on the urban agenda in 1979.[36] Even the very names of the respective documents suggest a shift in thinking. The former emphasizes "urbanization" as a *process* that affects the worldview and culture of virtually everyone. It speaks of a "world radically changed," of a "new age of metropolis" and an "urban revolution" in the making. This 1963 proposal clearly reflects an era in which both church and society were awakened to new social responsibilities by the civil rights and antiwar movements. Therefore it has the tone of a call to action rallying Christians to be "pioneer saints."

In contrast, the 1979 report is a more measured and pragmatic document. As the name "Urban Agenda" suggests, there is more emphasis on the *problems* of the city than on the *process* of urbanization, and more weight put on public policy issues as these affect urban life.

The practical implications of this theoretical paradigm shift are especially evident with respect to the recommended structures for urban mission and ministry in the United Church of Christ. There has always been a tension between those who viewed the local congregation as the primary instrument for urban ministry and those who called for new forms and para-parochial strategies as the best hope for renewed urban mission. In the earlier 1963 proposal, not a single illustration cited as relevant "action programs" involved in the renewal of existing congregations or planting new congregations in urban areas. In contrast, without disregarding the need for para-parochial structures, the 1979 report began to emphasize the need for renewing urban congregations and developing new congregations, especially among racial and ethnic minorities, in our cities. In the next section, we will see how the 1981 pronouncement formalized this shift in emphasis.

III. The Quiet Withdrawal from Urban Ministry: 1980-91

One of the recommendations approved at General Synod XII in 1979 was the appointment of an urban task force to prepare for the next general synod a pronouncement on "The Future of Urban Life in America." This document was presented to General Synod XIII in 1981,[37] and it clearly favored both the theoretical and practical positions of the 1979 report.

---

35. "Advance Reports," General Synod IV, 1963, pp. 233ff.
36. "Minutes of General Synod XII," 1979, pp. 83ff.
37. "Minutes of General Synod XIII," 1981, pp. 37ff.

Though recognizing that the term "city" could be used in a "symbolic" sense, the authors of the pronouncement state that they use the term to refer to "specific realities" in a "concrete entity." Significantly, after detailing the mounting problems of American cities and recognizing the small and declining number of UCC congregations in central cities, the pronouncement concludes: "A new commitment to founding new congregations and renewing existing congregations in urban settings is an *essential* element of contemporary mission."[38] With respect to the option of creating and supporting alternative structures for urban ministry, the pronouncement is much more equivocal:

> New structures for mission *may* be necessary, which can build upon a heritage of urban mission exemplified in City Missionary Societies, the Minister of Metropolitan Missions program, settlement houses and others.[39]

The two major sections of the pronouncement having to do with recommendations are divided into public policy recommendations and recommendations to churches. Again, it becomes clear that urban life is not viewed as a process that requires new forms of response but as a set of problems and issues that demands advocacy at the national level and more committed urban congregations at the local level. To put it otherwise, the pronouncement on "The Future of Urban Life in America" calls more for "problem solving" than for fundamental transformation.

Attached to this pronouncement were four other motions that are especially critical:

1. The 13th General Synod requests that the United Church Board for Homeland Ministries, the Office for Church in Society, the Office for Church Life and Leadership, and the Commission for Racial Justice report to the 14th General Synod concerning the implementation of this pronouncement.
2. The 13th General Synod recommends that, by adopting this pronouncement, urban ministries and urban issues which are highlighted in the pronouncement be considered in the priority process of the 14th General Synod.
3. The 13th General Synod requests that a study guide be prepared and

---

38. "Minutes of General Synod XIII," 1981, p. 39; emphasis mine.
39. "Minutes of General Synod XIII," 1981, p. 40; emphasis mine.

that both the pronouncement and the study guide be made available in Spanish and in English.

4. The 13th General Synod requests that policies enacted within this general pronouncement be linked to program implementation including New Initiatives in Church Development.[40]

Whatever its emphasis, the 1981 pronouncement is especially important because, to my knowledge, this is the last specific reference to urban ministry made by a general synod of the United Church of Christ. Nor, as far as I can ascertain, were the requested report and study guide ever prepared. Moreover, urban ministries have never received priority standing in the priority process of the United Church of Christ since that time.

Finally, the fourth motion was far more significant than it might seem on the surface. New Initiatives in Church Development (NICD) was a major national fund drive recommended by the Division of Evangelism of the United Church Board for Homeland Ministries. As initially conceived, it involved a strategy going back to the post–World War II emphasis by targeting new church development in the "Sun Belt States" as the new "high potential" areas. There was considerable resistance to this as the exclusive emphasis of the program, especially among conference ministers. The fourth motion, made from the floor, resulted in funds being available for the renewal of existing congregations in cities throughout the country, along with the development of minority congregations.

Nonetheless, the silence of the national church on urban ministry since 1981 is deafening indeed. The last remaining identifiable urban program within the United Church Board for Homeland Ministries, the Ministers for Metropolitan Mission program, was disbanded in the mid to late 1980s. Clearly, the United Church Board for Homeland Ministries, after having spearheaded a variety of urban ministries in the 1960s and 1970s, now has other priorities.

Though there are still many within the United Church of Christ who labor in the vineyards of our cities and metropolitan areas, one has to wonder about the future of urban ministry in this denomination, at least from the perspective of the national church and its instrumentalities. Perhaps the greatest sign of hope is that several leaders elected in the 90s to prominent positions in the United Church of Christ all come out of urban ministry and have strong commitments to urban concerns; these include Paul Sherry, president of the church; Bennie Whiten, conference minister

40. "Minutes of General Synod XIII," 1981, p. 41.

in Massachusetts; and Valerie Russell, director of the Office of Church in Society. Moreover, Yvonne Delk, a major national leader, has moved to head the Community Renewal Society, and new leadership is in place at the Board for Homeland Ministries. Whether, with shrinking resources, the attention of the denomination can be refocused from institutional survival to mission, including urban mission, remains to be seen. We can only hope that future years will bring renewed zeal in the United Church of Christ for God's mission in urban America.

Postscript. Since the writing of this chapter, some new stirrings in urban ministry have appeared in the United Church of Christ. Largely initiated by a group of inner-city local church pastors, but supported by two City Missionary Societies,[41] a new UCC National Urban Network has been formed with funding from the United Church Board for Homeland Ministries. Several Steering Committee meetings, consultations, and national gatherings have been held during 1993-1995. Plans are underway to establish several "Covenant Academies for Urban Ministries" involving groupings of local churches in urban settings. Clearly, new hope and new energy are emerging from the grassroots of those who labor in ministry to the city.

---

41. The Community Renewal Society, Chicago, and the Christian Activities Council, Hartford.

• 10 •

Urban United Methodism:
Structures and Strategies, 1945-90

LOYDE H. HARTLEY, WILLIAM E. RAMSDEN,
AND KINMOTH JEFFERSON

OVER THE PAST FIFTY YEARS, Methodists[1] have relied on five traditional strategies for engaging church members with city issues: (1) congregational extension and development, (2) interdenominational cooperation, (3) missionary enterprise, (4) pan-urban denominational agencies and coordinating structures, and (5) independent Methodist movements operating outside of judicatory oversight. Deeply rooted in Methodist history, this repertoire of strategies has remained basically unchanged in number and form since World War II. None of the five has been totally abandoned; none has been added. Important changes have occurred, however. The relative confidence Methodists placed in each of the five strategies has changed, as has the proportion of the denomination's resources committed to each. Theological understandings of the city have gone through a series of modifications, both in regard to the city's moral fiber and the city church's mission. In most large cities, the neighborhoods in which Methodist churches were and are located have proceeded through at least two, often more, ethnic successions. Each new ethnic group, insofar as they were Methodist, has used some combination of the five strategies to accommodate to the urban environment.

More telling of the denomination's changing urban fortunes, the

---

1. The term *Methodist* is used to refer to the United Methodist Church and its predecessors: the Methodist Church and the Evangelical United Brethren Church (EUB).

proportion of city people who are Methodists has decreased sharply over the past fifty years, peaking in the 1950s but reaching a twentieth-century low in the 1980s. No fundamentally new urban strategies, however, have resulted from any of these changes. Even with changes in the social and religious goals that the strategies were intended to accomplish, the strategies themselves have persisted in a kind of system of checks and balances, being periodically reorganized and renewed to meet emerging urban circumstances. Clearly, each strategy, in addition to apparent strengths, has its own inherent defects that, if allowed to proceed unchecked by the other strategies, lead to socially, theologically, and morally unacceptable results.

This chapter aims briefly to identify the origins and fundamental characteristics of each of the five strategies, including their aberrant expressions, then to trace in more detail their evolution through four identifiable time periods of American urban life since World War II, and finally to describe how the United Methodist Church's capacity for shaping its urban future has been reflected in its altering, recasting, and combining of the strategic options it has chosen to use.

Methodist urban policy has arguably proceeded through four distinct but overlapping time periods during the past fifty years, each with its own predominant theme: (1) suburban church extension from the 1940s to early 1960s, (2) urban racial crisis and new church forms in the 1960s and early 1970s, (3) ethnic and racial transition of communities and churches in the 1970s and early 1980s, and (4) new urban ethnic congregations in the 1980s and 1990s. The main themes of the four time periods do not stand alone, however. Each is accompanied by both discordant and harmonic counterpoints and a leitmotif to presage rising dominant themes in successive time periods. Moreover, they overlap each other, having indistinct demarcations between them. The structure of this chapter, therefore, may be understood as a matrix — five strategies traced through four time periods of urban church policy.

I. Some Origins of Methodist City Strategy

Tracing postwar developments requires a review of prewar history. Methodist city strategies did not emerge de novo following World War II but have their roots in the nineteenth century and earlier. From its inception, Methodism has been associated with cities. Following English Methodism, the principal strategy of American Wesleyans was to establish local societies anywhere interested people could be assembled, resulting in the establishment of a "First" Methodist church in most frontier settlements during the nineteenth-century westward expansion. As settlements grew into cities, the conferences founded a host of neighborhood-oriented local churches drawing on the resources of the mother churches and, eventually, the church extension societies.[2] All branches of nineteenth-century Methodism followed this basic extension pattern in virtually all U.S. cities. This local system was controlled by the bishops and annual conferences; they decided where churches would be established and who would be assigned to them as pastors.[3]

By the early 1800s, Methodists, along with other Protestants, recognized that the local system was by itself insufficient to cope with growing city problems. Additional measures were necessary to evangelize recently arrived rural migrants, to reach the city's children and poor families, and to maintain order in society. A host of cooperative efforts was launched to ameliorate city problems, the most important of which were Sunday schools, city revivals, charitable and relief societies, Bible and tract societies, and the YMCA and YWCA. For the most part, civic-minded laypeople organized and controlled these cooperative endeavors, including large numbers of women who experienced religious calls but were excluded at that time from pastoral appointment. These cooperative movements remained mostly outside the jurisdiction of the Methodist conferences, but with few exceptions were enthusiastically endorsed by Methodist laity and clergy alike.[4]

A third strategy, beyond that of church extension and cooperative programs, is reflected in the emergence of denominational city missions,

2. Wilbur Chapman Hallenbeck, *Urban Organization of Protestantism* (New York: Harper and Brothers, for the Institute of Social and Religious Research, 1934). The appendix includes an incomplete list of Methodist city church extension and mission societies and the names of their executives. Methodist mission and church extension societies were founded in Boston (1867), Pittsburgh (1880), San Francisco (1884), Chicago (1885), Cleveland (1886), and Los Angeles (1904).

3. Sweet makes the point that Methodists were less dependent than other denominations on missionary agencies for advancement on the western frontier. Circuit riders relied on support, no matter how meager, from the people to whom they ministered. This practice partly accounts for the wide distribution of Methodism in nineteenth-century cities. See William Warren Sweet, *Religion in the Development of American Culture, 1765-1840* (New York: Scribners, 1954).

4. For competent summaries of the emergence of extra-parochial urban religious movements, see Raymond A. Mohl, "The Urban Missionary Movement in New York City, 1800-1825," *Journal of Religious History* 7, no. 2 (December 1972): 110-28; and Paul S. Boyer, *Urban Masses and Moral Order in America, 1820-1920* (Cambridge: Harvard University Press, 1978).

home missions societies, and philanthropic institutions. City missions were particularly adapted to address the city's social ills.[5] Five Points Mission, for example, was launched by a group of Methodist women in 1850 in one of New York City's most distressed districts and, shortly thereafter, Methodist missions began in several other cities in order to reach the poor, the destitute, and the immigrant.[6] The Methodist Episcopal Church, South, founded similar missions, as did other Methodist bodies.[7] By the close of the nineteenth century there were many Methodist city missions, institutional churches, social settlements, hospitals, asylums, orphanages, and neighborhood houses, each designed along missionary lines to reach particular constituencies and people with special needs outside the local church. An order of deaconesses was established to staff and manage the rapidly growing missionary programs.[8] These agencies, in distinction from the cooperative efforts started earlier in the nineteenth century, were largely Methodist owned and operated.

The early twentieth century saw the emergence of the final two strategies related to city ministry — denominational agencies officially assigned to city work and independent Methodist movements. The first strategy established the official denominational boards and agencies expressly related to city concerns, for example, the Council of Cities and the Bureau of Foreign Speaking Work, both instruments of the Board of Home Missions and Church Extension of the Methodist Episcopal Church. Denominational agencies were created to coordinate support for the growing number of missions and eleemosynary institutions, many of which were city oriented, and to provide a formal denominational structure for concerns about the city. They also provided a forum for the exchange of ideas, offered financial aid to some city ministries, and supported the conferences in city church extension efforts. The Council of Cities sponsored twelve national city ministry conferences between 1916 and Methodist unification in 1939.

5. See, for example, Frank Mason North, "City Missions and Social Problems," *Methodist Review* 75 [i.e., series 4, vol. 9] (March-April 1893): 228-39.

6. For a listing of materials regarding the Five Points Mission, see the subject index of Loyde H. Hartley, *Cities and Churches: An International Bibliography* (Metuchen, N.J.: Scarecrow, 1992).

7. Tochie Williams [Mrs. Robert W.] MacDonell, *The Story of the Years in City Mission Work* (Nashville: Woman's Missionary Council, Methodist Episcopal Church, South, [1916?]); a pamphlet. See also by MacDonell, *A Neighbor to New Americans* (Nashville: Women's Department, Board of Missions, Methodist Episcopal Church, South, [1923?]).

8. For a history of Methodist women's work in Chicago, see Lucy Rider Meyer, *Deaconesses: Biblical, Early Church, European, American — The Story of the Chicago Training School for City, Home and Foreign Missions and the Chicago Deaconess Home* (Chicago: Message Publishing Company, 1889).

The second to be implemented in the early twentieth century is illustrated by the Methodist Federation for Social Service (MFSS), founded in 1908 by Harry F. Ward, Frank Mason North, Worth M. Tippy, and others especially concerned with city work.[9] The MFSS, operating as a nominally Methodist voluntary organization outside the jurisdiction of the Methodist hierarchy, found it possible to promote social justice, the rights of labor, and radical religion in a manner not possible within official Methodism. Notwithstanding its deliberately peripheral status, MFSS grew to become highly influential in matters of Methodist social teaching and policy. Ward was largely responsible for the adoption of the 1908 Methodist Social Creed, which became the basis for the statement on the rights of laborers adopted by the Federal Council of Churches.[10] A series of semiofficial and unofficial federations, networks, and caucuses have followed in the footsteps of MFSS.

Methodist Reunification

By 1939, when Northern and Southern Methodists reunited, all five city ministry strategies emergent in the nineteenth and early twentieth centuries, with their attendant bureaucracies, were functioning and sometimes competing with each other.

In the reunified denomination, a single Board of Missions and Church Extension combined denominational agencies for home and foreign missions. The new board was organized in sections, each comprised of one or more departments. Two sections — Home Missions and Church Extension — were related to city ministry. The Section of Home Missions had four departments, three of which were concerned with city issues — City Work, Goodwill Industries, and Negro Work.[11] The Department of City Work was

9. Well before the founding of the MFSS, several Methodist urban leaders were cautiously interested in Christian aspects of socialism, particularly in regard to its potential for creating a more just society. See Frank Mason North's series of articles titled "Christianity and Socialism," *Zion's Herald* 69 (January 18, 1891): 25; (February 4, 1891): 34. Although he falls short of a total endorsement of socialism, he does conclude that socialism applies many Christian principles to everyday life.

10. Donald K. Gorrell, "Methodist Federation for Social Service and the Social Creed," *Methodist History* 13, no. 2 (January 1975): 3-32. Gorrell traces how the 1908 Methodist Social Creed became widely accepted in interdenominational circles, with particular attention to the role of the MFSS.

11. Ludwell H. Estes, ed., *Journal of the First General Conference of the Methodist Church, Atlantic City, N.J., April 24–May 6, 1940* (Nashville: Methodist Publishing House, 1940), pp. 614-20.

restricted largely to the support of Methodist city mission and extension societies and the Council of Cities. The Department of Negro Work was mandated to promote missionary work among African Americans in cooperation with the Department of City Work, the Central Jurisdiction, the Colored Methodist Episcopal Church,[12] and several other Methodist denominational agencies. The Central Jurisdiction represented the principal way in which the Methodist church accommodated its system of church extension and support to ethnic minorities.[13] The Section of Church Extension assumed responsibility for new church development in both city and noncity locations, and administered denominational funds loaned for construction of church buildings and parsonages.

Apart from the churches' participation in national mobilization efforts,[14] World War II had two profound effects on Methodist city strategy. First, it slowed the flow of church resources toward the growing suburban areas and, second, it increased the rate of African and Hispanic Americans migrating to northern cities to work in war industries.[15] Well before the war, denominational officials had measured the effects of the population shift away from center cities. The prevailing church extension maxim of "into the city and up" (e.g., Chicago Temple's building, in 1924 the tallest

12. Prior to reunification, the Northern Church had separate conferences of African American churches (including some congregations in southern states), while the Southern Church supported a separate denomination of African American churches — the Colored Methodist Episcopal (CME). At the time of church union, the existing African American conferences of the Northern Church were organized in a separate nongeographical judicatory named the Central Jurisdiction, while the CME continued as a separate denomination. The Department of Negro Work was abolished in the early 1950s, being replaced with an associate secretaryship that carried forward the department's mandates and added to them concerns for other minorities. In 1968, when the United Methodist Church was formed, the Central Jurisdiction was eliminated, and all churches were attached to geographic conferences.

13. In addition to the Central Jurisdiction, Methodism also had a conference for oriental churches in California that included Chinese, Filipino, and Korean congregations, as well as a Japanese Provisional Annual Conference. The Japanese conference became an instrument through which Methodists addressed the crisis of wartime detainment of Japanese Americans in "evacuation areas." Another example is the Oklahoma Indian Missionary Conference, which at one point had sixty-seven pastors and more than ten thousand members.

14. Ministry in defense areas continued well after the war in sites such as the Savannah River hydrogen bomb plant.

15. African American migration had been well underway long before this time. Shortly after the Civil War, J. C. Hartzell anticipated the causes: Blacks seeking economic betterment and oppressive political persecution. Northern cities and states, he feared, were ill prepared to add more people to the rolls of paupers. He cites evidence that the migrating blacks were industrious and able to care for themselves, given the chance. See J. C. Hartzell, "Negro Exodus," *Methodist Quarterly Review* 61, no. 4 (October 1897): 722-47.

structure in the world for its steeple) had been challenged, if not refuted, by the research of H. Paul Douglass on the importance of suburbs for the future of the church.[16] Channing Richardson, the superintendent of City Work following Methodist reunification, observed that existing city churches simply failed to reach suburban dwellers.[17] W. V. Cropper, head of the Section of Church Extension, named six targets for extension: dilapidated or obsolete country churches, churches in suburban areas, churches in industrial areas, churches suffering disasters, churches serving distinctive racial groups (Mexicans, Native Americans, Cubans, and African Americans), and churches near military camps.[18] Conspicuously absent from Cropper's list is any reference to extension of traditional city churches.

By the end of the war, Methodist leaders were ready, well primed, and highly motivated for massive suburban church extension efforts. They were not, however, similarly prepared to respond to the northerly migration of African Americans and Hispanics, many of whom were Methodists. Moreover, Methodist leaders became increasingly fearful about the future of traditional city churches and of the cities themselves. The 1945 report of the Department of Cities cites two major urban problems: deteriorating buildings and infrastructure, and the heterogenous mixtures of races and national ethnic groups. Both were viewed as destructive and divisive, and the church was called to build a unified citizenship for the city and for the kingdom of God.

II. Methodism and the Postwar Urban Expansion: 1945-65

Methodists relied on the five well-tested prewar urban strategies in the postwar era. Along with other Protestant denominations, their first priority was developing a suburban church extension strategy, with renewal or closing of troubled city churches as a second priority.[19] For Methodists, the suburban extension plan involved the conferences acquiring property located where suburban expansion was anticipated. When a central-city church closed, its assets were usually sold and the proceeds given to erect

16. Harlan Paul Douglass, *The Suburban Trend* (New York: Century, 1925).
17. Channing A. Richardson, "The Challenge of the City's Change," *World Outlook*, n.s. 1, no. 6 (February 1941): 43ff.
18. W. V. Cropper, "Modern Methodism Needs Church Extension," *World Outlook*, n.s. 3, no. 5 (January 1943): 13-14.
19. Referred to in several annual reports of the Section on Church Extension as the "Great church extension task of building sanctuaries for modern America."

new buildings on suburban sites, sometimes before the first houses were started. A great deal of foresight was needed to implement such a plan, and assorted models were rapidly developed as the secular discipline of urban planning gained prominence. Cooperation among Protestants, under comity agreements established before the war, guided decisions about which denominations would develop churches in which suburbs. Denominations, competing for their fair share of prime development sites, relied on comity arrangements to prevent "over-churching" of affluent suburbs and, theoretically, "under-churching" of poor neighborhoods. Overdevelopment was often controlled by comity arrangements, but underdevelopment in poor areas remained a problem.

The suburban trend continued throughout the 1950s and well into the 1960s. In 1955 the *World Outlook* celebrated the extension goal of a new Methodist church every day. Although the pace had slowed somewhat by the beginning of the 1960s, ambitious projections were still being made. In the Northeastern Methodist Jurisdiction alone, according to Albert Adams' estimations, church extension needs for the years 1963 to 1968 would require a total of 331 new churches (mostly in suburbs), 292 relocations (mostly to suburbs), and 326 mergers (mostly rural, some small-city congregations) at a cost of nearly $68 million for site purchase, first-unit construction, and church budget subsidy.[20]

Denominational urban planning was not limited to the suburbs, however. It involved the development of strategic plans for entire metropolitan areas. Conferences, in cooperation with the denomination, employed field researchers during the 1950s to study most metropolitan areas to develop a comprehensive regional strategy and to make specific recommendations regarding troubled central-city churches. Characteristically, the sociological inquiries amassed demographic data, church statistics, and questionnaires completed by church members, and from these the researchers induced a set of social trends and church policy alternatives. Strategic recommendations for local churches — merge, close church, sell property, adopt new approaches, revive old approaches, hold on for a while longer, welcome neighborhood newcomers — were accompanied by suggestions for denominational plans for the city as a whole.[21] Studying an entire metropoli-

20. Albert S. Adams, *Work Book: Church Extension Opportunities and Needs, 1962-1968, in the Northeastern Jurisdiction of the Methodist Church* (Philadelphia: Division of National Missions of the Board of Missions of the Methodist Church, 1963).

21. For several years, the National Council of Churches maintained a library collection of church-related sociological field studies. Although far from being exhaustive of all such

tan region led the researchers not only to provide planning information about the growing parts of the city, but also to call attention to the inner cities' worsening social conditions, the effects of racial change in neighborhoods, and the negative impact of urban renewal and highway construction on existing local churches.

Moreover, the ruinous effects of "white flight" to the suburbs became increasingly apparent. Shippey, for example, notes that by 1951 all white Methodist churches located in predominantly African American sections of Newark, New Jersey, had either moved out of the area, merged with other churches outside the area, or closed.[22] Ethnically and racially changing urban neighborhoods were seen, notwithstanding eloquent appeals for racial integration, largely as strategic problems for existing local churches coping with crises, rather than as opportunities for new Methodist growth. The appeals of black Methodist church leaders for church extension aid to help them respond to rapidly growing numbers of blacks migrating to northern cities went largely unheeded, sounding a leitmotif prescient of the urban crisis years in the 1960s.[23]

The Department of City Work sponsored quadrennial urban convocations during the 1950s and early 1960s for the purpose of alerting city churches to the rapidly changing conditions they faced and to the alternative approaches they might adopt in order to increase their effectiveness. The series of twenty-one pamphlets generated by the convocations reflects both the denominational leaders' understanding of urban problems and the methods they hoped churches would embrace in dealing with them. The problems included: a lack of awareness in congregations regarding the implications of urban social dynamics, white flight to suburbs, apartment dwellers' lack of interest in religion, expressways changing community

---

studies, the index of this collection does list 151 Methodist urban-related studies produced from 1945 to 1969. The principal producers of these studies were: Wayne Artis, Earl D. C. Brewer, James H. Davis, Douglas W. Johnson, Murray H. Leiffer, Lyle E. Schaller, Frederick A. Shippey, Herbert E. Stotts, Roy A. Sturm, and Robert Leroy Wilson. Both Leiffer and Shippey used the studies as a basis for monographs on city church issues, while Davis and Wilson wrote a substantial amount of denominational literature on urban ministry. See Earl D. C. Brewer and Douglas W. Johnson, *An Inventory of the Harlan Paul Douglass Collection of Religious Research Reports* (New York: National Council of Churches, 1970).

22. Frederick A. Shippey, *Methodism in Newark [N.J.]: A Study of Church Trends and Characteristics, 1900-1951* (New York: Department of Research and Survey, Board of Missions and Church Extension, the Methodist Church, [1951?]).

23. Ralph A. Felton, *The Ministry of the Central Jurisdiction of the Methodist Church* (Madison, N.J.: Drew University Theological School, [1954?]).

boundaries, rising costs of property and limits on church expansion, unavailability of people for standard times of worship and church activity, and, most importantly, changes in racial composition of neighborhoods.

Local churches were urged to develop radically new ideas about how to deal with these issues. Recommendations, often using the language of church renewal, were couched largely in case studies of new models, exemplary congregations that had devised a modified approach that appeared to be working in the city, e.g., weekday church programs, relocation of churches into apartment buildings, and, above all, racial integration in the churches. "Adapt or die" was the none-too-subliminal message. Many churches actually did adopt the recommended innovations, and some integrated, although largely on the basis of continued white cultural patterns in worship and white clergy. Most ethnically white churches, however, relied on their long-standing members commuting greater distances to ensure their survival. And many did survive — longer than grocery stores and movie theaters, longer than office buildings and shopping districts, longer than denominational officials expected.

Constituency specialization and program adaptation were commended not only for suburban and central-city churches, but also for others affected by the urban industrial expansion of the 1950s. For example, Edgar Wahlberg, a Methodist pastor in an industrial section of Detroit, lists eleven types of activities and interests that evidence the church's alliances with labor and involvements in industrial concerns: (1) seminary classes in industrial relations; (2) interseminary conferences on labor issues; (3) denominational departments of industrial relations; (4) industry-employed chaplains; (5) church-employed industrial chaplains; (6) clergy employed by labor unions; (7) priest workers; (8) company-owned churches; (9) church-supported programs among laborers, e.g., textile workers and miners; (10) labor churches; and (11) parish churches cooperating with labor groups.[24] Church-labor relations were given new poignancy during the 1950s by the attempts to pass right-to-work laws in many states. The Methodists' opposition efforts were led by the Methodist Federation for Social Action (MFSA, successor to the MFSS). Because the MFSA persisted in its justice emphasis and its interests in socialism, some of its leaders were accused of being Communists.

City missions, neighborhood houses, settlements, and institutional

---

24. Edgar M. Wahlberg, "Serving Industrial Workers," *City Church* 6, no. 1 (January 1955): 9-10ff. A number of these activities were implemented by Methodist churches, and later taken up by the Detroit Industrial Mission.

churches, many of which were organized before World War II, were pressed
to offer an increasingly wide range of social services directed toward greater
numbers of individuals, especially to African Americans and Hispanics;
many city missions became racially integrated for the first time. They were
caught, even more than local churches, in city changes that sometimes
contributed to their growth, but more often led to decline in their programs.
Halstead Street Institutional Church, Chicago, provides an example. At the
turn of the century it prospered, offering some of the more innovative social
services of the era. By 1950, even though some of the members recalled
with nostalgia the halcyon days of the church's booming social service
programs, most agreed that the church was in irreversible decline — the
result of deteriorating housing, increased industrial land use, and new
highways that split apart the old neighborhood.[25]

Concern over rapid urbanization and suburban growth resulted in
several ecumenical emphases on city ministry, beginning with the Convocation on the City Church sponsored in 1950 by the National Council of
Churches. Methodists and members of the Evangelical United Brethren
Church (EUB) participated fully in these conferences and other emphases,
contributing and deriving much of their understanding of urban dynamics
and theology of the city.

By the end of the 1950s church leaders gradually became convinced
that the old parish patterns of city ministry would not suffice in the emerging city, and perhaps even the best that church renewal could offer (as with
urban renewal) would fall short. Increased social services and specialized
ministries, sometimes called functional ministries, were commended for all
sorts of potential urban church constituencies, e.g., language groups, African and Hispanic Americans, industrial workers, apartment dwellers, alienated youth, single adults, business and professional groups, and "trailer
park" residents.[26] East Harlem Protestant Parish, a most unconventional
church by any traditional measures, seemed an exotic but impossible ideal
to emulate even though it was repeatedly described in the church and
secular presses as the epitome of urban relevance. Walter Mphasis, writing
in 1960, summarized the antitraditional parish opinion that gained ascendancy among leaders of that time by maintaining that

25. Murray Howard Leiffer, *Halstead Street. Institutional Church* (Evanston, Ill.: Bureau
of Social Research, Garrett Biblical Institute, 1954). Similar findings are reported in another
study by Leiffer and Charles Klosterman, *The Methodist Community House, Grand Rapids: Final
Report of Survey* (Evanston, Ill.: Bureau of Social Research, Garrett Biblical Institute, 1946).

26. Bonneau Pernell Murphy, *The Call for New Churches* (New York: Board of Missions
of the Methodist Church, 1961), pp. 120-21.

the typical Protestant parish conception will not fit [the] new city. Missions will be needed to experiment with new functional ministries. In downtown areas where urban renewal housing projects are established, the mobile populations may require a number of such centers rather than a conventional church institution with large capital investment and expensive parish overhead.[27]

Traditional parish ministries were to undergo increasingly harsh criticism in the early 1960s. Methodist policy began to shift from local church extension and cultural methods toward functional ministries for addressing specific urban issues and missionary methods. The shift became apparent on all organizational levels, but was promoted most strongly at the national level and resisted most often at the local level. While denominational offices were developing new racially integrated inner-city ministries, some city churches were establishing endowments intended to allow the exclusively white membership to continue control indefinitely, or until the church closed.

III. Methodism and Cities in Racial Crisis: 1960-75

Denominational leaders, concluding that urban conditions were fundamentally cruel and that congregations were basically ill equipped to do anything about them, turned away from the church extension strategies of the 1950s toward a new set of missionary strategies. Ecumenical experiments — youth ministries, apartment churches, inner-city cooperative parishes, industrial chaplaincies, civil rights marches — stirred excitement and hope. The whole ecumenical movement, with its emphasis on cooperation, gained influence in cities as denominations discovered they had by themselves too few resources to make much impact on city conditions. The National Council of Churches' "Crisis in the Cities" program and the World Council's work on "Missionary Structures of the Congregation" drew heavy Methodist participation and helped provide direction for Methodist and EUB action.[28] The catchphrase "Let the world write the agenda" reflects

27. Walter G. Muelder, "The Road Ahead in America," pp. 79-90 in *The Christian Message Today* (New York: Abingdon Press, for the Board of Missions and Board of Education of the Methodist Church, 1960).

28. The Methodist Church, Board of Education, Division of the Local Church, *The Church for Others: A Quest for Structures for Missionary Congregations* (Nashville: Board of

best the shift toward theological secularism during this era. If the church could not be trusted to embody the spirit of Christ in the city, then society itself would bear his stamp. East Harlem Protestant Parish began to look more practical than it had in the 1950s; certainly it appeared more relevant to city conditions, and perhaps it could even be reproduced in many cities. Cooperation with other denominations and secular agencies, largely eclipsed during the 1950s, reemerge as a dominant theme in denominational literature on the city.[29] As civil rights protests appeared to be influencing national legislators in the direction of greater racial justice, a new optimism among church leaders arose, even as the cities swirled in a deepening eddy of crisis. A new reformation if not a total renascence was afoot.

At the pinnacle of the urban crisis years, 1968, several organizational strands happened to come together, giving new shape to United Methodist urban ministry. Union between the Methodist and the EUB churches was effected, incidentally creating the peak membership of the new denomination. Membership totals have decreased annually since union. At the same time and in the spirit of racial integration, the Central Jurisdiction was eliminated, with the result that the more urban annual conferences suddenly acquired a constituency of African American churches — and African American Methodists lost traditional structures of service, communication, and decision making.

Hope-filled new forms of ministry required a "new breed" of clergy. Those who aspired to urban church leadership had to be retrofitted with new theology, new action skills, and an ecclesiology suited to the new forms of urban ministry. Seminarians were recruited for cooperative inner-city ministries, social activism, and industrial chaplaincies. The Metropolitan Urban Service Training (MUST) was devised to train church and community people for urban action, primarily in New York City. Methodists United for Service and Training (MUST-II) extended the effort by encouraging action training in annual conferences. Community organizing methods

Education, Division of the Local Church, Methodist Church, 1965). Service to others is the theme of this draft report of the Western European Working Group, the Missionary Structure of the Congregation Study of the World Council of Churches. The full report was published as: World Council of Churches, Department on Studies in Evangelism, Western European Working Group, *The Church for Others and the Church for the World: A Quest for Structures for Missionary Congregations* (Geneva: the Council, 1967).

29. See Hartley, subject index headings: City churches — Protestant sources — 1960-1969; Cooperative ministries.

were encouraged, particularly in terms of United Methodist sponsorship and participation in the efforts conducted by Saul Alinsky's Industrial Areas Foundation. Alinsky's confrontational tactics proved controversial, but controversy was inevitable as the old passed and the new dawned.

The enormity of urban problems undoubtedly underlined local church inadequacies and helped forward the new emphasis on cooperative mission and strategy. Cooperation became central in Methodist efforts, both within the denomination and with other denominations and secular allies. MUST became a prototype for the sort of ecumenical programs that all United Methodists were encouraged to support. Most of the urban training programs for clergy and laity that affiliated in the Action Training Coalition had significant United Methodist participation and support.

Ed Carothers, associate general secretary of the National Division of the United Methodist Board of Missions, was a key mover in the MUST innovations and called the church to respond to urban poverty.[30] The Office of Urban Ministries, a division under his leadership, became a strong force for moving the denomination toward activist ministries. Its increasingly influential staff ultimately reached a peak of six full-time people — Ernest May, Negail Riley, Kinmoth Jefferson, Cecil Pottieger,[31] John Hager, and James Sims. In addition, John Coleman staffed the Office of Community Developers, a denomination-wide program initiated by the Office of Urban Ministries. Coleman's office became a center of urgent activity for communications and strategic funding during the urban crisis.

While from the early eighteenth century onward heated debates were common between the advocates of extension strategies and proponents of missionary strategies, acrimony was especially sharp during the 1960s. Traditional local churches were criticized as being irrelevant at best and, at worst, dangerous to Christ's mission. Mere institutional survival, apart from addressing the city's problems, was deemed sinful. Traditional indicators of congregational success and failure — size of membership and offerings, Sunday school enrollment — were scorned as superfluous. Parishes that clung to old ways, resisting efforts toward racial justice and integration, were condemned as part of the city's problem and not part of its redemp-

30. See, for example, J. Edward Carothers, *How Does the Church Relate Itself to Issues of Economic Order?* (Washington, D.C.: General Board of Christian Social Concerns of the Methodist Church, [1963?]). See also his *Keepers of the Poor* (Cincinnati: Joint Commission on Education and Cultivation, Board of Missions of the Methodist Church, 1966).

31. From Pottieger's EUB days forward, he was especially involved in apartment house ministries. See his *Apartment House Ministry Handbook* (New York: Educational and Cultivation Division, Board of Global Ministries, UMC, 1980).

tion. Many white inner-city congregations, recoiling simultaneously from church leaders' vituperation and from surging social changes in their communities, grew resistant to any change and retreated into a survival mode or, worse, a siege mentality. There were, of course, notable exceptions, and these were heralded regularly as exemplars by the 1960s church press.[32] Methodist denominational funds were directed during these years mainly toward development of new models of parish life rather than toward maintaining existing parishes. New models included cooperative parish structures, citywide mission action or mission agencies (which were given the generic name of Metropolitan Ministry Agencies and were, as often as not, ecumenical in character), and other efforts aimed at achieving greater racial and economic justice.

Urban crisis was matched by crisis within the local churches. Membership declined in urban United Methodist congregations, and the rate of decline increased. Unalarmed, many denominational leaders believed that a new form of the church was emerging in cities and that old-style local churches simply were not in the vanguard.

Methodist city missions and service agencies also responded to the urban crisis. Community outreach efforts shifted away from providing direct social service to the needy toward systemic change for greater justice. Oppressive systems, not people with problems, were targeted for change. Advocacy, self-help and self-representation, and community empowerment were preferred over the more traditional remedies of charity and palliative aid. Even the task of determining what city people needed shifted from the denomination and its agencies toward the city people themselves. United Methodist colleges and universities established urban studies programs and United Methodist hospitals girded themselves for ministry to the casualties of the urban crisis.[33] City church workers came to recognize the political process as the primary arena in which justice could and should be sought.

One result of the emphasis on empowerment was that the white leadership of a predominantly white denomination came to a new awareness of the many racial and ethnic constituencies in the communities they sought to serve — and within the denomination itself. This insight helped pave the way for the denomination to return in the 1970s and 1980s to local church strategies, but with an important change — stress

---

32. See Hartley, subject index topic: City churches — Methodist sources — 1960-1969.

33. It should also be noted that during the 1960s some universities and hospitals faced unionization of their staff for the first time, themselves becoming the target of justice demands.

would be placed on the extension of racial, ethnic, and immigrant urban congregations.

IV. Methodists and Cities in Racial-Ethnic Transition: 1970-85

A sense of hopelessness became commonplace in urban churches during the 1970s, especially among those which in the 1960s made valiant efforts to bring about racial justice and improved social conditions. The city seemed unamenable to well-intended calls for change and even to the confrontation tactics of community organizers. The magnitude of city problems appeared to be far too great for a local church — or a denomination, or all of Protestantism, or even the federal government — to make any difference. In spite of all efforts to improve city conditions, matters grew manifestly and perversely worse. Promising new church forms of the 1960s vanished, taking with them the energy of optimism they had inspired.[34] During these years the Action Training Coalition disbanded, as did most of its member agencies. Industrial missions were phased out. Denominational agencies had much less money to spend for specialized urban ministry. Meanwhile, minority and immigrant urban populations continued to grow, precipitated in part by a 1965 change in U.S. immigration laws.

United Methodists' denominational emphasis returned to concerns for the local churches, stressing particularly communities and congregations in racial or ethnic transition. One sign of the changing emphases appeared in the Office of Urban Ministries when, under the leadership of Kinmoth Jefferson, Eli Rivera was employed to promote Hispanic church extension and development. Staff members William Thomas Robinson and Charles Brown enabled the office to deal more effectively with African American churches, concerns, and community groups. Another staff member, Marjorie Lutz, contributed administratively to this change in direction.

Many Anglo urban congregations had managed to survive the 1960s, albeit in reduced circumstances, long after their surrounding communities had changed racially or ethnically. While some of the first generation following suburban flight were willing to travel back into the city to their churches, subsequent generations lacked sustained interest. Local churches, once change-resistant, now agreed more readily with denominational

---

34. Lee Ranck, ed., "The Ethnic Minority Local Church: In the Midst of Social and Economic Issues," *Engage/Social Action* [thematic issue] 9, no. 5 (May 1981): 9-40.

leaders that transition was inevitable. If surviving Anglo congregations did not make changes in the composition of their membership, and if new ethnic congregations were not started, large sections of cities would be without any United Methodist congregations or witness.

Denominational literature spoke to the issues of justice and mission effectiveness during neighborhood transitions. In most actual situations, however, the concern for transition had more to do with preserving the future of an existing congregation or making use of an existing building than with promoting justice. Local church integration models of the 1950s and 1960s encouraged efforts to induce gradual transition from an all-white congregation to a racially integrated congregation, usually with a white pastor and with the basic white patterns of organization and worship remaining dominant. These efforts rarely produced major results. Other patterns of transition were required for the 1970s. With racial integration of local churches receding as an objective for urban ministry, multiculturalism — the affirmation that each culture has distinctive contributions to bring to the church and that each should be encouraged — gained ascendancy.

The simplest form of church transition was a transfer. When a white congregation declined and decided to disband, the property was transferred by the conference to a new racial-ethnic congregation, usually African American. Unfortunately, preaching barns built for Anglo crowds of years gone by were sadly ill suited to the requirements of their new ethnic occupants, and sometimes they were falling apart. Only in a few instances were the new congregations occupying old buildings able to avoid capital development expenses, a burden that impeded some fledgling congregations from rapid growth.

Facility sharing became another attractive response to neighborhood transition. Sometimes the sharing was seen as a permanent plan, sometimes as temporary until the racial-ethnic congregation grew large enough to afford its own building. In still other instances the white congregation was expected to die, leaving the racial-ethnic congregation to inherit the building. Bruce McSpadden's manual on facility sharing, the result of a three-year inquiry, describes the varieties of cooperative arrangements that emerged.[35]

Facility sharing may have been a particularly popular option in medium- and smaller-sized cities where, as the result of short commuting distances and surmountable community barriers, transition did not always

35. Bruce McSpadden, *Manual on Shared Facilities* (New York: General Board of Global Ministries, United Methodist Church, 1986).

portend the death of an Anglo congregation. Potential growth in the racial-ethnic populations was often insufficient in smaller cities to support separate new churches for each ethnic group. Shared facilities provided a ready solution. However, projects in smaller cities attracted minimal attention in the denomination's urban literature. The denomination's 1960s urban crisis emphasis aimed at New York, Chicago, and other larger cities. They, it was assumed, sufficed as paradigms for all urban ministry. By the mid-1970s the national Office of Urban Ministries began to shift its attention to medium and small cities, a trend that increased as the decade progressed.

Transitional churches and communities had direct impact on denominational policy. The most obvious manifestation was the denomination's emphasis on the "Ethnic Minority Local Church," inaugurated in 1976 and continued for twelve years. Denominational leaders wanted the church's admittedly diminishing urban ministry funds used to empower leaders of racial-ethnic congregations to accomplish objectives they themselves had determined, as opposed to priorities set by denominational officials. People at the local level were in a better position than those in distant offices to know how to deploy scarce resources. This emphasis reflected the denomination's recognition of growing racial-ethnic power in all aspects of city life and acknowledged the growing weakness of the church in financing its urban ministry objectives.

The rediscovery of the congregation as the critical agent of mission represented a conceptual change in ecclesiology. Specialized and segmented ministries for reaching out to the city's diverse people were replaced by the more holistic local church approaches. No matter what happened in the city, some local churches were prepared to stay. Survival capacity became a positive attribute. The development and redevelopment of congregations once again received the denomination's full attention as the main goal of church effort and funding. Resources were simply insufficient to replace the local church with substitutes, even if such replacement had been desirable. Moreover, some United Methodist congregations had demonstrated their capacity to survive beyond all expectations, even in the poorest of neighborhoods where virtually all other social institutions had failed. These congregations would become valued as the only community institution that could serve to introduce changes for social improvement in their neighborhoods.

The waning of denominational financial resources may have contributed to United Methodist leaders' growing attention to economic injustice in society. In any event, justice-related concerns did grow during the

252

1970s. The national Office of Urban Ministries played key leadership roles in the Joint Strategy and Action (JSAC) Task Force on Ministers to Business and Industry, and helped found the Interfaith Center on Corporate Responsibility. Kinmoth Jefferson became deeply involved with the National Council of Churches' Domestic Hunger and Poverty program, the Interreligious Economic Crisis Organizing Network, and its successor, the Federation for Industrial Retention and Renewal. In 1990 he played a key role in creating the Coalition for Justice in the Maquiladoras.

The loss of much of the denomination's readily available funding precipitated dramatic changes in its urban program, especially reductions of staff and program funds. Networking — the practice of linking people across the denomination in order to share their knowledge as a resource for mission — grew in importance. As the number of people on the national urban ministry staff began to diminish, networks helped fill the gaps. Similarly, efforts by the local urban ministry projects to find multiple funding sources grew, seeking support from their own communities and building coalitions to address specific urban issues with combined forces. In addition to urban ministry networks, other caucuses emerged during these years. Most ethnic minorities had United Methodist caucuses. Women, sexual minorities, and conservative interests organized coalitions and networks to advance their interests in United Methodist policy-making bodies.

V. Ethnic Predominance in Urban United Methodism: 1978-90

Trends toward racial-ethnic local church empowerment and the usage of multicultural models accelerated during this period. Some church buildings contained two or more congregations worshipping in different languages and/or ethnic styles with only one legal entity. Racial-ethnic membership grew. Korean churches became the most rapidly growing segment of the denomination. A new denominational program was launched because of increasing Native American migration to cities.

Racial-ethnic membership growth brought into question several United Methodist policies and procedures, especially in regard to new congregations and the credentialing and appointment of clergy. Urban ministry advocates — based on their commitments to racial justice, empowerment, congregational development, and church growth — sought more flexible standards for ordination, theological education in the language of immigrants, and improved channels for appointment across conference lines (policies resisted by many conference Boards of Ordained Ministry). Moreover, United Methodist commitment to racial-ethnic church membership is reflected in denominational programming during this period, for example, the twelve-year emphasis on the ethnic minority local church and the $16.5 million spent by the Board of Global Ministries, National Division, on salary support, church extension, and the outreach ministries of black, Asian, Native American, and Hispanic congregations.

By 1989, new initiatives among United Methodists were involving urban congregations and agencies in addressing the issues of substance abuse and related violence, AIDS, and homelessness. The denomination emphasized reconnecting existing urban congregations with their surrounding neighborhoods.

The local church empowerment emphasis led to creation of new and strengthening of old Methodist pan-urban agencies in order to provide mission development coordination. The term "Metros" was used for these bodies, one key purpose of which was to develop resources for congregations' mission. Metros typically had small staffs, often only a director with secretarial support. They aimed to help local churches by identifying mission, providing training, offering consultation, and assisting minimally with funding.[36]

If local church empowerment has resulted in greater emphasis on the Metros, it has meant less emphasis on ecumenical agencies and interdenominational cooperation. That change may have been one of the contributing factors to the near demise of the conciliar movement in the 1980s, and certainly to reduced United Methodist participation in multidenomination congregations. East Harlem Protestant Parish seemed like an artifact curiously surviving from a previous age. Ecumenical service and action ministries, however, proved an exception to the reduction in interdenominational cooperation. Problems of homelessness, poor housing, economic and other emergencies, and the range of human suffering in cities continued to be addressed through ecumenical auspices with United Methodist support. Most notably, church-based community organizing, always ecumenical or interfaith in membership, has become a powerful response to urban needs. Community organizing of the 1980s, in distinction from that of earlier years, became a powerful tool for those congregations willing to become involved.

36. For case studies of Metros, see William E. Ramsden and Clinton E. Stockwell, *Metropolitan Ministry Agencies: Profiles of Twenty Agencies across the United States* (New York: National Program Division, General Board of Global Ministries, United Methodist Church, 1989).

Funding available for urban ministry continued to decline during the 1980s, as it had in previous decades, both on local and denominational levels. A greater proportion of each dollar contributed was retained by congregations for local expenses. Costs of supporting clergy rose, especially pensions and health insurance. Mission contributions, as a proportion of local church expenses, reached a record low. Even United Methodist annual conferences began to have funding difficulties.

Urban United Methodism of the 1980s has become much more racially and ethnically oriented, less ecumenical, and more frugal in funding. Denominational-level staff with urban ministry portfolios had been reduced from six persons in the late 1960s to one in the 1990s. Congregations with all or mostly Anglo members continued to decline and close. National denominational agencies, having lost funding, also lost power and the position of being at the cutting edge of urban ministry. Power and position shifted toward the local.

VI. Methodism in the Urban Future

The purpose of this chapter has been to identify the origins of Methodist city strategies, to trace how the denomination's urban involvement has fared over the years following 1945, and to consider analytically what the concept of "urban ministry" has meant for United Methodists. Post–World War II strategies, it has been suggested, were largely adaptations of those devised well before the war. In all, five strategies were named, and they have remained largely the same over this fifty-year span, each persisting but falling in and out of relative favor according to the times. By way of contrast, objectives for the strategies have changed greatly, as have understandings of the church's mission, the relative power of urban Methodism, and the demography of Methodist urban church membership. The most obvious changes have been the reduction in the number of Methodist city churchgoers and the diminution of denominational urban ministry funds. Many of the churches prospering in cities during the 1950s are simply nonexistent in the 1990s, and many of those that survived have done so with their 1990 membership only 10 percent of the membership size in the 1950s.

What survives in Methodism, apparently longer than denomination urban ministry goals, even longer than the most durable of central-city Methodist buildings and infrastructure, is a set of procedures and organizations that a variety of people have found useful in accomplishing a range of goals. The five do not exhaust all possible strategic options open to urban Methodism. Methodists could, but do not, invest heavily in television, create urban lay apostolates, ordain ethnic religious leaders who lack college and seminary training, or encourage charismatic preachers to build urban superchurches; nor do they, notwithstanding over three decades of decline, abandon cities.

America's future will clearly be predominantly metropolitan. While rural villages will no doubt survive in places like northern New England, the Appalachian Mountains, Montana, and western Texas, urban-metropolitan life will be the norm for most Americans. United Methodism's future is inextricably linked to its condition in cities and suburbs. Suburban and urban fringe areas, currently perceived by some residents as rural, will increasingly be understood as urban. Both residence and employment for the majority of Americans are already suburban. Older suburbs are rapidly becoming more like the central cities. Small towns are becoming urbanized, having their own core of jobs to which people commute. People in older suburbs are moving to newer suburbs, and the people replacing them are, not surprisingly, religiously or ethnically or racially or socioeconomically different, repeating once again a cycle discernible not only over the past fifty years, but even in early-nineteenth-century cities.

Urban United Methodism has in some senses suffered greatly over the last four decades, at least in terms of membership statistics. Local churches and annual conferences that tried to preserve the ministries fitted for the social realities of previous decades found their efforts futile. National denominational urban ministry emphases have countered preservation efforts with encouragement to diversify, to reach out to meet new needs and new people, and to risk change, but results have at best been mixed. Bitter arguments and a great deal of sadness ensued as most urban local churches declined and many closed. Neither flagship nor neighborhood congregations were immune.

Yet, sadness and suffering do not tell the whole story. United Methodism, notwithstanding its history as a predominantly white denomination, has proved to be a usable tool for urban ethnic and racial minorities. Methodism now has the opportunity to learn from the growing experience and expertise of its new urban churches.

Whether or not the denomination as a whole regains health and vigor because of its new urban resources depends on how several critical questions are resolved. Such questions may of course be framed in a variety of ways, but the authors of this chapter believe dominant themes will be recurrent. Our list follows:

256

1. Will racial and ethnic minorities continue to find in Methodism an expression of their spirituality and faith as well as a usable structure?

2. Can white United Methodists find in the city a rich resource for their own spiritual health as opposed to seeing it merely as a target of missionary activity or charity? Can whites join the rest of humanity in city life, notwithstanding their retreat from it?

3. What do Methodist immigrants bring with them from their countries of origin for Methodism in the United States? What opinions of Methodism do non-Methodist immigrants have?

4. What is the impact of Methodist urban ministry in other parts of the world, especially the Third World nations of Central and South America, Asia, and Africa, on United Methodist urban work in the United States?

5. What does the recent trend of African American migration southward and westward in the United States mean for the urban church?

6. How do the urban experiences and understandings vary in Korean, Cuban, Puerto Rican, Mexican, Haitian, Indian, Native American, and Filipino United Methodist congregations?

7. Can United Methodist systems for the training, ordination, and placement of clergy be transformed to respond to contemporary urban church needs, especially those of racial-ethnic churches?

8. Will a new form of denominational structure emerge that spans the diversity of new ethnic congregations, integrated congregations, and surviving white congregations, thereby giving new voice to urban Methodism's witness?

· 11 ·

Urban Economic Development Strategies of African-American Baptist Clergy during the Cold War Era

JAMES MELVIN WASHINGTON

SEVERAL PROMINENT African American clergy have offered pivotal *national* leadership in creating a strategy to deal with the tragic social and economic legacy of slavery. Several recent professional studies[1] have emphasized the social and political history of African-American Baptist leaders without sustained attention to their contribution to solving the economic plight of their congregants. But most of these studies do not cover the twentieth century, and none sufficiently examines the complex development of the post–World War II era. The search for a viable strategy of economic development, especially during most of the Cold War years, 1945-90, is an indispensable and distinctive dimension of this critical story. Many prominent laypersons, such as Nannie Helen Burroughs, Rayford Logan, and Ralph Bunche,[2] also participated in this struggle. In fact, Logan

---

1. See Mechal Sobel, *Trabelin' On: The Slave Journey to an Afro-Baptist Faith* (Westport, Conn., and London: Greenwood Press, 1979); Leroy Fitts, *A History of Black Baptists* (Nashville: Broadman Press, 1985); James Melvin Washington, *Frustrated Fellowship: The Black Baptist Quest for Social Power* (Macon, Ga.: Mercer University Press, 1986); Sandy D. Martin, *Black Baptists and African Missions: The Origins of a Movement, 1880-1915* (Macon, Ga.: Mercer University Press, 1989); Evelyn Brooks Higginbotham, *Righteous Discontent: The Women's Movement in the Black Baptist Church, 1880-1920* (Cambridge: Harvard University Press, 1993).

2. See Kenneth Robert Janken, *Rayford W. Logan and the Dilemma of the African-American Intellectual* (Amherst, Mass.: University of Massachusetts Press, 1993), pp. 10-12,

and Bunche did not relate their public activities to their religious convictions. On the other hand, few African-American Baptist women gained the national public prominence of Burroughs as major players in shaping public policy.[3] The focus of this chapter, however, is upon strategies for economic development.

The reasons for clergy involvement in the struggle for an effective urban economic development strategy are obvious. Among these, one should note that all African American clergy, and Baptist clergy in particular, had to contend with the social crisis created by the urbanization of the African American community. Those who were most experienced in dealing with such problems were the pastors of the larger congregations in the urban centers both in the North and in the South. These congregations, as Carter G. Woodson reminds us in *A Century of Negro Migration*,[4] had been dealing with the distending urban crisis since the 1830s. Clerical leaders in the old congregations, formed in the late eighteenth and early nineteenth century, responded to fugitive slaves in the antebellum period; to mass migrations of ex-slaves during the Reconstruction period (1865-77); to the western movement, led in 1879 by such figures as "Pap" Singleton, a black Baptist preacher; and to the massive migrations of black Southerners when the "Boll Weevil" attacked the tender cotton plants and devastated the agricultural economy of the South. Pastors of congregations such as Abyssinian Baptist of New York, Olivet Baptist of Chicago, Third Baptist of San Francisco, Concord Baptist of Brooklyn, Shiloh Baptist of Washington, D.C., and Eighth Street Baptist of Kansas City, Kansas, responded to these crises with innovative programs that addressed the immediate needs of their new parishioners. But the problem was too great for them. Only government had the economic resources to address such a systemic economic problem that afflicted African American people.

23, 44; and Brian Urquhart, *Ralph Bunche: An American Life* (New York and London: W. W. Norton, 1993), p. 32.

3. Even Burroughs's political power was diminished somewhat because of her loyalty to the Republican Party, which lost its majoritarian status among African Americans during the 1930s. See Nancy Weiss's *Farewell to the Party of Lincoln: Black Politics in the Age of FDR* (Princeton, N.J.: Princeton University Press, 1983). Scores of Baptist women became powerful local leaders in denominational circles and civic affairs; several African-American Baptist women, such as Ella Baker, a former Baptist missionary, gained national prominence in the civil rights movement. See Vicki L. Crawford et al., eds., *Women in the Civil Rights Movement: Trailblazers and Torchbearers, 1941-1965* (Brooklyn, N.Y.: Carlson Publishing Co., 1990).

4. Carter G. Woodson, *A Century of Negro Migration* (1918; reprint, New York: Russell and Russell, 1969).

In the era of Jim Crow (1866-1965), between the end of the Civil War and the passage of the Voting Rights Act of 1965, legal racial segregation legitimized economic discrimination. Sporadic attempts during the period to overthrow Jim Crow largely proved to be either only partially successful or simply ineffective. The New Deal programs of President Franklin D. Roosevelt in response to the Great Depression, and World War II, were the key events that changed the attitudes of white Americans about economic justice. Progressive American religious leaders, both black and white, sensed this, and took full advantage of this change. They formed coalitions with black clergy and other organic intellectuals, to bring pressure for the application of economic justice along racial lines, rather than simply restrict this new mood to the white community.

Economic justice in America has only recently been recognized as a major public problem. That is especially true when it comes to economic justice for black people, the grandchildren of American slaves. No study did more to surface the social and economic plight of black America than Gunnar Myrdal's *An American Dilemma*.[5] With the financial sponsorship of the Carnegie Corporation, Myrdal, a distinguished Swedish social scientist, assembled the most gifted group of social scientists he could find. Many of them were important black researchers such as Ralph Bunche, Allison Davis, St. Clair Drake, E. Franklin Frazier, and Ira Dea Reid. In fact, *An American Dilemma* was a summary of important special reports written by fine scholars like these men, and therefore gained wide acceptance not only in the white power structure but also among black middle-class leaders. Myrdal argued that blacks were held back by the nation's refusal to give reparation as a consequence of their slavery experience. For Myrdal and his colleagues, the economic dilemma the "Negro problem" posed for America was a "pathological" one. Although they perceived that the problem was malignant, they did not conclude that it was absolutely fatal in the long run. They believed that "the American Creed," which offered "liberty, equality, and the pursuit of happiness" to all its citizens, could be realized by increasing educational opportunities and intensifying American industrialization. The "Negro problem" signalled a major crisis of faith in the American political and social credo. The shortfall between promises and fulfillment made the American Dream a nightmare for the black masses. In order to restore this faith, Myrdal and company suggested that only the complete

---

5. Gunnar Myrdal (with Richard Sterner and Arnold Rose), *An American Dilemma: The Negro Problem and Modern Democracy*, 2 vols. (1944; reprint, New York: Pantheon Books, 1975).

social, political, and economic conversion of the entire nation would lead to serious changes. They believed the problem to be systemic rather than isolated. Myrdal wrote:

> The American Negro problem is a problem in the heart of the American. It is there that the interracial tension has its focus. It is there that the decisive struggle goes on. This is the central viewpoint of this treatise. Though our study includes economic, social, and political race relations, at bottom our problem is the moral dilemma of the American — the conflict between his moral valuations on various levels of consciousness and generality.[6]

By making the race problem a moral and religious problem, Myrdal was functioning as a theologian and moralist. But he was also providing a remarkable rationale for the liberal Democratic projects of the Roosevelt and Truman administrations. Liberal capitalism could only be saved, he reasoned, if the American people faced up to the Negro problem as a moral and psychological dilemma.

But it was precisely the realization that the problem of racism was so deep on so many levels that led many black leaders to suspect the "good intentions" of white liberals. They realized that the temptation of the hypocrites is to believe that if they do just a little bit, God, or providence, or even the helpless themselves, would be able to finish it. Just provide them with the opportunity, and all would be well somewhere down the road. White leaders did not believe in what Barrington Moore Jr. calls "reciprocity." Moore argues that "without the concept of reciprocity — or better, mutual obligations — it becomes impossible to interpret human society as the consequence of anything other than perpetual force and fraud."[7]

If this is true, what recourse could the victims of injustice in America have? Better yet, what strategies have they employed to resist systemic unfairness? Since it is obvious from even a child's knowledge of American history that violent revolution has not been a common strategy, we must look elsewhere. The answer is simple and yet complex: they resorted to individual and group protest.

---

6. Myrdal, vol. 1, p. lxix.
7. Barrington Moore, *Injustice: The Social Bases of Obedience and Revolt* (White Plains, N.Y.: M. E. Sharpe, 1978), p. 506.

I. Background to Postwar Boycott Strategies

Blacks did not start organizations exclusively for the purpose of protest until the twentieth century, however. The first one was, of course, the National Association for the Advancement of Colored People (NAACP) in 1909. The other important organizations were the National Urban League in 1910, the Congress on Racial Equality in 1942, the Southern Christian Leadership Conference (SCLC) in 1957, and People United to Save Humanity (PUSH) in 1971. Of these five major protest organizations, three have always had significant religious bases and often equally powerful religious leadership: the NAACP, SCLC, and PUSH. And black ministers have had far more power in the NAACP than had been recognized before the Reverend Benjamin E. Hooks became its executive director. The Reverend Dr. Channing Tobias, the powerful national executive director of the Colored Young Men's Christian Association and a member of Roosevelt's "Black Cabinet," served for years as the chairman of the NAACP's Board of Directors.

Such strong black religious leaders have always been at the forefront of black protest. That ministers should have such a strong place in this movement is inconsistent with the general history of religion in America, as is seen if one reads such major histories of American religion as those by Sydney Ahlstrom and Winthrop Hudson.[8] Why then do we have this trend among black ministers? Perhaps the best reason for this development was put forth by the Reverend Dr. Benjamin E. Mays, onetime president of Morehouse College, in his classic study. Mays and Nicholson argue:

> It is the firm conviction of the writers that the Negro pastor is one of the freest, as well as most influential, men on the American platform today. This is due to various causes, but chief among them is the factor of the long-time prestige of the Negro minister, the respect for him and for religion; and the poverty and the financial freedom of the Negro church.[9]

The black church movement commenced in the late eighteenth century, and has been thriving ever since. It started out as a religious protest movement and quickly became the chief force behind many black social reform movements such as abolitionism, and the leader of resistance to Jim

8. Sydney E. Ahlstrom, *A Religious History of the American People* (New Haven: Yale University Press, 1972); Winthrop S. Hudson, *Religion in America* (New York: Scribner, 1965).
9. Benjamin Elijah Mays and Joseph William Nicholson, *The Negro's Church* (1933; reprint, New York: Arno Press, 1969), pp. 289f.

Crowism, tragic political inequalities, lynchings, and so on. And, as Mays and Nicholson argue with power and enthusiasm, the black church has been the major galvanizing force for the black community. But it had to maintain this position through much internal struggle and, most certainly, through much struggle with secular black competitors.

One of the chief means that black leaders have used to acquire large shifts of power has been the pressure tactic called the boycott. Economic boycotts are an old and very successful tool used by black Americans to extract as much power as possible from white America. One of the early uses of this tactic was in the abolitionist movement. White and black abolitionists organized the African Civilization Society partly in order to organize black people to resist the slave powers by refusing to buy any products made with cotton grown in the American South. In fact, Henry Highland Garnet, the first president of this society and the black pastor of the Shiloh Presbyterian Church of Brooklyn, New York, accompanied his fellow black Presbyterian brother, the Reverend Dr. James William Charles Pennington, to Frankfurt-am-Main to establish the first Antislavery Society in Germany; its chief goal was to institute a boycott against buying American cotton products. Although this movement was not very successful, it created a precedent that was not forgotten by future generations of black Americans.

During intermittent periods in the nineteenth century, especially after the emancipation of over four million slaves, African Americans used the boycott to protest against all forms of economic and social discrimination. This was their best defense against the absurd proscriptions of Jim Crow. From discrimination in seating on urban streetcars to discrimination in numerous other public facilities such as libraries and interstate vehicles, black leaders led their people in attempts to halt Jim Crow's advance. Bishop Benjamin W. Arnett, of the African Methodist Episcopal Church, for example, was instrumental in the passage of the Civil Rights Act of 1886, which prohibited discrimination on interstate vehicles. But to no avail. By the end of the 1880s black folk were still being discriminated against on trains and riverboats because state laws often superseded, in practice at least, the mandates of federal legislation and courts. The Interstate Commerce Commission, created in 1887, offered a solution temporarily acceptable to blacks, the "separate but equal accommodations" doctrine. The separate-but-equal idea was superseded in the 1930s by reappropriating the economic boycott strategy as a means for obtaining black economic power.

What happened in the interim? Although there were numerous attempts to use the boycott method on a local level, it never really gained wide recognition and use again until the success of the Reverend Adam Clayton Powell Jr. in the 1930s. But in the meantime, by 1896, the Supreme Court institutionalized the "separate-but-equal" doctrine in its famous *Plessy v. Ferguson* ruling. Furthermore, 1895 saw the temporary demise of the protest form of leadership in the death of the famous black protest leader, Frederick Douglass, and the rise to power of the famous black accommodationist, Booker Talifero Washington. As Louis Harlan suggests in both volumes of his now classic biography,[10] Booker T. Washington was involved in a serious power struggle against those black leaders who felt that social protest was a viable strategy. Ironically, the black leaders who provided him with the most support and the most opposition were the black ministers. Fellow teachers such as W. E. B. DuBois and I. Garland Penn, journalists such as T. Thomas Fortune and William Monroe Trotter, lawyers such as Archibald Grimke and T. McCants Stewart, and black politicians such as John Mercer Langston vigorously opposed Washington. It was not until the founding of the NAACP in 1909, nearly a year after the white citizens of Springfield, Illinois, instigated a race riot against blacks, that the use of protest as an important strategy was recovered.

Washington was largely successful in redirecting the tactics of his rival leaders because he was able to placate them with political patronage positions, or confuse them with a number of questionable business schemes. The scheme to found the National Negro Business League was very successful, not only because of Washington's tireless maneuvers, but because of strong support from clerical entrepreneurs such as the Reverend William Reuben Pettiford, the founder of the Alabama Penny Savings Bank and the pastor of the Sixteenth Street Baptist Church of Birmingham, Alabama. Other black ministers, like William W. Browne, who organized the True Reformers Bank; John R. Hawkins, who was the able financial secretary of the African Methodist Episcopal Church; and the Reverend W. F. Graham, populated the ranks of the National Negro Business League and helped black business leaders increase their profits and assets. In 1914 the league reported that black business ventures rose from 20,000 in 1900 to 40,000 in 1914, that banks increased from a pitiful 4 to 51, undertakers from 450 to 1,000, drugstores from 250 to 695, and retail merchants from 10,000 to 25,000. In fact, some blacks, like Madame C. J. Walker of St. Louis, a pioneer in black hair products, actually became millionaires. But it should be noted

---

10. See Louis R. Harlan, *Booker T. Washington: The Making of a Black Leader, 1856-1901* (New York: Oxford University Press, 1972), and *Booker T. Washington: The Wizard of Tuskegee, 1901-1915* (New York: Oxford University Press, 1983).

that much of their success came from capitalizing on the so-called Negro Market. Black community solidarity was one of its high points, largely because blacks were indeed an insulated social colony that either had to provide its own services or simply do without.

Only rarely did white people try to support black businesses. But they sometimes provided services for a few black people. It was not until after World War I that black urban communities began to receive the attention of white businesses as black migrants from the rural South quickly took over white communities. The white merchants left stranded were forced to service these black people. This was certainly true for the increasing number of merchants who were foreign immigrants and therefore trying to acquire quick capital. In an economic crunch, Jim Crow always took a back seat. As someone has said, when it came to the green of the dollar bill, Jim Crow was usually color-blind.

No persons or groups, whether black or white, helped these black rural migrants more than the black churches. The urban black churches and their pastors became havens in the heartless environs of the developing urban slums. They provided numerous social services that local governments refused to provide (or provided reluctantly) because they were only gradually accepting a social welfare outlook. Many churches, often called institutional centers, became employment bureaus, recreation centers, child-care centers, community centers for political forums and activities, and creditors. The list is lengthy, some of the outstanding churches being the Olivet Baptist Church in Chicago under the pastorate of Lacey Kirk Williams, Pilgrim Baptist Church under Junius Ceasar Austin, and Reverdy C. Ransom's Institutional Church and Social Settlement, which belonged to the African Methodist Episcopal Church. Few, however, surpassed the amazing accomplishment of the Reverend Charles Albert Tindley's Methodist church in Philadelphia. And in New York City William H. Brooks at Saint Mark's Methodist Episcopal Church, and Adam Clayton Powell Sr. at the Abyssinian Baptist Church, both provided model churches for this important response to the new black urban immigrants.

The continuous economic depression that the black masses had experienced since emancipation from slavery could not be resolved even by well-meaning black church leaders until the government faced up to the need for serious reparations for well over 350 years of unrequited labor. Roger L. Ransom and Richard Sutch are quite correct when they conclude that the nation's refusal to address this particular legacy of slavery has dealt a terribly unjust blow both to its own material and human well-being and also to black people themselves.

Unlike the indentured servants of Colonial America, blacks received no freedom dues: land redistribution was aborted and the blacks were forced to begin their lives as free men and women without money, without tools, without work animals, without any assets of any kind. Their economic, political and social freedom was under constant attack by the dominant white society determined to preserve racial inequalities. The economic institutions established in the post-emancipation era effectively operated to keep the black population a landless agricultural labor force operating tenant farms with a backward and unprogressive technology. What little income was generated in excess of the bare essentials of life was exploited by monopolistic credit merchants.[11]

The major difference between the post–World War I period and the post–Civil War era was that blacks were fast becoming exploited, unemployed urban serfs with little hope of owning anything but the blues. There were, however, a few black leaders, including the increasing middle-class-minded preachers, who really captured the attention of the black masses. After the death of Booker T. Washington in 1915, only one major mass leader was able to amass a huge following, the Jamaican-born Marcus Garvey. Garvey understood that what the black masses needed was a massive dosage of hope during one of the most vicious periods of racism in American history, the 1920s. While recognizing the significant accomplishments of the new black middle class that its major trumpeter called "The New Negro,"[12] we cannot dismiss the reality that black America was still in the grips of a major economic depression. We usually think of the 1920s in American history as a time of great prosperity. It was. But, as usual, it was not for black people. And the depression that held black folk in its relentless grip finally tried to strangle the nation itself after the great stock market crash of 1929. The unfortunate laissez-faire economic philosophy and praxis of over fifty years of Republican rule came to a close in the 1932 presidential election when Franklin Delano Roosevelt was elected on the Democratic ticket. He offered what Harvard Sitkoff calls a "new deal for blacks."[13]

The positive climate the Roosevelt era created encouraged able and

---

11. Roger L. Ransom and Richard Sutch, *One Kind of Freedom: The Economic Consequences of Emancipation* (New York: Cambridge University Press, 1977), p. 198.

12. Alain Locke, ed., *The New Negro: An Interpretation* (New York: A. and C. Boni, 1925; Atheneum, 1992).

13. Harvard Sitkoff, *A New Deal for Blacks: The Emergence of Civil Rights as a National Issue* (New York: Oxford University Press, 1978).

ever-ready black leaders to press even more vigorously for economic concessions from the federal government. Thousands of blacks and whites were employed under the numerous projects of the Works Progress Administration, as well as in the slow but determined economic revitalization of "private" industry. In the midst of this evolving economic resurgence, black leaders felt that it was imperative to press for jobs. Indeed, the black clergy were among the major leaders in this endeavor to acquire economic justice for the black masses.

The so-called Jobs for Negroes campaign was propelled not only by increasing black impatience with Roosevelt's economic reforms, but also by the founding of the National Negro Congress, the Civil Rights Federation, and the Fraternal Council of the Negro Churches. The 1930s ushered in a new era of white liberalism as seen in white friends in the Federal Council of Churches (reorganized in 1948 to form the National Council of Churches), the National Board of the Young Women's Christian Association, the Public Affairs Committee, and especially in the undaunted support of First Lady Eleanor Roosevelt. Strong, intelligent, and courageous black leaders like Mary McCleod Bethune, A. Phillip Randolph, and Roy Wilkins led the black masses with foresight and determination. Black ministers were also reaping tremendous benefits from the rising support for an educated clergy, as is so well documented by W. A. Daniel.[14] One of the trained young seminarians who quickly rose to power was the Reverend Adam Clayton Powell Jr., who received his graduate professional training at Union Theological Seminary, New York, and Columbia University.

II. Civil Rights and the Uses of Economic Boycotts

When Powell became the assistant pastor of his father's famous Abyssinian Baptist Church, he introduced a new style of ministry. He challenged the old Victorian values of his father's deacon board by marrying Isabel Washington, the star of the Cotton Club, the famous Harlem nightclub the younger Powell often frequented. The majority of the church and the Harlem community overwhelmingly supported young Powell when the deacons tried to unseat him. This touching personal triumph encouraged Powell to take bold public stands. Numerous opportunities came his way.

He led successful boycotts against the banning of black doctors from

---

14. W. A. Daniel, *The Education of Negro Ministers* (New York: George H. Doran, 1925).

Harlem Hospital, against stores on 125th Street that would not hire or serve black people, and against Con Edison Electrical Company, which he threatened by suggesting black folk could pay their bills with pennies. He finally led over six thousand blacks on a march to city hall to protest injustices against the black community. He won on all fronts. He was also shrewd enough to pay attention to the need to monitor the progress of the companies and the city. But this was a large undertaking. The solution was to lobby for public support. So Powell ran for a seat on the City Council and won. He later ran for Congress and became one of only two black congressmen at the time. But Powell became more important than just a congressman from New York. He became the symbol of a new kind of power that he, himself, called in 1965, "Black Power." He understood that there are different kinds of power, and that the most he could probably achieve in his day was "symbolic power." He was well suited for the role of the new "bad nigger," "the trickster," in an era when black folk were depicted on stage and screen as lazy, dumb, and helpless. But he never achieved greater notoriety than when he led the boycotts of the 1930s. He established the resurgence of the new protest leader who was more than the genteel breed one saw in A. Phillip Randolph. He was simply sassy and proud of it. No other noted black ministerial leader was able to surpass Powell's audaciousness and flamboyance. (Later Jesse Jackson appeared to be a close contender.) Yet, a leader without a program is like a nuclear submarine without a rudder. The search continues for a social protest technique that could impress the black masses yet not alienate white allies.

The boycott still struck many black leaders, especially ministers, as a viable option. But they had to learn how to focus this technique. One early, and often forgotten, experimenter was the Reverend Theodore J. Jemison, who in 1982 became the president of the huge National Baptist Convention, U.S.A., Inc. Jemison led a very successful boycott against the public transit system of Baton Rouge. Three years later Martin Luther King Jr., a young black Baptist pastor with a Ph.D., led a similar boycott in Montgomery, Alabama. He actually travelled to Baton Rouge to learn how Jemison conducted his campaign. King's boycott was more successful, however, because it led to the creation of the historic Southern Christian Leadership Conference (SCLC) in 1957. His economic philosophy did not lead him to a broader vision until it was evident in his August 1967 annual address as president of SCLC, the last address he gave to that annual meeting before his assassination the following year.

In the meantime, between 1959 and 1963, Rev. Leon Sullivan, pastor of the Zion Baptist Church of Philadelphia, refined the use of the boycott into what he called "Selective Patronage." Using the umbrella of the black church, Sullivan organized four hundred Philadelphia ministers. Their collective church membership of more than 250,000 people were called upon to redirect the buying habits of the black community.

The conditions that sparked the drive in Philadelphia included the following: no blacks drove soft drink, ice cream, bread, or oil trucks. Black truckdrivers, sales agents, white-collar executives, and secretaries were missing from the crowds that poured out of the banks and insurance companies.

In the three-year drive on industry in Philadelphia, some thirty companies that had committed the "corporate sin" of discrimination became targets for withdrawal campaigns. Some of the more notable were Pepsi-Cola, Gulf, Sun Oil, and Tasty Baking Company, which reportedly lost 40 percent in sales over a seven-week period.

According to Sullivan, the Philadelphia selective patronage program resulted in more than five thousand jobs, directly or indirectly, channeling more than $15 million in new income for black families.[15]

The negotiation process consists of five stages: information, education, negotiations, demonstrations, and reconciliation.

Information: Letters were sent to political targets requesting a listing of all job classifications, the total number of employees versus the number of blacks in each category, and the salary range. Government forms that companies submitted to the Equal Employment Opportunity Commission (EEOC) were requested. Virtually before the information was in their hands, the ministers could visualize the familiar employment patterns: blacks, if employed at all, were in the lowest-paying jobs that required little or no responsibility.

Demands for hiring and upgrading centered on the often disputed logic that if blacks made up 20 percent of the population they should have 20 percent of the jobs. For companies that served a predominantly black population, the demands were often increased to 30 percent. However, it was also taken into consideration that some companies were so far behind in black employment that a 20-percent to 30-percent increase would force them into bankruptcy.

Ministers were careful to couch their demands in terms of expectations. They demanded an increase instead of quotas, since the latter has always had a negative connotation when it meant black addition to the workforce. But when quota meant subtraction — last hired, first fired — or zero population in terms of blacks in upper echelon positions, the term

---

15. See Leon H. Sullivan, *Build, Brother, Build* (Philadelphia: McCrae Smith Company, 1969).

was acceptable, if not as a figure of speech, certainly as an expression of intent.

Education: What the ministers meant by education was nothing that had ever been taught in an urban or suburban classroom. The ministers would switch from the subject of lack of truckdrivers to Shadrach, Meshach, and Abednego without ever losing the beat of their Baptist cadence, which hopelessly confused some of the white officials. In their preaching-teaching sessions, the ministers also impressed upon the executives that by denying blacks the right to work they were the main contributors to their daily diet of social injustices, shoddy housing, and poverty.

Negotiation: In the spirit of their social gospel, these sessions always opened with prayer before the ministers changed into the posture of hatchet men. Prior to the meeting at least two hatchet men were selected; their job was never to be satisfied with anything. They were always radical, pushing at the need to get more from the company than was being offered. The executives were not allowed to stray from the issue of jobs, and were made to stay on the point of offering corporate solutions to the problem. A point that should not be overlooked is that the ministers were careful not to waste their time with company underlings who couldn't make decisions. Sullivan offers a pithy narrative of how the ministers organized themselves into "general gatherings" to plan strategies. There were four hundred ministers involved; and no one came closer to being the director of the movement than Sullivan himself. The ministers were especially good at getting the attention of recalcitrant executives.

> The four hundred, on gathering, then agreed upon the "company for visitation," the priority group leader was confirmed as spokesman for the campaign, and a "visitation team" was agreed upon, usually consisting of five ministers, including the spokesman. And at that point the campaign was ready to be initiated.
>
> The next day, arrangements were made for a meeting with the top executive of the company. If he chose to delay the meeting, the time would be compensated for further up the line. Later, when the deadline was given for meeting the requests of the preachers, the executive was informed that his time for meeting the requests had started the day he was called for the first meeting. He was reminded that the delay was not the fault of the ministers but the fault of the company. Executives soon ceased postponing meetings.[16]

16. See Sullivan, p. 72.

Demonstration: It was the hope of the ministers that negotiations would prevent the necessity of consumer withdrawal, that companies would submit to a program of economic justice without additional pressure. The basic tool used here was an appeal to the black community not to cooperate with "evil" as it was found in the target company. Direct action usually consisted of the following: (1) the ministers' call from the pulpit for selective withdrawal, (2) announcement over the ministers' radio broadcasts, (3) letters to supporters, (4) letters to stores requesting the removal of target products from their shelves, (5) winning the support of other community groups, (6) picketing of large-volume stores that did not remove the products, and (7) statements, primarily to the black press, explaining the rationale for the withdrawal.

Reconciliation: The conclusion of the direct action phase was to establish new relations of cooperation and assist in sensitizing company officials to their new black workers. This was a time of jubilation — often unwarranted — for the black community. Officials were encouraged to pose for press photographers to celebrate the victory and to emphasize their new corporate image in hopes the ghetto dollar would return. There is only one thing more difficult than calling for a boycott, and that is calling it off in the minds of consumers who have found other places to shop. Targets in the ghetto were not picked at random, and the majority deserved to be boycotted. Ministers sized up targets in terms of a sliding vulnerability scale. Targets were companies with low profit margins so that boycotts would have a quick, spiraling result. Ministers selected companies with strong competitors eager to absorb their markets, stores with few retail outlets, and businesses not conducted by phone or mail order. Ministers also took into account the image of the company. The more a company had worked to effect good race relations, the more sensitive it would be to adverse publicity.

Although the concept of organized consumer withdrawal was not new to the SCLC in light of the historic 381-day Montgomery bus boycott in 1955, the Reverend Leon Sullivan was called to Atlanta by Dr. Martin Luther King Jr. and the Reverend Ralph Abernathy to help set up a pilot project based on his experience in Philadelphia. As a result of the meeting, Operation Breadbasket was established as an official economic arm of SCLC in September 1962.

Having gained a reported five-thousand-plus new jobs in Atlanta, which included their first target, the Colonial Bread Company, SCLC established Breadbasket affiliates in eight southern cities. This success in the South, however, was minuscule compared to the depressed economic condition of black dwellers in the urban ghettos of the North. King's famous "I Have a Dream" speech on August 28, 1963, was the crowning achievement of a movement geared toward symbolic victories. King rightly understood that his movement was largely a powerful and effective "symbolic struggle." The hard-core material victories would come down the road; but they would come with grudging compliance. But King himself knew this would not be enough. He well understood that the significance of the civil rights movement would not be judged only by its psychic and spiritual achievements, but especially by the concrete gains it could acquire from a greedy, materialistic society that held fast to a Horatio Alger understanding of human opportunity, and felt that charity was an individual virtue rather than a reasonable human expectation. He argued that

> the struggle for rights is, at bottom, a struggle for opportunities. In asking for something special, the Negro is not seeking charity. He does not want to languish on welfare rolls any more than the next man. He does not want to be given a job he cannot handle. Neither, however, does he want to be told that there is no place where he can be trained to handle it. So with equal opportunity must come the practical, realistic aid which will equip him to seize it. Giving a pair of shoes to a man who has not learned how to walk is a cruel jest.[17]

With this realism in mind, King looked toward the North. Like the slaves of the nineteenth century, King and his cohorts came to the conclusion that the dethronement of the systemic racism in the North was of paramount importance.

Chicago was a natural location for King to test how effectively Operation Breadbasket might work in the North, not only because local black leaders like Al Raby were pressing to have King witness against racism there, but also because of the tradition of strong black political involvement in that great midwestern metropolis. Neither Detroit, New York, nor Los Angeles had the history of strong political successes that Chicago did, even though they had larger black and minority communities. This history of black political leadership in Chicago goes back to the first powerful patronage system established by the Reverend Archibald J. Cary Sr., who later became a bishop in the African Methodist Episcopal Church. It was really Cary who was the chief political protégé that made Oscar de Priest, the noted black congressman, into a powerful symbol of black achievement

---

17. Martin Luther King Jr., *Why We Can't Wait* (New York: New American Library, 1964), p. 136.

within the nation itself. Cary's mantle was picked up by his son, Judge Archibald Cary Jr. But when King finally came to Chicago in 1966, he found it difficult to win the confidence of the local leadership.

III. Jesse Jackson and Black Capitalism

It was Jesse Louis Jackson, then a young seminarian at the Chicago Theological Seminary, who was able to organize and mobilize the black community in preparation for the coming of Martin Luther King Jr. First of all, Jackson's charisma won the confidence of the ministers. There was a definite fire and fervent spiritual presence that joined the need to relate ministry to social and political change. One could, of course, argue that Jackson got his greatest inspiration from Martin Luther King Jr. That is true. But within that spiritual and intellectual presence he could never have won the support of stalwart assistants like the Reverends David Wallace (his protégé at Chicago Theological Seminary), George Riddick, Willie Barrows, Wilbur Reid, and Calvin Morris. These were all very charismatic figures in their own right. But there was an energy and contagion about this young man that demanded their best and their most faithful loyalty. And these servants delivered their best. Many of them still do. This charismatic attraction did not sustain many of these assistants past 1971 when Operation Breadbasket became Operation PUSH. But the main point to remember is that Jesse Jackson's charisma attracted and held their allegiance long enough to build a forceful movement of national and international viability.

The sobering event that solicited reconsideration of the place of these lieutenants in this movement was the assassination of Dr. King on April 4, 1968. After King's death, Jesse apparently underwent a conversion experience. He was ordained a month later in the midst of waging a fierce campaign to keep "The Poor People's Campaign" alive. Abernathy had appointed Jesse as the mayor of "Resurrection City," the camp constructed on the Washington Mall as the headquarters of the campaign. Apparently, this nitty-gritty job was dumped into Jesse's lap because the other disciples of the martyred King did not want it. Jackson later became the national director of Operation Breadbasket, but was encouraged to resign this post as a result of personality conflicts between himself and other SCLC staffers, especially Abernathy. There were other more formal reasons for the split, however. It was said that Jackson did not give a full financial accounting of his famous Chicago trade fair that he called "Black Expo." Instead of fighting about this matter, Jackson left Operation Breadbasket and took most of his famous Chicago followers with him in the formation of PUSH on December 25, 1971. But before discussing PUSH any further, we need to place its rise in a wider context.

Jackson was not only engaged in the internal power struggle within SCLC between 1968 and 1971, he was also beginning to mount a formidable attempt to meet the challenge of Nixon's "black capitalism" idea. Black capitalism began as a very suspicious idea put forth by Richard M. Nixon in his 1968 campaign for the presidency. After the massive urban riots following the assassination of Dr. King, Nixon offered the very opportunistic proposal that the nation needed a "new approach" to its racial problem. Under the rubric of black capitalism, he advocated more black ownership, pride, jobs, and political power. His rhetoric led many black entrepreneurs to try to seize this occasion to press for a far greater share of the economic pie. Nixon's concept of black capitalism included providing tax incentives that would encourage the "private sector" to risk venture capital in rebuilding and developing the underdeveloped ghettos. Hubert Humphrey, the Democratic Party's nominee, advanced a counterproposal: he called for a government-supported "Marshall Plan" similar to the very successful project put forth to rebuild Europe after the devastation of World War II. Both Nixon and Humphrey offered governmental assistance to solve the problem of black economic underdevelopment. But one offered indirect assistance while the other offered direct assistance. Nixon won the election largely because the nation was once again beginning a slow but determined drift back to a conservative mood. Yet the idea of black capitalism would not go away. In fact, it fit the conservative mood quite well. Other far more radical proposals were put forth, but they did not see the light of day.

Jesse Jackson's strategy and social theology (or social gospel) are comparable only to those of Powell, Sullivan, and Martin Luther King Jr. Powell led us in a civil political equality movement. Sullivan awakened us to what was the earliest architecture of the civil economics movement. King was primarily committed to a movement for civil social equality. But Jesse Jackson became all three and more. His strategy provided a viable philosophy and methodological vision that took seriously the need for bodily as well as psychic nurturance. His move to enhance the black pocketbook and black self-esteem represented an attempt to uplift the psyche as well as the material condition of black people. He has provided the synthesis that was so badly needed since the death of Dr. King.

Jackson concurred with the judgment that Dr. King himself had made: the next phase of the movement would have to be a quest to achieve economic justice. King said, in that historic film titled *From Montgomery to Memphis,* that there had been three stages of the movement. The first was concerned with public accommodations. The second phase, which was actually the main focus of the campaign in Chicago, was concerned with open housing. Who can forget Cicero, Illinois, which King dubbed the most racist city he had ever encountered? But King prophesied that the next phase of the movement must be geared toward the redemption of black America, and of all poor people in the United States and throughout the world. Thus his last powerful but ineffective gesture in this direction was the Poor People's Campaign.

As mentioned previously, Jackson became the mayor of Resurrection City. But this symbolic coincidence augured the new course for the civil rights movement. Jesse himself called this phase of the civil rights movement the "Civil Economics Movement."[18] How he structured such a movement will become our concern momentarily. But first we need to review the philosophical framework Jesse used to motivate his followers into such a new direction.

It has often been said that Jesse Jackson is nothing more than a poor, warmed-over Booker T. Washington. In fact, no one has levelled this half-truth more than Barbara Reynolds, a distinguished black journalist. She argued the point in this fashion:

> As in the era of Booker T. Washington, black capitalism is seen as a panacea to the race problem. It is in line with the work ethic. And there can be a plethora of individual "success" stories that create the impression that blacks are making great strides when the masses are standing still or at worst going backwards. . . .
>
> White capital, as it was with Washington, is a growing source of Jackson's influence. Washington's white benefactors were Andrew Carnegie, John D. Rockefeller, the President of Standard Oil, and Julius Rosenwald of Sears, Roebuck & Company. In Jackson's era they are Hugh Hefner, Jewel Tea Company, the Gulf Oil Company, Sears, Roebuck, & Company and the Ford Foundation.
>
> No other black man in America except Washington, has been given the green light by the czars.[19]

---

18. Jesse L. Jackson, "Completing the Agenda of Dr. King," *Ebony* 29, no. 8 (June 1974): 117.
19. Barbara A. Reynolds, *Jesse Jackson: The Man, the Movement, the Myth* (Chicago: Nelson-Hall, 1965), pp. 376-77. This book was later reprinted under a different title; see Barbara A. Reynolds, *Jesse Jackson: America's David* (Washington, D.C.: JFJ Associates, 1985).

It is very difficult to verify Reynolds's claims. But one thing is certain: those white friends who support Jackson do so not only because he is a charming and charismatic person. What they rightly perceive is that he has tremendous power and influence among the black masses. The sources of that power are rooted in a powerful economic patronage system that Jackson has constructed over several years of hard and intense labor. He has also constructed a very elusive but still quite reliable political network that is grounded primarily in the black church movement, while the economic one is related more to organizations like the National Business League. While Jackson receives support from these sources, it must be emphasized that his strongest support comes from black ministers. Without their help he would be far less effective in getting direct access to working-class black people. The reason Jackson commands this support is not always given the attention it deserves. He is first and foremost a minister, an esteemed colleague to over forty thousand ministers. And he espouses a theology much like their own. Because he only meets with his Operation PUSH "congregation" on Saturdays, he is able to crisscross the country preaching at various black churches on Sunday mornings. These travels not only provide public exposure, of which Jackson has an abundant share; they also provide a tremendous opportunity for Jackson to touch base with his primary support group.

Jackson preaches and teaches a simple but powerful gospel of black upward mobility in what he himself calls "the revolutionary, democratic traditions of the Black Church." It is a message that proclaims that the Christian's gospel is not only about individualistic sin. It is also about "corporate sin." This shift to the social, economic, and political implication of being a Christian is taken with deep seriousness by Jackson and those ministers who identify with him. Indeed, Jackson's passionate sense of religious vocation enhances his social and political philosophy. In fact, the two are so intertwined that it is difficult to discern where one ends and the other begins.

Jesse's philosophy is an excellent synthesis of King's civil rights philosophy, with its emphasis on psychic and material uplift, Black Power rhetoric, and American populist sentiments. Jackson has argued over and over again that

> The questions that have been asked of me the most are, "Why are you putting all this pressure on the victim instead of the victimizer? Why are you letting the 'system' off the hook?" I'm not arguing that the victimizer abdicate his responsibility, and I challenge the victimizer everywhere I

go. While I know that the victimizer may be responsible for the victim
being down, the victim must be responsible for getting up. The victim
is responsible for initiating change, determining strategy, tactics and
timing, and being disciplined enough to pull it off. No one has a greater
self-interest than the victim for getting up, while the victimizer does not
perceive it in his self-interest to help the victim to rise. In this relationship
between slave and slavemaster, I have never known of a retired
slavemaster.[20]

In order to continue the black-consciousness revolution taught him by his
chief mentor, Martin Luther King Jr., Jesse organized PUSH for Excellence
in Education in September 1977. But actually he had been promoting this
black self-esteem platform since the time he led the residents of Resurrection City in this famous chant: "I am somebody. I may be poor, on welfare,
uneducated, powerless, on dope or in jail, but I am still somebody." Jesse
actually states in a 1979 *Ebony* article, "PUSH for EXCELLENCE Can Be
One of the Cures," that this chant operates as the first part of a three-part
"litany" at PUSH-EXCEL rallies. He calls such a meeting a "motivational
rally." According to Dr. Jackson, "each part consciously addresses three
problems in the Black Community — all of which are important to solving
Black on Black crime." The "I am somebody" part of his litany addresses
the "psychological issue" of "self-identity." In the second part Jesse leads his
followers in this chant: "Down with dope and up with hope." Jesse says:

> The critical factor here is self-control. Since we are behind and do live
> in a racist society, we must be superior just to be looked on as equal.
> Thirdly, we say "Nobody will save us, from us, for us, but us." The issue
> here is self-determination. The resolution of self-identity, self-control
> and self-determination are critical factors that will contribute to the cure
> of Black on Black crime.[21]

Actually Jackson's attack against "Black on Black crime" is a very subtle
attempt to address the problem of group motivation and self-destruction.

It is important to note that for ten years Operation PUSH had the *S*
in PUSH stand for "save." Jesse Jackson is undoubtedly the most political
evangelist America has ever seen. He saw and conducted that phase of his
movement as a revivalistic campaign against the assaults on black humanity.

---

20. Jesse L. Jackson, "A Challenge to the New Generation," *Ebony* 33, no. 10 (August
1978): 164.
21. See *Ebony* 34, no. 10 (August 1979): 105.

It is often forgotten that this was the only country in the history of the world whose chief justice once said that "the black man has no rights that a white man needs respect." Justice Roger Brooke Taney's infamous words in the *Dred Scott* decision of 1854 gave public utterance to the widespread sentiment that black people are biological degenerates, on the edge of the human species, closest cousins to the apes. The very concepts of beauty and ugliness are measured against a racist society's tendency to define its own main tribe's characteristics as universal traits against which all others are to be judged. The struggle throughout black history to fight against this sort of dehumanization has been intense. The psychological fallout from this kind of stereotyping is incalculable. But few know and see its consequences with as much consistency as ministers like the Reverend Jesse Jackson. Of course, this social ploy of stereotyping black folk is a common one used by victimizers throughout the course of human history. But it is quite debatable whether or not there has been such a consistent and thorough degradation as represented in the term *nigger*. Jackson, his ministerial cohorts, and their spiritual forebears have always recognized this problem and addressed it with the spiritual power of black preaching. They have understood that black self-identity is indeed a large part of the spiritual quest of this community.

Jackson's emphasis upon the need for "self-control" is obviously rooted in his athletic background. He sees himself as a spiritual and moral athlete for social justice, minority political empowerment, and now economic parity. This is, as noted previously, a definite continuation of Dr. King's program. But where he diverges from Dr. King is at the point of accenting the need for black "self-determination." Jackson has actually transformed the old integration-versus-segregation debate. This, too, is related to his own religious outlook.

Details of Jackson's economic views can be found in several places, including the 1974 *Ebony* article mentioned above. But at this point we cannot focus on the details of Jackson's economic strategy, nor can we speculate about his plans for the coming decade. Rather, it is necessary to conclude by considering the story told here in the framework of this book's concern with urban ministry.

Social conditions in America for African-American Baptists were the same as for other black Christians, indeed, for black people as a whole. The legacy of slavery and Jim Crow has persisted throughout this century down to the present time. As blacks migrated increasingly into cities over the past century, churches developed many forms of ministry adapted to the new environment. Like the congregations of the Christian Methodist Episcopal

Church and the Church of God in Christ, described in other chapters, Baptist churches were truly community institutions, serving their members and neighborhoods as centers for employment, recreation, child care, youth activities, and political debate.

This chapter has not discussed that broad range of urban ministries, but has focused on urban economic development strategies as one specific form of ministry — one that I consider absolutely crucial. If African American churches, and their progressive friends, mobilized in the civil rights movement of the sixties, it was clear to many that civil rights involved more than laws on the books. It is one thing for legislation to open for blacks public accommodation, interstate travel, or the home housing market; but it takes economic resources to enjoy these "rights." A family mired in poverty will not buy a house, stay in hotels, or exercise their right to go to restaurants and resorts. Political rights must be supported by a sturdy economic base. So it belongs to the logic of the matter that Adam Clayton Powell Jr. and Leon Sullivan led boycott campaigns,[22] drawing on strategies used in the nineteenth century; Jesse Jackson articulated that logic when he insisted that the civil rights movement as a movement for social equality must be transformed into a "Civil Economics Movement."

Many African-American Baptist pastors, and their colleagues in other black denominations, have always understood the gospel to involve political and economic redemption. This theology is the prerequisite for pursuing urban economic development strategies as an indispensable form of urban ministry.

22. Sullivan also attempted (ineffectually in the view of his critics) to apply a similar approach to companies in South Africa through his "Sullivan Principles."

Seeking Community in the Metropolis:
Reflections for the Future

CLIFFORD GREEN

WHAT CAN WE LEARN from the rich and varied history recounted in the previous chapters? What enduring insights and promising experiments emerge from these stories? What problems and oversights appear from analyzing these histories? What should inform the thinking of pastors and congregations (suburban as well as urban), of judicatory, denominational, and ecumenical leaders, as they reflect on these chapters?

This chapter will address these questions in three parts. In the first two I will focus on the previous chapters, partly in review and partly to suggest some learnings; in the third section I will offer some personal reflections. Inevitably, this chapter must reflect the views of its author; it is not a consensus document composed by committee. But it is disciplined by the reports and analysis in the previous chapters, and informed by the critique of colleagues in the project who read it in draft.

I. Observations on the History

The obvious first comment, especially in comparison to the situation in the nineties, is the impressive degree of commitment to ministry in the city at the peak of the postwar period in the sixties and seventies. This commitment is evident in many ways: the number of people in urban parishes, in judicatories, in national church offices, in ecumenical organizations, and in training programs who were deeply concerned about urban life and convinced about the special responsibility of the Christian community to be engaged with the pressing issues of the cities. These people were supported by substantial funds in national church budgets, as well as by studies, reports, and resolutions of church bodies that professed commitment to ministry in the city. A spirit of innovation and experimentation was in the air, a hopeful spirit that cities could be rejuvenated and that urban churches could play an important part in that rejuvenation. To be sure, this commitment was not universal. The early part of the period showed most denominations preoccupied with moving into the suburbs, and the latter part has certainly seen a dramatic falling-off in the investment of attention, people, and resources in urban ministry. But even though the commitment was not universal or enduring at the same level, it was impressive. Although lists are inevitably fragmentary, they help us look at the expressions of this commitment from several angles.

When we consider the *issues addressed* we find the following range of interrelated problems, with the main items recurring like a litany throughout many chapters: jobs and economic development; housing and homelessness, especially for low-income, elderly, and minority people; civil rights and race relations; public education; urban renewal; environment; health care; drugs; AIDS; abortion; teen pregnancy; single-parent families; violence. The first five categories recur throughout the period and dominate most lists.[1] (Later in the chapter I will discuss this focus on issues as it bears on the conceptualization and overall strategy of urban ministry.)

In terms of the *constituencies,* or groups of people, the list of those with whom urban ministry programs were particularly concerned covers a broad range: migrants, both from overseas and intra-U.S. migration; African Americans and Hispanics, especially around civil rights issues; industrial workers; youth, including juvenile delinquents and gang members; refugees; artists; elderly, especially low-income seniors; apartment dwellers; single adults; prisoners; handicapped; business and professional groups; and unmarried mothers and AFDC mothers. To a significant degree, this list reflects the church's historic and biblical commitment to people who are suffering, and to the victims of society. In addition, the chapters reveal sustained efforts to

---

1. It is worth noting, in view of the discussion below about the problem of thinking primarily in terms of issues, that AIDS and homelessness appear on people's lists beginning about the mid-eighties and reflect, respectively, the spread of the disease and the impact of Reagan policies. Environmental issues and abortion have also become prominent in the latter half of the period. That is, issues get people's attention because they are there, and not necessarily because they derive from some urban analysis or priority of ministry strategy.

CLIFFORD GREEN

influence people who had the power to shape and improve urban life — politicians, city planners, corporate executives, bankers and investment managers, and so on — not to overlook church executives!

If we look at the *sectors of urban life* that churches tried to engage, we see represented, in some measure, local, state, and national government; businesses and stores; industry and labor; media; education; and health care.

When we consider the *services provided* by churches in urban ministry, we find the following: meeting places for community and civil rights organizations; office space and support for community organizers; low-income and elderly housing; social services (e.g., Catholic Family Services); infant day care and Head Start programs; recreation programs and summer camps; tutoring students and mentoring; counseling; homeless shelters; soup kitchens; emergency funds; and job training.

When we examine the *forms of ministry* in the previous chapters, it is clear that churches have engaged a broad spectrum of urban life with their witness, advocacy, and service. By forms of ministry I mean specific modes of organization and activity through which clergy and laypeople sought to influence and change various aspects of urban life, and to serve suffering and needy people. An attempt to categorize them yields a long list: intentional communities, settlement houses and community centers, legislative advocacy, coffeehouses, storefront churches, street ministry, industrial chaplaincies, and a national center on corporate responsibility.

Finally, if we consider the various *methods of ministry* — what people did (and in many places are still doing) to seek community in the city — we create a very long list. It includes activities that are quickly recognized as "ministry," such as the personal evangelism in the urban "war zone" carried out by the Church of God in Christ; the pastoral care, support, and socialization of black migrants by their congregations; running institutions such as hospitals, parochial schools, orphanages, and homes for unmarried mothers; mobilizing pan-urban denominational agencies; and pairing urban and suburban congregations. But the methods of ministry also included a range of less traditional activities, many oriented to the public world rather than congregations and individuals, yet all ways in which people were trying to respond to the gospel, love their neighbors, and live lives of faith, hope, and love. These activities include providing various of the services mentioned above; advocacy and lobbying with government, corporations, and foundations; marches, protests, and boycotts; education; community organizing; voter registration drives; issuing prophetic pronouncements; organizing ethnic caucuses; electing candidates to office;

282

neighborhood economic development; monitoring police, courts, and prisons; running credit unions; labor organizing; working in volunteer groups like St. Vincent de Paul; creating national networks of individuals (e.g., CCUM, IMPACT, Lutheran Human Relations Associations); and fund-raising and grant making (e.g., the Campaign for Human Development).

Lists like these, while documenting deep commitment and a broad range of activities, cannot convey the more holistic, systemic, and strategic thinking of many urban ministry leaders.[2] Therefore we must ask what are some of the main insights to be learned from these histories.

2. Some Learnings from the History

As we look to the future, the first point to be highlighted is that *the church must be confident about its own calling, identity, and message.* The Zeitgeist may not be as encouraging as it superficially seemed to be in the 1960s, for example; but then, the church is the community of the Holy Spirit of Jesus, not of the Zeitgeist. In his chapter Robert Franklin describes congregations of the Church of God in Christ as confident in "the unfolding will of God" and certain of "the future outcome of the war against evil." These "soldiers in the army of the Lord are authorized to celebrate Christ as the victor who makes our lives possible"; they have "a 'wartime' deliverance approach to ministry." This theology, Franklin writes, can combine both personal and social transformation, personal evangelism and concern for social justice and institutional, systemic change.[3]

The military metaphor is not the only way to express this confidence of being the people of God, the vanguard of the new humanity, created by the incarnation of God in Jesus Christ and his resurrected presence in the Holy Spirit. But words like those evoke the ethos of the pre-Constantinian church whose confidence in its Lord and its gospel was more than equal to its sufferings. When Athanasius told the story of the gospel early in the fourth century, it was above all the story of the incarnation of God in Jesus Christ and the life-giving power of his resurrection.[4] He lived in the confidence that the resurrection of Christ means nothing less than the re-

2. Richard Luecke, for example, writes of the "more unified intent . . . to get affected communities to *pose* problems prior to imposing solutions, and therefore to resist service providers whose solutions served to define the problems," adding that "this intent helps account for the central emphasis on community organizations" (letter of July 22, 1994).

3. See chapter 4 above, pp. 89-90.

4. See *The Incarnation of the Word of God*, in E. R. Hardy, ed., *Christology of the Later Fathers* (Philadelphia: Westminster, 1954).

creation of the world and the redemption of all humanity. He understood that ministry is witnessing to *God's* gracious action, *God's* faithfulness, *God's* life-giving and creative power, *God's* own saving and healing ministry in Jesus Christ. Earlier than Athanasius, the author of the letter to the church at Ephesus prayed for that congregation "that you may know what is the hope to which God has called you, what are the riches of God's glorious inheritance in the saints, and what is the immeasurable greatness of God's power in us who believe, according to the working of God's great might accomplished in Christ in raising him from the dead" (Ephesians 1:18-20a RSV rev.). That is a statement of the confident faith that will uphold the church in ministry — urban or any other context — in the coming decades.

Another basic point is theology. Metropolitan ministry must be rooted in full-blown *social and public theology.* This is the premise of the chapters above, even if we see it in glimpses rather than fully articulated. Far too often at urban ministry conferences and workshops, and in some literature, people only focus on the city theme. But it is quite inadequate to have snippets from the prophets talking about justice, or Jesus weeping over Jerusalem, or meditations on Nehemiah or the "new Jerusalem" from the book of Revelation. It is not just a "city theme" theology that is needed, but a theology that explicitly and comprehensively challenges the individualistic and subjective bias that too much of the church has adopted from a secular and commercial culture.

A social, communal, and public theology will know, with Bonhoeffer, "the social intention of all the basic Christian doctrines."[5] Its doctrine of creation will show how the co-humanity of human existence is the reflected "image of God," who is the God of pro-humanity.[6] Its doctrine of redemption will stress simultaneously the new relationship of faith to God and to the community of the new humanity God creates in Jesus Christ. Its doctrine of the Holy Spirit will celebrate the life-giving power of Christ to unite in one reconciled body people from all nations, races, and social classes, and to connect the liturgy of word, bread, and wine with an economy of shared goods. Its eschatology will describe the divine commonwealth as not only the fulfilling goal for the future but also the transforming paradigm for the present. As the community of the divine commonwealth in history, the church enacts parables of redemption and hope in the worship and

5. Bonhoeffer, *Sanctorum Communio* (London: Collins, 1963), p. 13. A new translation of the German critical edition of this text will be published by Fortress Press as part of the sixteen-volume Dietrich Bonhoeffer Works Translation Project.
6. See Bonhoeffer, *Creation and Fall* (New York: Macmillan, 1966), pp. 35ff., and Karl Barth on the *analogia relationis,* e.g., *Church Dogmatics* (Edinburgh: T. & T. Clark, 1958, 1960), III/1, pp. 194ff., III/2, pp. 220ff.

composition of the congregation, in its own form and purpose in the metropolis, and in the ministries of its members in their vocations and public roles. A new and vital appreciation is needed of how this is all summed up in Trinitarian theology and Eucharistic liturgy.

We must give special attention to ecclesiology, in particular asking how different forms of the church are congruent, or incongruent, with the shape and institutions of urban life. From a sociological perspective, what we have today are ecclesial forms that dimly reflect either the feudal structure of medieval society (e.g., Catholics, Episcopalians, Lutherans) or the small-town structure of early modern society (e.g., congregational polities). Without doubt, the congregation is the dominant form of the church in the United States. Unlike thirty years ago, nobody today is arguing that the congregation should be scrapped or bypassed; it is recognized as the basic unit of Christian community life. Yet a congregation, while congruent with a neighborhood (absent for a moment denominational divisions!), is certainly not congruent with urban-metropolitan life as a whole. But when we look at larger forms of the church, such as the diocese or synod, these display their own incongruities — either because of denominational divisions (see below), or because they are more forms of administration than forms of ministry and mission. So the urban reality forces us to recognize that ecclesiology is not simply concerned with *teaching about* the church, with a doctrine that exists in books and ideas, but also with the actual empirical *structure* of the church in its urban-metropolitan context.

A public theology, contextualized to its urban locus, must also be a critical theology in its social and cultural analysis. The decades of urban ministry documented in this book certainly reveal plenty of critical prophetic passion, especially around issues of racism and poverty. But just as we need a holistic approach to urban-metropolitan life, so we need deeper cultural and social analysis that dissects the fundamental doctrines of our social philosophy and economic institutions and practices.[7] These are the roots of which so many "urban issues" are the scarred fruit.

Church-based neighborhood renewal. That congregations can be powerful agents of neighborhood renewal, thereby revealing their congruity with a part of the metropolis (especially in ecumenical coalitions), is strikingly documented by the story of Bethel New Life, Inc., in Chicago. There is no need to repeat the story here,[8] but there is need to reflect on

---

7. I have in mind writings like those of Cornel West, Stanley Hauerwas, Robert Bellah and his coworkers, Beverly Harrison, and others.

8. See Richard Luecke's summary above, pp. 131-33.

Luecke's insight: *"community revitalization is not achieved through a housing project here, a new school principal there, a jobs program somewhere else. It begins to look like a circle of things."* The "circle of things" at Bethel were: a vibrant worshipping congregation that initiated the neighborhood redemption; a volunteer and sweat equity housing program; control of the rebuilding by local residents; increasing financial strength, enabling deals to be made with city government and banks; the joining of over twenty neighborhood congregations in an Isaiah plan for new housing; converting a failing hospital to a community center with programs for the elderly, day care for children, and art programs; cooperative efforts in sewing, home care, and recycling; and a creative experiment using welfare funds for a Self-Sufficiency Program. Over the course of twenty-five years Bethel New Life, Inc., had itself become the employer of nearly five hundred people, and ran a budget of over $6 million. Like the seed in the parable of the sower that fell on good ground, the congregation at Bethel had multiplied many times.

Stories like this can be told of other cities: Luecke also mentions the Nehemiah Project in East Brooklyn; the Church of the Savior in Washington, D.C., is another example. The moral is clear. Since human lives are not heaps of fragments but complex unities with many interrelated variables, so neighborhood renewal and community creation entail a holistic strategy dealing with the related aspects of worship, work, housing, mutual care, sharing of skills, care for the old and the young, recreation and art, and so on. The different variables are mutually reinforcing, and the effect is cumulative over the years.

Community organizing. The effectiveness of community organizing to mobilize and renew urban neighborhoods and congregations is clearly one of the most promising learnings from the experience of the last fifty years.[9] At the same time, organizing now is not the same as when Saul Alinsky began working in Chicago's "Back of the Yards" in the 1930s. As John McKnight and John Kretzmann point out, "conditions have changed dramatically in most working-class and poor urban neighborhoods"; further, the "targets" of Alinsky-style organizing are increasingly difficult to find. "New strategies," they argue, "must stress an organizing process that enhances and builds community, and that focuses on developing a neighborhood's own capacities to do for itself what outsiders will or can no

---

9. See, for example, the community organizing issue of *Christianity and Crisis* 47, no. 1 (February 2, 1987).

longer do." In short, "building community through the restoration of local political economies" is the new agenda.[10]

Churches have a leading role to play, because they are survival institutions in neighborhoods where political organizations and labor unions — two of Alinsky's other building blocks — are much weaker than formerly. There is a natural congruence between an urban neighborhood and a coalition of congregations in that community. Such neighborhood ecumenical coalitions of congregations have increasingly initiated community organizations by giving seed money to hire a start-up organizer, donating space, providing office facilities, and enlisting the support of members of their congregations. Further, suburban residents who are members of city churches get more deeply exposed to the problems of their congregation's urban community through the organizing project, as they are also able to bring resources of skills, money, and connections to it.

Not to be overlooked is the opportunity for evangelism and transformation of a congregation that involvement in a neighborhood organizing project can bring. Older city congregations often reflect the ethnic and class composition that neighborhoods had a century ago — Irish or Italian Catholics, German or Swedish Lutherans, etc. Meanwhile the neighborhood has changed and now has a diverse population of African Americans and Hispanics, whites and Asians. Church-based organizing can bring congregations and these neighbors together in a new way, which can result in new ethnic diversity, so that Pentecost as a microcosm of the peoples of the world becomes an operative paradigm for the congregation and not just an ancient memory. Such transformation is not just a matter of reconstituting white congregations; it can also happen when Caribbean people or Hispanics or Asians move into neighborhoods formerly occupied only by African Americans.

Community organizing is an effective neighborhood strategy that has traditionally empowered people to deal with a range of issues such as housing, education, public safety, health care, youth programs, and zoning; recently, community development and local economic initiatives have also moved to the top of the agenda. Here we find examples of community organization creating the local political economy and generating local productivity that McKnight and Kretzmann spoke about. The Nehemiah Project of East Brooklyn Churches, described in chapter 6 above, is one impressive case in point.[11]

---

10. "Community Organizing in the 80s: Toward a Post-Alinsky Agenda," *Social Policy* (Winter 1984): 15-17.

11. For an account of the first decade of the Nehemiah Project, see Jim Gittings,

Neighborhood ecumenical coalitions of congregations initiating community-organizing projects can thus be critical components of a holistic metropolitan church strategy and structure. But Wende Marshall, who worked as a community organizer in Central Harlem, poses a pertinent question: "How does the success of direct-action campaigns and the winning of a specific set of demands in any way alter control over city funding priorities?"[12] In other words, neighborhood-level action is indispensable, but beyond that lies the question of how the church will organize itself to address policies and decisions at the metropolitan level.

In the heyday of the sixties and seventies the necessity for *education and training* to equip people for ministry in the urban-metropolitan world produced for a time an impressive number of centers and programs.[13] The necessity is no less urgent today, but the question of what forms this training should take needs to be revisited. Obviously specific training and experience is needed to prepare people to take on a specialized role like community organizing.[14] But what should the role of seminaries be in coming decades? Why should they not take on the role of equipping both clergy *and laity* for their respective vocations in the urban-metropolitan world? The prospect of laity and clergy studying *together* in courses dealing with church and ministry in urban life is enticing, for laypeople could bring their expertise in economics, politics, media, and so on while clergy contributed their biblical and theological insights. It is symptomatic of our individualistic and psychologically oriented culture that *clinical pastoral education (CPE)* has been institutionalized in theological training during the decades since World War II. We urgently need programs of *urban pastoral education.*[15] For a quarter century now, especially under the impetus of liberation theology and theologians working in non-Western cultures, the contextual character of theology has become more and more evident.[16] In our training and theological education we need to acknowledge the urban-metropolitan

---

"Churches in Communities: A Place to Stand," *Christianity and Crisis* 47, no. 1 (February 2, 1987): 5-11.

12. "Organizing Community: Asking Questions," *Christianity and Crisis* 52, nos. 16-17 (November 16, 1992): 376.

13. See chapter 1, pp. 19-20, and the reference there to George Younger's study.

14. Cf. Richard Luecke above, p. 133: "some professional or skilled assistance is highly desirable, even necessary, in organizing the broader community."

15. The Seminary Consortium for Urban Pastoral Education (SCUPE) under the leadership of David Frenchak recognized this years ago.

16. See, for example, Stephen B. Bevans, *Models of Contextual Theology* (Maryknoll, N.Y.: Orbis, 1992).

world as the inescapable and formative context for our analysis, reflection, and church life.

It is a truism, which must nevertheless be repeated, that if American churches in the coming decades are to launch any major new urban initiatives, *funding* will be required. To this day the Catholic Campaign for Human Development[17] is an exemplary ongoing source of funds for urban and other ministries. But the funds Protestant churches poured into people and programs in the postwar period have largely dried up. To be sure, miracles have sometimes been done with very modest sums — for example, Bethel New Life, Inc., started with $9,600. Here is an area where ecumenical partnerships over a metropolitan area can often make a large difference; a coalition of twenty suburban churches should not have much trouble raising $50,000 each over several years, in order to begin a $1-million revolving loan fund for sweat equity housing. Much smaller amounts from a neighborhood ecumenical coalition of congregations can hire a community organizer for a year, who can then get grants from local foundations and over time leverage very considerable funds from corporations and government grants. Even some individual congregations of affluent people can often raise very substantial sums of money. But the theological issue is whether the church at large cares deeply enough about cities, and believes deeply enough in the body of Christ, to translate into dollars the biblical conviction that "if one member suffers, all suffer together; if one member is honored, all rejoice together" (1 Corinthians 12:26, RSV). The issue of funding very simply comes down to the question of where the priorities of churches are as we encounter the current plight of American cities. We may adapt the words of Jesus and say that where the heart is, there the treasure will be also (cf. Matthew 6:21).

III. Reflections

In this section I wish to address the central conceptual issue involved in the very idea of "urban ministry." What does "urban" mean as a formative context for ministry? How do our assumptions and definitions of the "urbs" inform both our reflection about the church and about the forms of ministry (or strategies) by which the Christian community engages urban life?

Reflection on ministry in a context as complex as the modern city

17. See chapter 8, pp. 202-4 above.

must be approached from several perspectives. My concern here is with *forms of the church* as they relate to ministry in cities. Reflection on urban church strategy can be ordered on three levels: the micro, the macro, and the metropolitan. Each of these is necessary for a comprehensive strategy.

In a land where the individual congregation is the dominant form of church organization and ecclesial thought, it may seem natural to begin with *congregations* in cities. The congregational approach is the micro level, because it focuses on the small units of church life; it does not focus on a national denomination, or a regional judicatory, but on the local unit of Christian community. At this level we can analyze the various forms of ministry, indigenous to urban areas, which are carried out by congregations; many examples are given in preceding chapters. A typology of congregations could be developed, correlating their theological emphases, their characteristic members, and the sorts of ministry that different types of congregation undertake in cities.[18] It is self-evident that in every strategy for ministry in cities, congregations will have an indispensable role; individual congregations are one necessary ingredient in a comprehensive urban strategy.[19]

At the other end of the spectrum is the macro level, where we view the forms of the church in the urban context from a national and sometimes international viewpoint. From its early centuries the church has had supra-congregational forms by which it related to larger social, political, and intellectual forces than those in the local parish. Similarly, as we consider American cities today, it is obvious that they are profoundly affected by events and activities on the national and international levels; and church

18. See, for example, David A. Roozen, William McKinney, and Jackson W. Carroll, *Varieties of Religious Presence* (New York: Pilgrim Press, 1984); Carl Dudley, *Basic Steps toward Community Ministry* (Washington, D.C.: Alban Institute, 1991); Carl Dudley and Sally A. Johnson, *Energizing the Congregation: Images That Shape Your Church's Ministry* (Louisville: Westminster/John Knox Press, 1993).

19. A congregation in a modern city, however, is a different social form compared with a congregation in the villages and small towns of colonial New England or an agrarian village society today. In the World Council of Churches' 1968 Urban Rural Mission document, "Becoming Operational in a World of Cities: A Strategy for Urban and Industrial Mission," the following comment is found: "Structurally the churches in the cities are still mainly organized in the form of parishes/congregations patterned on the village life. These draw their membership from a confined residential area which does not correspond to the larger units or zones of modern society. . . . The church must develop structures of its own by which it can relate to total metropolitan areas and can inter-relate its own different ministries to form a more comprehensive presence." Cited in Hugh Lewin, ed., *A Community of Clowns: Testimonies of People in Urban Rural Mission* (Geneva: WCC Publications, 1987), pp. 72ff.

forms have evolved that engage these systemic factors. Among the macro influences on cities are the following. Programs funded by the federal government, or cut from the national budget, heavily impact what happens in cities, from employment and transportation to health care and welfare. Popular culture is beamed from national media institutions into local cities by television. Airlines and cars move people so easily that some people live only part of their lives in the city of their official residence, and the "second home" is not an uncommon phenomenon. The ethnic composition of modern cities is often significantly changed by national economic trends, by wars overseas, and by political events in other countries. Drugs sold on the streets of American cities are often important economic products for peasants in foreign countries. Factors such as these highlight the truth that no city is an island.

To note these macro factors profoundly shaping life in individual cities is also to highlight the supra-local forms and structures of the church that are necessary to engage and shape them. Some of these forms have ancient beginnings; others are recent. National denominational organizations such as the National Conference of Catholic Bishops, national ecumenical organizations such as the National Council of Churches, national ecumenical advocacy organizations such as Interfaith IMPACT, organizations concerned with corporate ethics and influence such as the Interfaith Center for Corporate Responsibility — these, together with international church forms such as the Vatican, the Lutheran World Federation, and the World Council of Churches, may all be understood as macro forms of the church that have various functions, among which are efforts to affect the macro forces shaping urban life for good and ill.

Forms of the church at both the micro and macro levels have essential contributions to make in a comprehensive strategy of ministry in cities, and both the congregational and the national and international forms have had a good deal of attention over the years. I therefore wish to attend here to a third option — namely, to explore in these reflections what it would mean to focus on *the metropolis,* the whole urban metropolitan area, as an essential organizing paradigm for church ministry in cities. There are both *contextual* and *ecclesial* reasons for concentrating on the metropolitan paradigm.

The *ecclesial* reasons are implicit and often explicit in many of the chapters above. When George Todd and his colleagues in the Board of National Missions of the United Presbyterian Church produced an urban strategy document for their denomination's 179th General Assembly, they called it "Guidelines for Development of Strategy for Metropolitan Mission."[20] The urban specialists employed by the Presbyterian Board of National Missions were called "Director of Metropolitan Mission" and "Metropolitan Mission Coordinator." The United Church of Christ also had specialized people called "ministers of metropolitan mission." Gibson Winter's books clearly presupposed the metropolitan model.[21] His thinking surely influenced the naming of the Episcopal urban ministry journal *Church in Metropolis,* which came to be the ecumenical organ for sharing reflection. The United Methodists used the concept of a "Metro" to describe pan-urban denominational agencies that coordinate and support their congregations in a metropolitan area.[22] The ecumenical experiment in Philadelphia was also based on a metropolitan model as stated in its name: Metropolitan Associates of Philadelphia.

Furthermore, the urban training centers were informed by a metropolitan model. George Younger, who dedicated one of his books "to all who live in metropolis,"[23] writes:

> From the very beginning the action-training programs were committed to a metropolitan focus, which stressed the interrelatedness of urban society, while emphasizing the need to redress inner-city and minority injustice. . . . [They] kept a clear vision of the roots of the problems of the inner city that lay with institutions and people outside those blighted areas. This was not a popular emphasis, even at the height of the Civil Rights Movement and the War Against Poverty. Middle-class people, especially those living in suburban areas, preferred to see the residents of the inner city as responsible for their own plight and to treat them as objects of Christian service rather than the subjects of their own empowerment and liberation. Although there were many temptations to adapt to or adopt this reigning value system and faulty analysis, the action-training centers kept the kind of vision and emphasis that saw metropolitan areas and the whole urban society as an interrelated system in which most were victims, and only a few dominant institutions and

---

20. This is a very thorough example of a deliberate effort to think consistently with a metropolitan paradigm of both city and church.

21. See Gibson Winter, *The Suburban Captivity of the Churches* (Garden City, N.Y.: Doubleday, 1961) and *The New Creation as Metropolis* (New York: Macmillan, 1963).

22. See Hartley, Jefferson, and Ramsden above, p. 254. The Methodist usage is more restricted than my use of the terms *metropolis* and *metropolitan* as intrinsically ecumenical; nevertheless it goes in the right direction.

23. George Younger, *The Church and Urban Renewal* (Philadelphia: Lippincott, 1965).

members of the ruling power groups were able to control their own life and destiny.[24]

Perhaps the most ambitious effort to begin to think and act in a metropolitan paradigm was the Los Angeles Regional Goals Project. Following discussions in the National Council of Churches Urban Church Office, Calvin Hamilton, a Presbyterian layman and member of the NCC board, won a competition to become the chief urban planner for Los Angeles. Because his appointment had grown out of discussions in the church, Hamilton proposed that the project in Los Angeles should enlist the cooperation of the religious community. An Interreligious Committee was set up and John Wagner, a Lutheran pastor who had headed the NCC Urban Church Office, was funded by several denominations to lead it. The committee was a means by which "the church could participate in thinking through how a city establishes its goals for the future, against which all of the actions are appraised."[25] One of the strengths of the planning process was the unusually broad citizen participation in the planning effort. Forty congregations played a significant role in this, being designated "centers of choice" where citizens could participate in articulating visions and goals that would shape the future development of the city.[26] It is easy to see why the World Council of Churches adopted this project as part of its study on the Missionary Structure of the Congregation — though it is ironical to note that a *regional-metropolitan* urban project was adopted into an ecclesiological study using *congregation* as its central category! Nevertheless, Wagner points out that the new form of church cooperation in the Interreligious Committee also led to new thinking: "A lot of the topical areas [such as zoning, transportation] had never been thought of or talked about within the religious community and yet they were influencing every single congregation."[27] Creative spin-offs followed the conclusion of the project. One was an organization of architects from churches who worked to establish neighborhood parks and nonprofit housing; another was the Joint Health Venture, a partnership of colleges, hospitals, and congregations dealing with health services. In developments like these the WCC's "theology of

24. George Younger, *From New Creation to Urban Crisis: A History of Action Training Ministries, 1962-1975* (Chicago: Center for the Scientific Study of Religion, 1987), pp. 166f.

25. John Wagner, in transcript of September 1993 interview by Loyde Hartley; see following note.

26. For the Los Angeles Goals Project, see the chapter of George Todd above, the literature cited there (p. 169), and the transcripts of 1993 interviews of Wagner and others by Loyde Hartley.

27. Hartley transcript, p. 4.

the laity" from that period took root, and the organizations continue their work to this day.

To sum up: the actual practice of city ministry in the histories analyzed here found church leaders again and again devising ecumenical, metropolitan forms of the church. This *ecclesial* development was in response to the *contextual reality:* they understood the city systemically, holistically, as a metropolis, and so sought forms of the church that were congruent with that reality. Given the historic fracturing of the church into denominations, these metropolitan forms were usually ecumenical coalitions and programs of judicatories, congregations, and individuals that were ad hoc, experimental, and temporary.

The contextual understanding of urban reality according to the metropolitan paradigm is that cities are *systems, structural entities,* which must be understood as *wholes* comprised of *interdependent variables:* a city must be viewed holistically as a metropolis. The *polis* is not simply downtown, nor is it the inner city isolated from its suburbs. The *polis*[28] is the whole life-complex comprising areas of residence, work, and recreation. Work in the center city would not be possible without the numerous residents who commute from the suburbs; but these commuters could not live in the suburbs without the income and services provided by their work in the center city. This interdependence, or symbiosis, reminds us that the word *metro* in "metropolis" comes from the Greek word *mētēr,* meaning "mother." Originally referring to a city that was the "mother" of a region or country, because it was the capital, the metaphor can now remind us that it is the *whole* city, the *metropolis,* which is the mother of its people and necessary for their life. Urban-suburban apartheid must be overcome. Residence without work is no more viable than work without home.

Before exploring further the implications of the metropolitan paradigm, we need to ask why it did not give rise either to permanent new church forms or enduring structures of ecumenical cooperation designed specifically as vehicles for metropolitan ministry. There are certainly many reasons for this, including the continuing power of denominational traditions, the dominance of the congregational form, and the pervasiveness of subjective and privatized styles of Christianity that turn away from public life. But another question needs to be explored, namely, whether the metropolitan paradigm had to struggle for centrality with the tendency to define the urban context in terms of *issues.* This was a characteristic of the recent history of urban ministry in the United States, and it is certainly a habit of mind with powerful cultural endorsement. These issues were usually related to particular groups

28. It is interesting to note here the origin of our word *police.*

of people. The most obvious example is the civil rights movement, the struggle for freedom and equality for African Americans. This was certainly a dominant issue throughout the sixties, and it remains crucial today. Related to that is the issue of poverty. Churches responded out of their own gospel mandate to Lyndon Johnson's War on Poverty; but the problem of poverty intensified during the Reagan years, and in the eighties new aspects of the poverty issue became painfully obvious and claimed church efforts, especially hunger and homelessness, and the feminization of poverty. Low-income housing has been another enduring issue for urban ministry, as have jobs and public education. Most recently drugs, AIDS, urban violence, and teen pregnancy have been high on the issue list.

The prominence of the "issue" approach demands some critical reflection about this conventional habit of mind. Discerning readers of the chapters above will have noted how frequently authors have referred to "issues" engaged by urban ministry — indeed, the word almost seems to have the status of a technical term.[29] Now, from one point of view, it is simply necessary to identify those aspects of urban life that are problematic characteristics of the context and require special attention. Whether we call them issues or problems (or even "aspects"!), we have to name them. So I am not arguing that we should not attend to these urgent human issues. But a fundamental question is involved here. It concerns how we *conceptualize* urban life and the ministry of churches within it. Granted, these issues name real suffering and injustice, and the people involved must be embraced by Christian ministry. But the danger is that focusing on issues becomes a substitute for focusing on *the city as such*.[30]

29. This usage is found in many chapters. For a sampling see the following pages above: 25-26, 29, 33, 53-54, 58, 66, 103, 105, 110, 112, 153, 174, 183, 188, 207, 219, 230, and 254. Among the frequently mentioned issues are race relations, urban renewal, low-income housing, public education, and poverty. At one point Donald Steinle notes that "urban life is . . . viewed as . . . a set of problems and issues . . ." (above, p. 232).

30. See George Younger's comment that, among the American Baptists, "from the 1960s onwards, resolutions voted by delegates at the annual conventions . . . addressed many urban issues without saying much about urbanization itself" (p. 35). Younger notes the tension of *issues* and *systemic thinking* as follows. "There is no question that 'issues' were the major category used both for analysis and for strategizing. . . . This had several sources: the way in which lay persons perceive their own situation; the processing of information by the mass media; the approach used by many community organizing approaches; and American pragmatism which is concerned for 'problem-solving' and looking for what works. . . . The action training agencies (and many of the mission strategists in the denominations) kept a metropolitan perspective, and often had to remind groups working on particular issues that there was an interlocking of these issues that could not be ignored" (letter of July 30, 1994).

This matter has been perceptively noted by the authors of the Episcopal chapter. They rightly argue that "the urban agenda cuts across many issues and cannot be reduced to any single issue. Urban mission is hurt by single-issue agendas."[31] They point out, further, that

> our churches, like our society, are psyched up for short-term crusades [and] not long-term journeys or pilgrimages. We resonate with addressing problems that have immediate solutions. *Urban ministry is by its very nature systemic and therefore resistant to quick fixes.*[32]

One of the problems here is that a habit of focusing on issues can result in a *reactive* rather than creative posture. Another is that new issues come along and displace old issues, simply because — all issues being urgent — newness seems to create a self-evident priority. As the Episcopal authors write, "Urban work and racism are often demoted on the priority list by the 'hot' issue of the moment."

The issue approach was illustrated again when Vincent Harding quoted a Lilly-funded study on "Church and Family Life" in which 90 percent of the church leaders surveyed identified drugs, crime, and unemployment as the major *problems* faced by their communities. (Later Harding adds AIDS and heart disease especially to the list of issues.) Examining the churches' response to such critical issues, the study found that less than 5 percent of them had *programs* that directly addressed these problems.[33] Here is a good example of issue thinking, the response to which is "programs." Defining urban ministry for the future involves more than identifying burning issues of the nineties compared to those of the sixties. Harding points to the larger systemic question when he refers to a church-sponsored campaign in Dorchester, Massachusetts, to address urban violence by having young people turn in their guns. The youth agreed to do it if they could have jobs in exchange. Harding comments: "Urban ministry of the 1990s cannot avoid this direct politico-economic challenge without losing its central purpose and meaning." In other words, even the attempt to address one issue like violence among urban youth immediately involves urban economics and unemployment (especially among minority youth) as crucial in the systemic whole.

The tendency of churches to focus on *issues* reflects the same habit in the culture at large. The land of voluntary associations is full of special issue or

31. See Faramelli, Rodman, and Scheibner above, p. 121.
32. Faramelli, Rodman, and Scheibner above, p. 119 (italics mine).
33. Vincent Harding, "Churchz N the Hood," *Christianity and Crisis* 52, nos. 16-17 (November 16, 1992): 380.

interest groups, organizations concerned with every conceivable social problem. The daily mail documents this: every day we are bombarded with mailings that request our money and urge us to lobby Congress on behalf of all sorts of urgent social issues and good causes. Churches frequently behave like other voluntary associations in addressing now this, now that, critical urban issue.

My argument is that our thinking about ministry in the cities must begin with the paradigm of the metropolis; *within* this paradigm we can address the problems of urban life, considering the forms of the church and types of ministry that enable us to engage them more faithfully and effectively.[34] An "issues and programs" mentality cannot be our point of departure. Theological thinking cannot unconsciously and uncritically adopt the habits of mind of a secular culture. Beginning with the vision of the divine commonwealth Jesus announced and inaugurated, embodying the gospel of reconciliation and transformation as good news that promises community and peace for the city, churches must begin to explore again what it means for future ministry to think systemically and holistically about the metropolis. In this way we can build on one of the most important basic insights informing many of the chapters above. What follows are several observations that a metropolitan perspective quickly suggests.

1. In the first place, beginning with the metropolitan paradigm means questioning the conventional defining term of this project, which we still employ in the book's subtitle, that is, the very term "urban ministry" itself. Has it been understood to mean the ministry of the whole church in a metropolitan area, addressing crucial aspects of that whole urban complex? Has it meant the ministry to which suburban congregations were called and committed as much as those in the urban core? Simply to pose these questions is to know the answer: no. George Younger has pointed out that the word *urban* in "urban ministry" had come to mean "inner city" in mainline Protestantism by the mid-1960s; further, due to the white exodus to the suburbs in the postwar period, "urban" became a synonym for black or Hispanic.[35] In other words, while most practitioners of "urban ministry"

---

34. This is precisely the approach found in the Presbyterian "Guidelines"; see pp. 164-65, note 14 above.

35. Younger, *New Creation to Urban Crisis*, pp. 13, 179. Gibson Winter confirms this in his report that the Episcopal Urban Caucus once decided "that urban meant central city or the most impoverished areas of the cities"; see his "Urbanization in the Great City," *Religion in Intellectual Life* 7, no. 2 (Winter 1990): 69. The same point is made in the Presbyterian "Guidelines" quoted above (pp. 164-65), which refer to that church's growth in "understanding of urban mission from focus on the inner city to the search for patterns of interdependence among all churches of a metropolitan area" (p. 3).

had a deep commitment to the city and especially to its African American and Hispanic people, the key term "urban ministry" was itself a victim of the urban-suburban split they were trying to overcome. This helps to explain, I believe, the rise of the alternate term "metropolitan" noted above. Seeking community in the city and binding up its wounds, hostilities, and fears means using this inclusive metropolitan paradigm, and refusing to adopt a conceptuality and terminology that perpetuates the very bifurcation it is trying to overcome.

Incidentally, if the urban-suburban bifurcation in earlier postwar decades was also largely a black-white split in many cities, there is now a new element in the situation. Vincent Harding has pointed out that African American churches are now facing challenges similar to those encountered by white churches as a result of migration to the suburbs.

> Today urban ministry is carried on in the midst of a massive post-1960's black exodus from the inner city to the suburbs. The sociological literature of the past two decades has called our attention to that demographic shift. . . . However, the responses of the African-American urban churches to this suburban movement are not as clearly delineated. As the century ends, urban ministry is faced with the challenge of reconnecting middle-class and working-class black suburban church members with the central urban communities they have left.[36]

This "reconnecting" presupposes a metropolitan paradigm.

2. Secondly, thinking in a metropolitan paradigm highlights the self-evident fact that cities are no respecters of denominations and their sacred structures. If we consider precisely those urban issues that have occupied churches in recent decades, it is obvious that racism, poverty, housing, and public education, for example, simply do not line up along Catholic, Presbyterian, Methodist, Episcopal, and other denominational lines. Organization along denominational lines does not position churches well to deal with these problems. Another way to state this is to say that the denominational form of the church is simply not congruent with the modern metropolis, including the issues of urban life. Viewed historically, denominations are the legacy of confessional struggles and other factors; they were never intended to be structures of metropolitan ministry. They are simply not the best forms mobilizing church people and resources for advocacy with corporations and legislatures, for dealing with city government and

36. Harding, p. 379.

other bureaucracies, and so on. This is admitted every time denominational leaders band together to make a statement on a public issue or to visit a city official.

Denominations are not likely to disappear in the near future; we rarely hear preaching nowadays about the "scandal of division" that was standard ecumenical rhetoric at the beginning of our period. Therefore we must pursue two questions: (1) how can the denominational form of the church better serve metropolitan ministry? (2) how can churches transcend denominational limits in ecumenical modes that are more congruent with urban life?

To the first question, the greater loyalty congregations usually have to their own denomination can be turned to advantage. For example, denominational city mission agencies have often linked together urban and suburban congregations of a whole metropolitan area to pursue urban agendas, and this is no small feat.[37] If the denominational agency, or a structure like a synod or presbytery that included both city and suburban congregations, can intentionally work to overcome the urban-suburban split, this would be a major contribution. One might say that this only ameliorates the incongruence of denominations in the metropolis. But if few local ecumenical councils can attract the loyalty and involvement of congregations as strongly as their own denominational bodies or agencies, then the latter are better positioned to do it in a less than ideal world.

An analogous role in addressing the urban-suburban split can sometimes be played by certain congregations; at this point the micro and metropolitan levels overlap. There are congregations that have succeeded in joining in their membership suburban and urban families and individuals of considerable diversity ethnically, educationally, and in terms of economic class. The suburban families may have been members of the congregation for several generations, and their parents or grandparents may have previously lived in the urban neighborhood. Though the young people moved to the suburbs, they continued worshipping in the same church. Meanwhile, the neighborhood changed, bringing in people of different races, languages, and nationalities, and often with less education and affluence than the former middle-class population. If the congregation can

---

37. The case study of the Christian Activities Council in Donald Steinle's chapter 9 above on the UCC illustrates this, though he would be the first to admit that involvement by suburban churches is often token, and that special efforts (such as the CAC's Metropolitan Training Institute) are necessary to begin realizing the potential of a metropolitan denominational coalition of congregations.

"indigenize" itself to the new population by changes in its worship and its modes of ministry (program), and if the longtime suburban families can be taught the race- and class-transcending power of the gospel, such a congregation can be a parable of redemption and renewal.

Similarly, an old "high steeple" congregation may be almost entirely composed of suburban members, some of whom drive a significant distance into the city to attend its services and participate in its activities. When such a church accepts its urban-metropolitan calling and mobilizes the considerable talents of its members, it can become another important contribution to overcoming the urban-suburban split. Likewise, a council of churches composed of urban and suburban churches can link congregations in partnerships of "urban-suburban bridge building."[38] Even if such efforts do not by themselves constitute a comprehensive metropolitan church strategy, they are necessary ingredients.

The second question about adapting denominational facts to metropolitan reality was: how can churches transcend denominational limits in ecumenical modes that are more congruent with urban life? If churches are seriously to engage the systems and the crises of urban life over the long haul, they must do so ecumenically. This is one of the major lessons of this study. Chapter after chapter shows how the reality of urban life drove congregations and denominational agencies into ecumenical partnerships. If these were usually ad hoc and temporary coalitions, do we have more permanent ecumenical vehicles, or, theologically stated, forms of the church? What are the ecumenical forms through which local denominations and congregations can work together to engage government, corporations, and civic associations around the challenges of urban life?

The seemingly obvious answer is that most American cities have councils or conferences of churches that could serve this purpose. But presently they rarely serve the ecumenical function I am suggesting.[39] On the one hand, they are often voluntary groupings of congregations, many struggling to survive; unless they have at least a critical mass of congregations they will not have the resources to generate initiatives of their own or to engage the power structures of the metropolis. On the other hand,

---

38. For example, the Capitol Region Conference of Churches in Hartford, Connecticut, has had an urban-suburban, interracial bridge-building program for about a decade.

39. An interesting little research project would be to learn how many are constituted by judicatories, as distinct from individual congregations, and if any are designed to be vehicles of a comprehensive urban strategy. George Younger reports (letter of July 30, 1994) that Grace Ann Goodman made studies of many ecumenical metropolitan mission agencies, but that most of these have gone out of existence.

there is the attitude of the regional judicatories themselves. How often do they choose to use the local ecumenical council as the vehicle for their common metropolitan mission? My impression is that this is very rare nowadays. More often denominational judicatories may have an urban mission officer who works within the congregations of a particular denomination, and sometimes networks with counterparts in another denomination — if they exist. But to overcome the structural incongruity of denominations and the metropolis, the judicatories need to jointly build the local ecumenical council into a vehicle for a comprehensive, metropolitan strategy.[40]

3. Thirdly, thinking in a metropolitan paradigm brings to the foreground of theological reflection the *calling of the laity.* In the 1950s the World Council of Churches spearheaded a movement on the ministry of the laity. People like Hendrik Kraemer wrote books on the subject,[41] and Hans-Ruedi Weber gave Bible studies on Ephesians 4:12 about "equipping the saints for the work of ministry." The saints, he explained, are not the ordained clergy or members of religious orders. They are precisely the church, the *laos tou theou,* the people of God, who are called to serve God in the world. The role of the ordained is to equip the laity for just this service in the world.

While we may presently be seeing some revival of this theology of the laity in America,[42] it is safe to say that the movement has not made much substantial and lasting impact on our churches. For most people, clergy included, "lay ministry" is regarded chiefly as service *within* the congregation, whether as Christian educators, choir members, workers on various committees, etc. When Vatican II lifted up the role of the laity, the practical result of this was also to enhance the roles of laypeople in the inner life of Roman Catholic congregations, especially in light of the shortage of priests.

With some exceptions, this general picture holds for the foregoing chapters. Laity in their vocational and public roles are almost invisible. I

---

40. George Todd reports in his chapter (pp. 162-63 above) that in the 1960s new ecumenical urban ministry structures were created precisely by the urban ministry offices and staff of local judicatories. He argues that not only were the extant councils composed of congregations; the premium they put on unity led them to avoid controversial issues and confrontational situations.

41. Hendrik Kraemer, *A Theology of the Laity* (London: Lutterworth, 1958).

42. See, for example, books published during the 1980s by Richard Mouw, Mark Gibbs, William Diehl, Verna Dozier and Celia Hahn, James D. Anderson and Ezra Earl Jones, Anne Rowthorn, Dolores Lecky, and Davida Crabtree.

must immediately hasten to qualify this. The urban training centers explicitly set out to include laypeople as well as clergy in their training, though this turned out to be mainly laypeople who were professionals in community organizing, civil rights work, and similar roles, i.e., they were full-time, paid, professional, lay "urban ministers."

A notable exception to the picture of the invisible laity was found in MAP, Metropolitan Associates of Philadelphia. An ecumenical venture initiated by the American Baptists, and informed by the World Council of Churches study on "The Missionary Structure of the Congregation" (initiated at the New Delhi Assembly in 1961), MAP set out to mobilize and train laypeople in their vocational roles and institutional settings.

> The program was defined initially as consisting of "research on the character of the church's influence and witness in the public, holistic, productive, and secularized spheres of industrialized society" through lay presence, and "experiments in missionary action across the major sectors of the metropolis."[43]

MAP gathered people such as doctors, lawyers, and government employees into groups for training and support; it helped them engage, through their work, issues of urban society in light of Christian faith and ethics. A related emphasis on the laity was found in the industrial mission movement.

But MAP and industrial mission were exceptions. What George Younger wrote of the urban training programs also applied elsewhere: "their training activities principally enrolled professionals and had been unable, in most cases, to build a significant lay constituency."[44]

Why emphasize the calling and role of the laity in metropolitan ministry strategy? First, there is the theological point already mentioned: the laity are the people of God already present in that metropolitan world which is our concern. Failure to acknowledge this is to operate with a truncated, clerical model of the church — albeit unintentionally. Taking seriously this theological starting point leads, second, to awareness of the strategic location of church members throughout metropolitan institutions. Church members are found in government, industry, education, law, business, finance, medicine, the media — all the institutions that bear on the life and crises of modern cities are already populated to some degree by Christian laypeople. They are paid to make decisions and exercise power

43. Younger, *New Creation to Urban Crisis*, p. 125.
44. Younger, *New Creation to Urban Crisis*, p. 160.

day by day. Whereas clergy and community organizers seek access to power and influence from the outside, the laity are already there on the inside. Whether the issue is racial integration in schools, access to health care for teen mothers, city housing policy, community economic development, or dozens of similar issues, laypeople are already working on these issues.

But this lay presence, while large in numbers, is a scattered, uncoordinated diaspora. What is needed to support lay ministry in public life? First of all we need ways to identify and bring together church members from different sectors — government, business, voluntary associations — who are working on a given aspect of urban life. Because they come from different congregations and different denominations, few of these people even know each other, nor have they had the opportunity to explore fruitful ways of cooperation and new initiatives. Is it inconceivable even to imagine new forms of the church that would parallel, not supersede or compete with, present congregations?[45] Short of that, coalitions, perhaps focused on a particular issue (e.g., economic development, urban education) or organized along a professional or industry line (e.g., media, health care, law), can be created with modest resources, given the necessary leadership. Whether a coalition or a new form of the church, such groupings would serve several purposes: (1) as an opportunity to study the Bible, theology, and ethics in relation to their work and the issues of the metropolitan area; (2) as a cooperative group with expertise where people could explore policy options and plan strategies that might be pursued in their institutions; (3) as a source of support as laypeople struggle to live faithfully in the public world.

Doubtless someone will suggest that congregations should play this role of equipping laypeople for engaging the problems of urban life. While agreeing that all congregations, suburban and urban, should encourage and nurture this vision of metropolitan lay ministry, there are structural limits in the nature of congregations themselves. For one thing congregations gather people according to denominations, not according to their functional responsibilities in the metropolis; once again we run into the insight that cities are no respecters of denominations. (The commonplace observation that denominations today are more porous than previously does not negate this truth.) Again, few congregations would have resource people with the specialized expertise to address the complex issues of modern society. A small group of laypeople from one congregation would

---

45. The Evangelical Academies in Germany, while not exactly what I have in mind here, are probably the closest to serving this purpose. MAP experimented along these lines also.

certainly be able to undertake a neighborhood low-income housing project. But to engage problems like racial segregation in schools along urban-suburban lines, or the economic viability of a radically changing downtown area, we need ecumenical and supra-congregational groupings. To advocate such coalitions or forms of the church is not to polarize congregations and ecumenical bodies. This was an error of some involved in the earlier stage of urban ministry. Regarding the congregation as reactionary, they argued for "parachurch" forms. Congregations and ecumenical forms are complementary, not competitive. Coalitions of congregations have indispensable roles to play, especially in relation to their neighborhoods.

4. Yet another implication of thinking in a systemic, metropolitan paradigm is to alert us to the issue of the *size* of a given metropolis, and to consider whether the *small city* should receive special attention. In thinking about urban ministry there seems to have been a bias to thinking in terms of the very large city, the megalopolis — at least the small city does not appear to have been the subject of systematic reflection. New York and Chicago seem to have functioned as unexamined paradigms in American thinking. Perhaps that is not surprising: until recently New York was the headquarters for many denominations, and Chicago was the home, and still is, for agencies like the Urban Training Center, ICUIS, and more recently SCUPE and International Urban Associates. (This megalopolis paradigm also is presupposed in the frequently quoted statistics about megacities in various continents, and the large numbers of people who will live in relatively few cities in a decade or so.)[46]

In keeping with this bias toward the megalopolis, there is no discussion in our chapters highlighting the issue of small cities, i.e., urban areas under about 250,000 people. At present most American cities are small cities.[47] The question is: Does it make a difference to metropolitan ministry if churches are in small cities rather than in a large city or a megalopolis? In fact, it may be that the massiveness, complexity, and seeming intractability of the problems in cities like New York have inhibited thinking in a

46. The mission statement of International Urban Associates states that it "seeks to empower God's people in the largest cities of the world. . . ."

47. The director of research of the Advisory Commission on Intergovernmental Research, John Kincaid, wrote in 1987 that "the United States may be about 75 percent urban, but it is only about 25 percent 'citified' in a big-city cultural sense. Approximately 75 percent of the American people live in communities having populations of 100,000 or less" (letter to Ronald Pasquariello, Churches Center for Theology and Public Policy, October 6, 1987). Critical here is the definition of "communities," whether it means a relatively freestanding unit, or whether it is a self-governing suburb that is in fact part of a larger metropolitan area.

metropolitan paradigm. What we need to explore is whether scale is a relevant difference. Some of the questions to investigate include:

a. Is the small city more comprehensible because of its modest size? It seems that it is easier to know and understand the interaction of its various sectors, and that the relationships between its problems are relatively intelligible.

b. Does it make it easier to get things done when one can fairly easily know who the major players are in the corporate, government, community organization, and church worlds? Does it help when relations between all the players have a face-to-face quality?

c. Because of the relative smallness of the city, it is difficult for these racial, ethnic, and economic groups not to interact with each other as a general rule. Can this interaction of diverse groups lead to better cooperation and positive results?

d. Church leaders, both ordained and lay, can be significant voices and actors in the small city. In addition, congregations with a high concentration of institutional leaders have the potential for significant impact. Do we have evidence confirming these possibilities?

Research on the small city is necessary to investigate these questions.[48]

5. Empirical support for the metropolitan paradigm comes from the research of David Rusk in his *Cities without Suburbs*.[49] Rusk, sometime mayor of Albuquerque who has worked on urban issues all his career, studied 522 central cities in 320 metropolitan areas through the period 1950-90. He argues that "racial and economic segregation is the heart of America's 'urban problem' . . . [which] is the toughest issue in American society. It goes right to the heart of the deep-rooted fears about race and social class that have had so much to do with shaping urban America today."[50]

Rusk's argument runs as follows. In 1950, 70 percent of those who lived in metropolitan areas lived in central cities; in 1990, however, 60 percent of metropolitan residents lived in suburbs, where a majority of jobs

48. One person working on this question from the church side is Prof. Loyde Hartley of Lancaster Seminary, Pennsylvania. See also the work of David Rusk (below, note 49) who notes that "debate over urban policy has focused on only a handful of America's largest cities (p. 1)."

49. Published in 1993 by the Woodrow Wilson Center Press in Washington, D.C., *Cities without Suburbs*, by David Rusk, is distributed by the Johns Hopkins University Press.

50. Rusk, pp. xiiif.

were located by then. During those forty years, America's minority population (including Native Americans) doubled from 14 percent to 27 percent; over 80 percent of minorities now live in metropolitan areas. Given this demographic and economic picture, Rusk analyzes cities according to the criterion of "elasticity." An elastic city is one with the capacity to grow, typically acquiring new territory by annexation, thus linking older central city and newer suburb in one metropolitan whole. Inelastic cities are those which cannot grow — because they are already dense within their boundaries, or cannot expand their boundaries; this situation is common in the Northeast and Midwest. By contrasting pairs of comparable cities — elastic cities like Houston, Columbus, Nashville, and Indianapolis, and inelastic cities like Detroit, Cleveland, Louisville, and Milwaukee — Rusk reached some telling conclusions.

Whereas virtually all metro areas have grown, "inelastic cities suffered catastrophic population losses."[51] Cities that did not grow did not remain stable but lost population dramatically. The inelastic areas, where central city is divorced from its suburbs, are much more segregated. If "the city-suburb per capita income ratio is the single most important indicator of an urban area's social health," inelastic cities have marked disparities between per capita income of city and suburbs, while in elastic cities the income levels were equal; poverty, consequently, "is more concentrated in inelastic cities than elastic cities." Conversely, "the smaller the income gap between city and suburb, the greater the economic progress for the whole metropolitan community." The more a metro area is fragmented into multiple local governments — which correlates to inelasticity — the more segregated it is likely to be, both racially and economically. Similarly, "public education in inelastic areas is characterized by a single, but shrinking, central-city school system surrounded by multiple suburban systems"; these fragmented structures of public education are much more segregated than a centralized and unified system.

Rusk's elastic cities have clearly been doing much better on issues that church leaders in ministry to cities have been animated about for decades, such as race, poverty, housing, and education. Indeed, some of his "laws of urban dynamics" have an almost theological ring to them and could be paraphrases of biblical texts: *"fragmentation divides; unification unites"; "ties do bind"; "ghettos can only become bigger ghettos."* The passion that drives his analysis is "redeeming inner cities and the urban underclass," and the

51. Citations in this and the next paragraph are found on the following pages of Rusk: 14, 31, 41f., 40, 35, 38, 41, 47, 122.

motive for doing this is a moral vision of shared responsibility throughout a whole metropolitan community. At such a point the theological conviction of churches and the empirical analysis of urban research coincide.

Perhaps that is the most appropriate point for this essay to end — where theology and urban research intersect. Ministry to cities needs, on the one hand, research that yields intentional, systematic, and analytical conceptualization of what modern American cities are. In this Rusk and many of the urban church leaders writing in this volume have converged on the metropolitan paradigm to diagnose the ills and search for the cure of contemporary urban life. In both cases their analyses have been deeply informed by profound moral and theological convictions about good human communities. Ministry to cities needs, on the other hand, a renewal of faith vigorous enough to meet the challenge of the urban context. Will biblical faith be revived that is as hopeful of public redemption as of personal salvation, of social justice as of peace of mind? Will churches order their priorities to meet the challenges of contemporary urban life? Will a new and enduring practice of lay vocation in public life arise? Will theological education meet the challenge that the crises of urban, national, and international disparities reveal? Will a new ecumenism be born to serve the new millennium? The formidable challenge of renewing American cities exposes the equally formidable task of renewing the American church. *Veni Creator Spiritus!*

• 13 •

Urban Church Literature: A Retrospection[1]

LOYDE H. HARTLEY

I. Dimensions of City Church Literature

As a topic of inquiry, churches' relationships with cities have universalizing characteristics. Most of what has been written about the church over the past fifty years can be construed to have some urban relevance, even when the "urban ministry" banner is not clearly displayed. The topic extends beyond the internal operation of churches in cities to myriad interconnections with industry, labor organizations, law enforcement agencies, municipal governments, charities, community organizations, hospitals, and the range of metropolitan institutions. Moreover, much written in secular urbanology has relevance to churches, and much of twentieth-century theology has addressed questions precipitated by urbanization, industrialization, and technological developments. Religion is a topic of importance in the literatures of all ethnic, racial, and national groups. Urban church problems have inspired a host of innovations, accommodations, specializations, and responses to segmentation, all of which have attendant literatures. Even the smallest sect or cult has made some contribution. The result is not a unified body of materials about city-church relationships, but rather an array of divergent literatures on such topics as ethnic churches, industrial ministries, inner-city churches, suburban churches — all of them proceeding independently without much awareness of each other.

1. The author expresses appreciation to George Younger and George Todd for their critical readings of this essay, as well as to the authors of preceding chapters, who offered suggestions for their particular denominations.

308

This essay attempts to summarize published contributions to the urban church literature produced by or extensively circulated in U.S. main-line Catholic and Protestant denominations since World War II — books, articles, pronouncements, formal reports, and periodicals. A sprawling, disorganized corpus of unpublished materials also exists — local church records (including decisions to expand or reduce programs, to remain in the city, merge, or close), correspondence, planning documents, judicatory actions, architects' drawings, evaluation reports, drafts of resolutions, minutes of formal church actions and resolutions, sermons, personal journals, proposals, funding requests, photographs, lecture notes, materials assembled hastily in the face of emergencies, even some heated debates and terse exchanges on the role of churches in cities — all of which are more immediate to pivotal decisions than published materials. These, regrettably, await analysis and, in many cases, location and preservation. Consequently, they are for the most part omitted from this essay. Writings discussed herein represent only a fragment of the total published literature, which is more comprehensively listed in a bibliography I collected and published under the title *Cities and Churches: An International Bibliography* (Metuchen, N.J.: Scarecrow Press, 1992), hereinafter referred to as *Cities and Churches*. That bibliography contains 19,358 citations and over 10,000 separate subject classifications. Of those citations, 73 percent were written after 1945.

All references herein to names, titles, and subjects are mentioned also in *Cities and Churches*, most with brief annotations. The majority of them are listed in one of the databases used for library cataloging (RLIN or OCLC) or, for periodical literature, in *Religion Index*.

II. Collections, Archives, and Bibliographies

1. Collections

For the most part, urban ministry literature is scattered in an assortment of theological libraries, denominational archives, and old filing cabinets of retired church leaders. Many theological seminary libraries offer respectable collections of published materials, but policy documents, research reports, city and church newspaper articles, and local church publications are more difficult to locate. Some fugitive materials for the 1940s through the 1960s, principally denominationally sponsored citywide religious surveys, were amassed for the H. Paul Douglass Collection at the National Council of Churches. Sadly, this collection was disassembled in the early 1970s, but microfiche copies are located at Lancaster Theological Seminary, Hartford Seminary, and Emory University. An index for the collection was prepared by Earl Brewer and Douglas Johnson titled *An Inventory of the Harlan Paul Douglass Collection of Religious Research Reports* (National Council of Churches, 1970).

In the late 1960s and through the 1970s, the Institute on the Church in Urban-Industrial Society (ICUIS, Chicago) offered a documentation service that drew urban ministry articles, reports, and other fugitive materials from around the world. ICUIS collected these materials for the purpose of supporting people actively engaged in urban and industrial ministries. It reported to them what was happening in other places and made available information produced by and about a wide range of urban ministry experiments. It published abstracts and kept files of materials. In 1989 a large part of those files was placed in the archives of the University of Illinois at Chicago. Access to the ICUIS collection is best approached through their periodical bibliography titled *Abstract Service* and by contacting the archives of the University of Illinois at Chicago. In the early 1960s a sizable urban ministry library was assembled (and produced) by Chicago's Urban Training Center, an effort now lost to fire, although major parts of its materials were transferred to the ICUIS collection in 1972 and to other libraries.

No systematic collection of urban ministry materials was attempted during the 1980s, although the Seminary Consortium for Urban Pastoral Education (SCUPE, Chicago) prepared several bibliographies and, in the 1990s, is attempting to build a comprehensive collection.

2. Archival Collections

No archives specialize in urban church materials. Each denomination has its own archives or, in the case of denominations with mergers in their history, several archives. Information about denominational archives is listed in section 8 below, with some indication of the kinds of urban ministry materials preserved there. As a whole, denominational archives suffer from three major liabilities. First, only a few urban church leaders over the past fifty years have bequeathed papers to the archives. Second, archives customarily arrange materials by names of people, churches, or denominational agencies, not by topics that relate to inquiries about the urban church. Users of these archives need to know the relevant names before starting any inquiry. Third, and most annoying, much of the material that archives have collected from the past fifty years is sealed, with access delayed until sometime in the twenty-first century.

Beyond denominational archives, several others deserve passing mention. The Urban Archive Center of Temple University has some church materials, limited mostly to Philadelphia-related items. Archives for the Federal Council of Churches and its successor, the National Council of Churches, are maintained by the Presbyterian Historical Society, Philadelphia. The University of Illinois at Chicago has amassed a sizable collection, including the surviving files of the now defunct ICUIS and UTC. The Billy Graham Library in Wheaton, Illinois, has resources regarding evangelical approaches to the city and city missions. Miscellaneous papers and documents for Martin Luther King Jr. are located in the Mugar Memorial Library of Boston University and in the Center for Nonviolent Social Action, Atlanta. Georgia State University archives for John Gates Ramsay have among them church-related documents, owing to Ramsay's church and labor interest. Also, the labor archives at Wayne State University, Detroit, include church and labor materials. East Harlem Protestant Parish has placed its papers at Union Theological Seminary Library, New York City. Papers for the Joint Strategy and Action Committee (JSAC), an interdenominational organization committed to cooperative church planning, are located in the Methodist Library at Drew University, Madison, New Jersey, and include a manuscript by John DeBoer titled *JSAC's First Twenty Years* (JSAC, 1988). Church Women United (CWU), an organization of Protestant and Orthodox laywomen, maintains an archival collection with information about their urban-related programs, also at Drew University. Of particular interest is CWU's "Urban Causeway" program during the 1970s. The YMCA and YWCA both have useful archives in New York City. Some state and city historical societies maintain church-related archival materials, but no comprehensive listing of these has been attempted since the Historical Records Survey of the early 1940s.

Some of the larger and older urban local churches, particularly African American churches, have maintained small archives for their own histories and even have designated local historians among their leaders. Often their records and documents have not yet been placed in libraries or other conserving collections.

3. Bibliography of Bibliographies and Other Helpful Lists

Beyond the bibliographies appended to books and articles, a total of 184 bibliographies published between 1945 and 1991 is listed in *Cities and Churches*. In addition to the manual for the H. Paul Douglass Collection, notable among these compilations of items published during the 1940s and 1950s are: Urban Church Lending Library, *Urban Church Booklist* (Green Lake, Wisc., 1963); Carolyn Odell, *Bibliography for the Urban Church* (Protestant Council for the City of New York, 1958); and ongoing bibliographic notes in two National Council periodicals: *City Church* (passim) and *Information Service* (see, for example, October 23, 1965). The National Council's Department of Urban Church also produced a mimeographed series of resource listings (1960), and Union Theological Seminary (1960, 1964) developed an Urban Education Collection that was summarized in bibliographies by Virginia Clifford. Nelson Burr's *Critical Bibliography of Religion in America* (Princeton University Press, 1961) includes some citations about urban churches.

Bibliographies and lists about specialized ministries of the late 1950s and 1960s include Ira Harrison, *Selected Annotated Bibliography on Store Front Churches* (Syracuse University Youth Development Center, 1962); Grace Goodman, *The Church and the Apartment House: A Listing of People and Programs* (Board of Missions, UPUSA, 1965); and Carl Siegenthaler, *A Select Bibliography for Churchmen Involved or to Be Involved in Neighborhood and Community Organization* (Urban Training Center, 1966). P. Beffa et al. document the urban and social ministry interests of the World Council in *Index to the World Council of Churches' Official Statements and Reports* (WCC, 1978).

Urban crisis years (1967-72) produced a spate of hastily prepared although often helpful bibliographies aimed at supporting church leaders in the front lines of conflict. Foremost among these are the bibliographies produced by the Institute on the Church in Urban-Industrial Society (ICUIS) — *Notes on Urban-Industrial Mission Literature and Training* (beginning in 1969), *Abstract Service* (beginning 1970), *Justice Ministries* (beginning 1978), and a sheaf of specialized bibliographies prepared by Richard Poethig and Bobbi Wells Hargleroad. In the same vein are E. Warren Rust, *A Select Bibliography on Urban Life* (Home Mission Board, Southern Baptist Convention, 1978), and Geno Baroni, *A Select Bibliography on Neighborhoods* (U.S. Department of Housing and Urban Development, 1978). Concerns about racially transitional communities in the 1970s precipitated Kinmoth Jefferson's *Bibliographies for National Workshop on Church Strategies in Transitional Communities* (Office of Urban Ministries, UMC, 1976).

Bibliographies were compiled in seminaries and universities to support urban studies programs. Examples include Richard Gowan and Martin Marty, *Bibliography on the History of the Churches in the American City* (University of Chicago Divinity School, 1966), and Francis DuBose, *A*

Bibliographic Outline of the Urban Church (Golden Gate Baptist Theological Seminary, 1968). Some sociological studies about urban churches are indexed by Morris Berkowitz's *Social Scientific Studies of Religion* (University of Pittsburgh Press, 1967) and in Canada by Stewart Crysdale's *La Religion au Canada* (York University, 1974). These were updated by Blasi and Cuneo in *Issues in the Sociology of Religion* (Garland, 1985 and 1990). The Council of Planning Libraries developed a bibliographic series wherein some numbers deal with urban ministry: Anthony White, *Religion as an Urban Institution* (1973); Bryan Thompson, *Ethnic Groups in Urban Areas* (1971); and Dale Casper, *Religious Groups in Urban America* (1983).

Among notable African American church bibliographies are those included in C. Eric Lincoln, *The Black Church in the African American Experience* (with Lawrence Mamiya; Duke University, 1990); William Fisher, *Free at Last: A Bibliography of Martin Luther King* (Scarecrow, 1977); and the *Newsletter of the Afro-American Religious History Group of the American Academy of Religion,* edited by Randall Burkett (beginning in 1976).

Business ethics and transnational corporations became topical in the 1970s, leading to the publication of Donald Jones, *A Bibliography of Business Ethics, 1971-1974* (University of Virginia Press, 1977); Harry Strharsky, *United States' Churches and the Transnational Corporation* (WCC, 1977); and Carl Mitcham, *Theology and Technology* (with Jim Grote; University Press of America, 1984).

In the 1980s the most extensive bibliographic work was undertaken at the Seminary Consortium for Urban Pastoral Education (SCUPE), particularly from the hand of Clinton E. Stockwell, such as: *A General Bibliography for Urban Ministers* (1980), *The Christian in the Workplace* (1981), *Hunger, Food and Poverty* (1982), *Biblical and Theological Resources for Urban Ministry* (1982), and *Resources for Urban Ministry* (1984). Also in the 1980s some Protestant evangelicals began producing substantial bibliographies: Harvie Conn, *Urban Mission: An Annotated Bibliography* (Westminster Seminary, 1986); Roger Greenway and Timothy Monsma, *Cities: Mission's New Frontier* (Baker, 1989). A journal titled *Urban Mission* (Westminster Theological Seminary, beginning in 1983) regularly reviews the rapidly growing evangelical urban ministry literature.

III. Pre-1940 City Church History

During and shortly following World War II several scholars undertook histories of nineteenth-century and early-twentieth-century urban religion.

Especially notable are: Aaron Abell, *The Urban Impact of American Protestantism, 1865-1900* (Harvard, 1943) and *American Catholicism and Social Action* (Hanover House, 1960); Henry May, *Protestant Churches and Industrial America* (Harper, 1949); Charles Hopkins, *The Rise of the Social Gospel in American Protestantism, 1865-1915* (Yale, 1940) and his *History of the YMCA in North America* (Association, 1951).

These were superseded but not entirely replaced by histories that focus on specific aspects of urban religion: Robert Handy, *The Social Gospel in America, 1870-1920* (Oxford, 1966); Paul Boyer, *Urban Masses and Moral Order in America, 1820-1920* (Harvard, 1978); Norris Magnuson, *Salvation in the Slums* (Scarecrow, 1977); Esther McBride, *Open Church* (Starline, 1983); Donald Gorrell, *The Age of Social Responsibility: The Social Gospel in the Progressive Era, 1900-1920* (Mercer, 1988); Kevin Christiano, *Religious Diversity and Social Change: American Cities, 1890-1906* (Cambridge, 1987); Jay P. Dolan, *The American Catholic Parish: A History from 1850 to the Present* (Paulist, 1987); Ralph Janis's study of religious groups in Detroit titled *Church and City in Transition* (Garland, 1990); and Kenneth Fones-Wolf, *Trade Union Gospel* (Temple University Press, 1989). James Lewis's *At Home in the City* (University of Tennessee, 1992), a study of two congregations in Gary, Indiana, challenges the thesis that Protestants were severely alienated from the city. Lewis's history illustrates the value of careful analysis of archival materials.

During the 1970s and 1980s a plethora of articles appeared in historical journals regarding nineteenth-century and early-twentieth-century urban religion. Illustrations include: Jay Dolan, "Immigrants in the City" (*Church History* 41, September 1972, pp. 354-68); Raymond Mohl, "The Urban Missionary Movement in New York City, 1800-1825" (*Journal of Religious History* 7, December 1972, pp. 110-28); Patrick Carey, "Voluntaryism: An Irish Catholic Tradition" (*Church History* 48, March 1979, pp. 49-62). Moreover, urbanization was an early interest of historian Martin E. Marty: *The New Shape of American Religion* (Harper and Row, 1959), *Second Chance for American Protestants* (1963), *Babylon by Choice* (Friendship Press, 1965), and *The Search for a Usable Future* (Harper and Row, 1969).

IV. Post-1940 Benchmarks

Urban ministry literature burgeoned in mainline churches following World War II. Church press, popular literature on church life, action research, and scholarly inquiry about city churches leaped in geometric progression. If one author, one city, and one denomination were selected to typify urban church literature for each decade since 1940, what would the list of nominees look like? Here is my perhaps oversimplified attempt at such a list, offered as deliberate artifice for summarizing mountains of materials. Nominees for particular decades, it should be noted, are not necessarily connected with each other by common themes.

For the 1940s, my list would be: author — H. Paul Douglass; city — Philadelphia; denomination — the Methodist Church. Although Douglass's major theoretical and methodological treatises were written before 1940 (*The St. Louis Church Survey,* 1924; *The Suburban Trend,* 1925; *The Springfield [Mass.] Church Survey,* 1926; *1000 City Churches,* 1926; *How to Study the City Church,* 1927; *Church Comity,* 1929; and *Protestant Cooperation in American Cities,* 1930), he produced thirty-nine city church studies in the 1940s, more than he had in any previous decade and more than any other researcher during the 1940s. Several of Douglass's studies had to do with the impact of the war and defense communities on city churches and, later in the decade, they focused on suburban expansion of the church as well as on weakening conditions of inner-city churches. The 1950s cadre of religious survey experts were mostly Douglass protégés, a fact supporting his nomination. By the end of the 1950s, the Religious Research Association was formed as a professional society dedicated to the kinds of research Douglass had pioneered; it publishes the *Review of Religious Research.*

I chose Philadelphia as the city that typifies the 1940s because it epitomizes the decade's major developments in all northern and northeastern U.S. cities — its heavy involvement in the war industry, its expanding population of migrating African Americans and Puerto Ricans during and following the war, and its rapid suburban expansion that would grow into an array of satellite cities such as Levittown (see further, *Cities and Churches,* subject index: Philadelphia).

As the result of the 1939 reunification, Methodists became the largest Protestant denomination and were particularly well positioned to build new churches during the postwar suburban expansion (see further, *Cities and Churches,* subject index: Church development, new — Methodist sources).

My three nominees for the 1950s: author — Ross Sanderson; city — Newark, New Jersey; denomination — the Congregational Christian Churches. Sanderson was on the National Council's urban ministry staff during the 1950s and early 1960s. He was instrumental in facilitating a series of ecumenical urban church convocations and edited the *City Church* (a periodical published by the NCC, 1950-64). He wrote *The Strategy of*

City Church Planning (Harper, 1932), *The Church Serves the Inner City* (National Council, 1954), and *The Church Serves the Changing City* (Harper, 1955). He was a major figure in promoting local interdenominational cooperation, in helping churches keep pace with urban expansion, in raising consciousness about inner-city conditions, in encouraging urban planning models for the church, and in stressing the importance of racial integration in churches.

Newark commends itself for nomination in the city category because it was one of the first U.S. cities where "white flight" pushed suburban expansion to the point of massive urban neglect and decay; see, for example, Frederick Shippey, *Methodism in Newark* (Board of Missions, Methodist Church, 1951).

The Congregational Christian Churches were chosen for the denominational category because they promoted cooperative urban ministries and engaged secular disciplines in the service of church planning. See in particular the writings of congregationalists Truman B. Douglass, Yoshio Fukuyama, J. Archie Hargraves, Joseph W. Merchant, George W. Webber, and, of course, Sanderson. In 1950, the Christian Century Foundation published *Great Churches of America*, which featured the ministries of several large Congregational churches along with descriptions of other denominations' leading urban congregations.

A digression is required before proceeding to the 1960s nominees. In Europe during the late 1940s and 1950s a spirit of experimentation and theological venturesomeness arose that inspired many U.S. city church innovations in the late 1950s and 1960s. Illustrations are literature pertaining to missionary forms of the church, industrial missions, and worker priests (all listed in *Cities and Churches*). Particularly important are: Georges Michonneau, *Paroisse, communauté missionnaire: conclusions de cinq ans d'expérience en milieu populaire* (Paris: Editions du Cerf, 1946; English translation: *Revolution in a City Parish* [London: Blackfriars, 1950]); Edward R. Wickham, *Church and People in an Industrial City* (Lutterworth, 1957) and *Encounter with Modern Society* (1964); Jacques Loew, *Journal d'une mission ouvrière* (Cerf, 1959); Ernest William Southcott, *The House Church* (British Council of Churches, 1954) as well as his *The Parish Comes Alive* (Morehouse-Gorham, 1957); Hendrik Kraemer, *A Theology of the Laity* (Lutterworth, 1958); Horst Symanowski, *Gegen die Weltfremdheit: Theologische Existenz heute* (Chr. Kaiser Verlag, 1960; English translation: *The Christian Witness in an Industrial Society* [Westminster Press, 1964]); and the writings of George F. MacLeod et al., at the Iona Community in Scotland, published largely in their periodical titled the *Coracle*.

The 1960s are especially difficult to narrow to one nominee for each category, but my list of finalists would be: author — George W. Webber; city — Chicago; denomination — Baptist churches, especially the National Baptist Convention, the Progressive National Baptist Convention of America, and the American Baptist Churches in the U.S.A. Webber's selection is based on work with the East Harlem Protestant Parish, a widely acclaimed, innovative cooperative ministry in New York City that generated a large part of the 1960s' city church literature. See his *God's Colony in Man's World* (Abingdon, 1960), *Missionary Structures of the Congregation* (Ph.D. diss., Columbia, 1963), and *The Congregation in Mission* (Abingdon, 1964). Equally worthy for nomination is Gibson Winter for his *Suburban Captivity of the Churches* (Doubleday, 1961) and *The New Creation as Metropolis* (Macmillan, 1963). Winter, more than any other writer of the period, challenged denominations' suburban biases and called into question prevailing church extension policies, namely, selling old city church buildings to finance new suburban churches. To the efforts of Webber and Winter must be added Harvey Cox's seminal study, *The Secular City: Secularization and Urbanization in Theological Perspective* (Macmillan, 1965) — see further, *Cities and Churches*, subject index: "Secular City debate."

Chicago is a fairly obvious nomination for the city category for the 1960s. It was the location of innovative action training programs (Urban Training Center for Christian Mission; the Institute on the Church in Urban-Industrial Society and its predecessor, the Presbyterian Institute on Industrial Relations; the Ecumenical Institute; the Community Renewal Society), all of which produced heaps of new urban church literature. George Younger's *From New Creation to Urban Crisis* (Center for the Scientific Study of Religion, 1987) traces the history of action training centers in Chicago and other cities. Chicago served as a laboratory for church renewal, prompting Robert Lecky to ask, *Can These Bones Live? The Failure of Church Renewal* (with Elliot Wright; Sheed and Ward, 1969), with answers based on Chicago experiences. Additionally, Chicago's Woodlawn area was the setting for some of the more celebrated and controversial community organization projects undertaken by Saul Alinsky's Industrial Areas Foundation, and a lively literature resulted. Discourses by Alinsky that were influential among the churches include: *Reveille for Radicals* (Vantage, 1946), *From Citizen Apathy to Participation* (IAF, 1957), and *Rules for Radicals* (Random House, 1971). Even more important, Chicago was a major center for the civil rights movement during this decade.

When I chose Baptist churches for the 1960s denominational category, I had in mind particularly the importance of African-American Baptist congregations, the civil rights movement, and the ministry of Martin Luther King Jr. The American Baptist Convention was instrumental in the urban training programs of the 1960s (see listings in *Cities and Churches* for George Younger, Harvey Cox, Norman Greene, Robert Hoover, Paul O. Madsen, Robert Frerichs, Lawrence Janssen, Howard Moody, Robert Spike, and Jitsuo Morikawa). Interest in urban ministry began to arise even in certain Southern Baptist circles, a denomination historically preoccupied with rural and small-town ministries (see listings in *Cities and Churches* for F. Russell Bennett, G. Willis Bennett, Francis DuBose, and Leonard Irwin).

Because of the "church and community in transition" theme recurrent in the 1970s, I nominate for this decade: author — Geno C. Baroni; city — Kansas City, Missouri; denomination — the Roman Catholic Church. Baroni adopted a controversial position regarding community development. He reasoned that, if cities were to be saved, planning ought to begin with helping those people who wanted to live there — the traditional ethnic communities — rather than with renewal plans aimed at attracting alienated people back into the cities or programs that poured money into unstable communities without any prospect of change. If life was made secure for the people who wanted to live in the city, and if their communities were made sound, then urban leaders would have a strong base from which to work with the more unstable communities. His position is best articulated in *Who's Left in the Neighborhoods?* (National Center for Urban Ethnic Affairs, 1977). His organization, the National Center for Urban Ethnic Affairs, sponsored neighborhood and commercial revitalization in several cities during the late 1970s. In addition to Baroni, several other Roman Catholics advocated the rights and views of ethnics; among others, see: Michael Novak, *The Rise of the Unmeltable Ethnics* (Macmillan, 1972); Andrew Greeley, *Neighborhoods* (Seabury, 1977); and Silvano Tomasi's historical monographs at the Center for Migration Studies.

During the 1970s most U.S. cities experienced disruptive neighborhood transitions, some more advanced than others, but none more typically than Kansas City, Missouri. See, for example, John DeBoer's article "Housing Miracles" in the *JSAC Grapevine* (August 1978), and materials related to the Linwood United Ministries (Kansas City) listed in *Cities and Churches.*

Risking nominations for the 1980s is probably unwise; not enough time has elapsed for perspective to emerge. Undaunted, I nominate: author — Harold Recinos; city — Los Angeles; and denomination — African American Pentecostal churches. I chose Recinos because of the importance of ethnic churches as reflected in his *Hear the Cry! A Latino Pastor Challenges the Church* (Westminster, 1989). Antonio Stevens-Arroyo, who wrote

318

Prophets Denied Honor: An Anthology of the Hispano Church of the United States (Orbis, 1980), would also be an acceptable nominee, he dealing from a historical perspective while Recinos describes the plight of the contemporary Hispanic church. Of course, the faith story of almost any ethnic minority population in cities during the 1980s might suffice to epitomize city churches of that decade — inter alia, African American, Native American, Korean, Samoan, Vietnamese, Haitian, Mexican; see Stephan Thernstrom's *Harvard Encyclopedia of American Ethnic Groups* (Harvard, 1980) for a more complete list of candidates. Most denominations published guidebooks for establishing and strengthening ethnic minority congregations (see *Cities and Churches*, subject index: Minority churches; Social change and church; and names of specific ethnic groups).

Los Angeles typifies the 1980s because of its diverse immigrant and ethnic population and its many multiple-language churches. Both Fuller Theological Seminary and the School of Theology at Claremont produced many dissertations on ethnic minority ministries during this decade. Various patterns of cooperation among ethnic congregations arose in Los Angeles. Such congregations became an important force for stability and justice following the 1992 urban riots there. Of African American Pentecostal denominations, the Church of God in Christ (COGIC) and the United Holy Church of America (UHC) stand out. COGIC, having formed itself during the years of African Americans' northerly migration following both of this century's world wars, very likely became in the 1980s the fastest-growing religious body in cities. Without any announced urban ministry programs or urban missionary emphases, African American Pentecostal churches have found ways to uphold urban people and their aspirations. Moreover, one of their ministerial sons became pastor of New York City's stately Riverside Church (James Forbes, UHC), and another the dean of Washington's National Cathedral (Nathan Baxter, COGIC).

V. Some Secular Sources

More than any other scholarly discipline, sociology has provided church leaders handy interpretations both of the city and of the city church itself. From the time of Robert Park and Ernest Burgess's *The City* (University of Chicago, 1925) to David Riesman's *The Lonely Crowd* (Yale, 1950) to Lewis Mumford's *The City in History* (Harcourt, 1961) to Theodore Roszak's *The Making of the Counter Culture* (Doubleday, 1968), city life was described mainly in terms of crowds, apathy, anomie, loneliness, estrangement, distortion, distress, alienation, depersonalization, and dehumanization. Arguably, literary and intellectual views of the city reflected a similar anti-urban tone (see, for example, Morton and Lucia White, *The Intellectual versus the City* [Oxford, 1962, 1977]). More recently, negative views of city life have been challenged by such sociologists as Claude Fischer; see his *The Urban Experience* (Harcourt, 1976) and *To Dwell among Friends* (University of Chicago Press, 1982). Fischer contends, in what is called a subcultural theory of urbanism, that city life strengthens rather than weakens human relationships; see also the essays and books of sociologists Barry Wellman, Kenneth Jackson, and William Whyte.

The social criticism explicit in Michael Harrington's *The Other America* (Penguin, 1962) evoked urban church responses. Jane Jacobs attacks city planning in her *The Death and Life of the Great American Cities* (Vintage, 1961), promoting a greater role for neighborhoods in determining their futures. Economic theories about cities gained the attention of religious leaders during the 1970s and 1980s; see Jane Jacobs, *The Economy of Cities* (Random House, 1969) and *Cities and the Wealth of Nations* (1984).

Secular sociologists and social historians have turned their investigative eyes toward the urban church ever since the late nineteenth century, more recently in such essays as: Sabino Acquaviva, *The Decline of the Sacred in Industrial Society* (Harper and Row, 1979; originally in Italian, 1961); Bryan Wilson, *Religion in Secular Society* (Watts, 1966); Jeffery Hadden, *The Gathering Storm in the Churches* (Doubleday, 1969), which alerted readers to the widening gap between clergy and laity on civil rights and other social issues; Michael Ducey, *Sunday Morning: Aspects of Urban Ritual* (Free Press, 1977); and Peter Hawkins's edited volume, *Civitas* (Scholar's Press, 1986), which applies the discipline of sociolinguistics, broadly conceived, to the question of the religious significance of the city. Charles Glock et al. describe two distinct orientations in the church to injustice and suffering in *To Comfort and to Challenge* (University of California Press, 1967), a reflection of bitter division in many urban congregations; see also Glock's *Religion and Society in Tension* (with Rodney Stark; Rand McNally, 1965).

During the 1960s, the sociological and economic writings by and about African Americans had a formative impact on denominational urban policy. Increasingly urgent reports began to emerge following World War II, and some of them were addressed to the religious community. The body of civil rights and Black Power literature is large and, in addition to those listed in section 8 below, these benchmarks require mentioning: Gunnar Myrdal, *An American Dilemma: The Negro Problem and Modern Democracy* (Harper, 1944); St. Clair Drake, *Black Metropolis: A Study of Negro Life in a Northern City* (with Horace Cayton; Harcourt, Brace, 1945); Oscar Handlin, *The Newcomers* (Harvard, 1959); John H. Griffin, *Black Like Me* (New American Library, 1961); Franz Fanon, *The Wretched of the Earth* (Grove, 1961); James Baldwin, *The Fire Next Time* (Dial, 1963); Charles Silberman, *Crisis in Black and White* (Random House, 1964), which includes an analysis of the Woodlawn section of Chicago; *The Autobiography of Malcolm X* (Grove, 1964); Claude Brown, *Manchild in the Promised Land* (Macmillan, 1965) and the video sequel titled *Manchild Revisited* (PBS Video, 1987); Stokely Carmichael, *Black Power* (with Charles Hamilton; Vintage, 1967); Fred Powledge, *Black Power — White Resistance: Notes on the New Civil War* (World, 1967); the various writings about the Black Panthers; H. Rap Brown, *Die Nigger Die* (Dial, 1968); Dick Gregory, *The Shadow That Scares Me* (Doubleday, 1968); Nathan Wright, *Black Power and Urban Unrest* (Hawthorne, 1968) as well as his *Ready to Riot* (Holt, Rinehart and Winston, 1968); Eldridge Cleaver, *Soul on Ice* (McGraw-Hill, 1968) — all in some sense anticipating James Foreman's demands of the "Black Manifesto" (Robert S. Lecky and H. Elliot Wright, eds., *Black Manifesto: Religion, Racism, and Reparations* [Sheed and Ward, 1969], among other places). In a similar vein, Piri Thomas, *Down These Mean Streets* (Knopf, 1967) and the sequel titled *Savior, Savior, Hold My Hand* (Doubleday, 1972) portray the social and economic conditions of Puerto Ricans. *The Report of the National Advisory Commission on Civil Disorders* (1968) was widely discussed among denominational leaders and served as the basis for designing church responses. The complete list is much longer. For interpretations of the importance of these developments, see Francis F. Piven and Richard Cloward, *Regulating the Poor* (Vintage, 1971) as well as their *Poor People's Movements* (1977), and Herbert Haines, *Black Radicals in the Civil Rights Mainstream, 1954-1970* (University of Tennessee Press, 1988). Vincent Harding's *Hope and History* (Orbis, 1990) provides an overview.

There exists, in addition to the above, a literature of secular views on city ministry in trade union periodicals, business journals and industrial house organs, public school newsletters, social work periodicals, law journals, and municipal government publications. These await thorough bibliographical study and analysis. Two articles appearing in the *Washington University Journal of Urban and Contemporary Law* summarize a part of the relevant legal literature: Susan L. Goldberg, "Gimme Shelter: Religious Provision of Shelter to the Homeless as a Protected Use under Zoning Laws" (vol. 30, Spring 1986, pp. 75-114), and Robert L. Crewdson, "Ministry and Mortar: Historic Preservation and the First Amendment after Barwick" (vol. 33, Summer 1988, pp. 137-63).

VI. Interdenominational and Ecumenical Sources

From its inception in 1948, the World Council of Churches has maintained high interest in urbanization and its consequences for churches. This concern was expressed in a series of official pronouncements; see P. Beffa, *Index* (cited above). In the 1950s the World Council conducted a special inquiry on rapid social change that generated such study documents as J. H. A. Longmann's *The Characteristics of Urban Centers in the East* (Department of Church and Society, WCC, 1956) and eventually issued in Egbert de Vries's *Man in Rapid Social Change* (Doubleday, 1961). Also, in 1956, Hans-Ruedi Weber began editing the *Laity Bulletin* (WCC, 1956 to 1968), which provided theological stimulation for experiments in urban ministry, as did the World Council's *Monthly Letter on Evangelism* (WCC, also beginning in 1956). In the 1960s, the World Council's highly important study on the Missionary Structure of the Congregation was in the vanguard of those promoting new church models for cities. This study stimulated much of the theology and philosophy underlying denominational urban ministry programs. See: Colin Williams, *Where in the World?* (National Council, 1963); Thomas Wieser, ed., *Planning for Mission: Working Papers on the New Quest for Missionary Communities* (WCC, 1966); *The Church for Others and the Church for the World* (WCC, 1967); and Herbert Neve, *Sources for Change: Searching for Flexible Church Structures* (WCC, 1968). In the 1970s and 1980s the World Council conducted inquiries about science and technology, the ethical practices of multinational corporations, and the church's participation in economic development, all of which have relevance to urban churches. A long-lived program emphasis titled Urban Industrial Mission (beginning in the late 1960s, later renamed Urban Rural Mission [URM] in recognition of the interconnections between urban and rural issues) ensured that urban issues remained in the forefront of the World Council's agenda. Representative publications include: Bobbi Wells Hargleroad's edited volume titled *Struggle to Be Human: Stories of Urban-Industrial Mission* (WCC, 1973) and Leon Howell, *People Are the Subject: Stories of Rural-Urban Mission* (WCC, 1980). See also the Council's *URM Newsletter* (beginning in 1983); Hugh Lewin, *A Community of Clowns* (WCC, 1987); and *Abstract Service* published by ICUIS, which indexed many of the documents generated around the world by this emphasis.

The National Council of the Churches of Christ in the U.S.A. (NCC) has a similar record of interest in matters urban, continuing the long tradition of its predecessor, the Federal Council of Churches. Shortly after its founding, the NCC sponsored in 1950 a national convocation on urban ministry, which resulted in a spate of denominational follow-up convocations and inaugurated the NCC's journal titled the *City Church* (cited above) and sponsored by the Department of City Church. Until its demise in 1964, this, more than any other periodical, kept abreast of urban church developments. Under the leadership of Ross Sanderson, the Department of City Church also published occasional planning studies for various cities and denominations. In 1952 the NCC's Department of the Church and Economic Life, headed by Cameron P. Hall (see listing in *Cities and Churches*), sponsored a conference on "The Christian and His Daily Work," as well as some subsequent conferences. Simultaneously, this department issued a sequence of pamphlets and reports on a variety of urban social and economic conditions. In 1953 the NCC Department of the Churches and Social Welfare launched a periodical titled *Christian Social Welfare* to facilitate communication between social workers and church-sponsored social welfare institutions.

The NCC's Missionary Education theme for 1954-55 dealt with the city, leading to the publication of Janette Harrington's *Look at the City* (Friendship Press, 1954), among other materials. Analyses of urban ethnic groups were prepared by Bertha Blair et al., *Spanish Speaking Americans* (NCC, 1959). *Information Service,* a newsletter continuing from Federal Council days, offered intelligence on various urban issues and happenings. The NCC's Broadcasting and Film commissions sponsored a regular radio and television program, often featuring urban issues. In 1962 the council issued a pronouncement titled *The Churches and Immigration* that advocated the abolition of the quota system for restricting immigration into the United States. This federal policy was in fact changed a few years later, setting the stage for increasing emphasis on ethnic minority urban ministries in the 1970s and 1980s. Other NCC and Federal Council pronouncements about urban and industrial issues include: "Pronouncements on Religion and Economic Life" (1947), "Narcotics" (1952), "The Churches and Segregation" (1952), "Union Membership as a Condition of Employment" (1956), "Ethical Issues in Industrial Relations" (1959), and "Resolution on Crisis in the Nation" (1967), the latter announcing a program emphasis that generated a large amount of materials.

During the 1960s, the National Council of Churches was in the forefront of the search for "new forms" of the church. Radical aspects of the church's mission mandated finding models additional to, if not moving beyond, the local church. The city itself and various sectors of it became the arena for mission. The NCC participated in planning for new cities, as witness Stanley J. Hallett's essay titled *Working Papers in Church Planning,*

Columbia, Maryland (NCC, 1965). John Perry prepared a report on coffee-house ministries (NCC, 1965), representative of the council's interest in innovative urban church programming. John Fry edited a volume on churches and urban development titled *The Church and Community Organization* (NCC, 1965). It reports an NCC conference where heated conflicts emerged among church leaders regarding Saul Alinsky's organizing tactics (a meeting recalled by some participants as a "head bumping event"). In one experimental "new form," part of a metropolitan planning commission actually thought of itself as a church; see John Wagner, "Los Angeles Region Goals Project Interreligious Committee" (*Church in Metropolis*, no. 12, Spring 1967, pp. 24-25). Reports on apartment house ministries, the urban crisis (a major NCC emphasis), and the churches' war on poverty appeared regularly in the later 1960s. Ann L. Werneke's paper titled "Guidelines for Aid to Victims of Riot" (NCC, 1968) reflects the turmoil of the times. In the 1970s the NCC experienced drastic budget cuts and, as a result, its urban church publications virtually halted. The NCC's urban interests were continued in part, however, through such agencies as the Interfaith Center on Corporate Responsibility (ICCR), which generated a series of reports on church investments in corporations with ethically questionable practices.

The Joint Strategy and Action Committee (JSAC) took up the "new forms" banner when the NCC urban office was closing. Starting with only three denominations especially concerned about urban ministry and community organization — Episcopal, UCC, and United Presbyterian — JSAC eventually attracted several other denominations into its circle, including the Southern Baptists, and its focus broadened. The *JSAC Grapevine* (cited above) is one of the better sources for intelligence on urban ecumenical efforts in the 1970s and early 1980s. The *Grapevine* was preceded by a periodical titled *Church in Metropolis,* originally an Episcopal publication that became the first JSAC organ. *Church in Metropolis* was edited for a time by Earl K. Larson Jr., formerly executive of the art department for *Better Homes and Gardens;* it received accolades for its graphic excellence. Additional citations of "new forms" literature appear in section VIII, below, with the materials listed for specific denominations. See also the heading "Experimental ministries" in the subject index of *Cities and Churches.*

Several other ecumenically supported organizations dealt with single sectors or aspects of urban ministry, each of which generated attendant literatures. Among these are: National Industrial Mission (beginning in 1966), Interreligious Foundation for Community Organizing (IFCO, 1967), Operation Connection (formed by church and business leaders, 1968),

Action Training Coalition (1968), Interreligious Coalition for Housing (1969), and United Ministries in Public Education (UMPE, 1969). These organizations served as vehicles for the churches' participation in broader coalitions dealing with urban social concerns.

In addition to literature stemming directly from ecumenical organizations, many individual authors attempted a broader perspective on urban ministries than could be afforded within denominational confines. John H. Fish et al., *The Edge of the Ghetto* (Seabury, 1968), is an example, as is the volume edited by Kendig Cully and F. Nile Harper that asks *Will the Church Lose the City?* (World Publishing, 1969). John C. Bennett et al., *Christian Values and Economic Life* (Harper, 1954), combines the insights of theologians and economists regarding ethics and social welfare, an effort continued in Horace Cayton, *The Changing Scene* (with Setsuko Nishi; NCC, 1955), and F. Ernest Johnson, *Religion and Social Work* (Harper, 1957). Ernest Q. Campbell's study of clergy responses to desegregation — *Christians in Racial Crisis* (with Thomas Pettigrew; Public Affairs Press, 1959) — had important impact on the civil rights ministries of most mainline denominations. In 1972, Richard Luecke, a Lutheran writing in an ecumenical vein, produced *Perchings: Reflections on Society and Ministry* (Urban Training Center) in which he traced the economic aspects of ministry and described various approaches to urban theological education. Concern over the deterioration of urban public policy generated such jointly authored essays as *Redeeming the City: Theology, Politics and Urban Policy* (Pilgrim, 1982) by Ronald Pasquariello, Donald Shriver, and Alan Geyer; to which may be added the whole range of materials generated by the Center for Theology and Public Policy. Pastors and laity in ecumenical and nondenominational churches have contributed to urban church literature; for example, Elizabeth O'Connor, *The Call to Commitment* (Harper and Row, 1963), *Journey Inward, Journey Outward* (1968), *The New Community* (1976), and *Letters to Scattered Pilgrims* (1982). MUST, a training program for clergy and laity in New York City, created a literature surrounding its development and programs in the 1960s, as did all the urban training programs (see Younger, *From New Creation to Urban Crisis*, cited above). Publications of ICUIS and SCUPE are ecumenically based; see *Signs of the Kingdom in the Secular City* (Covenant Press, 1984), edited by David Frenchak et al. Moreover, many citations listed below in section VIII, "Denominational Sources," have had largely ecumenical audiences and impacts notwithstanding their denominational origins.

325

LOYDE H. HARTLEY

VII. Theology of the City

Theology that has informed city church policy and programs has been, over the past fifty years, at the innovative edge and the prevailing theology of the times. For Protestants this has meant that the Social Gospel and the theologies of cultural Protestantism dominated during the years immediately following World War II. A historical treatment of how these two perspectives informed local city churches' programs is offered in James Lewis's *At Home in the City* (cited above). Ecumenical theology, with emphasis on mission and evangelism, began playing an important role in urban church circles during the late 1940s and 1950s, often under the motto Let the Church Be the Church. See, for example, listings for Johannes C. Hoekendijk in *Cities and Churches,* as well as in the subject index under Theology, ecumenical; Theology, Protestant; and Theology (of the city). Ecumenical theology reached its peak of influence in the 1960s, the result of flourishing innovative and cooperative urban programs. By the late 1950s, neo-orthodoxy had become increasingly important, with emphasis on the sovereignty of God and the church's responsibility for prophetic ministries; see especially the tomes of Karl Barth, Hendrik Kraemer, Dietrich Bonhoeffer, H. Richard Niebuhr, Reinhold Niebuhr, and Paul Tillich. Early postwar Roman Catholic theology was influenced strongly by the social encyclicals, beginning with *Rerum Novarum* (1891), a direction reinforced by writings of Catholic theologians following Vatican II. Moreover, ethnic interpretations of Catholic theology emerged in many of the national churches, sometimes with unique local variations that reinforced identity and heritage against city forces that promoted assimilation. In the 1970s and following, liberation theologies gained influence in many urban churches, especially those with ethnic minority memberships.

Usually theologians do not deal extensively with "city" as a concept, although some few do. Tracing the labyrinthine linkages between urban ministries and the theologies that have informed them is beyond the scope of this essay. Alternatively, using a typology of storytelling, a brief overview is offered regarding ways in which "city" is employed as a concept by some theologians.

James Hopewell suggests that the ordinary stories religious people tell, when analyzed using the literary criticism theories of Northrop Frye, can provide an experimental methodology for assessing the social dynamics of local churches: *Congregation: Stories and Structures* (Fortress, 1987). Frye's theories may also provide a framework for describing how theolo-

326

gians, who are among other things storytellers, tell the city's story, although such an application is not actually mentioned by Hopewell. The argument for such a use of Frye's and Hopewell's categories, which share the conceptual problems of any typology based on polar adjectives, is stated here only in summary. The typology is used principally as a mechanism for pointing out relative differences among the ways theologians have interpreted the city or have used "city" as a theological concept. As with all typologies, differences rather than similarities are stressed. Subtleties are suppressed or ignored. Particular illustrations are consigned to types that seem, at least initially, to deplete them of their richness and variability. These sacrifices are exacted for the sake of identifying and clarifying options that would remain adumbrated were the juxtaposition not forced. The following typology draws particularly on the notion of "worldview" in narratives.

The worldview of some story lines, Hopewell suggests, moves from a state of confusion and complexity toward a state of coherence and unity. Things "work out" at the end of these stories, no matter how improbably. Frye calls this type of story comic, and Hopewell renames it gnostic. The theology underlying Cox's story of the "secular city" (cited above) cautiously moves along a similar pattern — that is, from the crisis of faith in modern cities and churches to the reinstatement of faith in secular city structures. Dismay about the decrepit state of religion and religious institutions will yield, gradually, hopefully, to the realization that secular society has in some sense preserved religious values. The secular city has taken responsibility to fulfill needs met formerly by religious institutions. The city, in short, exhibits positive religious values. It is a sign of hope. Poor migrants often view the city in a similar optimistic way, at least initially before their hopes are crushed; see Peter Lloyd's *Slums of Hope? Shanty Towns of the Third World* (Penguin, 1979). The theologian's task is to enlighten those who cannot see the city's religious values, to foster in doubters an inner awareness of the city's fundamental trustworthiness, and to support the expectant in their efforts to precipitate the hopeful promises of city life. Theologians must search secular arenas for signs of God's work and for unusual manifestations of the church. See the subject index in *Cities and Churches* under the heading Secularization (religion) for other examples.

In diametric opposition to the comic line of story development, other stories start with a unified and coherent worldview, and then dissolve into disintegration and perplexity — a pattern labeled tragic by Frye and canonic by Hopewell. City conditions, if not the city itself, spiral downward in such stories. The French theologian Jacques Ellul's understanding of the city tends to fit this pattern; see his *The Meaning of the City* (Eerdmans, 1970). For Ellul, the city is the epitome of sin and fallenness, notwithstanding the fact that it represents the greatest of human achievements. In the city, people try to do without God, but fail. Much of the theology written using neo-orthodox paradigms came to this conclusion, as have contemporary evangelical Protestant theologians. Cities are basically hopeless places from which people need to be saved by means of God's extra-historical intervention. Nevertheless, Christians must go as missionaries to the city, no matter how evil it may become, and share the lot of those who suffer there. Such costly service is demanded by the sovereign God. Theologians, in this view, must interpret God's word and revealed will to city dwellers and inspire those who serve God in the city.

Two other types of worldview in stories are described by Frye and Hopewell. They, like the former two, are diametric opposites, and their axis bisects the line running from the comic to the tragic at right angles. With the third type of storyteller's worldview, then, narration moves from the factual toward the supernatural. It progresses from well-established data toward infinite variety and mystery, from uniformity toward variety. Frye calls such stories romantic; Hopewell calls them charismatic. Benjamin Tonna's *A Gospel for the City: A Socio-Theology of Urban Ministry* (Orbis, 1982; originally published in Italian, 1978) might be called romantic in Frye's sense of the word. Tonna, a Maltese Roman Catholic priest, sees the city as being neither sinful nor righteous, but as the arena in which God's great drama is being worked out, the setting for a great adventure. God is in favor of the city. God is at home in the city. It is the "tent" of God's reconciliation with humankind, and of humanity with itself. The theologian's task is to call people to discern God's mysterious work in cities, to trust God's providence and blessings, and even more important, to join God's great urban adventure.

Opposite the romantic story Frye places the ironic (Hopewell's empiric). Such stories are based on empirical data, testable by the five senses, and straightforwardly objective. The story line runs from the unknown (supernatural, mysterious) toward the known (natural, evident), from variety toward uniformity. Realism is praised, and the city is seen as being neither necessarily righteous nor demonic, but susceptible to both. Edward Wickham tells the story of the industrial city in this way in *Church and People in an Industrial City* (cited above). He analyzes why the church is not an important part of working people's lives, and concludes that the church must break away from its parochial moorings and meet people in their workplaces. The problem lies not with cities, but with the church's sluggish adaptation to the city. Church planners, demographers, and researchers tend to tell empiric stories. See the reports written by H. Paul Douglass, Earl Brewer, Murray Leiffer, Everett Perry, Meryl Ruoss, Leland Gartrell, Edmund de S. Brunner, Robert L. Wilson, and others who have conducted social surveys for the church. Because theology is implicit and usually unspoken in their treatises, these authors are often in error assumed to be atheological. Their theology is most apparent in their ecclesiologies. Cities place constraints on churches, which must be understood and taken into account. The theologian's task is to depict with integrity the real world and to help people perceive accurately what is happening around them in the city and in the church. Theology itself must change as it helps the church evolve in its response to urban environmental pressures.

Four different ways in which theologians have used "city" as a concept can be conjectured, if only in a preliminary way, using the categories of Frye and Hopewell. Each can readily be illustrated from the citations listed in *Cities and Churches;* see particularly the subject index topics Theology (of the city), Bible, City of God (metaphor), Secular City debate, Babylon (metaphor), Theology (Kingdom), and Theology (evangelical Protestant).

VIII. Denominational Sources

Bibliographic materials are summarized in the following paragraphs for those denominations and denominational groups that are treated in the preceding chapters of this book. Almost all persons and organizations mentioned have multiple citations in *Cities and Churches.* Sources cited consist largely of books, articles, and program materials published by church presses. Monographs, formal pronouncements, denominational periodicals, and archives are discussed in subsections under each denomination.

Although authors are listed by denominational affiliation, many of the writings are ecumenical in scope and have little to do with the urban programs of specific religious denominations. Cooperative publishing efforts were particularly prevalent during the 1960s and early 1970s. The fact that denominational urban church leaders had ecumenical audiences for their writings, some of them have observed, increased their influence in their own denominations.

1. African-American Baptist Bodies

a. Monographs, Reports, and Essays

Several historical and sociological studies relate to the whole field of African American urban churches, including Baptists and Methodists. See, for example: Carter Woodson, *History of the Negro Church* (Associated Publishers, 1921); Benjamin Mays and Joseph Nicholson, *The Negro's Church* (Institute of Social and Religious Research, 1933); Joseph Merchant, *A Study of Urban Problems of Home Mission Boards of Negro Denominations Constituent to the National Council of Churches* (NCC, 1954); E. Franklin Frazier, *The Negro Church in America* (Schocken Books, 1964); Ronald Johnstone, "Negro Preachers Take Sides" (*Review of Religious Research* 11, pp. 81-89); C. Eric Lincoln, *The Black Church Since Frazier* (Schocken, 1974); Randall Burkett and Richard Newman, *Black Apostles* (Hall, 1978); John B. Childs, *The Political Black Minister* (Hall, 1980); Ida Faye Rousseau Mukenge, *The Black Church in Urban America* (University Press of America, 1983); Gayraud Wilmore, *Black Religion and Black Radicalism* (Orbis, 1983); James H. Harris, *Black Ministers and Laity in the Urban Church: An Analysis of Political and Social Expectations* (University Press of America, 1987); Edward D. Smith, *Climbing Jacob's Ladder: The Rise of Black Churches in Eastern American Cities, 1740-1877* (Smithsonian Institution, 1988); Samuel Proctor's autobiography titled *Samuel Proctor: My Moral Odyssey* (Judson, 1989); and especially C. Eric Lincoln and Lawrence Mamiya, *The Black Church in the African American Experience* (Duke University Press, 1990).

Historical study of African-American Baptists, an ongoing project of James M. Washington, has resulted in the publication of his *Frustrated Fellowship: The Black Baptist Quest for Social Power* (Mercer, 1987). This first volume deals with the nineteenth century. Although Washington's efforts are resulting in the first comprehensive history of African-American Baptists, it is preceded by a host of shorter articles and books, collections of sermons, suggestions for church planning and programs, dissertations, biographies and autobiographies of notable clergy, sociological studies, and partial histories. Among these are: Adam Clayton Powell Sr., *Against the Tide: An Autobiography* (Smith, 1938) and his *Riots and Ruins* (Smith, 1945); Lewis Durden, *The Small Negro Church in Washington, DC* (thesis, Howard University, 1942); Evans Crawford, *The Leadership Role of the Urban Negro Minister* (thesis, Boston University, 1957); and Martin Luther King's writings, including *Our Struggle* (CORE, 1957), *Stride toward Freedom* (Harper, 1958), *Letter from Birmingham Jail* (American

Friends Service Committee, 1963, and elsewhere), *Why We Can't Wait* (Harper, 1964), *Where Do We Go from Here: Chaos or Community* (Harper, 1967), *The Crisis in America's Cities* (SCLC, 1967), and many other essays and articles. See also: William Fisher's bibliography on King titled *Free at Last* (cited above).

Other materials about or by notable clergy are: David Friedrichs, *The Role of the Negro Minister in Politics in New Orleans* (thesis, Tulane, 1968); an autobiography by Adam Clayton Powell Jr. titled *Adam by Adam* (Dial, 1971); Weptanomah Carter, *Black Minister's Wife* (Progressive National Baptist Publishing House, 1976); Floyd Massey and Samuel McKinney, *Church Administration in the Black Perspective* (Judson, 1976); William Jones, *God in the Ghetto* (Progressive National Baptist Publishing House, 1979); V. Simpson Turner, *Compassion for the City* (Progressive National Baptist Publishing House, 1979); an autobiography by Martin Luther King Sr. titled *Daddy King* (Morrow, 1980); Barbara A. Reynolds, *Jesse Jackson: The Man, the Movement, the Myth* (Nelson Hall, 1975); and J. Alfred Smith, *For the Facing of This Hour* (Progressive National Baptist Publishing House, 1981). Leon H. Sullivan's economic strategies for black churches are discussed in his *Build, Brother, Build* (Macrae Smith, 1969) and *Alternatives to Despair* (Judson, 1972). See also: Joseph H. Jackson, *The Story of the Christian Activism: The History of the National Baptist Convention* (Townsend, 1980); Jackson, the convention's president for many years and an associate of Chicago mayor Richard Daley, loudly opposed the tactics of Martin Luther King Jr. and other civil rights leaders.

Other sources include William H. Gray, a Philadelphia pastor and former U.S. congressman, who became an influential spokesperson for urban concerns in the 1970s and 1980s. His congressional speeches, often rooted in his urban church experience, sometimes referred directly to religious concerns. Also relevant to an understanding of African-American Baptists are Wyatt T. Walker's studies on church music — *Somebody's Calling My Name* (Judson, 1979) is an example — and Gardner C. Taylor's published sermons.

b. Periodicals

See especially a periodical bibliography edited by Randall K. Burkett titled *Newsletter of the Afro-American Religious History Group of the American Academy of Religion* (beginning in 1976). The National Baptist Convention, U.S.A., publishes the *National Baptist Voice* (beginning in 1916), which includes news of urban churches.

c. Archives

The archives for Martin Luther King Jr., mentioned above, have related materials for urban African-American Baptist churches. Martha Riggs's *The Kelly Miller Smith Papers* (Vanderbilt University, 1989) inventories 111 boxes of materials written and collected by the prominent Baptist pastor and civil rights activist in Nashville, Tennessee. These documents are housed in Vanderbilt University's Heard Library. The American Baptist Historical Society maintains many African-American Baptist records, even for churches not affiliated with the ABC, in the Samuel Colgate Collection at Colgate Rochester Divinity School, Rochester, New York. The ABC/USA archives at Valley Forge, Pennsylvania, also have a general collection of African-American Baptist materials.

2. African American Methodist Bodies

a. Monographs, Reports, and Essays

General essays on African American churches, listed at the beginning of the section above on African-American Baptists, apply also to African American Methodists. Additionally, several histories about the emergence of African American Methodist denominations exist, including: Daniel A. Payne and Charles Spencer Smith, *A History of the African Methodist Episcopal Church* (AME Church, 1891, 1922); Howard Gregg's recent work of the same title (AME Church, 1980); and Richard Allen's autobiography written in 1820 and published by Abingdon in 1960. Urban involvements of the Christian Methodist Episcopal Church are discussed in Othal Hawthorne Lakey's *History of the CME Church* (CME Publishing House, 1985).

b. Periodicals

The *AME Zion Quarterly Review* occasionally publishes articles on urban church concerns; for example: K. Logan Jackson, "Victimization and Community Violence within Metropolitan Washington" (January 1988, pp. 8-17). Intelligence about city church activities may be found in the *Star of Zion*, also an AMEZ publication. The African Methodist Episcopal Church publishes the *AME Christian Recorder* and the *AME Review*. The Christian Methodist Episcopal Church issues the bimonthly *Christian Index* with current news about churches.

c. Archives

The Methodist Archives at Drew University maintain materials on African American Methodist denominations. The Interdenominational Theological Center in Atlanta, Georgia, has assembled an important collection.

3. American Baptist Churches in the U.S.A.

a. Monographs, Reports, and Essays

Lawrence Janssen, James Scott, and Norman Green conducted several planning studies for ABC churches in the 1950s and 1960s, all of which demonstrate the denomination's commitment to urban church development. In the 1960s, George Younger, Jitsuo Morikawa, and Robert Hoover were especially influential in shaping denominational policy. See Younger's *The Bible Calls for Action* (Judson, 1959), *The Church and Urban Power Structure* (Westminster, 1963), and *The Church and Urban Renewal* (Lippincott, 1965). Morikawa's contribution is reflected mainly in denominational policy statements and reports; see his *The Urban Church and Evangelism* (American Baptist Home Mission Society, 1960) and *The Functional Purpose of MAP* (Metropolitan Associates of Philadelphia, 1965). He and other American Baptists were instrumental in founding the Metropolitan Associates of Philadelphia (MAP) program (see subject listing in *Cities and Churches*), an effort to train laity for urban action ministries that was quickly joined by other denominations and widely cited as an important experiment in new forms of the urban church. Morikawa's contributions are summarized in a brief biography by Hazel Morikawa, *Footprints: One Man's Pilgrimage* (Jennings Associates, 1990).

Pastors Howard Moody and Robert Spike wrote several essays and books on urban ministry; see, for example, Spike's *In but Not of the World* (Association, 1957). Both Moody and Spike had clergy standing with the Baptists and Congregationalists. See also the sermons of Harry Emerson Fosdick for views of city life and city ministry; his autobiography is titled *The Living of These Days* (Harper, 1956). Harvey Cox's writings are rooted in his Baptist background, including *The Secular City* (cited above) and his subsequent reconsiderations of the secular city. Martin Luther King's insights owe much to his American Baptist heritage and theological training. In the 1980s, Raymond Bakke produced a series of articles and books on urban ministry from a decidedly evangelical perspective, among which are: *The Expanded Mission of Old First Churches* (with Samuel Roberts; Judson, 1986) and *The Urban Christians* (with Jim Hart; InterVarsity, 1987).

b. Pronouncements and Policies

Among the resources for tracing American Baptist denominational policy regarding urban issues are: "Resolutions Adopted by the American Baptist Convention, Denver, Colorado, May 15, 1953" (Council on Christian Social Progress, 1953); Lawrence Janssen's article titled "Priorities of the Church Strategy Program: American Baptist Convention" (*City Church* 15, November 1964, pp. 18-19); and "Metropolitan Ministries" (*American Baptist Quarterly* 5, June 1986, p. 138).

c. Periodicals

Periodicals with several urban ministry–related articles are: *Chronicle, Foundations, American Baptist Quarterly, American Baptist Urban Newsletter,* and a short-lived newsletter of the Church Strategy Program titled *The Church in Metropolis and Space* (Division of Church Missions, American Baptist Home Mission Societies, 1967).

d. Archives

Archives are maintained by the American Baptist Historical Society at the Samuel Colgate Baptist Library, Rochester, New York, and at the denominational headquarters in Valley Forge. Materials related to local and regional programs tend to be stored in Rochester, while denominational materials are more often available at Valley Forge. Andover Newton Theological School, Newton Center, Massachusetts, has significant resources in its library.

4. The Church of God in Christ (COGIC)

Originating in the southern states in the early twentieth century, COGIC migrated northward with the African Americans who sought employment in major industrial cities during and following this century's two world wars. Of necessity, their movement was urban in nature, but they have had no literature designated as "urban ministry" nor official pronounce-ments about urban conditions. Ministry was unsegmented; ministry was whole, without any qualifying adjectives. Only in recent years have the documents of early COGIC history been sought for preservation; see, for example, the autobiography titled *The Life and Works of Mother Mary Magnum Johnson, Founder of the Church of God in Christ in the State of Michigan* (unpublished manuscript). The stories of other early COGIC leaders in northern industrial cities are also being sought for preservation and publication. A compendium listing over one thousand biographical sketches of Pentecostal leaders, including many in COGIC and many with urban churches, is provided in Sherry Sherrod DuPree's *Biographical Dictionary of African-American Holiness-Pentecostal, 1880-1990* (Middle Atlantic, 1989).

COGIC histories have been written by James O. Patterson et al., *History of the Formative Years of the Church of God in Christ, with Excerpts from the Life and Works of Its Founder, Bishop C. H. Mason* (COGIC Publishing House, 1969), and Douglas J. Nelson, *A Brief History of the Church of God in Christ* (Duke University, 1986); as well as autobiographies by COGIC clergy such as *A Man Called Famous: Elder Famous Smith* (West Memphis 15th Street COGIC, 1985). James C. Austin Sr., pastor of Chicago's St. Luke's COGIC, has produced a video of C. H. Mason's life titled *Legacy of a Leader* (Charles Harrison Mason Foundation, 1991). These histories reflect the urban character of COGIC churches, as do the data presented in James O. Patterson et al., *Church of God in Christ Directory* (COGIC Publishing House, 1980).

Urban concerns become explicit in George McKinney's *I Will Build My Church* (Open Door Press, 1977), which describes techniques used in founding and building St. Stephen COGIC in San Diego, California. Robert M. Franklin's article "Church and City: Black Christianity's Ministry" (*Christian Ministry* 20, March 1989, pp. 17-19) suggests that a mission of the rapidly growing Holiness Movement is to humanize the city by means of its worship styles. The importance of worship is reflected also in Donna M. Cox, "Contemporary Trends in the Music Ministry of the Church of God in Christ" (*Journal of Black Sacred Music* 2, Fall 1988, pp. 96-101), and in Beverly Boggs, "Some Aspects of Worship in a Holiness Church" (*New York Folklore* 3, nos. 1-4, 1977, pp. 29-44). Women's work in cities is emphasized in Cheryl T. Gilkes, "The Role of Church and Community Mothers: Ambivalent American Sexism or Fragmented African Familyhood" (*Journal of Feminist Studies in Religion* 2, Spring 1986, pp. 41-59).

5. Episcopal Church

a. Monographs, Reports, and Essays

Several Episcopalians writing in the 1930s and earlier were to have important influence on the postwar views of the urban church in that denomination. Among these are Niles Carpenter, who wrote *Sociology of City Life* (Longmans, Green, 1931), as well as *The Church and Changing Social Work* (National Council, PEC, 1934) and *The City and Its People* (1938?); William B. Spofford, founder of the periodical titled *The Witness;* Spencer Miller, who produced *The Church and Industry* (with Joseph Fletcher; Longmans, Green, 1930), *American Labor and the Nation* (University of Chicago Press, 1933), and *The Church Must Decide* (Morehouse, 1934); and Vida Dutton Scudder, a Christian socialist, whose later corpus includes *The Christian Attitude toward Private Property* (Morehouse, 1934) and the autobiographical *On Journey* (Dutton, 1937). Scudder's biography by Theresa Corcoran is also helpful: *Vida Dutton Scudder* (Twayne, 1982). Christianity's relationship to industry was a topic frequently debated in Church Congress meetings: see, for example, *Honest Liberty in the Church* (Macmillan, 1924) and *Christ in the World of Today* (Scribner's, 1927).

Following the war, urban church concerns were discussed in the writings of Theodore and Cynthia Wedel: the former wrote *The Christianity of Main Street* (Macmillan, 1950) while the latter authored "Health and Welfare Needs of the Nation and the Place of the Church Agency" (Diocese of New York, PEC, 1954) and "Employed Women and the Church" (NCC, 1959). Modernity is a major theme in Joseph F. Fletcher's edited volume *Christianity and Property* (Westminster, 1947) and his *Situation Ethics* (1960). A large body of materials was written during this era about the construction and programs of cathedrals; see, for example, information about the building of the Washington Cathedral and the books by George Edmed DeMille. The Episcopal Fellowship of Urban Workers, comprised mainly of church social workers in inner cities, began publishing materials in 1948. A history of Episcopal social work in Los Angeles was produced in the same year by Thomas Chalmers Marshall titled *Into the Streets and Lanes* (Saunders Press). G. Paul Musselman became interested in experimental urban church models during the 1950s; see his "The Episcopal Church Research Centers" (*City Church* 6, November 1955, pp. 9-11) and *The Church on the Urban Frontier* (Seabury, 1960). Chauncie Kilmer Myers's *Light the Dark Streets* (Seabury, 1957) graphically portrays the plight of youth caught in urban problems.

As with other denominations, the Episcopalians produced a large amount of urban-related literature in the 1960s. "Metabagdad," the name for a series of one-day urban ministry conferences held in several dioceses, stimulated comment in the Episcopal Church and ecumenical presses. Francis Ayres's *Ministry of the Laity: A Biblical Exposition* (Westminster, 1962), written when he was residing in the Plainfield Community in Michigan, became influential among urban church leaders. Hugh White and Scott Paradise wrote about nonparochial ministries; see Paradise's *Detroit Industrial Mission* (Harper and Row, 1968), a program based on the European models of church industrial work, namely Wickham and Loew (both cited above). Earlier writings on the Detroit Industrial Mission include: Hugh C. White Jr. and Robert C. Batchelder, "Mission to Metropolis: A Total Strategy" (*International Review of Missions* 54, no. 214, April 1965, pp. 161-72), and Batchelder's *Men Who Build: Some Human Problems in the Construction Industry* (Detroit Industrial Mission, 1963), the latter being a pamphlet with a set of case histories with laypeople's reflections on the theological significance of their labor. William Stringfellow, an attorney and controversial Episcopal layperson living in New York City, wrote pointed social criticism: *A Private and Public Faith* (Eerdmans, 1962), *My People Is the Enemy* (Holt, Rinehart and Winston, 1964), *Dissenter in a Great Society* (Abingdon, 1966), and *An Ethic for Christians and Other Aliens in a Strange Land* (Word Books, 1973). A city planner, Perry Norton, produced *Church and Metropolis: A City Planner's Viewpoint of the Slow Changing Church in the Fast Changing Metropolis* (Seabury Press, 1964); Norton frequently wrote for the National Council of Churches. The problems of affluence are discussed in *The Church in a Society of Abundance* (Seabury, 1963), edited by Arthur Walmsley. Malcolm Boyd advocated radical approaches in his *On the Battle Lines* (Morehouse-Barlow, 1964) and *The Underground Church* (Sheed and Ward, 1968), while John Harmon encouraged secular ministries that would include the dispossessed: *Toward a Secular Ecumenism* (Kellog Lectures, 1966). Gibson Winter's articles expanded his suburban captivity thesis, mentioned above in section IV. Innovative urban ministries are reflected in Brian Shaw, *Night Pastor* (Graywood, 1968), and Lester McManis, *Handbook on Christian Education in the Inner City* (Seabury, 1966). Bishop E. Paul Moore's writings on urban issues attracted a wide readership: *The Church Reclaims the City* (Seabury, 1964) and *Take a Bishop Like Me* (Harper and Row, 1979). Pierre Berton's disaffection with the church precipitated his *The Comfortable Pew* (Lippincott, 1965), an indictment of the church and its practices. Although a Canadian, Berton was widely read in the United States.

During the 1970s, Norman Faramelli's concern about technology and industry led to the publication of his *Technethics: Christian Mission in an Age of Technology* (Friendship, 1971) and "Distributive Justice in an Era of Material Scarcity" (Boston Industrial Mission, 1976). See also Faramelli's "Ecological Responsibility and Economic Justice: The Perilous Links between Ecology and Poverty" (*Andover Newton Quarterly* 11, November 1970, pp. 81-93) in which he asks if the cost for ecologically sound policy will fall unduly on the urban poor. An experimental, ecumenical theological education program called INTER-MET, located in Washington, D.C., was conceived by John C. Fletcher, an Episcopalian, and is best described in Celia Hahn, ed., *INTER-MET: Bold Experiment in Theological Education* (Alban Institute, 1977). INTER-MET archives are located at Lancaster Theological Seminary. William Jennings offered suggestions of how the church needed to change if it was to respond to the poor in *Poor People and Church Goers* (Seabury, 1972). Loren Mead and the Alban Institute recommended new strategies for parishes in such reports as *New Hope for Congregations* (with Elisa Des Portes; Seabury, 1972) and other Project Test-Pattern publications. The Church of the Redeemer in Houston, Texas, became the site of experimental ministries: see Michael Harper, *A New Way of Living* (Logos International, 1973) and W. Graham Pulkingham, *They Lifted Their Nets* (Morehouse-Barlow, 1973). Pastoral strategies are discussed in the writings of Urban T. Holmes, *Ministry and Imagination* (Seabury, 1976) and *The Priest in Community* (1978). David Sheppard, an influential Church of England priest who eventually became the bishop of Liverpool, England, developed a widely influential and controversial thesis about the urban poor: *Built as a City* (Hodder and Stoughton, 1974) and *Bias to the Poor* (1983).

The Episcopal Urban Caucus, organized in the early 1980s, generated a city ministry literature. Various models for urban ministry are reported in *To Build the City — Too Long to Dream* (Alban Institute, 1982), edited by William Yon. In Britain, the Church of England initiated a major urban emphasis at mid-decade with the report of the Archbishop of Canterbury's Commission on Urban Priority Areas titled *Faith in the City* (Church House, 1985), which generated a host of articles, criticisms, and implementation plans for various dioceses throughout England. The commission's report, highly influential among all denominations in Britain, regrettably was barely noticed in the United States — evidence of decline in urban church interests in all U.S. denominations during the 1980s. Robert Iles's *The Gospel Imperative in the Midst of AIDS* (Morehouse, 1989) reports Episcopalian views on the emerging urban health crisis. Gibson Winter summarized much of his thinking about cities in *Community Spiritual Transformation* (Crossroads, 1989). G. H. Jack Woodard, long associated with Episcopal urban ministries, is in processs of writing his personal reflections under the working title *Struggle to Light the Dark Streets* (unpublished manuscript), a deliberate play on C. Kilmer Myers's title of 1957.

b. Pronouncements and Policies

Regarding the development of social policy in the Protestant Episcopal Church, see the following, listed by date of publication: "Christian Doctrine in Social Action" (Protestant Episcopal Church in the U.S.A., National Council, 1928); Spencer Miller and Joseph Fletcher, *The Church and Industry* (Longmans, Green, 1930); Paul Schulz, *The Bishops on Social Problems* (Church League for Industrial Democracy, [1930s?]); "Episcopal Social Work" (Protestant Episcopal Church in the U.S.A., National Council, 1936); William Manning, ed., "The Church and Slum Clearance" (PECUSA, National Council, 1937); Niles Carpenter et al., "The City and Its People" (1938?); "An Inventory Outline for Parish Committees on Christian Social Relations" (1942); "Management and Labor" (Bishop's Conference on Capital and Labor, 1945); "The Church's Mission in Urban Industrial Areas" (Protestant Episcopal Church in the U.S.A., National Council, 1950); "Episcopalians at Work in the World" (1952?); M. Moran Weston, *Social Policy of the Episcopal Church in the Twentieth Century* (diss., Columbia University, 1954); Bishop John Hine's "Address to the [General] Convention" in 1961; James P. Morton, "Metabagdad" (PECUSA, National Council, 1963); various early editions of the periodical titled *Church in Metropolis* (1964-70); and Reinhart Gutmann et al., "The Church and Community Development: A Position Statement" (Episcopal Church, Executive Council, 1966).

To these must be added various documents and reports regarding the General Convention Special Program (GCSP), a hotly disputed denominational mechanism intended to raise funds in response to urban riots and James Foreman's appeals, in *Journals of the General Convention* (from 1969 to 1973), and especially "Learnings from GCSP: A Report on Five Years' Experience with the Episcopal Church's Most Controversial Program" (*Episcopalian* 137, November 1972, pp. 47-51). See also: "Asiamerica Ministry" (Episcopal Church, Executive Council, 1977); Jean C. Lyles, "A Mission to the Urban or the Urbane? Urban Bishops Coalition of the Episcopal Church" (*Christian Century* 95, May 17, 1978, pp. 524-25); Joseph Pelham, ed., "To Hear and to Heed: The Episcopal Church Listens and Acts in the

City" (Forward Movement Publications, 1978); "Episcopalians Recently Established a Church Structure for Ministry to the Cities" (*Christianity Today* 24, April 4, 1980, p. 49); Robert L. DeWitt, "Bishops Ponder Urban Apocalypse" (*Witness* 64, March, April, and June 1981); Peyton Craighill, "The Ministry of the Episcopal Church in the USA to Immigrants and Refugees: A Historical Outline" (*Historical Magazine of the Protestant Episcopal Church* 51, June 1982, pp. 203-18); "The Episcopal Church and the Hispanic Challenge" (National Hispanic Consultation, 1985); James Perkinson, "Taking Action for Economic Justice: A Theological Assessment" (a report from the Michigan Diocese to general convention, July 1988). A summary of formal statements is provided by Robert Hood's *Social Teachings in the Episcopal Church* (Morehouse, 1990).

c. Periodicals

Among the Episcopal journals that carry articles on urban church concerns are: *Alban Institute Action Information, Anglican Theological Review, Crucible* (Church of England), *Church in Metropolis, Historical Magazine of the Protestant Episcopal Church,* the *Witness* (Ambler, Pennsylvania), and, in the 1980s, the Episcopal Urban Caucus's *Urban Networker.*

d. Archives

The main archives for the Episcopal Church are found at the Library and Archives of the Church Historical Library in Austin, Texas, although a small collection is maintained at the National Council offices in New York City. General Theological Seminary has a fairly large assemblage of urban-related materials as part of its main library collection.

6. Lutheran Bodies

a. Monographs, Reports, and Essays

Much of the Lutheran city ministry literature of the 1940s and 1950s was generated by the Inner Mission programs, a charitable effort based on similar programs originating in nineteenth-century Germany. See, for example, Ethel Brubaker, *Case Work for Children* (National Lutheran Inner Mission Conference, 1939) and Walter Miesel's dissertation titled *The Development of the Lutheran Inner Mission Societies in the LCA* (University of

Pittsburgh, 1947). Also, during these decades, Carl Rasmussen conducted urban planning studies; Martin Anderson wrote about church finances and extension in *Planning and Financing the New Church* (Augsburg, 1944); and Harold Letts explored Christian economics in *Christian Social Responsibility* (Muhlenberg, 1957, especially vol. 1), *Teacher's Guide for Christian Action and Economic Life* (United Lutheran Publications, 1950), and *Christian Action in Economic Life* (Muhlenberg, 1953). John Daniel's book titled *Labor, Industry, and the Church* (Concordia, 1957) describes Lutheran perspectives on church-labor relations. Missouri Synod parishes are the subject of Ross Scherer's sociological study titled *The Lutheran Parish in an Urbanized America* (Lutheran Education Association, 1958).

Lutherans produced a large literature about urban concerns in the 1960s. Walter Kloetzli defended traditional Lutheran planning approaches to urban issues and sharply criticized the community organization theories of Saul Alinsky. See Kloetzli's *Urban Church Planning* (with Arthur Hillman; Muhlenberg, 1958), *Eight City Churches* (National Lutheran Council, 1960), *Lutheran Central Areas Study* (same), *The Church and the Urban Challenge* (Muhlenberg, 1961), *Challenge and Response in the City* (Augustana, 1962), and *Chicago Lutheran Planning Study* (National Lutheran Council, 1965). Planning models, especially those involving ecumenical cooperation, were the subject of H. Conrad Hoyer's writings: *The Lutheran Church in Metropolitan Areas* (National Lutheran Council, 1959), *Consultation on Cooperative Church Planning* (Massachusetts Council of Churches, 1965), and *Ecumenopolis, USA* (Augsburg, 1971). Edgar Trexler wrote a series of articles for the *Lutheran*, a periodical, citing examples of city church renewal, an interest eventually resulting in books titled *Ways to Wake Up Your Church* (Fortress, 1969) and *Creative Congregations* (Abingdon, 1972). Similarly, Wallace Fisher, a pastor in Lancaster, Pennsylvania, advanced the church renewal approach to urban church problems in *From Tradition to Mission: An Old Church Discovers the Secret to New Life* (Abingdon, 1965), *Preaching and Parish Renewal* (1966), and *Preface to Parish Renewal* (1968). Roy Blumhorst's *Faithful Rebels* (Concordia, 1967) describes innovative approaches to apartment house ministries. Political aspects of urban development are discussed in Karl Hertz's *Politics as a Way of Helping People* (Augsburg, 1974), based on his experience of church and city planning in the 1960s. David Schuller's essay, in a similar vein, stresses the importance of politics in the task of restoring a sense of community to cities: see Schuller's *The New Urban Society* (Concordia, 1966), *Emerging Shapes of the Church* (1967), and *Power Structures of the Church* (1969). James Manz's *The Church in an Urbanized World* (Concordia, 1964) provides an overview of city church issues and controversies, based on case studies in the Missouri Synod. Arthur Simon's *Faces of Poverty* (Concordia, 1966) calls for Lutheran responsiveness to the poor, as does Henry Whiting's *The Church and the Relief Client* (Board of Social Ministries, LCA, 1968). Under ecumenical auspices, Lutheran pastor John Wagner Jr. produced several reports related to the experimental Los Angeles Region Goals Project in the late 1960s and early 1970s.

Throughout the 1970s, Lutherans produced curriculum materials for urban churches that tended to stress the city, not as problem, but as resource. See, for example: Rolf Aaseng, ed., *The City: Viewpoints, Christian Perspectives on Social Concerns* (Augsburg, 1979); Joseph Barndt, *Liberating Our White Ghetto* (1972); *Hey, God, Hooray!* (and others in this series, Lutheran Church Press, 1970, 1972); *The Big Idea* (Board of Parish Education, LCA, 1972); and *Educaid, Educational Resources for the Urban Church* (1973). The growing importance of non-Germanic ethnic Lutherans is reflected in the National Hispanics Lutheran Assembly's *Directory of Hispanic Lutheran Ministries in the USA and Puerto Rico* (The Assembly, 1977).

Richard Diehl wrote in the 1980s about "Plant Closings" (Division for Mission in North America, LCA, 1985), and the church's role in corporate responsibility: "The Church as Shareholder" (same). Granger Westberg's ministry with churches operating health clinics gained national recognition; see his *Parish Nurse* (Augsburg, 1990). In the late 1980s, inner-city stories by Walter Wangerin gained an appreciative audience: *The Ragman and Other Cries of Faith* (Harper and Row, 1984) and *The Manger Is Empty* (Harper, 1989). Wayne Stumme edited a volume about different models of Lutheran urban ministries titled *The Experience of Hope: Mission and Ministry in Changing Urban Communities* (Augsburg, 1991).

Several Lutheran sociologists have been interested in urban church issues: Nicholas Demerath's thesis at the University of California was titled "Social Stratification and Church Involvement among Urban Lutheran Parishioners" (1962). Peter Berger's discourses deal broadly with urbanization and secularization: *The Noise of Solemn Assemblies* (Doubleday, 1961), *The Sacred Canopy* (1967), *The Social Construction of Reality* (with Thomas Luckmann; same), and *A Rumor of Angels* (1969). Several articles by Samuel Mueller in sociological journals deal with urban Lutherans; see his "Changes in the Social Status of Lutheranism in Ninety Chicago Suburbs, 1950-1960" (*Sociological Analysis* 27, Fall 1966, pp. 138-45). In 1980, Russell Hale produced *The Unchurched: Who They Are and Why They Stay Away* (Harper and Row).

b. Pronouncements and Policies

Lutherans have issued several formal statements about cities and urban issues. Among the resources for studying these are: "The Church Speaks on Labor" (United Lutheran Church of America, Board of Social Missions, 1946); Harold C. Letts, *Christian Social Responsibility* (Muhlenberg, 1957); "Social Statements of the United Lutheran Church in America, 1918-1962" (United Lutheran Church of America, Board of Social Missions, [1962?]); Henry J. Whiting, "The Churches Speak: A Bibliography of Official Statements and Study Reports" (Lutheran Council in the U.S.A., 1969); "Social Criteria for Investment" (Board of Social Ministry, 1972); "LCA Ministry in the City: A Position Paper" (LCA, Division for Mission in North America, 1977); "A Statement on Immigration Policies: Undocumented Persons" (Lutheran Council in the U.S.A., 1981); Charles Lutz, "Public Voice: Social Policy Development in the ALC, 1960-1987" (Office of Church and Society, LCA, 1987); Christa Klein and Christian Dehsen, *Politics and Policy: The Genesis and Theology of Social Statements in the LCA* (Fortress, 1989).

c. Periodicals

Lutheran general interest publications with occasional urban ministry articles include: *Dialog, The Lutheran, Lutheran Forum,* the *Lutheran Standard,* and the *National Lutheran.* Specialty periodicals dealing specifically with urban issues are represented by *Inner City: A Newsletter for Lutherans* (1964-68); *Lutheran Social Welfare* (Lutheran Social Welfare Conference, 1961-71); *Urban Newsletter* (LCA, 1970-87); *Renewal* (Lutheran Center for Church Renewal, St. Paul, Minnesota, beginning in 1980).

d. Archives

The Archives of the Lutheran Church in America at the Lutheran School of Theology, Chicago, has the most complete collection. Additional locations include the Lutheran Archives Center at Philadelphia, the Archives of Cooperative Lutheranism in Chicago, and the Concordia Historical Institute, St. Louis, Missouri. Bertha Paulssen, a leading Lutheran seminary professor in urban studies, collected materials during the 1940s and 1950s that are located at the Lutheran Theological Seminary, Gettysburg, Pennsylvania.

7. Presbyterian Church (U.S.A.) and Predecessor Denominations

a. Monographs, Reports, and Essays

Pre–World War II Presbyterian leaders who had important impact on the denomination's postwar urban policies include: Charles Stelzle, among whose prolific writings is *A Son of the Bowery,* his autobiographical recollections of Presbyterian church-labor relations (Doran, 1926); William P. Shriver, a denominational executive who authored *Projects for City Churches* (PCUSA, 1929), *The Presbyterian Church in the City* (Board of National Missions, PCUSA, 1938), and *Missions at the Grass Roots* (Friendship, 1949); and Jacob Avery Long, a seminary professor who wrote *Scotch, Irish, and* — (Board of National Missions, PCUSA, 1943) and *The Labor Temple, New York* (1944). Following the war, several Presbyterians conducted sociological urban church planning studies, including David Barry, Meryl Ruoss, Everett Perry, and Charles Thorn. Carolyn Odell conducted planning studies for local Presbyterian churches. William Biddle encouraged the development of communities in *The Cultivation of Community Leaders* (Harper, 1953) and *Community Development Process* (with Loureide Biddle; Holt, Rinehart and Winston, 1965). Samuel Blizzard's research on ministerial roles during the 1950s, which took into account urban and rural distinctions, is summarized in *The Protestant Parish Minister* (Society for the Scientific Study of Religion, 1985). The Presbyterian Institute of Industrial Relations (PIIR) operated an urban training program for clergy and seminarians in Chicago from 1945 until 1972, when it merged with the ecumenically sponsored ICUIS. Marshal Logan Scott was dean; see his *The Church Goes to Town* (Board of National Missions, UPUSA, 1951), *A Proposal for Strengthening Presbyterian Churches of Industrial Communities through Adult Education* (diss., Columbia, 1953), and several articles on training for industrial ministry. Scott also wrote occasional newsletters to PIIR alumni, only some of which have been preserved. Southern Presbyterian church urban policy is described in Thomas Currie's pamphlet titled *Our Cities for Christ* (Board of Church Extension, PCUS, 1954).

Presbyterians continued a strong emphasis on urban training throughout the 1960s. Robert Lee edited collections of readings widely used in theological seminaries titled *Cities and Churches* (Westminster, 1962) and *The Church in the Exploding Metropolis* (John Knox, 1965). Lee's views of Saul Alinsky's community organization work in the 1960s are recorded in *The Schizophrenic Church* (with Russell Galloway; Westminster, 1969). Robert Bonthius contributed to the development of action training methods for urban clergy, and George Todd wrote various articles on urban church issues; see listings for both authors in my *Cities and Churches*. A series of reports on innovative church programs was developed by Grace Ann Goodman, among which is "Rocking the Ark: Nine Cases of Traditional Churches in Process of Change" (Board of National Missions, UPUSA, 1968). Goodman's approach, with its emphasis on collecting stories and offering alternative models and "new forms" for the church, is in marked contrast to the earlier church planners' emphasis on demography, local church extension, and survey data collection. Letty M. Russell produced curricular material for children and adults, stemming in part from her involvement with East Harlem Protestant Parish and the World Council of Churches; see "Equipping Little Saints" (*Adult Teacher* [Methodist] 15, May 1962) and *Missionary Structure of Christian Education* (Westminster, 1967). More recently, Russell edited a volume titled *The Church with AIDS* (Westminster, 1990). Earl K. Larson Jr. edited a volume for the General Assembly describing radical and innovative ministries titled *How in the World* (1966?). John Fry commented on growing urban problems in *The Immobilized Christian* (Westminster, 1963) and *The Metropolitan Crisis* (United Campus Christian Fellowship, 1964). His sharpest criticism of the church was reserved for his *The Trivialization of the Presbyterian Church* (Harper and Row, 1975), where he assails theologies of reconciliation and conflict avoidance. Charles West, writing from a modified Marxist perspective, produced *Technologists and Revolutionaries* (National Council of Churches, Committee on the Church and Economic Life, 1966), and M. Richard Shaull began introducing a liberation perspective in his "Christian Theology and Social Revolution" (*Perkins School of Theology Journal* 21, nos. 2-3, Winter-Spring 1967, pp. 5-12).

Richard Poethig, executive for ICUIS, wrote and edited many reports from the late 1960s to the early 1980s, including some related to his earlier ministry in Manila, Philippines, among which are: "Guidelines for an Urban-Industrial Ministry" (Committee on Industrial Life and Vocation, 1966), "The Squatter Community" (Philippine Sociological Society, 1969), "Urban Mission in Southeast Asia" (East Asia Christian Council, 1970), "The Church in the Multinational Age" (ICUIS, 1974), "Forming a Theology of Urban-Industrial Mission" (with Bobby Wells; 1975), and *The Shape of Urban Ministry in the 80s* (ICUIS, 1979), an edited volume. Robert Worley wrote about church renewal strategies in *Change in the Church* (Westminster, 1971), *Dry Bones Breathe* (Center for the Study of Organizational Behavior, 1978), and *A Gathering of Strangers* (Westminster, 1983). Donald Allen describes his house church experiences in *Barefoot in the Church* (John Knox, 1972). An observer of city churches in the

South, Donald Shriver called for compassion and charity in city life in his *Is There Hope for the City?* (with Karl Ostrom; Westminster, 1977). Dieter Hessel emphasized the social ethics of urban issues in *The White Problem* (with Everett Perry; Department of Church and Society, UPUSA, 1970), *A Social Action Primer* (Westminster, 1972), "How to Become a Poor Church and Save Faith" (Office of Social Education, UPUSA, 1978), "Rethinking Social Ministry" (Office for Education Services, 1980), and *Social Ministry* (Westminster, 1982). His edited volume, *Theological Education for Social Ministry* (Pilgrim, 1988), continues the denomination's interest in training for urban clergy.

The emergence and development of black theology are summarized by Gayraud Wilmore; see his *Black Theology: A Documentary History, 1966-1979* (with James Cone; Orbis, 1979), *Black Religion and Black Radicalism* (Orbis, 1983), and *Black and Presbyterian* (Geneva Press, 1983). Carl Dudley, using largely sociological paradigms, wrote a series of books dealing with urban church problems: *Where Have All Our People Gone?* (Pilgrim, 1979), *Building Effective Ministry* (Harper and Row, 1983), *Developing Your Small Church's Potential* (with Douglas Walrath; Judson, 1988), and *Basic Steps toward Community Ministry* (Alban Institute, 1991). His research in the late 1980s and 1990s was in connection with the Church and Community Ministries Program. Glenda Hope, pastor of Second Presbyterian Church in San Francisco, produced several articles on innovative ministry and educational models stemming from that congregation; see listing for her in *Cities and Churches*. Denominational strategy in light of urban membership decline is a major topic in Milton Coalter et al., *The Mainline Protestant "Decline": The Presbyterian Pattern* (Westminster/John Knox, 1990) and *The Diversity of Discipleship* (1991). Robert Linthicum, of World Vision International, produced *City of God and City of Satan* (Zondervan, 1991) and *Empowering the Poor: Community Organizing among the City's Ragtag and Bobtail* (MARC, 1991), both with a worldwide orientation and a somewhat more evangelical perspective than typical in publications of earlier Presbyterian authors. Harvie Conn, an Orthodox Presbyterian and professor at Westminster Theological Seminary, wrote prolifically from an evangelical Presbyterian perspective during the 1980s; see his *Evangelism: Doing Justice and Preaching Grace* (Zondervan, 1984) and *A Clarified Vision for Urban Mission* (1987).

b. Pronouncements and Policies

Among resources for studying official Presbyterian urban policy are the following: "Official Pronouncements of the General Assembly of the Presbyterian Church in the USA Relative to Social and Industrial Relations and Social and Moral Welfare" (Office of the General Assembly, 1936); "Church and Society" (Board of Christian Education, UPUSA, 1937); "The City, USA: 152nd Annual Report . . . to the General Assembly . . ." (Board of National Missions, UPUSA, 1954); "Study of the Inner City" (1956?); "From Missions to Mission" (1962); a study of Protestant policies in the 1950s and 1960s directed by Robert Lee titled "Research Notes on the Role of the Churches in Urban Renewal and Development" (Institute of Ethics and Society, 1963-64); Daniel Little, "Commentary out of Denominations: Priorities of the Department of Urban Church, UPUSA" (*City Church* 15, November 1964, pp. 17-18); "The Church and Community Organization" (Board of National Missions, UPUSA, 1966); "Urban Affairs Pronouncements of the Presbyterian Church US, 1947-1966, [and] the United Presbyterian Church in the USA" (Office of Church and Society, UPUSA, 1967); *Guidelines for Development of Strategy for Metropolitan Mission* (Board of Missions), a policy document developed under the leadership of George Todd adopted by the 179th General Assembly in 1967; George Chauncey and Jacqueline Rhoades, eds., "Social Pronouncements of the Presbyterian Church in the US" (Board of Christian Education, PCUS, [1969?]); "Investment Policy Guidelines" (*Church and Society* 61, July 1971, pp. 38-54); Richard Poethig, "Historical Overview of the Urban/Metropolitan Mission Policies of the UPUSA, with Important Dates and Events" (General Assembly Mission Council, 1978; reprinted in *Journal of Presbyterian History* 57, Fall 1979, pp. 313-52); "A Joint Urban Policy for the United Presbyterian Church in the USA and the Presbyterian Church in the US" (Program Agency of the UPUSA, 1981; reprinted in *Cities* 1, July 1981, pp. 32-33); "The Church in Economic Affairs: The Policies of the Presbyterian Church, USA, 1930-1980" (*Church and Society* 74, March 1984, pp. 82-102).

In 1985, the Committee on a Just Political Economy issued its report titled "Toward a Just, Caring, and Dynamic Political Economy." General Assembly pronouncements on social and economic issues are reported regularly in *Church and Society,* usually in number 6 (July-August) of each volume. See, for example, "The Church and the Urban Crisis," *Church and Society* (vol. 82, no. 6, July-August 1992, pp. 5-17) for a response typical of Protestant denominations to the 1992 Los Angeles riots.

c. Periodicals

Among periodicals with articles regarding Presbyterian urban churches and programs are: *A.D.* (Presbyterian edition), *Church and Society, Coracle* (a

Scottish journal published by the Iona Community), *Journal of Presbyterian History, Presbyterian Life, Presbyterian Survey, Social Progress, City Church South,* and *The Church in Mission.*

d. Archives

Archives for the Presbyterian Church (U.S.A.) and predecessor denominations are located at the Presbyterian Historical Association and Archives in Philadelphia. Both Princeton Theological Seminary and Pittsburgh Theological Seminary have important collections. Some of the materials associated with PIIR are preserved among the Marshal Scott papers in the archives of McCormick Theological Seminary. A substantial amount of urban mission resources, mainly from an evangelical perspective, have been collected by the Orthodox Presbyterian Westminster Theological Seminary.

8. Roman Catholic Church

a. Monographs, Reports, and Essays

Following World War II, many Catholic leaders wrote about urban-oriented concerns, although the term "urban" was used less frequently than in Protestant circles. Catholics more often used the language of labor, ethnic, and pastoral issues. John Francis Cronin wrote *Catholic Social Action* (Bruce, 1948), *Catholic Social Principles* (Bruce, 1950), *The Church and Labor* (Sign, 1955), and *The Catholic as Citizen* (Helicon, 1963). Dorothy Day's leadership of the Catholic Worker Movement resulted in the publication of her largely autobiographical memoirs: *The House of Hospitality* (Sheed and Ward, 1939), *On Pilgrimage* (Catholic Worker Books, 1948), *The Long Loneliness* (Harper, 1952), and *Loaves and Fishes* (Harper, 1963). Francis J. Haas, longtime labor advocate, wrote *The Wages and Hours of American Labor* (Paulist, 1937) and *Jobs, Prices, and Unions* (Paulist, 1941). Joseph Fichter's controversial *Southern Parish: Dynamics of a City Church* (University of Chicago Press, 1951) applied sociology to the study of parish life in New Orleans, as did his *Social Relations in an Urban Parish* (University of Chicago, 1954). Joseph Schuyler reported similar sociological studies in *Northern Parish: A Sociological and Pastoral Study* (Loyola University Press, 1960). John La Farge articulated and defended the church's position on racial matters in *The Catholic Viewpoint on Race Relations* (Hanover House, 1956) and *An American Amen: A Statement of Hope* (Farrar, 1958), as well as in his earlier piece, *The Race Question and the Negro* (Longmans, Green, 1943).

In the 1960s, Geno Baroni began writing about the war on poverty, neighborhood development, and American ethnic groups — themes he would amplify in the 1970s. Andrew Greeley, prior to his fame as a novelist, produced *The Church in the Suburbs* (Sheed and Ward, 1959), one among several sociological studies. John J. Egan, who was instrumental in founding Catholic offices of urban affairs in many cities, defended the Alinsky approach in Chicago in various articles and reports; illustrations are: *Politics of Urban Renewal* (Archdiocese of Chicago, 1964) and *Citizen Participation and Neighborhood Renewal* (UPUSA, 1964). Egan's biographer is Margery Frisbie, *An Alley in Chicago: The Ministry of a City Priest* (Sheed and Ward, 1991). The history of the Archdiocese of Chicago's relationship with Alinsky is provided by P. David Fink in *The Radical Vision of Saul Alinsky* (Paulist, 1984); Fink also discusses Rochester's FIGHT organization there. Dennis Clark wrote about city planning and the "urban crisis" in *Cities in Crisis* (Sheed and Ward, 1960) and *The Ghetto Game* (Sheed and Ward, 1962). Rapid urban change is the subject of Robert Howes's *Crisis Downtown: A Church Eye-View of Urban Renewal* (NCC, 1959). See also by Howes, *Steeples in Metropolis* (Pflaum, 1969). At the decade's end, Daniel Berrigan began radical protest against the Vietnam War in such treatises as *They Call Us Dead Men* (Macmillan, 1968) and *The Trial of the Catonsville Nine* (Beacon, 1970). Silvano Tomasi launched a career of migration studies with *Migration in Light of Vatican II* (Center for Migration Studies, 1967).

For the 1970s, in addition to the citations noted in section IV above, see Joseph Fitzpatrick, *Puerto Rican Americans* (Prentice-Hall, 1971) and Philip Murnion, *Parish, Community, and Human Development* (Catholic Committee on Urban Ministry, 1979). CCUM was responsible for several important reports during this era. Pope Paul VI included three paragraphs about the city in the encyclical *Octogesima Adveniens* (1971).

Two major Roman Catholic documents were produced in the 1980s. The first, the encyclical of Pope John Paul II titled *Laborem Exercens* (1981), stimulated a great many interpretive discussions, such as Gregory Baum, *The Priority of Labor* (Paulist, 1982). See also by Baum, *Work and Religion* (Seabury, 1980). The second document is the National Council of Catholic Bishops' pastoral letter on the U.S. economy titled *Economic Justice for All* (1986), which generated lively debate and elicited antagonistic comments from some business leaders. A summary of the status of Catholic urban ministries at the decade's end is provided in Philip Murnion and Ann

Wentzel's *Crisis of the Church in the Inner City* (Pastoral Life Center, 1989) as the public press headlined troubles of inner-city Catholic churches; for example, Cardinal Szoka of Detroit closing thirty central-city churches. Angry debates about closing urban churches and parochial schools rapidly spread to other cities.

The tradition of papal encyclicals on social questions, started by Leo XIII's *Rerum Novarum* (1891), was continued by John Paul II's *Centesimus Annus* (1991). An overview of Catholic thought about economic matters is found in Michael Budde, *The Two Churches: Catholicism and Capitalism in the World System* (Duke University Press, 1992).

Frequent depiction in commercial motion pictures might warrant a dissertation titled "The Urban Catholic Church from Bing Crosby to Whoopi Goldberg." *The Bells of Saint Mary's* and *Sister Act* are but part of Hollywood's yield.

b. Pronouncements and Policies

In addition to the encyclicals and pastorals listed above, see also: Joseph Husslein, ed., *Social Wellsprings* (Bruce, 1940); Janelle Cahoon, *Tensions and Dilemmas Facing Organized Christianity in the Contemporary United States as Recognized in Official Church Statements* (diss., Fordham University, 1963); three pastorals of Richard Cardinal Cushing — "The Christian and Community," "The Church and Public Opinion," "The Servant Church" (Daughters of St. Paul, 1966); "Hear the Cry of Jerusalem: A National Pastoral Statement" (National Federation of Priests' Councils, 1978); "The Hispanic Presence, Challenge, and Commitment" and "National Pastoral Plan for Hispanic Ministry" (National Conference of Catholic Bishops, National Catholic Conference, 1984 and 1988, respectively). Many of the major documents are reproduced in David O'Brien and Thomas Shannon, eds., *Catholic Social Thought* (Orbis, 1992).

c. Periodicals

Catholic periodicals that feature articles on urban issues include: *City of God* (St. Maur, 1968-73, 1979-81); *America* (America Press, beginning in 1909, a Jesuit publication); *American Catholic Sociological Review; Catholic Charities Review; Catholic Historical Review; Commonweal; New Catholic World; New City — Man in Metropolis* (Catholic Council on Working Life, 1962-69); *Church* (National Pastoral Life Center, beginning in 1985); and *Records of the American Catholic Historical Society.*

d. Archives

Archives at the University of Notre Dame and the Catholic University of America have a considerable amount of urban ministry materials. Also, several diocesan seminaries have amassed materials for their respective archdioceses, among them St. Joseph's Seminary in New York City and St. Charles Borromeo in Philadelphia. St. Charles also houses the Archives of the American Catholic Historical Society.

9. United Church of Christ and Predecessor Denominations

a. Monographs, Reports, and Essays

Following World War II, leaders of both predecessor denominations — Congregational Christian and Evangelical and Reformed — were heavily involved with urban church concerns. Truman Douglass, head of the Board for Homeland Ministries, wrote *Mission to America* (Friendship, 1951) and *The New World of Urban Man* (with Konstantinos Doxiades; Oxford, 1965). His article, which appeared in *Harper's Magazine* with the title "The Job Protestants Shirk" (November 1958), accuses the church of anti-urban bias and attributes the urban failure of Protestantism to middle-class morality. Yoshio Fukuyama conducted inquiries into racial discrimination in churches: *Segregation and Inclusiveness of Protestant Churches in Metropolitan Chicago,* and *Church Housing Survey* (both Church Federation of Chicago, 1955), a thread of interest that ran throughout Fukuyama's career; see further his *The Ministry in Transition* (Pennsylvania State University, 1972). In 1956 and again in 1962 Fukuyama conducted studies of congregations aided by grants from the denomination's Board of Home Missions (both preserved in the H. Paul Douglass Collection). Joseph Merchant and Stanley North also conducted studies during this era that were aimed at influencing the denomination's urban church policy; see their *City Churches and the Cultural Crisis* (Board of Home Missions, 1958), and *The Inner-City Church* (UPUSA, 1959). John Shope produced similar studies for the Evangelical and Reformed Church. Liston Pope, editor of *Social Action,* included many urban-oriented articles in that journal. His influential books include *Millhands and Preachers* (Yale, 1942) and *The Kingdom beyond Caste* (Friendship, 1957). Ross Sanderson's writings, as noted above in section IV, were copious and largely ecumenical in orientation. Victor Obenhaus's *Ethics for an Industrial Age* (Harper and Row, 1965) deserves mention, as does his jointly authored volume with Widick Schroeder titled *Suburban Religion* (Center for the Scientific Study of Religion, 1974). Max Stackhouse's *The Ethics of Necropolis* (Beacon, 1971) uses urban imagery in his critique of the military-industrial complex. His interest in the moral aspects of urban life is continued in his *Ethics and the Urban Ethos: An Essay in Social Theory and Theological Reconstruction* (1972). Frederick Herzog's *Justice Church* (Orbis, 1980) provides theological underpinnings for the late-twentieth-century North American church from a liberation perspective.

UCC people among the founders of East Harlem Protestant Parish produced a large literature; for example, J. Archie Hargraves wrote *Stop Pussyfooting through a Revolution* (UCC, 1963), along with several articles; Donald Benedict's lifelong interest in community organization is recapitulated in *Born Again Radical* (Pilgrim, 1982); and some of the works of George W. Webber are noted above in section IV. Throughout the 1960s, UCC leaders were heavily involved in ecumenical endeavors and in the emerging action training programs for urban church lay leaders; see, for example, Ted Erickson's essay titled "Can the Church Be an Effective Resource for the Ministry of the Laity?" (Metropolitan Associates of Philadelphia [MAP], 1966). The MAP program is evaluated in Erickson's later paper titled "Cluster Development" (Board of Homeland Ministries, 1969). See above in the section on American Baptists for additional information on the ecumenically sponsored MAP program. A UCC denominational emphasis on city ministry produced a substantial amount of church-school curricular and discussion materials during the 1960s; examples include Florence Schultz, *Friends and Neighbors* (Pilgrim, 1962), two sound moving pictures titled *Leaven for the City* (produced by Robert F. Newman, Board for Homeland Ministries, UCC, 1963) and *City of Necessity* (same), and a series of theme-related articles in *Social Action*, the *United Church Herald*, and the *Church School Worker*, all UCC periodicals. The denomination's Urbanization Emphasis Committee produced a pamphlet titled "United Church of Christ Emphasis: The Church and Urbanization" (1963).

Chicago UCC leaders contributed greatly to the research on transitional churches in the 1970s. For example, William R. Voelkel edited *Churches-in-Transition National Consultation — Proceedings* (Community Renewal Society, 1977) and Walter Ziegenhals wrote *Urban Churches in Transition* (Pilgrim, 1978), along with several articles and progress reports on the Churches in Transition Project. Elsewhere in the denomination, Walter Brueggemann provided biblical and theological commentary on urban-related problems in such books as *The Land* (Fortress, 1977) and

Living toward a Vision (United Church Press, 1982). John DeBoer addressed urban church issues in *Discovering Our Mission* (UCC, 1969), *What American Churchmen Can Learn from the New Town Experience in England and Scotland* (UCC, 1974), *Are New Towns for Lower Income Americans, Too?* (with Alexander Greensdale; Praeger, 1974), and *Energy Conservation Manual for Congregations* (JSAC, NCC, 1980). A case study by Jeffrey Hadden and Charles Longino titled *Gideon's Gang* (Pilgrim, 1974) describes an experimental issue-centered UCC church. Gaylord Noyce offers a theology for suburban ministry in *The Responsible Suburban Church* (Westminster, 1970) and addresses questions about the nature of mission in *Survival and Mission for the City Church* (1975). Specific conflicts gave shape to UCC urban concerns; see, for example, Paul Sherry and Robert Strommen's article in *Christianity and Crisis* titled "The Textile Workers vs. J. P. Stevens" (April 4, 1977). In the late 1970s and throughout the 1980s Alfred Krass's writings for the periodical *The Other Side* address urban issues from a more evangelical approach than had been customary in UCC circles. See also his *Evangelizing Neo-Pagan North America* (Herald Press, 1982) and *Five Lanterns at Sundown: Evangelism in a Chastened Mood* (Eerdmans, 1978). A long list of various specialized ministries operating in UCC churches is given in David King's *No Church Is an Island* (Pilgrim, 1980), most of which are either urban or suburban. Geneva Butz's stories about her inner-city pastorate in Philadelphia have gained a following: *Color Me Yellow* (Pilgrim, 1986) and *Christmas Comes Alive* (1988). The emerging importance of urban ethnic churches is reflected in Edwin O. Ayala's *Evangelism and Church Development in UCC Hispanic Churches* (United Church Board for Homeland Ministries, 1991). Eleanor S. Meyers's edited volume *Envisioning the New City* (Westminster, 1992) provides a series of short articles on experimental ministries, several of which are UCC related; for instance, Valerie Russell's two contributions titled "A Lesson in Urban Spirituality" and "The Uprooted Poor: A Mandate for Mission."

b. Pronouncements and Policies

Resources for the study of UCC urban-related pronouncements and policies include: "Social Pronouncements of the Evangelical and Reformed Church, 1934-1947" (Commission on Christian Social Action, E and R Church, [1947?]); "United Church of Christ Emphasis: The Church and Urbanization" (Urbanization Emphasis Committee, UCC, [1963?]); "The Right to a Useful and Remunerative Job" (General Synod, UCC, 1976); and "UCC Covenants for Churches in Change" (*Christian Century* 94, November 16, 1977, p. 1055). The general synod passed resolutions titled "Toward a New Urban Agenda" (1977), "Report and Recommendations on the Urban Agenda" (1979), and "The Future of Urban Life in America" (1981). The latter called for yet another urban pronouncement, but general synod failed to produce such a document. Some interest in reviving the practice of the general synod making urban pronouncements was advanced in 1993.

c. Periodicals

Of the UCC periodicals with frequent urban-oriented articles, the longest running is *Social Action* (1934-72). It was continued following 1972 by the joint United Methodist–UCC publication titled *Engage/Social Action*. See also *A.D.* (UCC edition, 1971-81); *United Church Herald;* the particularly important *Renewal Magazine* (Community Renewal Society, 1960-71); the *Chicago Reporter* (beginning in 1972), a monthly information service on racial issues in metropolitan Chicago; *Urban Timepiece* (an occasional publication of the Board for Homeland Ministries [BHM] in the 1960s); *Journal of Current Social Issues* (also BHM, UCC, beginning in 1971); and *Strategies for City Churches* (an occasional newsletter produced by the Evangelical and Reformed Church in the 1950s).

d. Archives

Archives of the United Church of Christ are housed at Lancaster Theological Seminary, Lancaster, Pennsylvania, as are the archives for the Evangelical and Reformed Historical Society. Congregational materials are maintained in the Congregational Library, Boston. Some city societies, especially Chicago's Community Renewal Society, maintain collections of their own materials. Union Theological Seminary in New York City, Yale Divinity School, and Chicago Theological Seminary have many urban materials, particularly from Congregational sources, maintained as a part of their regular collections.

10. United Methodist Church and Predecessor Denominations

a. Monographs, Reports, and Essays

The Methodist literature on urban and industrial ministry is large, owing in part to the efforts of the Council of Cities, the Board of Missions, and the Methodist Federation for Social Action. Among materials produced in the early 1940s, see especially G. Bromley Oxnam's *The Ethics of Jesus in a Changing World* (Abingdon, 1941), *Labor and Tomorrow's World* (Abingdon, 1945), and *The Church and Contemporary Change* (Macmillan, 1950). See also Robert Miller's biography titled *Bishop G. Bromley Oxnam: Paladin of Liberal Protestantism* (Abingdon, 1990). Methodist interest in the welfare of laborers is also reflected by Charles C. Webber's *Industrial Conflicts* (National Council of Methodist Youth, 1937) and *Religion and Labor* (AF of L and CIO, [1950?]), as well as by the continuing essays of Harry F. Ward: *Democracy and Social Change* (Modern Age, 1940) and "Organized Religion, the State, and the Economic Order" (*Annals* 256, March 1948, pp. 72-83). Sermons published by Ralph Sockman in the 1940s and earlier reflect strong concern for city churches. Frederick Shippey began conducting urban church studies shortly after the end of World War II, a result of the denomination's growing awareness of the importance of postwar urban changes (see listing of Shippey's studies in *Cities and Churches*).

During the 1950s and continuing into the early 1960s several Methodist researchers produced empirically oriented urban church studies. See, for example, listings in *Cities and Churches* for Roy Sturm, Murray H. Leiffer, Earl D. C. Brewer, Robert McKibben, and, of course, Shippey. Walter G. Muelder and Harold DeWolf wrote theology relevant to urban issues. See especially Muelder's *Religion and Economic Responsibility* (Scribner, 1953), *The Foundations of Responsible Society* (Abingdon, 1959), and *Methodism and Society in the Twentieth Century* (Abingdon, 1960). DeWolf's article titled "A Theology for an Urban Church" (pp. 47-60 in Edwards and May, eds., *The Church in Urban America* [Methodist Service Center, 1966]) provides a helpful summary. Clair M. Cook wrote widely about Protestantism and the labor movement, although his writings are associated more often with the Religion and Labor Council of America than with Methodist structures. See, for example, his *The Modern Samaritan* (Board of Social and Economic Relations of the Methodist Church, 1956).

Empirical studies of urban churches and conditions continued well into the 1960s. To the list of those doing such studies in the 1950s must be added Robert Leroy Wilson, James Hill Davis, Douglas W. Johnson, and Lyle Schaller. See especially Davis's *The Outsider and the Urban Church* (Board of Missions, Methodist Church, 1962), *Changing Churches and Changing City* (1964), "Types of Community Organization" (1966), and "Toward a Racially Inclusive Methodist Church" (same). Conclusions from Wilson's many studies of city churches are summarized in his *Methodism in the Inner City* (Board of Missions, 1958), *Questions City Churches Must*

Answer (1962), and *The Church in the Racially Changing Community* (with Davis; Abingdon, 1966). See also Wilson's "Issues Related to the Churches' Involvement in Community Organization" (Board of Missions, 1965) for comment on the Alinsky movement. Philip C. Edwards, often in collaboration with Ernest V. May, wrote and edited program pamphlets during the 1960s for Methodist urban churches, all published by the denomination's Board of Missions: *Financing the Urban Church* (1961?), *The Minister and the Urban Church* (1958), *Echoes and Challenges* (1962), and *The Church in Urban America* (1966). Clifford C. Ham's writings focused on the church's response to urban planning and redevelopment, as did those of Stanley J. Hallett, the latter mainly in Chicago. Robert Raines and James Armstrong represent pastors of large Methodist churches who wrote on urban crisis issues. Cecil Pottieger, of the Evangelical United Brethren Church, specialized in apartment house ministries. Lyle Schaller's *Planning for Protestantism in Urban America* (Abingdon, 1965) is illustrative of his long series of advice-giving books for clergy. Colin Williams (see above, section VI) articulated theology for the Missionary Structure of the Congregation Study, an inquiry sponsored by the World Council of Churches in which Methodists were heavily involved. J. Edward Carothers's *Keepers of the Poor* (Board of Missions of the Methodist Church, 1966) and *The Church and Cruelty Systems* (Friendship Press, 1970) alerted the church to increasing urban social injustice. A study coordinated by Harold Garman and titled *Church in Metropolis: Emerging Strategies for Mission* (General Board of Education, UMC, 1968) emphasizes Methodist participation in ecumenical inner-city parishes, describes judicatory structures for city ministries, and encourages citywide strategies.

Ernest V. May's edited volume, *The Church in Transitional Communities* (Board of Global Ministries, 1972), sounded the familiar theme for the 1970s when Methodists, as well as most other denominations, were particularly concerned about the changing ethnic composition of urban neighborhoods and church membership. See also regarding this theme: James H. Davis and Woody W. White, *Racial Transition and the Church* (Abingdon, 1980). Social change, similarly, is a recurrent motif in the 1970-79 writings of Jackson Carroll, Philip Amerson, Stanley J. Hallett, Ezra Earl Jones, Kinmoth Jefferson, Douglass Johnson, Theodore McEachern, Eli Rivera, and Robert L. Wilson, Ellen Clark, Helen Kromer, Connie Meyer, Elaine Magalis, and Tracy Early (the latter five writing for the *New World Outlook*, a Methodist mission periodical). See listings of articles and reports produced by these authors in *Cities and Churches*. The Office of Urban Ministries, under the leadership of Negail Riley and, later, Kinmoth Jefferson, produced many resources for churches in transitional communities. Among urban pastors who contributed to the 1970s and 1980s urban church literature is Cecil Williams, who served at San Francisco's Glide Memorial Church. His *No Hiding Place* (Harper, 1992) recounts that congregation's extensive ministry to addicted people. Neal Fisher offers an alternative to secularism in the city with his *Theological Reflections: The Basis of Hope for Urban Ministries* (with Norman Faramelli; Board of Global Ministries, UMC, 1974). See also Fisher, *Trends and Issues for Metropolitan Ministry* (Northeast Jurisdiction, UMC, 1975), for a discussion of the church's responsibility to the poor.

Two non–North American Methodist authors writing during this time are important to note. John Vincent, who eventually became president of the Methodist Church in England, wrote radical Methodist theology for urban life; see his *The Secular Christ* (Abingdon, 1968), *Alternative Church* (Christian Journals, 1976), *Stirrings: Essays Christian and Radical* (Epworth, 1976), *Starting All Over Again: Hints of Jesus in the City* (World Council of Churches, 1981), and *Into the City* (Epworth, 1982). José Míguez Bonino began a series of important writings about social conditions in Latin America.

In the 1980s, United Methodist attention shifted markedly toward ethnic minority churches in urban areas. This direction became increasingly obvious, not only in publications produced by official United Methodist agencies and judicatories, but also in the writings of United Methodist authors generally. It is especially apparent in the doctor of ministry dissertations produced by United Methodists and others at United Methodist theological seminaries. Representative examples include: Ulisese E. Sala, "A Theology of Samoan Christian Immigrants in the United States" (Claremont, 1980); Amos Ree, "Stabilizing and Vitalizing the Church Membership of Central Korean Church" (Drew, 1981); Dewitt McIntyre, "A Program for Revitalizing an Urban Black Church Sunday School . . ." (Drew, 1981); Suk-Chong Yu, "An Inclusive Church: Korean Ministry . . ." (Claremont, 1983); Won Kie Kim, "Evangelization of the Korean Immigrants . . ." (Perkins, 1983); George Schreckengost, "The Effect of Latent Racial, Ethnic, and Sexual Biases on Open Itineracy . . ." (Lancaster Theological Seminary, 1984).

Descriptive of urban church conditions in the 1980s are: Philip Amerson, *Tell Me City Stories* (SCUPE, 1988); William Ramsden, *The Church in a Changing Society* (Abingdon, 1980); Tex Sample, *Blue-Collar Ministry* (Judson, 1984); and Harold Recinos, *Hear the Cry* (cited above) and his more recent *Jesus Weeps* (Abingdon, 1992). Also notable are Arthur Gafke and Bruce McSpadden's unpublished manuscript titled "Pastor-as-Organizer" (various editions, 1989) and John W. Edgar's volume titled *Reconnecting the Urban Neighborhood Church* (Columbus United Methodist Office of Urban Ministry, 1990). Howard Snyder offered Wesleyan theology as a resource for urban church issues: *The Radical Wesley and Patterns of Church Renewal* (InterVarsity, 1980) and *Liberating the Church* (InterVarsity, 1983). Several United Methodist pastors published regarding urban issues and problems, including Ted Loder, *No One but Us: Personal Reflections on Public Sanctuary* (Lura Media, 1986), and Gilbert Rendle, "Third Class Ministry: Urban Ministry in the Smaller City," *Quarterly Review* (with Frank Sanders; vol. 7, Summer 1987, pp. 24-37). By the end of the decade, United Methodist leadership was becoming increasingly aware of the need for dramatic new strategies for ministry in cities. See, for example, Lori Miller, "Methodist Bishop Confronts Drug Abuse" (*Washington Post,* June 2, 1990, p. B2), regarding the ministry of Bishop Felton May, and *The Burning Heart: Vision for Asian American Missional Congregations* (General Board of Global Ministries, 1990). Ignacio Castuera's *Dreams of Fire, Embers of Hope* (Chalice, 1992) reproduces sermons preached on the Sunday following the 1992 Los Angeles riots. Robert H. Terry has written a history of a Methodist City Mission in Harrisburg, Pennsylvania, titled *Neighborhood Center: An Urban Love Story* (Mennonite Publishing House, 1992).

b. Pronouncements and Policies

The Journal of the First General Conference of the Methodist Church (Ludwell Estes, ed., Methodist Publishing House, 1940) lists the denomination's urban policy and describes the organizational structures provided for implementing it in the newly reunited denomination. Additional information about social policy may be found in "Methodists Speak on Christian Social Concerns" (General Board of Christian Social Concern, 1964); James R. Wood and Mayer Zald, "Aspects of Racial Integration in the Methodist Church: Sources of Resistance to Organized Policy" (*Social Forces* 45, December 1966, pp. 255-56); "Statements, '69" (*Engage* 2, December 1, 1969, insert); Allen Brockway, "Statements on Social Principles" (*Engage* 2, September 1, 1970, pp. 5-39); "Statement of Investment Policy" (General Council on Finance and Administration, 1978); Jan Kindwoman and Ron Ozier, eds., *Journey toward Justice: Commemorating the 80th Anniversary of the Social Creed of the People Called the Methodists* (Methodist Federation for Social Action, 1978); *Source Book: United Methodist Urban Ministries Strategies* (Board of Global Ministries, UMC, 1979); "Developing and

Strengthening the Ethnic Minority Local Church" (Interagency Coordinating Committee, UMC, [1981?]). The United Methodist *Discipline,* published quadrennially, carries the social statements and describes denominational organization related, inter alia, to urban concerns.

c. Periodicals

Urban ministry–related articles appear frequently in the following United Methodist publications: *Engage* and its successor, *Engage/Social Action; Methodist History; Motive; World Outlook* and its successor, *New World Outlook; Together; Behold;* and the *MultiEthnic Center for Ministry News.*

d. Archives

United Methodist Archives are located at Drew University, although the Board of Global Ministries, which manages most of the denomination's urban ministry programs, has not placed many of its materials in that collection. Much of the material in the United Methodist Archives remains uncatalogued and is, as a result, inaccessible. Seminary libraries with notable collections include Wesley in Washington, D.C., United in Dayton, Ohio, and Candler School of Theology in Atlanta.

IX. Conclusion

The purpose of this essay has been to summarize urban church literature produced by mainline denominations in the United States since World War II. A preliminary periodization can be conjectured for this literature, with discernible stages in the evolution of religious leaders' thinking about cities and in the strategies they chose to follow. A caution to the conjecture, echoed from the first lines of this essay, bears repeating. The urban ministry literatures discussed herein are by no means exhaustive. A great many related literatures are touched here, if at all, only in passing — among them secularization, smaller Protestant denominations' urban programs, evangelical Protestant materials, Pentecostal church materials, urban church fiction and poetry, urban church art and architecture, laws and court cases, sect and cult literatures, liturgical materials invented for urban church use, academic literatures about the religious aspects of cities, Judaism and the city, Islam and the city, urban church materials dealing with Europe (also Asia, Africa, and Latin America), as well as the several hidden literatures of poor churches and ethnic religious bodies. Moreover, this essay does not deal extensively with the sector approach to urban ministry, that is, those efforts started or inspired by church leadership that rapidly became secularized in their sponsorship and direction. The following generalizations about periods of development in religious thought about cities do not apply to these other bodies of materials, therefore, but only to the corpus considered in this essay. The complete picture of religion's encounter with the city, if it is ever adequately portrayed, will consist of multiple histories in support of varied dreams, not a unified history with a compelling, integrated vision.

Notwithstanding these exceptions and limits, however, a series of four major turning points demarcating five distinct periods can be posited for the principal program thrust of mainline American urban churches. Before World War II, the main concern of church urbanologists was to extend the church and its cause throughout the city. "Into the city and up with the buildings" was the main strategy. Church architecture especially reflected the desire to make a statement in and to the city — the church intended to be significant among urban institutions. Although some cooperative endeavors were undertaken among denominations, such as comity agreements, most of the church extension energy was generated inside denominational bounds. The war proved to be the first turning point. Concern about suburban growth emerged. Many judicatories and local churches actually sold their city properties to finance suburban construction. "Follow the suburban American dream," the churches seemed to be saying. Planning, based on sociological paradigms and demographic data, was touted as the solution to pressing urban problems, including those of the urban church. Integration would, eventually, hopefully, eradicate segregation and racial prejudice in churches and cities. Comity agreements became highly influential in shaping church extension, with denominations agreeing with each other not to compete in new suburban communities. Urban church research drew heavily on demography and sociology, following the lead of H. Paul Douglass, and sought to provide survey data on which church planning could be based.

By the end of the 1950s, and ever more strongly throughout the 1960s, the suburban strategy was called into question, producing a second turning point. The city crisis became the city church crisis, and the literature was suffused with radical innovations and new models for the church. Many church leaders who wanted to address urban problems departed the church for secular agencies, which appeared to be doing more than the church to ameliorate crying city needs. Some church leaders openly questioned the

360

relevance of traditional local congregations. "Mere survival is not enough," the literature proclaimed, mainly to the white churches. "Renew the church for the sake of social relevance, or die." Some local churches did die, but most of them survived the 1960s, albeit with reduced numbers of members. This decade of feverish urgency saw many "new forms" of the church emerge, often under ecumenical sponsorship. Denominational urban ministry staffs grew to their largest size for any period following World War II, a contributing factor to the bulk of literature generated during the 1960s. Sociological paradigms informed church leaders' views of the city, the most important variable of which was "residence" and attendant social justice issues such as open housing, school desegregation, and "white flight" to suburbs. A new approach to urban church research, focused mainly on describing and evaluating "new forms" for mission and ministry, gradually replaced the earlier emphasis on demography and survey data.

In the 1970s, transition in racial and ethnic composition of urban communities and churches became a major theme — a third turning point. Integration was seen as a failed strategy, first by African Americans and then increasingly by leaders of white denominations. If integration was not going to work, denominations would need to help, cajole, or force white enclave congregations into entirely new memberships drawn from the urban ethnic groups. Ethnic pluralism remained the ideal for membership composition, but a new ethnically homogeneous membership was more often the reality. Many studies of transitional congregations were conducted, and several patterns emerged, such as multiple ethnic congregations in the same church building, and rental of church facilities to new ethnic groups. Innovations promoted in the 1960s — coffeehouses, action training programs, industrial missions, apartment ministries, secular ministries — fell on hard times; most dropped from sight. Fewer ecumenical projects were undertaken, and funds expended for new church construction reached a low in 1975 (*Current Constructions Reports*, C-30-8912, December 1989, U.S. Department of Commerce, Bureau of Census). Church leaders' heavy dependence on sociological paradigms was in part supplanted with greater attention to economic systems, corporate responsibility, and economic justice. Urban church research sought to identify survival strategies for churches in ethnically transitional communities.

By the mid-1980s, yet a fourth turning point became apparent — an ethnic urban ministry literature that not only deals with current issues but also traces the history of urban ethnic religious groups. The urban church literature of the 1970s and early 1980s was still written largely by whites about the problems of largely white churches in cities. Local leaders in white city churches struggled for their institutions' survival, and many questioned the relevance of costly denominational programs and offices, a development requiring restructuring of several denominations as funds dwindled drastically. As the 1960s had threatened local churches' existence, the 1980s threatened denominational staffs. Although economic justice issues emerged as a central concern of denominational leaders, decimated staff size and program budgets meant that only minimal influence could be exerted to implement denominational policies related to these issues. Urban ministry staffs numbered their lowest since World War II; most mainline denominations closed their city church departments altogether. In their place remained a loosely connected network of individuals and groups committed to urban church issues. While the total amount of urban church literature written during the 1980s was not smaller than in previous decades, it was more often produced by this network of individuals who had personal interest in the topic than by denominational urban church officers doing denominationally sponsored research.

As the 1980s progressed, the voices of ethnic minority church leaders and scholars were heard more strongly. They produced a new urban ministry literature, became the most recent innovative edge for urban churches, and represented the best hope for mainline denominations' future in cities. Their writing reflects the vigor of fresh, firsthand encounters with city life and teems with prophetic insights. One of the foci of urban church research in the 1980s was the recovery and appreciation of the earlier history of the urban ethnic congregations. There is, moreover, among them a resurgence of interest in church-based community organization, especially in urban areas where all other social institutions have fled or failed. Simultaneously, evangelical Protestants produced an ever increasing proportion of the city church literature, written principally from a missionary perspective, including demographic literature in support of urban evangelistic ministries and church growth.

Change has been the constant diet of urban churches since World War II, and church literature produced during these years reflects those changes — from booming, exclusively white churches dominating central cities, to suburban expansion with central city churches declining, to experimental "new forms" for racially integrating urban churches, to strategies for making transition from white to ethnically varied churches to diverse, rapidly growing ethnic congregations. H. Paul Douglass's early-twentieth-century observations about urbanization and religion anticipated these sorts of changes. "So far as the city is adversary," he wrote seventy years ago, "it is one with whom to agree quickly before the ultimate penalty is exacted. So far as the city is friend, no more dependable one exists with respect to the upbuilding of the church" (*The City's Church* [Friendship Press, 1927], p. x). Perhaps better than any other social institution, churches have adapted to urban changes and survived where others have failed. The urban church has become in many ways the city's institution of last resort. Literature produced over the past fifty years, summarized in this chapter, has borne out Douglass's expectations about the churches' remarkable persistence notwithstanding changing fortunes and great costs. In the same volume, he describes the mechanism that allows churches to survive rapid urban changes when others cannot: "The continuous re-creation of the church on varying levels, and especially out of the lowlier substratum of incoming immigrant population of all sorts, is tremendously impressive evidence of the power of religious tradition and its ability to re-root itself in the city. The ecclesiastical propagation of the church is able and admirable, but not so wonderful as this. Religious faith is a marvelously persistent thing, and urban change, though modifying it, shows no real signs of destroying it" (pp. 52-53).

Contributors

NORMAN FARAMELLI   Norman Faramelli works as Director of Transportation and Environmental Planning at MassPort Authority and is a member of the Episcopal City Mission executive committee. An Episcopal priest, he serves as consultant to the Episcopal Diocese of Massachusetts, and has served as interim pastor in various urban and suburban congregations in the Boston area. He currently serves on the Economic Justice Implementation committee of the Episcopal Church.

ROBERT MICHAEL FRANKLIN   Robert Michael Franklin is a Program Officer in the Rights and Social Justice department of the Ford Foundation. He previously served as Associate Professor of Ethics and Society, and Director of the Program of Black Church Studies, at the Candler School of Theology, Emory University, Atlanta, Georgia. He is author of "Church and City: Black Christianity's Ministry," in the *Christian Ministry* (March 1989) and *Liberating Visions: Human Fulfillment and Social Justice in African American Thought* (Minneapolis: Augsburg Fortress Press, 1990). From 1981 to 1983, Dr. Franklin served as a hospital chaplain in an inner-city emergency room (St. Bernard Hospital, Chicago), and has been active in small-group ministry with unchurched African American men.

CLIFFORD GREEN   Clifford Green is Professor of Theology at Hartford Seminary, Hartford, Connecticut. Educated in Australia and Europe, and at Union Theological Seminary, New York, he previously taught at Wellesley College and Goucher College. His work on urban ministry, and the church and poverty, is a practical expression of research and publications on Bonhoeffer and Barth. He also serves as Executive Director of the Dietrich Bonhoeffer Works Translation Project.

LOYDE H. HARTLEY   Loyde H. Hartley is Professor of Religion and Society at Lancaster Theological Seminary. Formerly pastor of inner-city churches in Detroit and Dayton, he is author of urban church study reports and of the three-volume urban ministry bibliography *Cities and Churches* (Scarecrow Press, 1992).

KINMOTH W. JEFFERSON   As a seminary student at Drew Theological School, Kim Jefferson began work in urban ministry in Newark, New Jersey, in 1959. During 1962-63 he was a Ford Foundation Fellow at the Rutgers Urban Study Center. Ordained in the United Methodist Church in 1963, he continued to work in urban ministry in Greater Newark until 1968, when he served as a Field Representative in the Office of Urban Ministries; in 1975 he became Executive Director of the Office of Urban Ministries of the National Division of the United Methodist Church, a position he held until 1992. He coauthored publications on metropolitan ministry, cooperative parish ministry, congregational transformation, and strengthening small membership churches. An active leader in national ecumenical bodies, he was a founder of the Interfaith Center on Corporate Responsibility and was active in other organizations relevant to urban ministry including National Interfaith IMPACT for Justice and Peace and the Religious Task Force of the Federation for Industrial Retention and Renewal.

RICHARD LUECKE   Richard Luecke was Director of Studies for the Urban Training Center in Chicago from its formation in 1963, after pastorates in Chicago and Princeton, New Jersey. During the urban training period he also taught at Yale Divinity School and helped develop the Urban Ministry Project in Oxford and London, England. He subsequently taught philosophy at Valparaiso University and served as director of studies for the Community Renewal Society, conducting programs on work, health, and the constitution of cities, and communicating with broader constituencies through *TheCityThatWorks* newsletter. UTC preaching was illustrated in his *Violent Sleep* (Fortress, 1969), and UTC methods were described in his *Perchings* (UTC/Fortress, 1972).

FREDERICK J. PERELLA JR.   Frederick J. Perella Jr. worked for nineteen years in urban ministry. He was Assistant Education Coordinator of the U.S. Catholic Conference's Campaign for Human Development from

1971 to 1976; and served as Executive Director of the Office of Urban Affairs, Archdiocese of Hartford, from 1976 until 1990. He is currently the Assistant to the President of the Raskob Foundation for Catholic Activities in Wilmington, Delaware. Mr. Perella has been a Board Member of the Roundtable, the association of Catholic Diocesan Directors of Social Action, of Catholic Charities U.S.A., and the American Sociological Association. He has published articles on social ministry in the *Living Light, New Catholic World,* and *New Catholic Encyclopedia.* He has authored or edited several books for the U.S. Catholic Conference and Paulist Press on the subjects of poverty, social justice, and justice education. He has taught at the Catholic Committee on Urban Ministry Summer Institute, University of Notre Dame, at Washington Theological Union, and numerous conferences.

WILLIAM RAMSDEN   After more than thirty years' involvement with urban ministry, Bill Ramsden is now Executive Director of Religious Opportunities Institute — a research and development effort for leadership productivity in churches. Working in cooperation with the Office of Urban Ministry of the United Methodist Board of Global Ministries, he has produced several reviews of urban ministries. *Inner Vitality, Outward Vigor* contained studies of missionally effective urban parishes. *Metro: Channel for Urban Ministry* and *Metropolitan Mission Agencies* reviewed that major emphasis in United Methodism. Studies of special dimensions of urban ministry included *Urban Cooperative Parishes,* the urban church profiles for *New Visions for Small-Membership Churches,* and contributions on church-based community organizing for *Biblical Justice and Community Integrity* (the last published by ICUIS, the others by the National Program Division of the United Methodist Board of Global Ministries).

EDWARD RODMAN   Edward Rodman is the Canon Missioner of the Episcopal Diocese of Massachusetts, who has also served as a consultant to the Urban Bishops Coalition, the Episcopal Urban Caucus, and the Union of Black Episcopalians. He is also convener of the Black Leaders and Diocesan Executives component of the Episcopal Commission for Black Ministries.

ANNE P. SCHEIBNER   Anne P. Scheibner was a founding lay board member of the Episcopal Urban Caucus in 1980 and was staff to the Urban Bishops Coalition hearings in Newark, Seattle, and Washington, D.C. She currently serves on the Economic Justice Implementation Committee of the Episcopal Church. She also served as staff to ecumenical efforts on plant closings and economic dislocation through the National Council of Churches and the Interreligious Economic Crisis Organizing Network.

LUTHER E. SMITH   Luther E. Smith Jr., Ph.D., is Associate Professor of Church and Community at Candler School of Theology, Emory University. He was an organizer for the East Saint Louis Welfare Rights Organization, the organizer and Executive Coordinator of the St. Louis Metropolitan Ministerial Alliance, and the Executive Coordinator of Eden Theological Seminary's Education for Black Urban Ministries Program. In Atlanta he continues to serve on many boards that direct the urban work of church and social agencies. He is the author of *Howard Thurman: The Mystic as Prophet,* editor of the *Pan-Methodist Social Witness Resource Book,* and has written numerous articles on the black church, church and community issues, and the relationship of Christian spirituality to prophetic witness.

DONALD R. STEINLE   Donald R. Steinle is Executive Director of the Christian Activities Council, a social service organization sponsored by thirty-four congregations of the United Church of Christ in the Hartford area. An ordained UCC minister, he received his undergraduate education at Northwestern University and did his graduate work at Yale University Divinity School, where he also served on the faculty. From 1970 to 1981 he was pastor of an urban congregation in Passaic, New Jersey, where he also founded and directed a nationally recognized community organization, Neighborhood Resources, Passaic.

GEORGE E. TODD   George E. Todd headed the Urban Ministry office for the United Presbyterian Church U.S.A. (1963-73) and the World Council of Churches' Urban-Industrial Mission office (1973-82). He was a member of the Group Ministry, East Harlem Protestant Parish (1951-59). He taught urban ministry courses at Pittsburgh Seminary; Union Theological Seminary, New York; and Tainan Theological College, Taiwan; and he lectured on urban ministry at many schools and conferences. He was an active participant in the founding of the Interfaith Center for Corporate Responsibility, the Interreligious Foundation for Community Organizing, and the Asian Committee for People's Organizations. He served for a number of years on the boards of the Chicago Urban Training Center and of the journal *Christianity and Crisis.* He was also director of the Wieboldt Foundation (1981-85), making grants to programs responding to urban need, and was Executive Presbyter for the Presbytery of New York City (1986-90).

CONTRIBUTORS

JAMES MELVIN WASHINGTON   James Washington is Professor of Church History, Union Theological Seminary, New York. Among his many publications on African American Christianity are: *Frustrated Fellowship: The Black Baptist Quest for Social Power* (Mercer, 1986); *Conversations with God. Two Centuries of Prayers by African Americans* (HarperCollins, 1994); *A Testament of Hope: The Essential Writings of Martin Luther King, Jr.* (Harper and Row, 1986); and *I Have a Dream: Writings and Speeches That Changed the World* (HarperSanFrancisco, 1992).

GEORGE D. YOUNGER   George D. Younger, retired executive minister, American Baptist Churches of New Jersey, served his full ministerial career in urban ministry as local pastor, denominational staff member, and director of urban training programs. He is the author of *The Bible Calls for Action* (Judson Press, 1958), *The Church and Urban Power Structure* (Westminster, 1962), *The Church and Urban Renewal* (Lippincott, 1965), and *From New Creation to Urban Crisis* (Center for the Scientific Study of Religion, 1987).

Index

Abernathy, Ralph, 43, 271, 273
Abyssinian Baptist Church, 78
Action Training Coalition, 248, 250
Adair, Eugene, 154
Adair, Thelma, 154
African American Baptist clergy, 258-79
Ahlstrom, Sydney, 7, 262
Ahmann, Mathew, 189
Alban Institute, 161
Alinsky, Saul, 20, 127, 129, 165-66, 191,
    192, 286
Allen, J. Claude, 56
Allen, Richard, 101
Allen Temple Baptist Church, 40
Allin, John, 109, 110, 112
American Baptist Churches, 23-51
American Baptist Women, 45
Anderson, Jesse Sr., 104
Apolinaris, Yamina, 35, 42, 46
Appalachian People's Service Organiza-
    tion, 115
Arnett, Benjamin W., 263
Asian Americans, 44, 101, 102, 118,
    119, 145n.33, 159, 175, 177, 178, 211,
    254
Assembly of God, 83
Asylum Hill Organizing Project,
    138n.24
Atlanta, GA, 60, 161, 175, 271

Augsburg Confession, 124
Augusta, GA, 69
Austin, Junius C., 265

Baker, Ella, 259n.3
Baltimore, 101, 126, 131, 193, 194, 199
Barndt, Joseph, 144
Baroni, Geno, 12, 186, 198, 200-202
Barrows, Willie, 273
Barth, Karl, 156, 284n.6
Bartley, Richard, 130
Batchelder, Robert, 172
Batten, Samuel Zane, 23
Becker, Donald, 142
Beck, Natlia, 112
Bellah, Robert, 285n.7
Benedict, Donald, 42, 126, 215, 216,
    222, 225, 226
Berdyaev, Nicholas, 156
Bergh, Alvin, 142
Berkeley, CA, 61
Bernhard, Leopold, 130
Bethel Chapel African Methodist Epis-
    copal Church, 78, 101
Bethel New Life, Inc., 132, 285-86, 289
Bethune, Mary McCleod, 267
Bird, Van Samuel, 104
Birmingham, AL, 60
Black American Baptists, 43

INDEX

Black capitalism, 274
Black Catholic Congress, 199
Black, Don, 172
Black Manifesto, 107, 108
Black Panther Party, 40, 61
Black Power movement, 15, 62-67, 268, 276
Bonhoeffer, Dietrich, 156, 284
Bonner, J. W., 60
Boston, 43, 102, 104, 105, 172, 188, 193, 199, 216
Broholm, Richard, 31, 33
Bronx, the, 137, 144
Brooklyn Ecumenical Council, 167
Brooklyn, NY, 81, 133, 188, 259, 263
Brooks, William H., 265
Brown, Charles, 250
Browne, William W., 264
Buffalo, 216, 224, 227
BUILD (Baltimore), 210
Bunche, Ralph, 258, 260
Bunton, Henry C., 60
Burgess, Bishop, 108, 113
Burns, Charles, 198
Burroughs, Nannie Helen, 258, 259

Campaign for Human Development, 188, 194, 196, 202-4, 209, 289
Cardijn, Joseph, 184, 191
Carmines, Al, 38-39
Carothers, Ed, 248
Carter administration, 177, 201
Carter, Jimmy, 132
Carter, Marmaduke, 139, 141
Carter, Rosalynn, 132
Carver, George Washington, 86
Cary, Archibald Jr., 272
Cary, Archibald J. Sr., 272
Castle, Robert, 104
Catholic Charities, 204-6, 209
Catholic Committee on Urban Ministry (CCUM), 193
Catholic Worker, 182, 209
Caution, Tillie, 103, 108
Chandler, Edgar, 193
Chavez, Cesar, 173
Chicago, 7, 29, 37, 60, 69, 77, 81, 91-92,

102, 126, 139, 140, 141, 142, 146, 147, 152, 164, 165, 167, 168, 172, 176, 177, 183, 185, 191, 199, 216, 220, 224, 227, 245, 252, 259, 265, 275, 272, 273, 304
Chrisman, Jesse, 171
Christian Activities Council, 217-20, 299
Christian Methodist Episcopal Church, 52-76, 278
Christiansen, Jim, 171
Christison, James A., 33-35
Church and City Conference, 104, 110, 114, 115
Church and industry, 244
Church-based neighborhood renewal, 285-86
Church extension and growth, 9, 24, 26, 28, 34, 35, 44, 46, 213, 214, 222, 235, 236, 237, 240, 241, 246
Churchill, Winston, 11
Church in Metropolis, 105, 163, 292
Church of God in Christ, 77-96, 279
Church of the Savior, 286
Church planning, 21, 154
Cicero, IL, 172, 275
Cincinnati, 172, 199
City missionary societies, 216-20
Civil Rights Act (1964), 106
Civil rights movement, 13, 42, 60, 90, 91-92, 98, 103, 106, 133, 142, 185, 246, 272, 275, 292
Claude, Judy, 35
Clemmons, Ithiel, 84
Clergy and Laity Concerned about Vietnam, 133
Cleveland, 37, 42, 63, 145, 161, 167, 177, 193, 207, 216, 224, 227
Coalition for Human Needs, 109, 115, 120
Cober, William K., 35
Cochrane, John, 135
Coffey, Lillian Brooks, 81
Cold War, 11
Coleman, C. D., 67
Coleman, John, 248
Coles, Joseph C., 71

370

Colored Methodist Episcopal Church, 240
Columbia, MD, 170
Columbus, OH, 130
Communities Organized for Public Service (COPS), 131, 166, 194
Community organizing, 20-21, 126, 129-31, 138, 160, 162, 164-67, 177, 191-95, 203, 209, 221, 224, 226-27, 228, 247, 254, 286-88
Community Renewal Society, 222
Confessing Church, 125
Congregations, 56, 114, 116, 162, 176, 231, 235, 252, 290
Congress of National Black Churches, 70, 76
Congress on Racial Equality, 13, 262
Cortes, Ernesto, 131
Council on Christian Social Progress, 24
Cox, Harvey G., 31, 49, 103
Cropper, W. V., 241
Crouch, Samuel, 81
Curran, Charles, 182

Dallas, 58
Daniels, David D., 84, 87n.19, 89
Davis, Allison, 260
Davis, A. R., 56
Day, Dorothy, 182
Dayton, 63, 193
de Dietrich, Suzanne, 157
de Foucald, Charles, 133n.17
de Hueck, Catherine, 182
Delk, Yvonne, 234
Denominational Ministry Strategy, 138n.24
Denominations, 3, 162, 298-301
Denver, 143, 145
de Priest, Oscar, 272
Detroit, 56, 57, 77, 81, 143, 144, 164, 167, 172, 177, 190, 193, 201, 224, 227, 229, 272
Detroit Industrial Mission, 157, 158, 171, 229
Dougherty, Cardinal, 183
Douglas, H. Paul, 125, 241
Douglas, Jesse L., 60

Douglass, Frederick, 264
Douglass, Truman, 216, 222
Drake, St. Clair, 260
Driver, E. M., 81
Du Bois, W. E. B., 89n.21, 264
Dudley, Carl, 176

East Brooklyn Churches, 166, 210, 287
East Brooklyn Clergy, 133
East Harlem Protestant Parish, 19, 133, 157, 158, 215, 224, 226, 228, 245, 247
East St. Louis, IL, 62
Ecclesial forms, 231, 236, 257, 249, 285, 290-305
Ecclesiology, 252
Economic boycotts, 263, 268
Economic development, 195, 201, 259
Ecumenism, 3, 17, 84, 120, 122, 133, 153, 162-63, 176, 185, 186, 194, 215, 223, 225, 228, 229, 235, 248, 254
Ecumenism, Decree on (Second Vatican Council), 191
Egan, John, 184, 187, 191, 192
Eisenhower, Dwight D., 60
Ellul, Jacques, 156, 214
Ellwanger, Joe, 144
Episcopal Church, 31, 97-122
Episcopal Church Women, 105
Episcopal Urban Caucus, 112, 114, 115
Erikson, Ted, 228
Ethnic caucuses, 159
Ethnic churches, 152, 236
Ethnic consciousness, 44
Ethnic Minority Local Church, 252
Eucharist, 87, 134, 142, 184-85, 285
Evangelical Academies, 157
Evangelical Lutheran Church in America, 18, 123-50
Evangelical United Brethren Church, 235n.1, 245
Evangelism, 30, 35, 46, 211, 287
Evjen, John Olaf, 127
Experimental communities, 157

Fair Employment Practices Act, 53, 56
Faniel, Leon, 154
Faramelli, Norman, 172

Finks, David, 198
Fish, John, 165
Flood, Pat, 131
Ford, Louis Henry, 79, 81, 90, 91-94
Forman, Jim, 107
Fortune, T. Thomas, 264
Foster, Harold, 131
Franklin, Robert, 282
Frazier, E. Franklin, 260
Frenchak, David, 288
Frerichs, Robert T., 29
Friendship House, 209
Fry, John, 142

Gallaudet, Thomas Hopkins, 217
Garnet, Henry Highland, 263
Garvey, Marcus, 266
Gary, IN, 56, 167, 201, 227
General Convention Special Program, 106, 120
George, Bryant, 154
Gilmore, Marshall, 63, 64
Glock, Charles Y., 126n.5
Gollwitzer, Helmut, 156, 157
Goodman, Grace Ann, 162, 300
Gorbachev, Mikhail, 11
Gossner Mission, 157
Graham, W. F., 264
Grand Rapids, MI, 227
Great Migration, 6, 54, 77, 81, 99, 101, 153, 183, 241, 259
Griffin, William, 141
Grimke, Archibald, 264
Groppi, James, 186
Gutiérrez, Gustavo, 150

Habitat for Humanity, 132
Hager, John, 248
Hallett, Stanley, 170
Hamilton, Calvin, 293
Handy, Robert, 16-17
Haney, Oliver, 90
Harding, Vincent, 296, 298
Hargleroad, Bobbie Wells, 153
Hargraves, Archie, 215, 225, 226
Harlan, Louis, 264
Harlem, 71, 78, 101, 102, 104

Harlem Churches for Community Improvement, 167
Harms, Oliver, 141
Harrington, Michael, 103
Harrison, Beverly, 285n.7
Hartford, 193, 194, 207, 216, 228
Hartford Areas Rally Together, 194
Hartley, Loyde, 293n.25, 305n.48
Hartman, Orville, 130
Hauerwas, Stanley, 285n.7
Hawkins, Edler, 154
Hawkins, John R., 264
Hawley, David, 217
Head Start, 14, 186
Heinemeier, John, 133, 134, 137, 149
Herbster, Ben, 222, 223
Herrin, J. C., 26, 44
Hertz, Karl, 128
Hicks, E. B., 26, 44
Hillerbrand, Reynold, 184
Hillman, Arthur, 126
Hines, John, 105, 106, 107, 108
Hispanics, 44, 101, 102, 118, 119, 138n.24, 145n.33, 155, 159, 175, 177, 178, 183, 186, 188, 208, 211, 203, 240, 245, 254, 257
Hoekendijk, Hans, 31
Hollowell, Donald L., 60
Honolulu, 224
Hoover, Robert C., 32, 34
Horning, Ron, 117
Housing and Urban Development, Dept. of (HUD), 11, 127n.7, 160, 201
Housing, 9, 29, 33, 34, 58, 100, 152, 162, 167-68, 174, 183, 193, 203, 219
Houston, 58, 81, 143, 193
Houston, Eugene, 154
Hoyt, Robert, 131
Hrbek, George, 146
Huber, Louis, 220
Hudson, Winthrop, 9, 262
Huess, John, 104
Humphrey, Hubert, 274
Hurston, Zora Neale, 86

Ignatius, L. Faye, 45
Illich, Ivan, 149

Index

Immigrants, 180, 216, 250, 257

Indianapolis, 37, 63, 104

Industrial Areas Foundation, 130, 165, 209, 210, 248

Industrial chaplaincy, 246

Industrial mission, 21n.45, 105, 120, 250

Institute for Policy Studies, 130

Institute on the Church in Urban Industrial Society, (ICUIS) 21, 153

Integration, 155, 159, 243, 244, 248, 251

Interfaith Center on Corporate Responsibility, 21, 172, 253, 290

Interfaith IMPACT, 168, 291

InterMet, 161

International Urban Associates, 304n.46

Interreligious Foundation for Community Organizing (IFCO), 131, 193, 227

Iona Community, 157

"Isaiah" plan, 132

Isom, Dotcy I. Jr., 61, 64

Jackson, Jesse, 90, 141, 268, 273-78

Jackson, Kenneth T., 9-10

Jackson, Mance, 61, 65, 69

Jackson, MI, 63

Jackson, TN, 56

Janssen, Lawrence H., 34

Jefferson, Kinmoth, 248, 250

Jefferson, Thomas, 119, 214

Jemison, Theodore J., 268

Jersey City, 102, 105, 164

John XXIII, 19, 185

Johnson, Alonzo, 84

Johnson, Joseph A., 62, 64

Johnson, Lyndon, 12, 14, 93, 160, 295

Johnson, Robert, 168

Joint Strategy and Action Committee (JSAC), 19, 50, 163, 253

Joint Urban Program, 104, 108; and "Metabagdad," 104

Jones, Absalom, 101

Jones, Kelsey A., 63

Jones, O. T. Sr., 81, 82, 88

Jones, Richard, 31, 33, 35n.15

Jubilee Ministry, 113, 114, 115, 116, 120

Judson, Edward, 23

Judson Memorial Church, 23, 38-39

Kansas City, KS, 259

Kansas City, MO, 145, 164

Kelly, Otha M., 81

Kennedy, John F., 14, 185

Kerner Report, 106, 143

Kilgore, Thomas Jr., 44

Kincaid, John, 304n.47

King, Martin Luther Jr., 4, 12-16, 43, 60, 63, 81, 89n.21, 92, 130, 268, 271-73, 274, 276, 277

Kloetzli, Walter, 125, 126, 127, 131

Korean churches, 253, 257

Korean War, 11

Kotler, Milton, 130

Kraemer, Hendrik, 301

Kretzmann, John, 286-87

Kretzmann, O. P., 140

Labor unions, 152, 173, 176, 177, 180

La Farge, John, 184

Laity, 4, 31-32, 72-73, 75, 190, 200, 211, 293, 301-4

Lakey, Othal Hawthorne, 55, 57

Langston, John M., 264

Latinos, 132, 227

Lawrence, Charles, 109

Lazareth, William, 129, 135, 146

Lenski, Gerhard, 126n.5

Lichtenberger, Arthur, 105, 115

Lincoln, C. Eric, 95n.22

Lindsay, John, 213

Linsey, Nathaniel, 60

Liturgy, 133, 158

Logan, Rayford W., 258

Los Angeles, 29, 37, 44, 57, 77, 79, 81, 102, 139n.29, 164, 167, 194, 224, 272

Los Angeles Regional Goals Project, 21, 293

Louisville, 69, 175, 227, 224

Lovett, Leonard, 79, 84

Luecke, Richard, 283n.2

Lueking, F. Dean, 124

Lutheran Church—Missouri Synod, 31

Lutheran Human Relations Association of America, 140

Lutheran Metropolitan Ministry Association, 145
Lutheran World Federation, 291
Luther, Martin, 127, 138n.25, 142
Lutze, Karl, 140
Lutze, Richard, 145
Lutz, Marjorie, 250

Macon, GA, 63
Madsen, Paul O., 26, 28
Malcolm X, 89n.21, 91, 107
Mallory, Arenia C., 81, 91, 92
Mamiya, Lawrence, 95n.22
Marshall, Wende, 288
Mason, Charles Harrison, 80, 81, 82, 83, 85, 90, 96
Matsushita, Eiichi, 131
May, Ernest, 248
Mayer, James, 146
Mays, Benjamin E., 262
McCann, Martha, 85, 88-89
McCarthy, Joseph, 11
McDaniel, Jim, 154
McGehee, Coleman, 116
McGowan, Raymond, 181
McKinney, Edward A., 42
McKinnon, U. Z., 56
McKnight, John, 286-87
McSpadden, Bruce, 251
Memphis, 59, 60, 63, 80, 90, 93
Merchant, Joseph W., 222, 223, 224, 225, 227, 229, 230
Meredith, James, 14
Methodist Federation for Social Service, 239
Metropolitan Associates of Philadelphia (MAP), 19, 31-33, 35, 49, 229, 292, 302
Metropolitan Lutheran Ministry, 145
Metropolitan Ministry (American Baptist), 41-42
Metropolitan Ministry Agencies, 249
Metropolitan Mission, 143
Metropolitan paradigm, 4, 104, 189, 164, 175, 180, 189, 203, 219, 242, 291-306
Metropolitan Training Institute, 219, 299n.37

Metropolitan Urban Service Training (MUST), 33, 161, 226, 247
Mexicans, 153
Meyer, Cardinal, 191, 192
Michonneau, Georges, 157
Millison, Irvin C., 59
Milwaukee, 126, 131, 137, 143, 144, 186, 193, 209
Minear, Paul, 157
Ministers for Metropolitan Mission, 221, 223-25, 233
Minneapolis, 43, 194, 224
Missionary Structures of the Congregation, 246
Mission de Paris, 157
Moellering, Ralph, 142
Montgomery, AL, 13, 60, 268
Moody, Howard, 38-39
Moore, Barrington Jr., 261
Moore, Jenny, 102
Moore, Paul, 102, 109
Morikawa, Jitsuo, 30-31, 33-35, 49
Morris, Calvin, 273
Morris, John, 103
Morton, Jim, 104
Muelder, Walter, 245
Muilenberg, James, 157
Mundelein, Cardinal, 183
Musselman, Paul, 103
Myers, Kilmer, 104
Myrdal, Gunnar, 13, 260

NAACP, 56, 61, 69, 73, 93, 262
Nashville, 69
National Baptist Convention of America, 43
National Baptist Convention U.S.A., Inc., 43
National Catholic Conference for Interracial Justice, 189-91, 193
National Catholic Welfare Conference, 181
National Conference of Bishops, 199
National Conference of Catholic Bishops, 291
National Conference of Catholic Charities, 181

National Conference on Religion and Race, 189

National Council of Churches, 18, 25, 27, 31, 49, 162, 245, 246, 267, 291, 293

National Low Income Housing Coalition, 168

National Urban Network (UCC), 234

Native Americans, 44, 132, 141, 143, 145, 253, 254

Naugatuck Valley Project, 210

Nehemiah Project, 286, 287n.11

Neigh, Kenneth, 160

Nelson, David, 131

Nelson, Mary, 131, 147

Neuhaus, Richard John, 133

Neumark, Heidi, 134n.18

New Haven, 102, 216

New Orleans, 139, 183, 188, 199

New Wine Exchange, 144, 147-49

New York City, 23, 29, 33-34, 37, 77, 81, 102, 104, 105, 139n.29, 144, 152, 160, 164, 166, 172, 175, 182, 183, 190, 193, 199, 201, 222, 247, 252, 259, 265, 272, 304

Newark, NJ, 104, 167

Nicholson, Joseph, 104, 262

Niebuhr, H. Richard, 156

Niebuhr, Reinhold, 20, 156

Nixon administration, 201

North, Frank Mason, 239

Norton, Perry, 104

Oakland, 29, 40, 144

O'Brien, David, 179n.1, 180n.2

Office of Urban Ministries (United Methodist), 248, 250, 253

O'Grady, John, 182

Omaha, 193

Operation Breadbasket, 64, 271, 273

Operation PUSH, 64, 69, 262, 273

Ordination, 257; of women, 109, 110

Overton, Kermit, 154

Pape, William, 145

Paradise, Scott, 105, 172

Parish, 99, 136-37

Parkhurst, Charles, 151

Parks, Rosa, 12

Patterson, James O., 82, 85, 90

Paul VI, 204

Paulssen, Bertha, 125, 135

Peace Corps, 103

Pelham, Joseph, 97n.1, 111

Penn, I. Garland, 264

Pennington, J. W. C., 263

Perkinson, James, 117

Peters, Harvey, 135

Pettiford, William R., 264

Pettigrew, Jasper M., 56, 60

Philadelphia, 31-33, 37, 77, 78, 81, 104, 109, 137, 164, 199, 265, 269

Philadelphia Central City Lutheran Parish, 134

Phoenix, 143

Pittsburgh, 37, 138n.24, 152, 176

Pluralism, religious, 95

Populorum Progressio, 204n.21

Pottieger, Cecil, 248

Poverty, 3, 103, 112, 113, 114, 119, 163, 152, 157, 162, 163, 174, 191, 193, 202, 248, 270

Powell, Adam Clayton Jr., 264, 267, 274, 279

Powell, Adam Clayton Sr., 265

Presbyterian Church (U.S.A.), 18, 151-78

Presbyterian Institute of Industrial Relations, 152, 171

Progressive National Baptist Convention, 43

Providence, RI, 224

Public education, 25, 153, 162, 167, 174

Puerto Ricans, 138, 153

Putz, Louis, 184

Queens Citizens Organization, 167

Raby, Al, 272

Race, 98, 112, 113, 119; and racial justice, 250; and racism, 3, 9, 83, 88, 95, 106, 122, 144, 153, 155, 159, 163, 167, 182, 200, 202, 214, 226, 266, 272, 275, 277, 278

Raleigh, 161
Randolph, A. Phillip, 267, 268
Ransom, Reverdy C., 265
Ransom, Roger L., 265
Rauschenbusch, Walter, 23
Reagan administration, 177, 209
Reagan, Ronald, 12, 295
Reddick, Lawrence L. III, 72n.33
Reid, Ira D., 260
Reid, Wilbur, 273
Rhoades, William H., 33
Richardson, Channing, 241
Riddick, George, 273
Riley, Negail, 248
Rivera, Eli, 248
Roberts, William, 81
Robinson, James, 154
Robinson, Jimmy Joe, 154
Robinson, Lizzie Woods, 81
Robinson, William Thomas, 250
Rochester, NY, 37, 104, 172, 198, 207, 227
Rollins, Metz, 154
Roman Catholic Church, 17, 50, 179-211
Roosevelt administration, 261, 262
Roosevelt, Eleanor, 267
Roosevelt, Franklin D., 260, 266
Rosenbaum, Irving, 193
Rucker, Joseph W., 63
Ruehle, Susan, 143
Rusk, David, 305-7
Russell, Valerie, 234
Ryan, John A., 181

St. Louis, 56, 57, 63, 104, 140, 183, 188, 190, 199, 207, 220
St. Paul, MN, 188, 193, 194, 207, 224
San Antonio, 131, 194, 199
San Francisco, 102, 207, 224, 259
Santmire, H. Paul, 138
Schaller, Lyle E., 214, 243n.21
Schmidt, Reuben, 141
Schramm, John, 144
Schultz, Stanley K., 10
Schulze, Andrew, 139, 140
Scott, James A., 27-28, 29n.11

Scott, Marshall, 152-53
Sears, Charles Hatch, 23
Seattle, 224
Second Vatican Council, 19, 185, 206, 301
Sedillo, Pablo, 199
Self-Sufficiency Program, 132
Selma, AL, 141, 189
Seminary Consortium for Urban Pastoral Education (SCUPE), 42, 288
Sennett, Richard, 129n.11
Sering, Richard, 145
Sessions, Jim, 173
Settlement houses, 218, 220-21, 244
Seymour, William J., 79, 83
Sheehan, James, 190
Sheen, Bp. Fulton, 198
Sheffield Industrial Mission, 157
Sherry, Paul, 233
Shippey, Frederick A., 243
Shorts, R. B., 60
Siefkes, James, 143
Silberman, Charles, 165, 193
Simpkins, Julian, 104,
Sims, James, 248
Sinnott, Thomas G., 137, 138
Sitkoff, Harvard, 266
Sittler, Joseph, 127, 128
Smith, B. Julian, 60
Smith, J. Alfred Jr., 40
Smith, Virginia Thrall, 218
Social Gospel, 23
Society of Friends, 31
Sorteberg, Warren, 143
South Bronx Churches, 134, 167
Southeast Community Organization (SECO), 194
Southern Christian Leadership Conference (SCLC), 13, 43, 61, 63, 69, 73, 262, 268
Spann, Ron, 116
Spike, Robert, 38
Springfield, IL, 262
Stafford, I. S., 81
Stallings, James, 42
Standing Commission of the Church in Metropolitan Areas, 113

Steinbruck, John, 144
Steinle, Donald, 295n.29
Stewart, T. McCants, 264
Still, Douglas, 168
Streufert, Victor, 131n.15
Stritch, Cardinal, 192
Student Non-Violent Coordinating
    Committee, 13, 63
Suburban churches, 4, 187, 121
Suburbs, 7, 8, 98, 100, 154, 156, 183
Sullivan, Leon, 268, 269, 271, 274, 279
Sutch, Richard, 265
Synan, Vinson, 83n.14
Syracuse, 69, 193

Taize Community, 157
Taney, Roger Brooke, 278
Tannenbaum, Marc, 193
Tarplee, Cornelius, 103
Tawney, R. H., 152
Theology, 95, 124, 147, 156-57, 184,
    192, 213, 230, 247, 274, 276, 279,
    284-85
Thompson, William P., 177
Thurman, Howard, 86
Tiemeyer, Arnold, 130, 131
Till, Emmett, 92
Tillich, Paul, 156
Tindley, Charles Albert, 265
Tippy, Worth M., 239
Tobias, Channing H., 56, 59, 262
Tocqueville, Alexis de, 214
Todd, George E., 291, 301
Traxler, Margaret, 190
Troeltsch, Ernst, 127
Trotter, William M., 264
Truman administration, 261
Tuller, Edwin H., 43
Twin Cities Organization (TCO), 194

Union of Black Episcopalians, 108, 109
United Church of Christ (UCC), 18,
    31, 212-34, 292
United Methodist Church, 17, 31, 292,
    235-57; and "Metros," 254
United Neighborhood Organization
    (UNO), 194, 210

United Presbyterian Church, 31, 291
Urban Bishops Coalition, 110, 111
Urbanization, 245
Urban League, 55-56, 61, 69, 73, 262
Urban ministry: defined, 2, 5-6; and
    emphasis on issues, 294-97
Urban pastoral education, 288
Urban planning, 242
Urban renewal, 11, 29, 126, 183, 188,
    193, 221, 225-26, 243, 246
Urban Training Center for Christian
    Mission, 104, 106, 126, 130, 141, 161,
    225
Urban training, 221, 225-26, 288
Urban violence, 15, 163-64
Urban-suburban partnership, 211, 229
U.S. Catholic Conference, 197, 202,
    208

Venture in Mission, 110, 111
Vietnam War, 11-12, 16, 39, 109, 196,
    167, 208
VISTA, 103
Voting Rights Act (1965), 106, 260

Wadsworth, Lincoln B., 25
Wagner, John, 293n.25
Wahlberg, Edgar, 244
Walker, C. J., 264
Walker, John, 110
Wallace, David, 173
Walmsley, Arthur, 106
Ward, Ed, 154
Ward, Harry F., 239
War on Poverty, 14, 63, 160, 194, 186,
    197, 205, 292, 295
Washington, Booker T., 77, 80, 84,
    89n.21, 264, 266
Washington, D.C., 102, 111, 139n.29,
    144, 161, 167, 183, 186, 193, 199,
    207, 227, 209, 259
Washington, Isabel, 267
Washington, Joseph R. Jr., 85
Washington, Paul, 109, 110
Waters, Shelton, 154
Watts, 102
Wayne, PA, 37

Weaver, Robert, 12
Webber, George, 215, 226
Weber, Hans-Ruedi, 301
West, Cornel, 95, 285n.7
West Indians, 101, 102, 138
Weston, Moran, 104
White, Hugh, 105, 112, 116, 171
White, Jack, 131
Whiten, Bennie, 233
Wickham, E. R., 105, 157
Wieser, Thomas, 31, 170
Wilkins, Roy, 267
Williams, Lacey Kirk, 265
Williamson, Henry, 69
Wilmore, Gayraud, 159
Winter, Gibson, 100n.2, 126, 213, 292, 297

Women's missionary societies, 24n.4, 25n.6, 45, 73
Woodard, Jack, 104
Woodlawn Organization, 165, 192
Woodson, Carter G., 259
World Council of Churches, 18, 31, 43, 153, 158, 246, 290, 293, 302
World Student Christian Federation, 157
Wright, G. Ernest, 157
Wright, Nathan, 104

Younger, George, 161n.12, 225, 292, 295n.30, 297, 302
Youngstown, OH, 176

Ziedler, Frank, 131
Ziegenhals, Walter E., 213, 215, 225, 228